A
Year with
Jesus

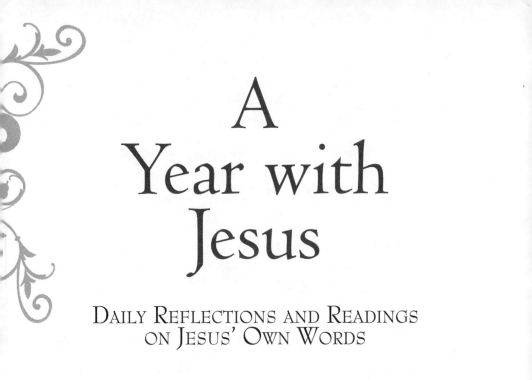

A
Year with
Jesus

Daily Reflections and Readings on Jesus' Own Words

R. P. Nettelhorst

Thomas Nelson
Since 1798

NASHVILLE   DALLAS   MEXICO CITY   RIO DE JANEIRO

Published in Nashville, Tennessee, by Thomas Nelson. Thomas Nelson is a registered trademark of Thomas Nelson, Inc.

Thomas Nelson, Inc. titles may be purchased in bulk for educational, business, fund-raising, or sales promotional use. For information, please e-mail SpecialMarkets@ThomasNelson.com.

Scripture quotations marked CEV are from the Contemporary English Version. ©1991, 1992, 1995 by American Bible Society. Used by permission.

Scripture quotations marked HCSB have been taken from the Holman Christian Standard Bible®, © 1999, 2000, 2002, 2003 by Holman Bible Publishers. Used by permission. Holman Christian Standard Bible®, Holman CSB® and HCSB® are federally registered trademarks of Holman Bible Publishers.

Scripture quotations marked MSG are from *The Message* by Eugene H. Peterson, © 1993, 1994, 1995, 1996, 2000, 2001, 2002. Used by permission of NavPress Publishing Group. All rights reserved.

Scripture quotations marked NASB are from the NEW AMERICAN STANDARD BIBLE®, © Copyright The Lockman Foundation 1960, 1962, 1963, 1968, 1971, 1972, 1973, 1975, 1977, 1995. Used by permission.

Scripture quotations marked NIV are taken from the HOLY BIBLE, NEW INTERNATIONAL VERSION®. NIV®. Copyright © 1973, 1978, 1984 by Biblica, Inc.™ Used by permission of Zondervan. All rights reserved worldwide. www.zondervan.com

Scripture quotations noted NKJV are from THE NEW KING JAMES VERSION. © 1979, 1980, 1982, Thomas Nelson, Inc., Publishers.

Scripture quotations marked NLT are taken from the *Holy Bible,* New Living Translation, ©1996, 2004. Used by permission of Tyndale House Publishers, Inc., Wheaton, Illinois 60189. All rights reserved.

Scripture quotations marked NRSV are taken from the NEW REVISED STANDARD VERSION of the Bible. © 1989 by the Division of Christian Education of the National Council of The Churches of Christ in the U.S.A. All rights reserved.

Library of Congress Control Number: 2010940847

ISBN: 978-0-8499-4699-8

Editor: Lila Empson Wavering

Associate Editor: Jennifer McNeil

Design: Whisner Design Group

Printed in the United States of America

11 12 13 14 15 QG 5 4 3 2 1

Jesus is not a figure in a book;
He is a living presence.

William Barclay

CONTENTS

CONTENTS

Arrogance and Humility

CONTENTS

Friends and Enemies

Belief and Disbelief

CONTENTS

Patience and Impatience

CONTENTS

Deserved and Undeserved

CONTENTS

Good and Evil

Fidelity and Treachery

CONTENTS

Life and Death

$\mathscr{T}$he best way to get to know other human beings is to spend time with them and to listen to what they have to say. We can then discover what matters to them and get a sense of their personalities. We have a wonderful opportunity to get to know Jesus through the Bible. We can hear directly from him with his own words spoken in a variety of circumstances to a variety of audiences. Through these words we can learn who Jesus is and what matters most to him.

What do we learn from listening to Jesus?

We learn that the kingdom of God has come to us and that the members of his kingdom are motivated by one thing: love for one another. Love does no harm to anyone, but instead seeks to bring out the best in each person. Love leads us to forgive rather than to seek vengeance. In fact, there is no room for vengeance at all. In its place, Jesus offers forgiveness and mercy.

Jesus was not concerned with whether a person deserved forgiveness and mercy. He didn't focus on whether the person was respected or important. Instead, he did what was best for each individual he met. Sometimes that meant healing people. Sometimes it meant answering people's questions. Sometimes it meant teaching or feeding them. Sometimes it meant eating a meal with them. And sometimes it meant criticizing them harshly. We learn from Jesus that love, though always seeking what's best for others, does not always feel good at first.

Spend a year with Jesus. Listen to his heart as you contemplate his words. You'll soon discover that what matters most of all to him is you. He knows what will make you happiest, and so he freely offers it to you—his Father's kingdom.

A
Year with
Jesus

God lives fully in Christ.

Colossians 2:9 CEV

Jesus Christ turns life right-side-up,
and heaven outside-in.

Carl F. H. Henry

LOVE AND HATE

Loving no matter how someone behaves is rare. We come closest in our relationships with our children. Babies give only sleepless nights and dirty diapers. They never mow the grass or do the dishes. And yet we love our babies. In the same way, God loves us. Hate, in contrast to real love, is entirely dependent upon performance and stands in opposition to love.

❀

Very rarely will anyone die for a righteous man, though for a good man someone might possibly dare to die. But God demonstrates his own love for us in this: While we were still sinners, Christ died for us.
Romans 5:7–8 NIV

KINGDOM NEWS

John came baptizing in the wilderness and preaching a baptism of repentance for the remission of sins. Then all the land of Judea, and those from Jerusalem, went out to him and were all baptized by him in the Jordan River, confessing their sins.

Now John was clothed with camel's hair and with a leather belt around his waist, and he ate locusts and wild honey. And he preached, saying, "There comes One after me who is mightier than I, whose sandal strap I am not worthy to stoop down and loose. I indeed baptized you with water, but He will baptize you with the Holy Spirit."

It came to pass in those days that Jesus came from Nazareth of Galilee, and was baptized by John in the Jordan. And immediately, coming up from the water, He saw the heavens parting and the Spirit descending upon Him like a dove. Then a voice came from heaven, "You are My beloved Son, in whom I am well pleased."

Immediately the Spirit drove Him into the wilderness. And He was there in the wilderness forty days, tempted by Satan, and was with the wild beasts; and the angels ministered to Him.

Now after John was put in prison, Jesus came to Galilee, preaching the gospel of the kingdom of God, and saying, "The time is fulfilled, and the kingdom of God is at hand. Repent, and believe in the gospel."

Mark 1:4–15 NKJV

※

*J*ohn the Baptist lived as he did, eating bad food and living far from other people, because he loved God and knew that God loved him. Like a man newly smitten who would willingly climb the highest mountain or cross the widest sea for his beloved, John so loved God that he was ready to do whatever God asked. God asked him to become his messenger, a prophet, and to proclaim the gospel of Jesus Christ.

Gospel is an old English translation of the Greek word that means "good news." The good news that John proclaimed about Jesus was threefold: first, the kingdom of God was near; second, repent of your sins; and third, believe in Jesus.

Repentance isn't simply about feeling bad for your sins. Repentance is about changing your mind. It means that you realize you're going the wrong way, so you turn around and take a different path.

Jesus' good news was that the kingdom is here. He and John taught that humanity has been going away from it in its pursuit of everything but love of God. Jesus showed us that we can turn our lives around and move toward God's kingdom by learning to love God and our neighbors as ourselves.

BEST FRIENDS FOREVE~

Jesus said to his disciples at the Last Supper:

"I have loved you, just as my Father has loved me. So remain faithful to my love for you. If you obey me, I will keep loving you, just as my Father keeps loving me, because I have obeyed him.

"I have told you this to make you as completely happy as I am. Now I tell you to love each other, as I have loved you. The greatest way to show love for friends is to die for them. And you are my friends, if you obey me. Servants don't know what their master is doing,

and so I do
vants. I sp
and I have told you
Father has told me.

"You did not choose me. I cho~ you and sent you out to produce fruit, the kind of fruit that will last. Then my Father will give you whatever you ask for in my name. So I command you to love each other."

John 15:9–17 CEV

※

*J*esus asked his disciples at the Last Supper to be his friends forever. He was going to die for them, as a friend might die to save a buddy in danger. In this case, the danger he would rescue them from was their sins.

He wanted them to understand that they were his friends, not his slaves or royal servants. In contrast, the leader of the Roman Empire, Caesar, was hailed as a god, and all the people in the empire were his servants. In fact, each year every person in the empire was supposed to perform a sacrifice and announce, "Caesar is Lord!" Only Jews were exempt from this duty, because the Greek word for *Lord* was the same Greek word that the most widely read translation of the Bible used for God's name. No Jew could call Caesar by that word.

Then Jesus, God himself, the Creator of the heavens and the earth, declared to his followers that they were not slaves. Slaves don't need to understand anything; all they have to do is obey orders. But friends do what they're asked to do because they understand and because they love each other. Jesus wanted us to realize that our relationship with God was not like the relationship between a master and his slaves. Unlike Caesar, the true God called his disciples his friends and asked for but one thing: that they love one another. Jesus is our friend, and so are all other Christians, whether they sit next to us in our church or live on the other side of the world. A friend of Jesus is a friend of ours.

PAYBACK TIME

Jesus said during his Sermon on the Mount:

"You know that you have been taught, 'An eye for an eye and a tooth for a tooth.' But I tell you not to try to get even with a person who has done something to you. When someone slaps your right cheek, turn and let that person slap your other cheek. If someone sues you for your shirt, give up your coat as well. If a soldier forces you to carry his pack one mile, carry it two miles. When people ask you for something, give it to them. When they want to borrow money, lend it to them.

"You have heard people say, 'Love your neighbors and hate your enemies.' But I tell you to love your enemies and pray for anyone who mistreats you. Then you will be acting like your Father in heaven. He makes the sun rise on both good and bad people. And he sends rain for the ones who do right and for the ones who do wrong. If you love only those people who love you, will God reward you for that? Even tax collectors love their friends. If you greet only your friends, what's so great about that? Don't even unbelievers do that? But you must always act like your Father in heaven."

Matthew 5:38–48 CEV

*J*esus asked for what seems impossible. He asked us to be nice to mean people. "Eye for eye" and "tooth for tooth" are phrases from the law of Moses known as the *lex talionis*. That "law of the tooth" was summarized as "Do to others as they have done to you." But the purpose of that old law wasn't what most people thought. It was designed to place limits on judicial punishment: a criminal could not be made to suffer more than his victim did. But by Jesus' day, the phrase had become twisted into a justification for vengeance. Jesus explained that that sort of thinking missed the whole point of what God was all about.

God is good to people who are not good to him or to anyone else. Loving those who love us is easy. God has called us to do something hard: to be like him and to love those who hate us.

God is good to us no matter what. His love is not dependent upon our performance. Jesus wants us to understand that real love is never based on performance. It can't be earned. And he wants us to treat other people the same way that he treats them and us. He wants us to love unconditionally.

LUMBER

During his Sermon on the Mount, Jesus said:

"Judge not, that you be not judged. For with what judgment you judge, you will be judged; and with the measure you use, it will be measured back to you. And why do you look at the speck in your brother's eye, but do not consider the plank in your own eye? Or how can you say to your brother, 'Let me remove the speck from your eye'; and look, a plank is in your own eye? Hypocrite! First remove the plank from your own eye, and then you will see clearly to remove the speck from your brother's eye.

"Do not give what is holy to the dogs; nor cast your pearls before swine, lest they trample them under their feet, and turn and tear you in pieces.

"Ask, and it will be given to you; seek, and you will find; knock, and it will be opened to you. For everyone who asks receives, and he who seeks finds, and to him who knocks it will be opened. Or what man is there among you who, if his son asks for bread, will give him a stone?

"Or if he asks for a fish, will he give him a serpent? If you then, being evil, know how to give good gifts to your children, how much more will your Father who is in heaven give good things to those who ask Him! Therefore, whatever you want men to do to you, do also to them, for this is the Law and the Prophets."

Matthew 7:1–12 NKJV

※

*J*esus regularly told his disciples and the crowds that the Scriptures didn't say what they thought they did. Much like the prophets of the Old Testament, he revealed what everyone should have already known.

The word *hypocrite* came from the Greek theater. It referred to the large masks actors wore showing either a smile or a frown. The masks displayed the emotion of a character that would otherwise be invisible to a distant audience in a world without close-ups and microphones.

We rarely have a complete picture of the lives of the people around us. Like the audience at the edge of a theater, we can judge only by the surface mask. Most often, we will judge wrong, seeing what we want to see, or projecting our own flaws. Better to not judge at all.

Ask yourself how you would like to be treated. Wouldn't you like people to give you the benefit of the doubt? The entire Old Testament—the Law and the Prophets that Jesus was talking about—is summed up by that concept of love, of doing to others as you'd like them to do to you.

UNDESERVED

Jesus went out from there and departed to the region of Tyre and Sidon.

And behold, a woman of Canaan came from that region and cried out to Him, saying, "Have mercy on me, O Lord, Son of David! My daughter is severely demon-possessed."

But He answered her not a word. And His disciples came and urged Him, saying, "Send her away, for she cries out after us."

But He answered and said, "I was not sent except to the lost sheep of the house of Israel."

Then she came and worshiped Him, saying, "Lord, help me!"

But He answered and said, "It is not good to take the children's bread and throw it to the little dogs."

And she said, "Yes, Lord, yet even the little dogs eat the crumbs which fall from their masters' table."

Then Jesus answered and said to her, "O woman, great is your faith! Let it be to you as you desire." And her daughter was healed from that very hour.

Matthew 15:21–28 NKJV

※

A modern, native-born Israeli is called a *sabra*. The *sabra* is the fruit of the prickly pear cactus. Israelis think of themselves as being like that fruit: prickly on the outside but sweet on the inside. One day, Jesus acted like a *sabra* with a Canaanite mother.

In the time of Joshua, God set the Canaanites of Palestine for extermination because of their idolatry. Nevertheless, a few repented and joined with the Israelites. Some of those Canaanites living in Tyre and Sidon ended up as friends of David and Solomon. Hiram, the king of Tyre, actually helped Solomon in the building of God's temple.

We should notice something intriguing about the story of the Canaanite woman. Jesus went out of his way to go to where she lived. After he talked to her, he went right back to where he had come from. Perhaps Jesus' purpose in going to the region of Tyre and Sidon was to heal the Canaanite woman's child, since that's the only thing he seemed to do there.

Jesus responded to her not out of cruelty but out of love. Jesus parroted what the disciples believed, that the Messiah belonged only to them. Just as Jesus taught the crowds that their understanding of what they imagined the Bible taught was flawed, Jesus instructed his disciples in the same way. God's love for us means that he intends to make us the best we can be.

COMPASSION

In those days when there was again a great crowd without anything to eat, [Jesus] called his disciples and said to them, "I have compassion for the crowd, because they have been with me now for three days and have nothing to eat. If I send them away hungry to their homes, they will faint on the way—and some of them have come from a great distance."

His disciples replied, "How can one feed these people with bread here in the desert?"

He asked them, "How many loaves do you have?"

They said, "Seven."

Then he ordered the crowd to sit down on the ground; and he took the seven loaves, and after giving thanks he broke them and gave them to his disciples to distribute; and they distributed them to the crowd. They had also a few small fish; and after blessing them, he ordered that these too should be distributed. They ate and were filled; and they took up the broken pieces left over, seven baskets full. Now there were about four thousand people. And he sent them away. And immediately he got into the boat with his disciples and went to the district of Dalmanutha.

Mark 8:1–9 NRSV

❋

*J*esus was motivated by love. It was love that moved him to feed the four thousand, just as it was love that motivated him to come to the world in the first place. Jesus' behavior makes sense only when one understands the power of love.

People will do for love what they would not do for anything else. When Moses led the Israelites from Egypt, the people despaired, imagining that God had brought them there only to make them die of hunger and thirst. Why did they have so little trust in God? In Egypt, Pharaoh was capricious. A kind act one day would be followed by cruelty the next. It was easy for them to think God would treat them just the same. When Jesus performed the miracle of feeding four thousand, it reminded his audience of Moses. But there was a difference: they were in no danger of starving, and they could easily have departed for home and found food within a day or so at most. Their need was not desperate. But Jesus fed them anyway.

God loves us. He takes care of us when we face disasters. He does not desert us during crises. God is also there for us during the flat tires, bounced checks, and inconveniences of life.

LEGALISM

[Jesus] set out from there and went to the region of Judea and across the Jordan. Then crowds converged on Him again and, as He usually did, He began teaching them once more. Some Pharisees approached Him to test Him. They asked, "Is it lawful for a man to divorce his wife?"

He replied to them, "What did Moses command you?"

They said, "Moses permitted us to write divorce papers and send her away."

But Jesus told them, "He wrote this commandment for you because of the hardness of your hearts. But from the beginning of creation God made them male and female.

> For this reason a man will
> leave his father and mother
> and be joined to his wife, and
> the two will become one
> flesh.

"So they are no longer two, but one flesh. Therefore what God has joined together, man must not separate."

Mark 10:1–9 HCSB

✻

Many people want to know the rules just so they can figure out what they can get away with. Many of those who were part of the religious establishment thought about the rules like that. They didn't love their neighbors. They didn't love God.

In Jesus' day, there were two schools of thought among the Pharisees concerning the issue of divorce. One group believed that divorce could happen for even the most trivial of reasons, such as a wife burning dinner. The other school of thought believed that divorce was permissible only in the most extreme of circumstances, such as adultery. The Pharisees wanted to know how they could get out of their marriages.

Jesus responded to their question with a question. He asked them what God had said about divorce. They responded merely with the relevant passage from the Bible, which in their mind they found inadequate, since God hadn't bothered to explain why they could get divorced. Jesus gave them another biblical passage, explaining that divorce existed not because God liked it, but because human beings were flawed and needed a way out of their mistakes.

Jesus pointed out that just because something is legal doesn't make it a good or right thing. The Pharisees were missing the point of the Bible and were asking the wrong question. It's easy to get so caught up in our own issues that we miss God's issues. He wants us to focus on loving him and loving others. When we do that, we don't need to think so much about the rules.

IS LOVE REALLY THE ANSWER?

Days after the triumphal entry, while Jesus was teaching in the temple:

One of the religion scholars came up. Hearing the lively exchanges of question and answer and seeing how sharp Jesus was in his answers, he put in his question: "Which is most important of all the commandments?"

Jesus said, "The first in importance is, 'Listen, Israel: The Lord your God is one; so love the Lord God with all your passion and prayer and intelligence and energy.' And here is the second: 'Love others as well as you love yourself.' There is no other commandment that ranks with these."

The religion scholar said, "A wonderful answer, Teacher! So lucid and accurate—that God is one and there is no other. And loving him with all passion and intelligence and energy, and loving others as well as you love yourself. Why, that's better than all offerings and sacrifices put together!"

When Jesus realized how insightful he was, he said, "You're almost there, right on the border of God's kingdom."

After that, no one else dared ask a question.

Mark 12:28–34 MSG

❈

*R*ight after watching a movie, if someone asked you what it was all about, you probably wouldn't have too much trouble giving an answer. But here's likely a much tougher question—what is life all about? Since loving God and loving people is the theme of the entire Bible, then we can summarize that love is what life is all about. But what is love?

Too often for the Israelites, they imagined that God could be manipulated in the same way they manipulated everything else in life. They were nice to their neighbors who were nice to them, and they expected kindness in return. So they thought God worked the same way. Rather than understanding their sacrifices and religious rituals as an expression of their love for God, they saw them as merely payments rendered in exchange for the stuff they wanted. Rather than a relationship with God, they had a superstition.

The sort of love Jesus was talking about means being kind to people regardless of how they respond and giving without expecting anything back. It's seeing your enemy's meter expire and dropping in a coin without ever letting him know you did it.

God's kingdom is near to those who understand the centrality of love. And it's far from those who don't. When we are kind to those who are unkind to us, and give to those who can't give to us, we are loving as Jesus loved us.

GIVING UNWISELY

Shortly after choosing the Twelve, Jesus taught them on a plain near the Sea of Galilee:

[Jesus said,] "I tell you who hear me: Love your enemies, do good to those who hate you, bless those who curse you, pray for those who mistreat you. If someone strikes you on one cheek, turn to him the other also. If someone takes your cloak, do not stop him from taking your tunic. Give to everyone who asks you, and if anyone takes what belongs to you, do not demand it back. Do to others as you would have them do to you.

"If you love those who love you, what credit is that to you? Even 'sinners' love those who love them. And if you do good to those who are good to you, what credit is that to you? Even 'sinners' do that. And if you lend to those from whom you expect repayment, what credit is that to you? Even 'sinners' lend to 'sinners,' expecting to be repaid in full. But love your enemies, do good to them, and lend to them without expecting to get anything back. Then your reward will be great, and you will be sons of the Most High, because he is kind to the ungrateful and wicked. Be merciful, just as your Father is merciful."

Luke 6:27–36 NIV

※

*I*n exchange for random acts of violence, Jesus expected targeted acts of kindness. Jesus asked people to act contrary to their natures, even contrary to what seemed like good sense. Rather than responding in kind to the people around us, he told people to respond with good, no matter how badly they were treated.

Jesus' words should raise an uncomfortable question. Are we kind to others because we hope that we'll get something out of it? Most of what we call *love* turns out to be the equivalent of paying for a performance: scratching a back to get ours scratched.

My wife occasionally asks, "Do you love me?" It is her joking way of asking me to do something. Often, however, we seriously, rather than jokingly, relate to God and one another in just that way. When we think God must do something good for us because we've been good, then we are not loving God. When we think he is waiting for us to be good before he'll bless us, then we are thinking God does not love us.

But God does love us, and that means he is good to us no matter what. Just as Jesus asks us to be kind without expecting repayment, so God doesn't expect anything back. Jesus asks us to love one another the same way God loves us: unconditionally.

GRATEFUL LOVE

A Pharisee invited Jesus to have dinner with him. So Jesus went to the Pharisee's home and got ready to eat. When a sinful woman in that town found out that Jesus was there, she bought an expensive bottle of perfume. Then she came and stood behind Jesus. She cried and started washing his feet with her tears and drying them with her hair. The woman kissed his feet and poured the perfume on them.

The Pharisee who had invited Jesus saw this and said to himself, "If this man really were a prophet, he would know what kind of woman is touching him! He would know that she is a sinner."

Jesus said to the Pharisee, "Simon, I have something to say to you."

"Teacher, what is it?" Simon replied.

Jesus told him, "Two people were in debt to a moneylender. One of them owed him five hundred silver coins, and the other owed him fifty. Since neither of them could pay him back, the money lender said that they didn't have to pay him anything. Which one of them will like him more?"

Simon answered, "I suppose it would be the one who had owed more and didn't have to pay it back."

"You are right," Jesus said.

Luke 7:36–43 CEV

*F*or Jesus, nothing ever happened by accident. Jesus knew that a disreputable woman would come to the party, he knew what she would do, and he knew how the Pharisee named Simon would respond. In fact, Jesus was counting on it.

Pharisees were one of the four major sects of Judaism in the first century, sort of like modern denominations within Christianity. The Pharisees were considered the progressives of their day. They believed that the Bible included all the books of the Old Testament, not just the five books of Moses. They believed in angels, demons, and Satan. And they believed in the resurrection of the dead. They took the Bible very seriously, and they believed that it was critical for the people of Israel to obey the laws of God completely and consistently in order to avoid a repeat of God's judgment.

When Simon saw a sinful woman touching Jesus, he was appalled. How could a prophet endure the presence, let alone the touch, of such a human being? Jesus used the situation as an opportunity to instruct a well-intentioned but misguided individual about the wonder of God's love and forgiveness. Simon took God for granted. Sometimes, like Simon, we need reminding about how great it is to have God's forgiveness. Then it will be easier for us to see worth in others and be more willing to forgive them ourselves.

PEST CONTROL

[Jesus and his disciples] arrived at the country of the Gerasenes, which is opposite Galilee. As he stepped out on land, a man of the city who had demons met him. For a long time he had worn no clothes, and he did not live in a house but in the tombs. When he saw Jesus, he fell down before him and shouted at the top of his voice, "What have you to do with me, Jesus, Son of the Most High God? I beg you, do not torment me"—for Jesus had commanded the unclean spirit to come out of the man. (For many times it had seized him; he was kept under guard and bound with chains and shackles, but he would break the bonds and be driven by the demon into the wilds.)

Jesus then asked him, "What is your name?" He said, "Legion"; for many demons had entered him. They begged him not to order them to go back into the abyss.

Luke 8:26–31 NRSV

❧

*E*arly in Jesus' ministry, after a rough trip across the Sea of Galilee, Jesus and his disciples arrived in the country of the Gerasenes. The population of the region seems to have been made up mostly of non-Jewish people.

When Jesus got out of the boat, a man infested with demons was waiting for him. The demons within him immediately recognized Jesus as the Messiah and were terrified. They referred to themselves collectively as "Legion." In the Roman army, a legion consisted of between 3,000 and 6,000 soldiers. Jesus wasn't intimidated or impressed by what they chose to call themselves. It was out of the ordinary for this man to be by the Sea of Galilee, meeting a man just stepping from a boat. Normally, the demon-possessed man avoided other people. The tombs he lived in were located far from shore, up in the hills. It was also out of the ordinary for demons to seek out Jesus, given what he consistently did to them. So the man had come to Jesus in order to be healed, likely struggling against his unwelcome inhabitants even to stand there.

Jesus relieved him of his deepest problems. Just as Jesus had calmed the raging storm on his trip across the lake to the country of the Gerasenes, so Jesus could calm the demon-possessed man. Whatever storms we face in life, whether natural or supernatural, Jesus has absolute control over them.

WHAT IS A WOMAN WORTH?

One Sabbath day as Jesus was teaching in a synagogue, he saw a woman who had been crippled by an evil spirit. She had been bent double for eighteen years and was unable to stand up straight. When Jesus saw her, he called her over and said, "Dear woman, you are healed of your sickness!" Then he touched her, and instantly she could stand straight. How she praised God!

But the leader in charge of the synagogue was indignant that Jesus had healed her on the Sabbath day. "There are six days of the week for working," he said to the crowd. "Come on those days to be healed, not on the Sabbath."

But the Lord replied, "You hypocrites! Each of you works on the Sabbath day! Don't you untie your ox or your donkey from its stall on the Sabbath and lead it out for water? This dear woman, a daughter of Abraham, has been held in bondage by Satan for eighteen years. Isn't it right that she be released, even on the Sabbath?"

This shamed his enemies, but all the people rejoiced at the wonderful things he did.

Luke 13:10–17 NLT

*W*ould you give up hope after suffering and praying for healing for eighteen years? For eighteen years, an unnamed woman had prayed for healing, and so had her family and friends. For eighteen years, it seemed that God was ignoring all their pleas.

Jesus never refused to help a person in need. While he was teaching, he took notice of her suffering. She had not requested that Jesus aid her. Instead, Jesus simply called her over and gave her what she wanted more than anything else.

Her response was to glorify God. The response of the synagogue ruler was something else entirely: he criticized what Jesus had done. Jesus reacted by pointing out the inconsistency in the ruler's thinking: The law allowed for the care of animals on the Sabbath. Weren't human beings of greater worth?

In his concern with doing the legal thing, the synagogue ruler had lost sight of the right thing. He'd forgotten the purpose for the laws: to make life better for human beings. If the laws stood in the way of that, then perhaps the laws were wrong—or at least they were being misunderstood and wrongly applied. We may go years or even a lifetime thinking God hasn't heard our prayers. But God hears every single prayer, and he will answer them in his way and in his timing.

SPEAKING TRUTH TO POWER

While Jesus was on the road to Jerusalem, teaching and healing:

Some Pharisees approached, saying to [Jesus], "Go away, leave here, for Herod wants to kill You."

And He said to them, "Go and tell that fox, 'Behold, I cast out demons and perform cures today and tomorrow, and the third day I reach My goal.' Nevertheless I must journey on today and tomorrow and the next day; for it cannot be that a prophet would perish outside of Jerusalem.

"O Jerusalem, Jerusalem, the city that kills the prophets and stones those sent to her! How often I wanted to gather your children together, just as a hen gathers her brood under her wings, and you would not have it!

"Behold, your house is left to you desolate; and I say to you, you will not see Me until the time comes when you say, 'Blessed is He who comes in the name of the Lord!'"

Luke 13:31–35 NASB

※

*J*esus did not always speak with kind and gentle words. Jesus purposely insulted the tetrarch of Galilee and Perea, Herod Antipas. Herod was the one who had killed John the Baptist. According to Jewish tradition, foxes were cunning but lowly animals. We have no way of knowing whether the Pharisees had a genuine concern for Jesus' safety or were simply hoping to scare Jesus away.

It's worth noting that Jesus, as the Messiah and a descendant of David, had a legitimate claim to the Jewish throne, while Herod did not. Herod was illegitimate, serving at the whim of the Roman occupiers. The law of Moses prohibited the cursing of a ruler, while New Testament authors spoke against saying evil things about one another. However, those prohibitions were not intended to prevent legitimate criticism of rulers by God's prophets, apostles, and people.

Jesus did not fear for his life. He intended to leave Herod's domain anyway and travel to Jerusalem. He knew he faced death in Jerusalem, but he went there on purpose, not because Herod chased him out of Galilee. Jesus' words with the Pharisees were designed to demonstrate that he was going where he wanted to go, when he wanted to go—and not because of what anyone else wanted of him.

God's will is accomplished in his timing. He won't let anyone else take credit for his actions. We are God's instruments, working to accomplish his desires. We don't manipulate God with our prayers; we ask him to do only what he is already ready and willing to do.

WHAT MATTERS

While Jesus traveled from village to village in Galilee:

Tax collectors and other notorious sinners often came to listen to Jesus teach. This made the Pharisees and teachers of religious law complain that he was associating with such sinful people—even eating with them!

So Jesus told them this story: "If a man has a hundred sheep and one of them gets lost, what will he do? Won't he leave the ninety-nine others in the wilderness and go to search for the one that is lost until he finds it? And when he has found it, he will joyfully carry it home on his shoulders. When he arrives, he will call together his friends and neighbors, saying, 'Rejoice with me because I have found my lost sheep.' In the same way, there is more joy in heaven over one lost sinner who repents and returns to God than over ninety-nine others who are righteous and haven't strayed away!

"Or suppose a woman has ten silver coins and loses one. Won't she light a lamp and sweep the entire house and search carefully until she finds it? And when she finds it, she will call in her friends and neighbors and say, 'Rejoice with me because I have found my lost coin.' In the same way, there is joy in the presence of God's angels when even one sinner repents."

Luke 15:1–10 NLT

*J*esus did not worry about what the neighbors thought. Instead, he simply did what was best for them. Reaching out to the sinners of the world was what was best for those sinners—and it was also best for those nosy neighbors who always criticized him for doing the loving thing instead of the correct thing.

In Jesus' day, most of the Jewish people were farmers, raisers of sheep or cattle, or fishermen. The parables he told and the word pictures he painted were designed to make sense to such an audience. He used the way shepherds cared about their lost sheep to illustrate how much God cared about lost people.

Pharisee means "separated." The Pharisees believed in separating themselves from sinners because they thought God hated sinners. Jesus wanted the Pharisees to understand that rather than hating sinners, God loved them. He compared sinners to lost precious things, hoping to get the Pharisees to understand how precious every human being was.

It gives us insight into the character of Jesus to note that he made sinners comfortable and enraged the righteous. How many sinners feel comfortable hanging out with most Christians? Perhaps we're not as much like Jesus as we like to imagine. Let's hope we can gain the same sense of compassion for the lost and broken people in our lives that Jesus had. Jesus always saw people with problems as wonderful opportunities, with boundless potential.

LOVE'S RESPONSE

[Jesus] entered Jericho and was passing through. There was a man named Zacchaeus who was a chief tax collector, and he was rich. He was trying to see who Jesus was, but he was not able because of the crowd, since he was a short man. So running ahead, he climbed up a sycamore tree to see Jesus, since He was about to pass that way. When Jesus came to the place, He looked up and said to him, "Zacchaeus, hurry and come down, because today I must stay at your house."

So he quickly came down and welcomed Him joyfully. All who saw it began to complain, "He's gone to lodge with a sinful man!"

But Zacchaeus stood there and said to the Lord, "Look, I'll give half of my possessions to the poor, Lord! And if I have extorted anything from anyone, I'll pay back four times as much!"

"Today salvation has come to this house," Jesus told him, "because he too is a son of Abraham. For the Son of Man has come to seek and to save the lost."

Luke 19:1–10 HCSB

※

Jesus did not worry about looking good. He was concerned only with doing good: with loving his neighbor as himself. Sometimes that neighbor was a genuinely evil person, like a tax collector. A tax collector gained his job by bidding on it. Whoever promised the Roman government the most money got the contract for the district or town. His pay came from whatever he could get above that promised amount. So tax collectors got rich by ripping off their neighbors. No one liked them. Their greed, their graft, and their legalized embezzlement branded them as sinners in the extreme.

It was such a man, and those like him, whom Jesus sought out and spent most of his time with. When Jesus saw Zacchaeus in the tree, Jesus did not tell him to give up his line of work. He did not tell him to change his lifestyle or to give back the money he had stolen. And yet Zacchaeus did just that: he accepted Jesus' request for lodging in Zacchaeus's house and responded by changing his own life.

That's the way it works for us today: we can't have God take up residence with us without profound implications. We are never the same afterward, any more than Zacchaeus was the same after having Jesus in his home. Meeting Jesus changes everything.

PARTY FAVOR

On the third day there was a wedding in Cana of Galilee, and the mother of Jesus was there. Jesus and his disciples had also been invited to the wedding. When the wine gave out, the mother of Jesus said to him, "They have no wine."

And Jesus said to her, "Woman, what concern is that to you and to me? My hour has not yet come."

His mother said to the servants, "Do whatever he tells you."

Now standing there were six stone water jars for the Jewish rites of purification, each holding twenty or thirty gallons. Jesus said to them, "Fill the jars with water." And they filled them up to the brim. He said to them, "Now draw some out, and take it to the chief steward." So they took it.

When the steward tasted the water that had become wine, and did not know where it came from (though the servants who had drawn the water knew), the steward called the bridegroom and said to him, "Everyone serves the good wine first, and then the inferior wine after the guests have become drunk. But you have kept the good wine until now." Jesus did this, the first of his signs, in Cana of Galilee, and revealed his glory; and his disciples believed in him.

John 2:1–11 NRSV

※

*J*esus was at a party. They ran out of wine. He made more. Jesus' first miracle tells us something surprising about him.

Jesus' mother knew he was the Messiah. She asked him to take care of a rather mundane problem. He warned her about the consequences of her request, but she insisted. With his obedience, he began the public ministry that would lead to his crucifixion.

No problem, however inconsequential, is beyond mattering to Jesus. Jesus loved his mother, and what was important to her was important to him because she was important. Jesus cared that the people at a party had fun, and that the hosts not be embarrassed.

People enjoyed spending time with Jesus, where they did not enjoy spending time with religious leaders. In fact, religious leaders criticized Jesus heavily for his relationships with sinners. In the minds of many of the religious leaders, Jesus was not religious at all.

And that is precisely the point. Religion does not and cannot fix the problems of the world, but a relationship with Jesus does, even if the problem is only a lack of wine at a wedding. We must concern ourselves with the welfare of the people around us and be willing to help out in any way we can. Don't ask if the people you're helping are worthy or if the task is important. Just ask what they need.

FEAR AND LOATHING

Jesus found an invalid by the Pool of Bethesda in Jerusalem:

When Jesus saw him lying there, and knew that he already had been in that condition a long time, He said to him, "Do you want to be made well?"

The sick man answered Him, "Sir, I have no man to put me into the pool when the water is stirred up; but while I am coming, another steps down before me."

Jesus said to him, "Rise, take up your bed and walk." And immediately the man was made well, took up his bed, and walked.

And that day was the Sabbath. The Jews therefore said to him who was cured, "It is the Sabbath; it is not lawful for you to carry your bed."

He answered them, "He who made me well said to me, 'Take up your bed and walk.'"

Then they asked him, "Who is the Man who said to you, 'Take up your bed and walk'?" But the one who was healed did not know who it was, for Jesus had withdrawn, a multitude being in that place. Afterward Jesus found him in the temple, and said to him, "See, you have been made well. Sin no more, lest a worse thing come upon you."

John 5:6–14 NKJV

※

*J*esus asked a disabled man a simple yes-or-no question. But instead of answering Jesus' question, the man told Jesus all about why he couldn't get healed. Too often we respond to God exactly the same way: rather than saying yes to him, we explain to God why what we most need is impossible to get.

Remarkably, Jesus did not wait for the poor man to say the right thing in the right way before he would help him—nor did he expect anything from the man at all. Jesus knew what the man really needed, even if the man didn't understand it himself.

Only after healing the man did Jesus warn him to stop sinning. Jesus' intervention was not dependent upon the man's repentance but rather upon his need. In contrast, the Pharisees' concern was not for the man or his needs. They couldn't see the sinner for the sin. For Jesus, the human beings who happened to be sinners werre what mattered. All that Jesus did was a means to an end: the restoration of those sinners rather than their condemnation. We need to recognize that loving others fulfills the law. We don't need to ask what is the right thing. Instead, all we need is to ask what is the loving thing. The right thing automatically follows.

THE TRUTH THAT FREES

In Jerusalem during the Festival of Tabernacles:

Jesus was saying to those Jews who had believed Him, "If you continue in My word, then you are truly disciples of Mine; and you will know the truth, and the truth will make you free."

They answered Him, "We are Abraham's descendants and have never yet been enslaved to anyone; how is it that You say, 'You will become free'?"

Jesus answered them, "Truly, truly, I say to you, everyone who commits sin is the slave of sin. The slave does not remain in the house forever; the son does remain forever. So if the Son makes you free, you will be free indeed. I know that you are Abraham's descendants; yet you seek to kill Me, because My word has no place in you. I speak the things which I have seen with My Father; therefore you also do the things which you heard from your father."

They answered and said to Him, "Abraham is our father."

Jesus said to them, "If you are Abraham's children, do the deeds of Abraham. But as it is, you are seeking to kill Me, a man who has told you the truth, which I heard from God; this Abraham did not do. You are doing the deeds of your father."

They said to Him, "We were not born of fornication; we have one Father: God."

John 8:31–41 NASB

*W*hat we think we already know often blinds us to the truth. When Jesus addressed the crowd during the Festival of Tabernacles, they already knew that the Pharisees believed he was a false prophet and a false Messiah. The crowd knew that the religious establishment wanted Jesus dead.

Many of those in Jesus' audience accepted his teaching and believed that he was from God. But enemy or sympathizer, they were all missing his point to such an extent that he had to tell them that rather than acting like the children of Abraham, they were acting like the children of the devil.

When Jesus told them that the truth could set them free, they thought he was talking about slavery. Since the people were not slaves, Jesus' words seemed pointless. But Jesus meant that the truth could set them free from sin. How so? Sin comes from believing lies: like the lie that God doesn't want what is best for us, or the lie that makes us believe today's pleasure matters more than tomorrow's consequence. We also sometimes believe lies that we may find comforting at the moment, but in the end will bring us disappointment and bitterness.

Jesus tells us that the truth can free us from the dishonesty that binds us to misery. Thanks to Jesus' death on the cross, God has removed those bonds from us forever.

LOVE FOR HIS SHEEP

In Jerusalem, after healing a blind man:

[Jesus] explained it to the Pharisees: "I tell you the truth, I am the gate for the sheep. All who came before me were thieves and robbers. But the true sheep did not listen to them. Yes, I am the gate. Those who come in through me will be saved. They will come and go freely and will find good pastures. The thief's purpose is to steal and kill and destroy. My purpose is to give them a rich and satisfying life.

"I am the good shepherd. The good shepherd sacrifices his life for the sheep. A hired hand will run when he sees a wolf coming. He will abandon the sheep because they don't belong to him and he isn't their shepherd. And so the wolf attacks them and scatters the flock. The hired hand runs away because he's working only for the money and doesn't really care about the sheep."

John 10:7–13 NLT

᙭

*J*esus thought that people mattered more than his own life. Their well-being was of greater worth than his. His love was that powerful.

Jesus sometimes spoke in allegory. In an agricultural society, his images were obvious and easy to get, though their implications were profound. Sometimes—perhaps most of the time—Jesus' audience missed his point altogether, whether that audience was the wider crowd or even his closest friends.

The picture of a shepherd taking care of his flock would have been easy for his audience to understand. But Jesus also alluded to the well-known Psalm 23, identifying himself with God as the protector of his people. Jesus was the gate into the sheepfold, so no one could get in without him knowing. Jesus was also the shepherd who took care of the sheep. He was not just a hired hand concerned only with his next paycheck. He loved the sheep more than anything.

Jesus wanted to give every person a rich and satisfying life. This echoed the psalm, which pointed out that goodness and mercy would be part of a believer's life forever. Only the lying wolf would make you think otherwise. It's easy to lose sight of the shepherd when the wolf appears.

Jesus pointed out that no matter what the sheep face, the shepherd is always with them. They are never alone. It should be comfort enough to know that we have the Good Shepherd with us. Jesus isn't getting paid to take care of us. Rather, he paid all that he had for the privilege. We matter more to him than his own life did.

NEVER SAY DIE

Jesus traveled to Bethany because his friend Lazarus had died:

When Jesus came, He found that he had already been in the tomb four days. Now Bethany was near Jerusalem, about two miles away. And many of the Jews had joined the women around Martha and Mary, to comfort them concerning their brother.

Now Martha, as soon as she heard that Jesus was coming, went and met Him, but Mary was sitting in the house. Now Martha said to Jesus, "Lord, if You had been here, my brother would not have died. But even now I know that whatever You ask of God, God will give You."

Jesus said to her, "Your brother will rise again."

Martha said to Him, "I know that he will rise again in the resurrection at the last day."

Jesus said to her, "I am the resurrection and the life. He who believes in Me, though he may die, he shall live. And whoever lives and believes in Me shall never die. Do you believe this?"

She said to Him, "Yes, Lord, I believe that You are the Christ, the Son of God, who is to come into the world."

John 11:17–27 NKJV

Don't underestimate God. Martha believed in the resurrection, but like everyone else, she thought of it only in terms of a distant future that had no effect on her life that day, as she faced the prospect of a future without her brother.

From her lips, Jesus received as strong an affirmation of faith as we ever got from Peter. Martha anticipated a resurrection that would soon, in just minutes, become a reality for her dead brother, Lazarus. But what did Jesus mean that whoever "lives and believes in Me shall never die"? Lazarus was already dead. And eventually Martha died. So has everyone who has ever been born. Jesus implied that our future resurrection hope has an effect on how we live now.

Jesus explained that *he* was the resurrection and the life. By trusting in Jesus, we gain that life that comes from his resurrection now, just as Lazarus had his life restored. Lazarus's death and restoration to life illustrate how Jesus transforms those who depend upon him. Death precedes resurrection. Resurrection must come before a new life can begin. Jesus' death and resurrection bring us a new life different from the old life we had before he came along. It is a life that we enjoy now, and will continue to enjoy for all eternity with him. We live our lives now because he lives in us and through us.

EVERYONE WILL KNOW YOU'RE DISCIPLES

During the Last Supper:

When [Judas] had gone out, Jesus said, "Now the Son of Man is glorified, and God is glorified in Him. If God is glorified in Him, God will also glorify Him in Himself, and glorify Him immediately. Little children, I shall be with you a little while longer. You will seek Me; and as I said to the Jews, 'Where I am going, you cannot come,' so now I say to you. A new commandment I give to you, that you love one another; as I have loved you, that you also love one another. By this all will know that you are My disciples, if you have love for one another."

Simon Peter said to Him, "Lord, where are You going?"

Jesus answered him, "Where I am going you cannot follow Me now, but you shall follow Me afterward."

Peter said to Him, "Lord, why can I not follow You now? I will lay down my life for Your sake."

Jesus answered him, "Will you lay down your life for My sake? Most assuredly, I say to you, the rooster shall not crow till you have denied Me three times."

John 13:31–38 NKJV

❈

*H*ow is "Love one another" a new commandment? Isn't love for our neighbors the theme of the Old Testament? And how many times had Jesus already told his disciples and the enormous crowds that followed him about the centrality of love?

What was new about his command to love was the meaning of it. The love Jesus was asking of his disciples went beyond desiring the best for someone else. It was more than just kindness. Jesus was about to give his life as a ransom for their sins. He was taking the command to love from the Old Testament and lifting it to a new and higher standard. The new love was a willingness to lay down our lives for one another—to give up everything for the sake of someone else. When we die for someone, there is no way for them to repay us. It's not like borrowing twenty dollars until payday. They can't offer to buy us lunch tomorrow.

The love that Jesus commanded went beyond any paybacks. It is the willingness to sacrifice all for someone else, knowing that we can receive no benefit from it at all. The love Jesus asks from us is a love we can give only by letting Jesus live through us and for us. Only by his strength can we have the strength to love as he does.

LOVE'S RESULTS

During the Last Supper, after Judas had left the Upper Room, Jesus said:

"If you love Me, you will keep My commandments. And I will ask the Father, and He will give you another Counselor to be with you forever. He is the Spirit of truth. The world is unable to receive Him because it doesn't see Him or know Him. But you do know Him, because He remains with you and will be in you. I will not leave you as orphans; I am coming to you.

"In a little while the world will see Me no longer, but you will see Me. Because I live, you will live too. In that day you will know that I am in My Father, you are in Me, and I am in you. The one who has My commands and keeps them is the one who loves Me. And the one who loves Me will be loved by My Father. I also will love him and will reveal Myself to him."

John 14:15–21 HCSB

❀

*W*hen Jesus told his disciples to pray, they didn't recognize the importance of his command. They didn't know how Jesus' request that they pray could matter more to them than their desire to sleep. Their ignorance and their love of themselves overwhelmed their love of Jesus.

Jesus was about to be betrayed. Judas had just left them, and within twenty-four hours Jesus would be dead. Jesus promised that once he was gone he would send them the Counselor: the Holy Spirit. He called it the Spirit of Truth, because the truth is what sets us free from sin. The truth is what allows us to see clearly what we need to do. The truth is what allows us to overcome temptation—like the temptation to sleep.

Had the disciples really understood what was about to happen that dark night that Jesus was betrayed, would they not have been able to resist the temptation to sleep? If they knew the truth, that Jesus was going to die for the sins of the world, would they not suddenly have been wide awake and praying desperately for Jesus to bear up? They would have joined with Jesus in his prayer to his Father, "Not my will, but yours." They would not have given in to the temptation to sleep.

Would we give in to the extra piece of chocolate cake if we saw the truth of what it would do to us? The extra pounds, the need for exercise, the rise in our cholesterol, the heart attack, the shortened life? If we saw the *whole* truth of whatever temptations we face, we would be much less likely to give in to them. The indwelling Spirit offers that kind of wisdom, that sort of truth, that sort of power, if we will only listen.

WHAT WE DO FOR LOVE

During the Last Supper, after Jesus predicted Peter's betrayal:

Judas (not Iscariot) said, "Master, why is it that you are about to make yourself plain to us but not to the world?"

"Because a loveless world," said Jesus, "is a sightless world. If anyone loves me, he will carefully keep my word and my Father will love him—we'll move right into the neighborhood! Not loving me means not keeping my words. The message you are hearing isn't mine. It's the message of the Father who sent me.

"I'm telling you these things while I'm still living with you. The Friend, the Holy Spirit whom the Father will send at my request, will make everything plain to you. He will remind you of all the things I have told you. I'm leaving you well and whole. That's my parting gift to you. Peace. I don't leave you the way you're used to being left—feeling abandoned, bereft. So don't be upset. Don't be distraught.

"You've heard me tell you, 'I'm going away, and I'm coming back.' If you loved me, you would be glad that I'm on my way to the Father because the Father is the goal and purpose of my life.

"I've told you this ahead of time, before it happens, so that when it does happen, the confirmation will deepen your belief in me. I'll not be talking with you much more like this because the chief of this godless world is about to attack."

John 14:22–30 MSG

※

*J*esus was about to die on the cross. For three days, his disciples would suffer great grief and fear. But after his resurrection, that grief would briefly turn to joy until he left them again.

On the threshold of their misery, Jesus promised to give his disciples a peace unlike the sort that the world gave. It was the peace they would have once the Holy Spirit moved inside them at pentecost.

The peace Jesus gave his disciples after he left them is the same peace Jesus gives us today. It is the peace that allowed them to turn the world upside down. The peace Jesus offered his disciples was not a life without pain, without trouble, or without stress. Rather, it was the peace that came of knowing that all their struggles were worth it.

For us, Jesus' peace gives us the strength to get out of bed even when our lives are coming undone. Jesus' peace makes it possible for us to love our neighbors even when there's nothing making it easy or natural to do so. Jesus' peace means that God reassures us each day that we're not alone. Jesus' peace helps us realize that even though we are not free of trouble, God loves us and will help us pass through it.

HARD PROMISE

During the Last Supper, Jesus said:

"If the world hates you, be aware that it hated me before it hated you. If you belonged to the world, the world would love you as its own. Because you do not belong to the world, but I have chosen you out of the world—therefore the world hates you. Remember the word that I said to you, 'Servants are not greater than their master.' If they persecuted me, they will persecute you; if they kept my word, they will keep yours also. But they will do all these things to you on account of my name, because they do not know him who sent me. If I had not come and spoken to them, they would not have sin; but now they have no excuse for their sin. Whoever hates me hates my Father also. If I had not done among them the works that no one else did, they would not have sin. But now they have seen and hated both me and my Father. It was to fulfill the word that is written in their law, 'They hated me without a cause.'"

John 15:18–25 NRSV

Although Jesus promised us an abundant life, we should no more expect a life free of stress than we would expect a beautiful rosebush free of thorns. On top of that, rosebushes need pruning, watering, and fertilizing. They go dormant in the winter. And the blossoms wilt and die eventually.

We'd like to believe that Jesus has promised us a life of ease and physical prosperity, because ease and physical prosperity are what most of us want. But Jesus promised thorns along with the rich blessings. Jesus wanted us to be just as happy as he was. He thoroughly enjoyed his life, even though all his life he knew he'd someday die—just as all of us know we'll die. Jesus experienced a violent and painful death upon a Roman cross. Jesus promised his disciples that the world would treat them no better than it had treated him.

Does this mean that if we're happy and prosperous, somehow we've been disobedient? No more than being miserable and suffering demonstrates a sinful condition. Jesus' life was abundant because he understood it was being lived for his Father's glory. He knew that his suffering had purpose. Likewise, we can have confidence that since God loves us, there is purpose in whatever we must endure. We want to have the mind of Christ—that is, we want to have the same perspective on life that Jesus had.

THE FATHER'S LOVE

Speaking to his disciples at the Last Supper, Jesus said:

"This is what I want you to do: Ask the Father for whatever is in keeping with the things I've revealed to you. Ask in my name, according to my will, and he'll most certainly give it to you. Your joy will be a river overflowing its banks!

"I've used figures of speech in telling you these things. Soon I'll drop the figures and tell you about the Father in plain language. Then you can make your requests directly to him in relation to this life I've revealed to you. I won't continue making requests of the Father on your behalf. I won't need to. Because you've gone out on a limb, committed yourselves to love and trust in me, believing I came directly from the Father, the Father loves you directly. First, I left the Father and arrived in the world; now I leave the world and travel to the Father."

John 16:23–28 MSG

When we pray, to whom are we really talking? We don't actually ask Jesus for anything. Instead, we ask his Father. In essence, we're telling the Father that "Jesus sent me and said you'd do this." And why do we ask for things from God? Jesus said we do it so we can be completely happy. And it isn't that Jesus then intercedes on our behalf with a reluctant deity when we invoke his name. God is not reluctant. Jesus wants us to understand that God loves us as much as he loves Jesus.

God knows what we really want, and he knows what we really need. Too often, we don't actually know what we want or need. We may think we do, but chances are that we are missing the big picture and are not asking for as much as God wants to give us.

We want a roommate, for instance, but what we really need is more income to pay the rent when it comes due every month. A roommate may be the way to do it, but God knows the root cause of what we're asking for and will satisfy *that* need rather than giving us what we think will satisfy that need. We're only human. God knows us better than we know ourselves. Don't doubt that God has the best of intentions for us; but it isn't all about us. There's a whole world interconnected to us as well. Our lives touch the lives of everyone else, and their lives touch ours. God works things together to benefit all of us.

UNITY

In the Garden of Gethsemane, Jesus prayed to his Father:

"I do not ask on behalf of these alone, but for those also who believe in Me through their word; that they may all be one; even as You, Father, are in Me and I in You, that they also may be in Us, so that the world may believe that You sent Me.

"The glory which You have given Me I have given to them, that they may be one, just as We are one; I in them and You in Me, that they may be perfected in unity, so that the world may know that You sent Me, and loved them, even as You have loved Me.

"Father, I desire that they also, whom You have given Me, be with Me where I am, so that they may see My glory which You have given Me, for You loved Me before the foundation of the world.

"O righteous Father, although the world has not known You, yet I have known You; and these have known that You sent Me; and I have made Your name known to them, and will make it known, so that the love with which You loved Me may be in them, and I in them."

John 17:20–26 NASB

※

One evening nearly two thousand years ago, Jesus himself got down on his knees, prayed specifically for us, and asked his Father to give us the glory that the Father had given to him.

What is glory? Glory is to accomplishment as sunlight is to the sun. Glory is the consequence—the effect—of accomplishment. True glory belongs to victors, to those who perform admirably beyond expectation or what is required.

God has given us the glory that Jesus has from the Father. We have been crucified with Christ and no longer live, except as Christ lives in us (Galatians 2:20). Our accomplishments are all thanks to him, and we have nothing left to boast about besides Jesus' cross (Ephesians 2:10; Galatians 6:14). We have become one with him and one with the Father. What they have, we have. What they are, we are. The glory that Jesus got the Father to give us is the glory of accomplishing his will, just as Jesus did; of living righteously and of living for others, just as Jesus did. Our righteousness isn't our doing; it is God's doing.

We do not think too highly of ourselves; rather, we do not think highly enough. Pride, boasting, and arrogance grow not from genuine greatness, but from insecurity. When the gold-medal winner tells his mom that he won, he is not boasting. He is merely describing what is. True glory eliminates boasting. We instead can merely declare what is: the glory we have in Jesus, thanks to his death and resurrection.

DAY 27

TEMPTATION

After leaving the Upper Room after the Last Supper:

[Jesus] went, as he so often did, to Mount Olives. The disciples followed him. When they arrived at the place, he said, "Pray that you don't give in to temptation."

He pulled away from them about a stone's throw, knelt down, and prayed, "Father, remove this cup from me. But please, not what I want. What do *you* want?" At once an angel from heaven was at his side, strengthening him. He prayed on all the harder. Sweat, wrung from him like drops of blood, poured off his face.

He got up from prayer, went back to the disciples and found them asleep, drugged by grief. He said, "What business do you have sleeping? Get up. Pray so you won't give in to temptation."

Luke 22:39–46 MSG

I can resist anything but temptation, so goes the old joke. What is temptation? Temptation is the desire to do something we shouldn't. It needs to be noticed that we can be tempted—enticed—to do only something that we would want to do. If you dislike liver, for instance, the offer of a steaming plate of liver and onions will do nothing for you. You won't be tempted at all. But change out that plate of liver for something you crave—a cheeseburger, for instance—and suddenly you *are* tempted.

Temptation is not a sin. Only giving in to the temptation is sin. Whether something is a sin is sometimes entirely dependent upon the context. After all, there is a time and place for a cheeseburger.

Jesus told his disciples to pray that they wouldn't give in to temptation. He asked them to pray for such protection at that particular moment because it had been a long day, it was late at night, and the one thing the disciples really wanted at that particular moment was something that in itself was usually a good thing: sleep. They needed to resist their natural urge to sleep. Jesus asked them to pray with him for strength for what he was about to face on the cross. But the disciples didn't understand. They didn't know what Jesus needed from them, and so they repeatedly gave in to their temptation.

Like the disciples, we don't always recognize the temptation we need protection from until it is too late. We should always be praying for protection from temptation.

VIOLENCE

In the Garden of Gethsemane:

While [Jesus] was still speaking a crowd came up, and the man who was called Judas, one of the Twelve, was leading them. He approached Jesus to kiss him, but Jesus asked him, "Judas, are you betraying the Son of Man with a kiss?"

When Jesus' followers saw what was going to happen, they said, "Lord, should we strike with our swords?" And one of them struck the servant of the high priest, cutting off his right ear.

But Jesus answered, "No more of this!" And he touched the man's ear and healed him.

Then Jesus said to the chief priests, the officers of the temple guard, and the elders, who had come for him, "Am I leading a rebellion, that you have come with swords and clubs? Every day I was with you in the temple courts, and you did not lay a hand on me. But this is your hour—when darkness reigns."

Luke 22:47–53 NIV

Jesus' disciples, the crowds that followed Jesus, and the religious establishment thought only in terms of earthly politics. They expected the Messiah to restore the Davidic monarchy, to overthrow the Roman hegemony, and to make Israel the most powerful kingdom on earth. When the soldiers came to arrest Jesus, his followers assumed that the war of liberation had begun. Instead, Jesus ordered surrender. The one act of bloodshed, Jesus corrected. He healed the victim of his disciple's sword.

Then he asked those who had come to arrest him if they really thought he was leading a rebellion. Of course, they did. But he was telling them, by the question and the words that followed, that they were mistaken.

Jesus was not about politics or government. The Talmud, an ancient Jewish commentary on the first five books of the Bible, states that saving a single soul saves a universe. Jesus was all about just that. He was about the kingdom of heaven, not the kingdom of man. And where was the kingdom of heaven being established? In the human heart. If you change the heart, Jesus knew, you change the individual. There's a whole world in a human heart. We can feed a hungry person; spend time with the lonely outcast; listen; take in a homeless, parentless child. We can do what is right regardless of how someone treats us. Our testimony to Jesus' sacrifice and resurrection will change society—has changed it—more than all the laws and all the armies in all the nations in all the world.

HE LOVES ME, HE LOVES ME NOT

Following Jesus' resurrection, he met his disciples at the Sea of Galilee:

After breakfast Jesus asked Simon Peter, "Simon son of John, do you love me more than these?"

"Yes, Lord," Peter replied, "you know I love you."

"Then feed my lambs," Jesus told him.

Jesus repeated the question: "Simon son of John, do you love me?"

"Yes, Lord," Peter said, "you know I love you."

"Then take care of my sheep," Jesus said.

A third time he asked him, "Simon son of John, do you love me?"

Peter was hurt that Jesus asked the question a third time. He said, "Lord, you know everything. You know that I love you."

Jesus said, "Then feed my sheep.

"I tell you the truth, when you were young, you were able to do as you liked; you dressed yourself and went wherever you wanted to go. But when you are old, you will stretch out your hands, and others will dress you and take you where you don't want to go." Jesus said this to let him know by what kind of death he would glorify God. Then Jesus told him, "Follow me."

John 21:15–19 NLT

❧

𝒫eter thought he didn't deserve Jesus' friendship any longer. He believed that he had failed him and that he was beyond forgiveness. Peter doubted that he really loved Jesus at all. Jesus made a special effort to show Peter that he was mistaken. Jesus showed Peter that despite everything he had done or failed to do, Jesus still loved Peter. And, perhaps more important, Jesus reassured Peter that he still loved Jesus.

The meaning of the word *love* becomes clear from paying attention to how Jesus used it. Peter denied Jesus three times, so three times Jesus asked him to affirm his love. Jesus reassured Peter. Just because Peter failed, it didn't mean that Peter didn't love Jesus. And it didn't mean that Jesus loved Peter any less. Peter was still Jesus' friend and was still a part of God's plan.

Peter had said he would die for Jesus, but when the time came, he'd protected himself instead. So Jesus revealed that Peter would take care of God's people, establish his church, and in the end, that he *would* die like Jesus on a cross. Peter's love for Jesus was not in doubt.

Jesus reassured his friend that failure today didn't mean failure for all time. Sometimes, like Peter, we may feel we haven't lived up to all that God wants of us. But God never gives up on us, even if we sometimes give up on ourselves.

❀❀❀❀❀❀❀❀❀❀❀❀❀❀❀❀❀❀❀❀❀❀❀❀❀❀❀❀❀❀

WHEN HATE BECOMES LOVE

After Paul was arrested in Jerusalem, he gave a speech about his conversion:

["Ananias said to me,] 'The God of our fathers has appointed you to know His will, to see the Righteous One, and to hear the sound of His voice. For you will be a witness for Him to all people of what you have seen and heard. And now, why delay? Get up and be baptized, and wash away your sins by calling on His name.'

"After I came back to Jerusalem and was praying in the temple complex, I went into a visionary state and saw [Jesus] telling me, 'Hurry and get out of Jerusalem quickly, because they will not accept your testimony about Me!'

"But I said, 'Lord, they know that in synagogue after synagogue I had those who believed in You imprisoned and beaten. And when the blood of Your witness Stephen was being shed, I myself was standing by and approving, and I guarded the clothes of those who killed him.'

"Then He said to me, 'Go, because I will send you far away to the Gentiles.'"

They listened to him up to this word. Then they raised their voices, shouting, "Wipe this person off the earth—it's a disgrace for him to live!"

Acts 22:14–22 HCSB

❀

Paul hated Christians and the Jesus they followed. Paul was certain that Christians were a danger to the well-being of Jewish society. But then one day Paul met Jesus, and everything changed for him.

Paul's transformation didn't stop with his conversion to Christianity. After Paul visited Jerusalem, Jesus told Paul to do something even more unsettling. He told Paul to preach to the Gentiles. Most Jews despised Gentiles. The word translated *Gentiles* literally meant "the Greeks." Two hundred years earlier, the Greek king Antiochus Epiphanes had tried to force the Jews to worship the Greek gods. He had even sacrificed a pig in the temple. The Jews had revolted and driven the Greeks out. Jesus sent Paul to talk to these very people.

Years later, when Paul shared what Jesus had asked him to do, the reaction of the Jewish mob in Jerusalem that was already angry with him was unsurprisingly negative. The prevailing view among Jewish people of Paul's time was that the Messiah would wipe out sinners. The sinners were the Gentiles, and the mob was not happy to hear that the Messiah loved Gentiles.

We like to hear that God loves us. We like to know that God loves our families and those who are on our side. But God also loves those who have hurt us and those who are fighting against us. God wants us to love our enemies the same way we love ourselves and the same way God loves us.

TRUTHS AND LIES

Lies are untruths told for the purpose of deception, usually to protect a person for fear that the truth will cause harm to himself. Or a lie may be told in the hope of causing a problem for an enemy. The lie may spring from hatred, a desire to win victory, or a desire to gain some other benefit or advantage. Truth aligns with reality. Philip K. Dick wrote, "Reality is that which, when you stop believing in it, doesn't go away." But truth is not always popular. Winston Churchill is quoted as saying, "Mankind will occasionally stumble over the truth, but most of the time he will pick himself up and continue on."

❈

The truth will set you free.
John 8:32 CEV

STRENGTH IN WEAKNESS

After John the Baptist identified Jesus as the Messiah:

Jesus was led by the Spirit into the wilderness to be tempted there by the devil. For forty days and forty nights he fasted and became very hungry.

During that time the devil came and said to him, "If you are the Son of God, tell these stones to become loaves of bread."

But Jesus told him, "No! The Scriptures say, 'People do not live by bread alone, but by every word that comes from the mouth of God.'"

Then the devil took him to the holy city, Jerusalem, to the highest point of the Temple, and said, "If you are the Son of God, jump off! For the Scriptures say, 'He will order his angels to protect you. And they will hold you up with their hands so you won't even hurt your foot on a stone.'"

Jesus responded, "The Scriptures also say, 'You must not test the LORD your God.'"

Next the devil took him to the peak of a very high mountain and showed him all the kingdoms of the world and their glory. "I will give it all to you," he said, "if you will kneel down and worship me."

"Get out of here, Satan," Jesus told him. "For the Scriptures say,

'You must worship the Lord your God and serve only him.'"

Then the devil went away, and angels came and took care of Jesus.

Matthew 4:1–11 NLT

❋

*T*he devil believes the Bible and takes it seriously. That's why, when he tempted Jesus in the wilderness, most of his temptations came with biblical citations. Satan imagined that Jesus would have to do what he said since it was biblical.

Satan's temptations were subtle lies, the consequence of his selective misreading and misunderstanding of the Bible. Satan, like many people, ignored the context of the passages he quoted. He went to the Bible looking for phrases to bolster his point of view. He imposed his agenda on the text, rather than looking for God's agenda.

Jesus responded to Satan by quoting the Bible back to him, challenging the devil's misunderstandings. Jesus was not willing to search the Bible to find a passage that would justify what he wanted to do. Instead, Jesus knew the Bible as a whole and then did what the Bible wanted him to do. It was easy for Jesus to see through Satan's lies.

Because Satan took the Bible seriously, Jesus' scriptural responses shut him down. Jesus' success against the devil demonstrated that knowing the Bible well is our best shield against temptation. We overcome Satan's lies when we use God's words against Satan.

THE BIBLE ENDURES

Jesus was speaking to his followers during his Sermon on the Mount:

"You are like salt for everyone on earth. But if salt no longer tastes like salt, how can it make food salty? All it is good for is to be thrown out and walked on.

"You are like light for the whole world. A city built on top of a hill cannot be hidden, and no one would light a lamp and put it under a clay pot. A lamp is placed on a lampstand, where it can give light to everyone in the house. Make your light shine, so that others will see the good that you do and will praise your Father in heaven.

"Don't suppose that I came to do away with the Law and the Prophets. I did not come to do away with them, but to give them their full meaning.

Heaven and earth may disappear. But I promise you that not even a period or comma will ever disappear from the Law. Everything written in it must happen.

"If you reject even the least important command in the Law and teach others to do the same, you will be the least important person in the kingdom of heaven. But if you obey and teach others its commands, you will have an important place in the kingdom. You must obey God's commands better than the Pharisees and the teachers of the Law obey them. If you don't, I promise you that you will never get into the kingdom of heaven."

Matthew 5:13–20 CEV

❀

*W*hen Jesus spoke of the law, he meant the Old Testament. The Old Testament is still important for us today. Jesus' arrival did not render the Old Testament, with all its rules and regulations, meaningless. The Old Testament did not stop being God's Word. Instead, Jesus affirmed its usefulness.

In fact, Jesus did not teach much that was truly new. Instead, he wiped off the dust and cobwebs that had hidden the Old Testament's meaning from the people of Israel. Like an antique painting being carefully restored by modern conservators, so Jesus revealed the word of God that had been obscured by centuries of bad interpretations and misreading. The Pharisees and teachers of the law may have wanted to do what the Old Testament said. But they all too often misunderstood and misapplied it.

The Old Testament is for us today. Ignoring it means ignoring three quarters of what God wants us to know about him. Jesus told us that we cannot live well without it and that we will suffer loss in God's kingdom if we try.

BROKEN KINGDOM

While Jesus preached in the towns of Galilee:

A demon-possessed man who was blind and unable to speak was brought to Him. He healed him, so that the man could both speak and see. And all the crowds were astounded and said, "Perhaps this is the Son of David!"

When the Pharisees heard this, they said, "The man drives out demons only by Beelzebul, the ruler of the demons."

Knowing their thoughts, He told them: "Every kingdom divided against itself is headed for destruction, and no city or house divided against itself will stand. If Satan drives out Satan, he is divided against himself. How then will his kingdom stand? And if I drive out demons by Beelzebul, who is it your sons drive them out by? For this reason they will be your judges. If I drive out demons by the Spirit of God, then the kingdom of God has come to you. How can someone enter a strong man's house and steal his possessions unless he first ties up the strong man? Then he can rob his house."

Matthew 12:22–29 HCSB

🌼

The religious establishment of Israel thought they had a way to show up Jesus. They brought him a demon-possessed man who was blind and mute. Since communicating with him was essentially impossible, they figured there was no way Jesus would be able to cast out the demon. According to widespread Jewish belief at that time, only the Messiah would be able to fix such a person, and the religious establishment had decided Jesus wasn't the Messiah. His failure would then prove them right.

But Jesus healed the man easily. The crowd was astonished. They couldn't help but think that Jesus must indeed be the son of David—that is, the Messiah—though, due to the presence of their religious leaders, they posed it as a question rather than making a clear statement.

Jesus consistently refused to take up residence in the box the religious establishment had built for the Messiah. But Jesus did wonders that only the Messiah could do, and so they finally accused Jesus of being powered by the devil. Otherwise, they'd have to acknowledge he was the Messiah, and that seemed more impossible to them than their ridiculous suggestion, which Jesus easily dismantled. People are willing to go to remarkable lengths to shore up their beliefs, especially when their pride is on the line. Too easily might we, like the Pharisees, find that we prefer the comfort of our cherished traditions to the truth. But we must choose to live with the truth rather than with the comfort of the cherished idols we've set up in our hearts.

UNPARDONABLE SIN

Jesus was talking to the Pharisees in a house near the Sea of Galilee, after healing a blind and mute demon-possessed man:

"Anyone who is not with Me is against Me, and anyone who does not gather with Me scatters. Because of this, I tell you, people will be forgiven every sin and blasphemy, but the blasphemy against the Spirit will not be forgiven. Whoever speaks a word against the Son of Man, it will be forgiven him. But whoever speaks against the Holy Spirit, it will not be forgiven him, either in this age or in the one to come.

"Either make the tree good and its fruit good, or make the tree bad and its fruit bad; for a tree is known by its fruit. Brood of vipers! How can you speak good things when you are evil? For the mouth speaks from the overflow of the heart. A good man produces good things from his storeroom of good, and an evil man produces evil things from his storeroom of evil. I tell you that on the day of judgment people will have to account for every careless word they speak. For by your words you will be acquitted, and by your words you will be condemned."

Matthew 12:30–37 HCSB

*W*hat happens when an irresistible force meets an immovable object? The old logic question may appear profound, but it's nothing more than a word game, since by definition something "irresistible" and something "immovable" cannot exist simultaneously. Can you commit the unpardonable sin? It is a similar sort of question.

But many decent people fear they have done something so bad that they can never be forgiven. Weighed down by guilt, they are convinced that they are beyond hope of redemption. Some respond to their guilty consciences by deciding that they might as well try to "eat, drink and be merry," for tomorrow they're going to die and there's nothing they can do to change their circumstances.

There is no one alive today who is guilty, or ever can be guilty, of the particular "unpardonable sin" that Jesus was referring to. The unpardonable sin was something that the religious leadership of Israel were guilty of when they attributed Jesus' miracles, done by the power of the Holy Spirit, to the devil. Their blasphemy against the Spirit of God, Jesus told them, would never be forgiven. And that was only because they didn't *want* to repent. They thought they were right. That's what made it "unpardonable" for them.

Jesus is not walking the earth now, and neither are those Pharisees who spoke against Jesus' demon casting. Jesus' death on the cross covers any sin that we have ever committed or ever will or can commit. Today, no one is beyond the hope of forgiveness. God will forgive us of anything we might do.

❋❋❋❋❋❋❋❋❋❋❋❋❋❋❋❋❋❋❋❋❋❋❋❋❋❋❋❋❋❋❋❋❋

BREAD MAKING

On their way to the other side of the lake, the disciples discovered they had forgotten to bring along bread. In the meantime, Jesus said to them, "Keep a sharp eye out for Pharisee-Sadducee yeast."

Thinking he was scolding them for forgetting bread, they discussed in whispers what to do. Jesus knew what they were doing and said, "Why all these worried whispers about forgetting the bread? Runt believers! Haven't you caught on yet? Don't you remember the five loaves of bread and the five thousand people, and how many baskets of fragments you picked up? Or the seven loaves that fed four thousand, and how many baskets of leftovers you collected? Haven't you realized yet that bread isn't the problem? The problem is yeast, Pharisee-Sadducee yeast." Then they got it: that he wasn't concerned about eating, but teaching—the Pharisee-Sadducee kind of teaching.

Matthew 16:5–12 MSG

❋

*T*he late Gilda Radner played an odd character on *Saturday Night Live* named Emily Latella, who was notorious for her misunderstandings and the long-winded rants they inspired. Once she railed for a long time against the movement to limit "violins on television." When told that the movement was, in fact, against "violence," she got quiet and then murmured, "Never mind."

Not long after the feeding of the four thousand, and right after a confrontation with a group of Pharisees and Sadducees, Jesus warned his disciples about the "Pharisee-Sadducee yeast." But his disciples thought he was scolding them for having forgotten to bring bread with them.

What was wrong with the teaching of the Pharisees and the Sadducees? They took the Bible seriously. They were concerned about sin. They were concerned about the survival of the Jewish nation. How could those be bad things?

The disciples missed the point of the Bible, which was how to love God and how to love one another. They approached Scripture the way a bureaucrat would approach paperwork. Getting the blanks filled, the boxes checked, and getting everything signed and stamped became their focus. But for Jesus, what mattered was not the forms but the people behind them. The religious establishment had lost sight of the fact that the rules that obsessed them existed to make sure people got help. They had misplaced priorities.

Jesus wants us not to lose sight of the purpose behind all the rules. God wants to make our lives better. The laws are summed up by the one rule, to love one another. The rules simply help us do that.

STATEMENT OF FAITH

When Jesus came to the region of Caesarea Philippi, he asked his disciples, "Who do people say the Son of Man is?"

They replied, "Some say John the Baptist; others say Elijah; and still others, Jeremiah or one of the prophets."

"But what about you?" he asked. "Who do you say I am?"

Simon Peter answered, "You are the Christ, the Son of the living God."

Jesus replied, "Blessed are you, Simon son of Jonah, for this was not revealed to you by man, but by my Father in heaven. And I tell you that you are Peter, and on this rock I will build my church, and the gates of Hades will not overcome it. I will give you the keys of the kingdom of heaven; whatever you bind on earth will be bound in heaven, and whatever you loose on earth will be loosed in heaven." Then he warned his disciples not to tell anyone that he was the Christ.

Matthew 16:13–20 NIV

Sometimes Jesus taught by telling stories. And sometimes he taught by asking pointed, open-ended questions. Asking questions like that is sometimes called the Socratic method, a technique used by the ancient Greek philosopher Socrates, who had died nearly four hundred years before Jesus was born. Sometimes when Jesus wanted his disciples to understand something new about himself, he started by asking them some questions. Jesus asked the questions because he knew his questions would get the disciples to recognize something that they might not otherwise understand.

Jesus' question about his identity was one that everyone must answer for himself or herself eventually. Who is Jesus? Is he a prophet? A teacher? Human? Divine? The author and apologist C. S. Lewis said that Jesus purposely narrowed the possibilities. Like Jesus' disciples, we must decide if Jesus is really God in human form or not. If he is not God, then he is either nuts or a con man. He's certainly not someone to follow or listen to.

As we think about Jesus, we have no other option, just as Peter and the disciples had no real choice in how they identified him. Once we start thinking about the possibilities, we know that Peter's conclusion is the only one that makes any sense given the facts. We must, like Peter, bow down and worship Jesus.

THE AFTERLIFE

During Jesus' last week in Jerusalem:

The Sadducees did not believe that people would rise to life after death. So that same day some of the Sadducees came to Jesus and said:

Teacher, Moses wrote that if a married man dies and has no children, his brother should marry the widow. Their first son would then be thought of as the son of the dead brother.

Once there were seven brothers who lived here. The first one married, but died without having any children. So his wife was left to his brother. The same thing happened to the second and third brothers and finally to all seven of them. At last the woman died. When God raises people from death, whose wife will this woman be? She had been married to all seven brothers.

Jesus answered:

You are completely wrong! You don't know what the Scriptures teach. And you don't know anything about the power of God. When God raises people to life, they won't marry. They will be like the angels in heaven. And as for people being raised to life, God was speaking to you when he said, "I am the God worshiped by Abraham, Isaac, and Jacob." He isn't the God of the dead, but of the living.

The crowds were surprised to hear what Jesus was teaching.

Matthew 22:23–33 CEV

The Sadducees were the traditionalists of their day. They were a sect of Judaism—think "denomination"—that was extremely strict and very conservative. They believed that only the first five books of the Bible, Genesis through Deuteronomy, were Scripture. Since they didn't accept the authority of any of the prophets or other Old Testament writings, they rejected the resurrection, demons, and angels. They thought Pharisees were adding dangerous innovations and silly speculations to God's true Word.

Jesus worked with people just as he found them. When Jesus solved the theological riddle that the Sadducees brought him, he took them to the parts of Scripture that they acknowledged were authoritative. He demonstrated that the concept of resurrection could be seen even in Genesis. They had missed what should have been obvious. After establishing that their truncated Bible taught the reality of an afterlife, he then challenged the presupposition underlying their riddle. Their assumption that life post-resurrection would be just as life was pre-resurrection was also mistaken. Their visions, their imaginations, their assumptions, Jesus pointed out, were too small. Like Jesus, when we teach we must not shy away from the truth. But we can put the truth in a context that will make sense. We need to learn to know our audience the way Jesus knew his.

PRESTIGE

In Jerusalem, just before Passover:

Jesus said to the crowds and to his disciples, "The scribes and the Pharisees sit on Moses' seat; therefore, do whatever they teach you and follow it; but do not do as they do, for they do not practice what they teach. They tie up heavy burdens, hard to bear, and lay them on the shoulders of others; but they themselves are unwilling to lift a finger to move them. They do all their deeds to be seen by others; for they make their phylacteries broad and their fringes long. They love to have the place of honor at banquets and the best seats in the synagogues, and to be greeted with respect in the marketplaces, and to have people call them rabbi. But you are not to be called rabbi, for you have one teacher, and you are all students. And call no one your father on earth, for you have one Father—the one in heaven. Nor are you to be called instructors, for you have one instructor, the Messiah. The greatest among you will be your servant. All who exalt themselves will be humbled, and all who humble themselves will be exalted."

Matthew 23:1–12 NRSV

※

*S*alute the uniform, not the man." It's an old saying in the military that grows from the sad reality that an individual in a position of authority may not be deserving of it. Jesus told his disciples to listen to what the Pharisees taught, since their positions of authority meant they had the right to be heard. But Jesus warned them not to imitate their lifestyles.

Then Jesus gave some illustrations to explain his point. In the Old Testament, God told his people to bind the Word of God to their hands and to hang it between their eyes. What God had meant metaphorically—that the Bible should be a guide in everything they did—the Jewish people took literally. Phylacteries were boxes containing Bible verses that they strapped to their wrists and foreheads. The Pharisees made their phylacteries especially large so that everyone could see just how religious they were.

The word *rabbi* in Hebrew means "my master" or "my teacher." Jesus warned his disciples—and us—that the Pharisees were wrong to exalt themselves that way. He also told us that looking up to people as if they could take the place of God was a serious mistake. Instead, we should be concerned only about the needs of others, not about our status among them.

SCORCHED-EARTH POLICY

[Jesus] began to teach by the sea. And a great multitude was gathered to Him, so that He got into a boat and sat in it on the sea; and the whole multitude was on the land facing the sea. Then He taught them many things by parables, and said to them in His teaching:

"Listen! Behold, a sower went out to sow. And it happened, as he sowed, that some seed fell by the wayside; and the birds of the air came and devoured it. Some fell on stony ground, where it did not have much earth; and immediately it sprang up because it had no depth of earth. But when the sun was up it was scorched, and because it had no root it withered away. And some seed fell among thorns; and the thorns grew up and choked it, and it yielded no crop. But other seed fell on good ground and yielded a crop that sprang up, increased and produced: some thirtyfold, some sixty, and some a hundred."

And He said to them, "He who has ears to hear, let him hear!"

But when He was alone, those around Him with the twelve asked Him about the parable. And He said to them, "To you it has been given to know the mystery of the kingdom of God; but to those who are outside, all things come in parables, so that

'Seeing they may see and not perceive,
And hearing they may hear and not understand;
Lest they should turn,
And their sins be forgiven them.'"

Mark 4:1–12 NKJV

❋

*I*s it true that Jesus wanted to keep the truth away from some of the people he talked to? Jesus explained that his parables fulfilled the words of the prophet Isaiah that said the people would hear and still not understand, because if they understood their sins would be forgiven.

When Jesus said that people would "hear but not understand," he was not explaining the purpose of his parables. Rather, he described how parables actually worked out in practice. Despite the fact that many people seemed to be listening, the reality was that they weren't listening to be changed or to find the truth. They were listening for justification. If people could actually hear with understanding, they would be changed. But as it was, that rarely happened.

The sad truth is that many people will never believe the gospel message no matter how clearly it is explained. They won't believe because they choose not to. We have to realize that much of the time, what we say will simply go in one ear and out the other. Or worse, it will be completely misunderstood. Our job as Christians is merely to tell people about Jesus. What they do with our words is up to them.

UNDERSTANDING PARABLES

Next to the Sea of Galilee, Jesus taught his disciples:

"Do you not understand this parable? How then will you understand any of the parables? The sower sows the word. These are the ones along the path where the word is sown: when they hear, immediately Satan comes and takes away the word sown in them. And these are the ones sown on rocky ground: when they hear the word, immediately they receive it with joy. But they have no root in themselves; they are short-lived. When affliction or persecution comes because of the word, they immediately stumble. Others are sown among thorns; these are the ones who hear the word, but the worries of this age, the seduction of wealth, and the desires for other things enter in and choke the word, and it becomes unfruitful. But the ones sown on good ground are those who hear the word, welcome it, and produce a crop: 30, 60, and 100 times what was sown."

Mark 4:13–20 HCSB

Jesus was disappointed that his disciples didn't understand him. In fact, he wondered if they were capable of understanding any parable at all.

Despite Jesus' frustration, he still explained the parable to them. He never gave up on the job of bringing them enlightenment. What made it so hard for the disciples to learn was how much they thought they already knew. They had a lifetime's worth of data in their minds, some of it true, much of it not. It was information they had gleaned from their surrounding culture, most of which was accepted and believed without thought. Everything that Jesus ever told them had first to pass through everything that was already in their minds. It was easy for them to think they already understood what Jesus was saying even when they didn't. Too often, they believed they'd already heard it all before. Jesus' words reminded them of stuff they thought they knew. It was easy for them to set it aside.

The biggest barrier any of us face in making sense of what Jesus says is the stuff we think we already know: the facts that aren't necessarily so, the incomplete understanding of other facts, and the just plain misunderstandings that come from not hearing clearly and from the gaps in our educations. We can learn only if we develop humility, if we come to grips with just how little we know or can ever know. We can learn when we realize that we need to learn.

PETER'S WILL

Jesus and His disciples went out to the towns of Caesarea Philippi; and on the road He asked His disciples, saying to them, "Who do men say that I am?"

So they answered, "John the Baptist; but some say, Elijah; and others, one of the prophets."

He said to them, "But who do you say that I am?"

Peter answered and said to Him, "You are the Christ."

Then He strictly warned them that they should tell no one about Him.

And He began to teach them that the Son of Man must suffer many things, and be rejected by the elders and chief priests and scribes, and be killed, and after three days rise again. He spoke this word openly. Then Peter took Him aside and began to rebuke Him. But when He had turned around and looked at His disciples, He rebuked Peter, saying, "Get behind Me, Satan! For you are not mindful of the things of God, but the things of men."

Mark 8:27–33 NKJV

※

Great insight can be followed by great blindness. After telling Jesus what the word on the street was about who Jesus might be, Peter announced his conclusion: that Jesus was the Messiah. Jesus immediately told his disciples to keep that information to themselves.

Jesus wanted his disciples to keep it a secret perhaps to ensure that his death came at the right moment in time and in the right way. As the author of Ecclesiastes wrote, there is a time to speak and a time to be silent. Jesus' disciples, at that moment, needed to be silent (Ecclesiastes 3:7). It was Jesus' intent to be crucified after the religious establishment rejected his claim to being the Messiah. It was not his intent to die by any other method or at any other time. The timing was significant because he wanted to die at Passover, since the Passover ceremony was a picture God had painted of Jesus' coming sacrifice. Had the establishment learned too early that Jesus was claiming to be the Messiah, they might have attempted to kill him earlier. Jesus needed to die in Jerusalem, on Passover, at the hands of the Romans. Certain things had to come together at just the right time, in just the right way, in order for Jesus' sacrifice to happen the way God wanted it to happen.

We can trust God's timing to be perfect, and we can know that he has good reasons for why things happen when they do, in the way they do.

RUMORS

In Jerusalem, just days before the Last Supper:

As [Jesus] walked away from the Temple, one of his disciples said, "Teacher, look at that stonework! Those buildings!"

Jesus said, "You're impressed by this grandiose architecture? There's not a stone in the whole works that is not going to end up in a heap of rubble."

Later, as he was sitting on Mount Olives in full view of the Temple, Peter, James, John, and Andrew got him off by himself and asked, "Tell us, when is this going to happen? What sign will we get that things are coming to a head?"

Jesus began, "Watch out for doomsday deceivers. Many leaders are going to show up with forged identities claiming, 'I'm the One.' They will deceive a lot of people. When you hear of wars and rumored wars, keep your head and don't panic. This is routine history, and no sign of the end. Nation will fight nation and ruler fight ruler, over and over. Earthquakes will occur in various places. There will be famines. But these things are nothing compared to what's coming."

Mark 13:1–8 MSG

The pyramids are so old and seem so unchanging that there is an old Egyptian proverb that says, "All things fear time. But time fears the pyramids." However, nothing physical lasts forever, not even the more than five-thousand-year-old pyramids. Jesus' disciples were impressed by the glory of the Jerusalem temple and its seeming imperviousness. Humans are easily impressed by massive architecture.

Jesus wasn't. The beautiful buildings that they thought were so great, the temple that was the focal point of all Judaism, were going to become piles of rubble in a generation, thanks to the Roman army. The temple wasn't what was important; the God behind it was what mattered.

Rather than wondering about the nature of God and how they would be able to worship him without a temple, the only question the disciples had was about the timing of the temple's demolition.

Jesus didn't give them the answer they wanted; they wanted a date. Instead, he warned them against focusing on gloom-and-doom prophecies and worrying about the timing of such destruction. He told them that many people would claim to be the Messiah. And many people would overemphasize the problems in the world. Jesus' disciples expected a revolution and were mostly concerned about physical change rather than spiritual change. It is easy for us to become so focused on our immediate problems and joys that we lose perspective and forget about the one thing that will last forever, the kingdom of God.

THE GOOD OLD DAYS

In Galilee, shortly after Jesus chose the twelve apostles:

[The Pharisees] said to [Jesus], "John's disciples often fast and pray, and so do the disciples of the Pharisees, but yours go on eating and drinking."

Jesus answered, "Can you make the guests of the bridegroom fast while he is with them? But the time will come when the bridegroom will be taken from them; in those days they will fast."

He told them this parable: "No one tears a patch from a new garment and sews it on an old one. If he does, he will have torn the new garment, and the patch from the new will not match the old. And no one pours new wine into old wineskins. If he does, the new wine will burst the skins, the wine will run out and the wineskins will be ruined. No, new wine must be poured into new wineskins. And no one after drinking old wine wants the new, for he says, 'The old is better.'"

Luke 5:33–39 NIV

H. L. Menken wrote of Puritans that they were the sort of people who had "the haunting fear that someone, somewhere, might be happy." The Pharisees were the Puritans of Jesus' day, wondering why the disciples were so happy.

The Pharisees usually set aside a day each week for fasting, and they made certain that everyone could tell. They didn't comb their hair, they didn't bathe, and they kept a pained expression on their faces so that everyone could see just how devoted they were to God.

Since the Pharisees never saw the disciples acting so miserable, they believed that they—and Jesus—must not be properly devoted to God. There was a lot behind the Pharisees' simple question about fasting. They were attacking Jesus' credibility and his commitment to religion.

The Pharisees failed to recognize the reality of their situation. Fasting and praying, of the sort that the Pharisees had in mind, was what people did when things were going badly, when someone was seriously ill, or when a war was on the horizon. It was proper to fast during Yom Kippur, the Day of Atonement. It wasn't proper to fast during Purim or First Fruits, times for rejoicing. Jesus' disciples had no reason to feel glum: the Messiah was there and they were with him. When you're at a wedding and you're part of the wedding party, is that the time to fast?

There are, indeed, times to mourn, but there are also times to rejoice! When life gets us down, we can rightly be sad. But we know that our sadness will someday pass. We will rejoice again, since our names are written in the Book of Life and we have a never-ending eternity ahead of us in paradise.

WHAT MATTERS

Not far from the Sea of Galilee:

One Sabbath when Jesus and his disciples were walking through some wheat fields, the disciples picked some wheat. They rubbed the husks off with their hands and started eating the grain. Some Pharisees said, "Why are you picking grain on the Sabbath? You're not supposed to do that!"

Jesus answered, "You surely have read what David did when he and his followers were hungry. He went into the house of God and took the sacred loaves of bread that only priests were supposed to eat. He not only ate some himself, but even gave some to his followers."

Jesus finished by saying, "The Son of Man is Lord over the Sabbath."

On another Sabbath Jesus was teaching in a Jewish meeting place, and a man with a crippled right hand was there. Some Pharisees and teachers of the Law of Moses kept watching Jesus to see if he would heal the man. They did this because they wanted to accuse Jesus of doing something wrong.

Jesus knew what they were thinking. So he told the man to stand up where everyone could see him. And the man stood up. Then Jesus asked, "On the Sabbath should we do good deeds or evil deeds? Should we save someone's life or destroy it?"

After he had looked around at everyone, he told the man, "Stretch out your hand." He did, and his bad hand became completely well.

The teachers and the Pharisees were furious and started saying to each other, "What can we do about Jesus?"

Luke 6:1–11 CEV

※

What is the meaning of the word *is*? The religious leaders in Israel enjoyed puzzling over that sort of question. The Pharisees, the Sadducees, the scribes—they concerned themselves with riddles regarding the law. The Pharisees and Sadducees believed that the commandment to "keep the Sabbath" was not as simple as it appeared. When God said that one must not work on Saturday, they wondered what he meant by *work*. Was harvesting grain work? Obviously. How about threshing grain? Also obviously. But then what was *harvesting*? What was *threshing*? By simply plucking a few ears of wheat from a field, the disciples had "harvested" the wheat according to the definition of "harvesting" developed by the Pharisees and Sadducees. By rubbing the husks off in their hands, they had also "threshed" it.

In response to this Pharisaical line of reasoning, Jesus pointed out that their interpretation resulted in absurdity if they tried to apply it to some of the characters and situations in the Bible. Jesus wanted them to understand that in interpreting the Bible, it was important to pay attention to the whole thing.

If we get lost in the details, we may simply get lost.

HOPE AND CHANGE

After Jesus had raised a widow's son from the dead in Nain:

The disciples of John reported to him about all these things. Summoning two of his disciples, John sent them to the Lord, saying, "Are You the Expected One, or do we look for someone else?"

When the men came to Him, they said, "John the Baptist has sent us to You, to ask, 'Are You the Expected One, or do we look for someone else?'"

At that very time He cured many people of diseases and afflictions and evil spirits; and He gave sight to many who were blind.

And He answered and said to them, "Go and report to John what you have seen and heard: the blind receive sight, the lame walk, the lepers are cleansed, and the deaf hear, the dead are raised up, the poor have the gospel preached to them. Blessed is he who does not take offense at Me."

Luke 7:18–23 NASB

❈

John had spent his last few years like a limo driver at an airport waiting for his passenger near the baggage claim and holding up a sign with the name "Messiah" scrawled on it. John's question about Jesus was not just a consequence of discouragement from being locked away in prison. His question grew out of what people in the day believed about the coming of God's kingdom.

The "Expected One" was the Messiah. According to Jewish tradition, there were two Messiahs coming, a Messiah son of David, who would rule and reign as king; and a Messiah son of Joseph, who would suffer and die. The idea of two Messiahs grew out of the two pictures of the Messiah in the Old Testament: one reigning and the other suffering and dying. John's question was not to wonder so much about the reality of Jesus' messiahship as it was to wonder which of the two he might be.

Jesus responded to John's question by healing the sick, casting out demons, and restoring sight to the blind. Then he sent John's messengers back to report what they had seen.

Why did Jesus end by telling John that the one who didn't take offense at Jesus would be happy? Because the Pharisees and other religious leaders were seeing the same thing that John's messengers saw, but they criticized only what Jesus was doing. Jesus believed that John's reaction was likely to be something different from that of the Pharisees.

Our reaction to Jesus should be like that of John the Baptist once he heard Jesus' response. When we see what Jesus has done in our lives and in the lives of so many others, we can respond to him with hope and faith.

WHAT COUNTS

In the region of Galilee, Jesus was teaching and healing:

As Jesus was speaking, one of the Pharisees invited him home for a meal. So he went in and took his place at the table. His host was amazed to see that he sat down to eat without first performing the hand-washing ceremony required by Jewish custom. Then the Lord said to him, "You Pharisees are so careful to clean the outside of the cup and the dish, but inside you are filthy—full of greed and wickedness! Fools! Didn't God make the inside as well as the outside? So clean the inside by giving gifts to the poor, and you will be clean all over.

"What sorrow awaits you Pharisees! For you are careful to tithe even the tiniest income from your herb gardens, but you ignore justice and the love of God. You should tithe, yes, but do not neglect the more important things.

"What sorrow awaits you Pharisees! For you love to sit in the seats of honor in the synagogues and receive respectful greetings as you walk in the marketplaces. Yes, what sorrow awaits you! For you are like hidden graves in a field. People walk over them without knowing the corruption they are stepping on."

Luke 11:37–44 NLT

Jesus used the issue of ceremonial washing as the opportunity to push a Pharisee outside his comfort zone in order to help him reassess his relationship with God. If Jesus had simply asked the Pharisee what was most important in the law, he would have received the proper prepared response about loving God and loving people. But those words had little to do with how the Pharisee conducted his life.

Like many religious people, this Pharisee concerned himself mostly with boundary issues: the quantifiable things that separated him—the "righteous" person he believed he was—from them, the "unrighteous" people who did what he didn't. It was easy to quantify and measure boundary issues. It was easy to make sure that he gave the penny to God from the dime he found on the street. Or—to put it in a modern context—that he said a prayer before he put any food in his mouth.

Jesus wanted the Pharisee to look at the hard things of righteousness, not the easy boundary issues. It is good to tithe and to pray. But it is more important for us to focus on how we care for the distressed and needy and how we treat our neighbors and our coworkers and family, let alone how we treat strangers like the clerks in the store or the beggar in the street.

RESURRECTION

In Galilee, Jesus responded to the Pharisees and Scribes who criticized him for spending time with sinners:

"The younger [son] said to his father, 'Father, give me the portion of goods that falls to me.' So he divided to them his livelihood. And not many days after, the younger son gathered all together, journeyed to a far country, and there wasted his possessions with prodigal living. . . .

"But when he came to himself, he said, 'How many of my father's hired servants have bread enough and to spare, and I perish with hunger! I will arise and go to my father, and will say to him, "Father, I have sinned against heaven and before you, and I am no longer worthy to be called your son. Make me like one of your hired servants."'

"And he arose and came to his father. But when he was still a great way off, his father saw him and had compassion, and ran and fell on his neck and kissed him. And the son said to him, 'Father, I have sinned against heaven and in your sight, and am no longer worthy to be called your son.'

"But the father said to his servants, 'Bring out the best robe and put it on him, and put a ring on his hand and sandals on his feet. And bring the fatted calf here and kill it, and let us eat and be merry; for this my son was dead and is alive again.'"

Luke 15:12–13, 17–23 NKJV

❋

*I*t is easy to believe the lies we tell ourselves. Why would we steer ourselves wrong? And yet all too often, we do precisely that.

In ancient Israel, the younger of two sons received a third of the property upon the father's demise. And it was possible for a son to ask for the inheritance ahead of time. But to do so was like telling a father, "I wish you were dead," since that's when an inheritance was normally given.

The younger son believed that his father was holding him back, standing in the way of his happiness. That's why he wanted the money and left home. He thought he had to get away in order to really enjoy life.

So when his life fell apart, he decided he had to go back home. But he pictured his father as the same man who had made him want to leave in the first place: a harsh taskmaster who didn't understand him, a man who would justly punish him for his mistake and make him suffer for it.

Jesus' point, of course, is that our heavenly Father is different from what we might think, just as the younger son's father was not the man he imagined him to be either. God is not waiting to lecture us or punish us. Rather, he's waiting for us with open arms.

DIVIDED LOYALTIES

In Galilee, Jesus taught his disciples:

"No worker can serve two bosses: He'll either hate the first and love the second or adore the first and despise the second. You can't serve both God and the Bank."

When the Pharisees, a money-obsessed bunch, heard [Jesus] say these things, they rolled their eyes, dismissing him as hopelessly out of touch. So Jesus spoke to them: "You are masters at making yourselves look good in front of others, but God knows what's behind the appearance.

"What society sees and calls monumental, God sees through and calls monstrous. God's Law and the Prophets climaxed in John; Now it's all kingdom of God—the glad news and compelling invitation to every man and woman. The sky will disintegrate and the earth dissolve before a single letter of God's Law wears out. Using the legalities of divorce as a cover for lust is adultery; Using the legalities of marriage as a cover for lust is adultery."

Luke 16:13–18 MSG

You can do all the right things, follow all the rules, and still be wrong. The religious leaders in Israel were concerned that they always did the right thing. Not because they wanted to do right, so much as they wanted to protect themselves and their reputations.

They consistently missed the point of the law, which is something that escapes the notice of all legalists everywhere. Legalists like the Pharisees were concerned only with figuring out how not to get into trouble for whatever it was they did.

Jesus pointed out that this attitude arose from a divided loyalty. To illustrate the problem, he used as an example how they treated their wives. The religious leaders knew that adultery was forbidden and that adultery meant a man having sex with a woman who wasn't his wife. But what if he wanted to have sex with a woman other than his wife? Then he found a way. He would divorce his current wife and then marry the other woman. When he tired of the other woman, he simply repeated the process. He could then have sex with whomever he wanted, whenever they wanted, and he never broke the law. The religious leaders were very good at making the law work for them.

And that was the problem: it was all about them. They didn't love God. They didn't love other people. They were misusing the law for their own selfish purposes. Their loyalties were divided.

Too often we may be mostly concerned about the perceptions of others and about what we will get from our actions. Instead, we can decide to focus on God and others with our actions and stop thinking so much about ourselves.

KINGDOM NOW

On his way to Jerusalem:

Jesus, grilled by the Pharisees on when the kingdom of God would come, answered, "The kingdom of God doesn't come by counting the days on the calendar. Nor when someone says, 'Look here!' or, 'There it is!' And why? Because God's kingdom is already among you."

He went on to say to his disciples, "The days are coming when you are going to be desperately homesick for just a glimpse of one of the days of the Son of Man, and you won't see a thing. And they'll say to you, 'Look over there!' or, 'Look here!' Don't fall for any of that nonsense. The arrival of the Son of Man is not something you go out to see. He simply comes.

"You know how the whole sky lights up from a single flash of lightning? That's how it will be on the Day of the Son of Man. But first it's necessary that he suffer many things and be turned down by the people of today."

Luke 17:20–25 MSG

People look for God in all the wrong places. When Jesus announced that the kingdom of God was at hand, he really meant it. He wasn't speaking metaphorically. He didn't mean it was "soon" in the sense that for God a thousand years is like a day, so that "soon" could be a really, really long time as far as mere mortals were concerned. Jesus was very clear with the Pharisees. He told them that the kingdom of God had arrived. It's right here, right now.

The Pharisees and, for that matter, Jesus' disciples and the bulk of the Jewish population, thought the kingdom of God was a physical kingdom. They believed that when the Messiah arrived, he would raise an army, defeat the Romans, and sit down on David's throne in Jerusalem, replacing Caesar and making the world a perfectly wonderful place. They thought they would all live happily ever after—well, except for the sinners—and the Pharisees had a list of who those were, who all would die miserably.

Jesus explained that they all—from the Pharisees to his own disciples— simply didn't get it.

God's kingdom wouldn't be like the Roman Empire at all. The kingdom of God existed in the hearts and minds of those who believed the gospel. It wasn't physical, even though it did have real-world implications that would be as obvious as a flash of lightning. God promises us a happy conclusion. But more than that, he promises he is with us now. There is relief for us now, if we choose to perceive the world through Him.

WHO'S YOUR FATHER?

Jesus was teaching in the temple and responded to a question about paying taxes to Caesar:

Some of the teachers of the law responded, "Well said, teacher!" And no one dared to ask him any more questions.

Then Jesus said to them, "How is it that they say the Christ is the Son of David? David himself declares in the Book of Psalms:

"'The Lord said to my Lord:
"Sit at my right hand until I
make your enemies a foot-
stool for your feet."'

"David calls him 'Lord.' How then can he be his son?"

While all the people were listening, Jesus said to his disciples, "Beware of the teachers of the law. They like to walk around in flowing robes and love to be greeted in the marketplaces and have the most important seats in the synagogues and the places of honor at banquets. They devour widows' houses and for a show make lengthy prayers. Such men will be punished most severely."

Luke 20:39–47 NIV

*P*eople don't like inconvenient questions, but that didn't stop Jesus from asking them. The hard questions forced people to look in places they'd rather not look, to think about what they'd rather not think about, and to see what they thought they believed in wholly new ways.

Jesus presented an uncomfortable bit of the book of Psalms that the religious establishment mostly tried to ignore. Jesus pointed out that David, the great king of Israel, referred to the Messiah as his Lord. If the Messiah was David's son, how could he call him that? Jesus wanted to know. In normal royal father-son relationships, the son might call his father lord, but never, ever the other way around. What could the psalmist have been thinking? What was going on? Jesus wanted the teachers of the law to puzzle over the problem, to face its implications.

Jesus was attempting to tweak the leaders' understanding of authority and relationships. They were all about being high and mighty. They wanted to be coddled and looked up to. Suddenly Jesus was casting their justification for that in doubt. Being the boss was not what mattered. Such attitudes were not how relationships worked in heaven, and it shouldn't have been how they worked on earth either.

When we face a hard or inconvenient question in the Bible, we can embrace it rather than shy away from it. Leadership for us is all about our service for others. Rather than thinking about the treatment we're getting, we should be focused on the treatment we're giving.

WHERE YOU'RE FROM

Jesus decided to go to Galilee. There he met Philip, who was from Bethsaida, the hometown of Andrew and Peter. Jesus said to Philip, "Come with me."

Philip then found Nathanael and said, "We have found the one that Moses and the Prophets wrote about. He is Jesus, the son of Joseph from Nazareth."

Nathanael asked, "Can anything good come from Nazareth?"

Philip answered, "Come and see."

When Jesus saw Nathanael coming toward him, he said, "Here is a true descendant of our ancestor Israel. And he isn't deceitful."

"How do you know me?" Nathanael asked.

Jesus answered, "Before Philip called you, I saw you under the fig tree."

Nathanael said, "Rabbi, you are the Son of God and the King of Israel!"

Jesus answered, "Did you believe me just because I said that I saw you under the fig tree? You will see something even greater. I tell you for certain that you will see heaven open and God's angels going up and coming down on the Son of Man."

John 1:43–51 CEV

Jesus couldn't be ignored. People had to make a decision about him, one way or the other. Philip quickly became convinced that Jesus was the long-awaited Messiah, so he asked Nathanael—elsewhere in the Bible referred to as Bartholomew—to come and meet Jesus.

Nathanael was doubtful. Nazareth had a bad reputation, and he couldn't see how Israel's Messiah could call such a place home. When Jesus saw Nathanael, he said something that Nathanael probably thought was mere flattery. So he asked Jesus a simple question: "How do you know me?"

Jesus' answer about seeing him under a fig tree convinced Nathanael that Jesus was the Son of God and the King of Israel. Jesus' few words convinced Nathanael of so much because no ordinary person could have known where Nathanael was or what he was doing. It meant Jesus really was the Messiah.

Jesus' response to Nathanael's expression of faith was to let him know that, in effect, he hadn't seen anything yet. Jesus would perform far more impressive miracles than something akin to what Sherlock Holmes or a stage magician might have been able to figure out.

Jesus inspired passion in the hearts and minds of everyone with whom he came in contact. We, too, should be like Jesus, becoming people who inspire passion, who affect our friends and community in such a way that they can't ignore us or the Lord we serve.

CONFUSION

One night while Jesus was staying in Jerusalem during Passover:

Nicodemus said to [Jesus], "How can these things be?"

Jesus answered him, "Are you a teacher of Israel, and yet you do not understand these things?

"Very truly, I tell you, we speak of what we know and testify to what we have seen; yet you do not receive our testimony. If I have told you about earthly things and you do not believe, how can you believe if I tell you about heavenly things? No one has ascended into heaven except the one who descended from heaven, the Son of Man. And just as Moses lifted up the serpent in the wilderness, so must the Son of Man be lifted up, that whoever believes in him may have eternal life.

"For God so loved the world that he gave his only Son, so that everyone who believes in him may not perish but may have eternal life."

John 3:9–15 NRSV

❁

*T*he Pharisees were generally well respected. Most people believed them to be good, upstanding citizens. And they believed in their own goodness. In fact, they were self-righteous. They took God and the Bible seriously, and their lives were consumed by being religious. Nicodemus belonged to that strict sect, and he also was a member of the Great Sanhedrin in Jerusalem, an assembly of seventy-one religious leaders, both Pharisees and Sadducees, who met six days a week, except during holidays. Those who became members of the Sanhedrin were the best of the best. To them was given the task of settling all disputes relating to the Bible and its interpretation.

The majority of the Pharisees and other members of that Sanhedrin did not like Jesus. So Nicodemus approached Jesus under cover of darkness one night. He was worried about what the other members of the Sanhedrin would think, but he needed to hear from Jesus directly. He was uncomfortable with relying on secondhand information and clearly biased and contradictory accounts of Jesus' activities.

Jesus explained that what he was teaching were things that Nicodemus, given his position and education, should already have known. Jesus wasn't offering new, strange ideas. His teachings came from what the Law and the Prophets—that is, the Scriptures—presented. The prophets had promised that the Messiah would finally take the sins of the world away because God loved the world and didn't want people to perish.

By the time Nicodemus had finished listening to Jesus, he believed in him. We today should present Jesus to others as clearly as possible.

NO CONDEMNATION

Jesus continued his conversation with Nicodemus:

[Jesus said,] "God did not send His Son into the world to condemn the world, but that the world through Him might be saved.

"He who believes in Him is not condemned; but he who does not believe is condemned already, because he has not believed in the name of the only begotten Son of God. And this is the condemnation, that the light has come into the world, and men loved darkness rather than light, because their deeds were evil. For everyone practicing evil hates the light and does not come to the light, lest his deeds should be exposed. But he who does the truth comes to the light, that his deeds may be clearly seen, that they have been done in God."

After these things Jesus and His disciples came into the land of Judea, and there He remained with them and baptized. Now John also was baptizing in Aenon near Salim, because there was much water there. And they came and were baptized. For John had not yet been thrown into prison.

John 3:17–24 NKJV

❧

*I*t's easier to believe that God loves sinners than to believe that God loves liars. But the popular belief, expressed by the Pharisees and the rest of the religious establishment, was that God hated sinners, regardless, and was bent on their destruction. They believed that when the Messiah came, among other things he would destroy the sinners and see to it that they were all appropriately judged.

Instead, Jesus explained to Nicodemus, the representative of the religious establishment who had come to meet with him, that God's plan for the human race—for sinners—was radically different from what they all imagined. Yes, sinners would be destroyed, not by killing them, but rather by killing their sin by nailing it to the cross. Belief in the Messiah would bring righteousness, while condemnation was merely the natural state of people before they believed. Jesus used the imagery of light and dark to differentiate between those two states of humanity. The imagery came from the Old Testament, as for instance with the creation story, when God said, "Let there be light," and he saw that it was good. Jesus knew that such imagery would make sense to such a "teacher of Israel" as Nicodemus.

Jesus was the Light of the World, and he brought light to everyone who listened and believed his message. Nicodemus had come to Jesus at night, but Jesus vanquished the darkness from his heart. We have the same opportunity today, to shine the light of Jesus on the darkness in our world. We can be ambassadors for Jesus, his instruments to transfer sinners into the ranks of the forgiven.

PROPHET

Jesus stopped by a well in Sychar, Samaria, and asked a woman for a drink:

Jesus said to [the Samaritan woman], "Go, call your husband, and come here."

The woman answered and said, "I have no husband."

Jesus said to her, "You have well said, 'I have no husband,' for you have had five husbands, and the one whom you now have is not your husband; in that you spoke truly."

The woman said to Him, "Sir, I perceive that You are a prophet. Our fathers worshiped on this mountain, and you Jews say that in Jerusalem is the place where one ought to worship."

Jesus said to her, "Woman, believe Me, the hour is coming when you will neither on this mountain, nor in Jerusalem, worship the Father. You worship what you do not know; we know what we worship, for salvation is of the Jews. But the hour is coming, and now is, when the true worshipers will worship the Father in spirit and truth; for the Father is seeking such to worship Him. God is Spirit, and those who worship Him must worship in spirit and truth."

The woman said to Him, "I know that Messiah is coming" (who is called Christ). "When He comes, He will tell us all things."

Jesus said to her, "I who speak to you am He."

John 4:16–26 NKJV

Jesus had a way of disturbing people. He regularly stepped beyond the bounds of social norms. A good Jewish man, married or not, did not commonly spend time alone with an unrelated woman. And the Jewish people were so loath to be with Samaritans that they would walk extra miles just to avoid them altogether. For him to be alone at a well with a Samaritan woman was peculiar, and she realized that.

Then Jesus invaded her privacy. He commented on details about her life that a stranger, especially a stranger who was Jewish, shouldn't have even known, let alone brought up. Realizing that he must be some kind of prophet, she asked him a question about one of the many things that divided the Samaritans and the Jewish people: where should they worship?

Jesus' answer to her question focused on more important issues: who could worship and what worship was. Despite what she and the Jewish establishment believed about Samaritans' being excluded from God, they weren't. God was accessible to anyone who truly believed.

Her recognition that the Messiah would someday cause everything to make sense prompted Jesus to reveal himself to her. Jesus' message of the kingdom was for all human beings, everywhere. Jesus excludes no one.

WITNESSES

In Jersualem, after healing a man on the Sabbath, Jesus told the religious leaders:

"If I were to testify on my own behalf, my testimony would not be valid. But someone else is also testifying about me, and I assure you that everything he says about me is true. In fact, you sent investigators to listen to John the Baptist, and his testimony about me was true. Of course, I have no need of human witnesses, but I say these things so you might be saved. John was like a burning and shining lamp, and you were excited for a while about his message. But I have a greater witness than John—my teachings and my miracles. The Father gave me these works to accomplish, and they prove that he sent me. And the Father who sent me has testified about me himself. You have never heard his voice or seen him face to face, and you do not have his message in your hearts, because you do not believe me—the one he sent to you."

John 5:31–38 NLT

*W*ho are you going to believe? Someone's words or his lying eyes? Affirming something doesn't make it so. Every defendant at trial is assumed to be not guilty; the prosecution must prove otherwise. Simple assertions of guilt are not enough. There must be evidence

In the Old Testament, Moses specified that for a crime to be proven there had to be at least two witnesses. A lone witness to an event could not be trusted. A single witness could be mistaken or malevolently biased. Jesus agreed with his critics that if he alone were claiming to be the Messiah, it proved nothing.

But Jesus wasn't the only one claiming he was the Messiah. John the Baptist claimed Jesus was the Messiah. But even more powerfully, the twin witnesses of his words and his miracles were enough to prove that the Father had sent him.

The fact that the religious establishment was standing as a witness against Jesus did not prove that Jesus wasn't the Messiah. Instead, it demonstrated the spiritual bankruptcy of the religious establishment of Israel. If they had really been the people of God, then they would recognize God when he showed up. Their failure to recognize Jesus as the Messiah—and their failure to keep God's words—demonstrated that they were clueless about God.

We can deny reality for only so long. Eventually it catches up with us. Jesus asks us to accept the reality that he loves us and gave us everything so we could become God's children and heirs to his kingdom.

MISSING THE OBVIOUS

In Jerusalem, facing criticism for healing on the Sabbath, Jesus told the religious leaders:

"You search the Scriptures, for in them you think you have eternal life; and these are they which testify of Me. But you are not willing to come to Me that you may have life.

"I do not receive honor from men. But I know you, that you do not have the love of God in you. I have come in My Father's name, and you do not receive Me; if another comes in his own name, him you will receive. How can you believe, who receive honor from one another, and do not seek the honor that comes from the only God? Do not think that I shall accuse you to the Father; there is one who accuses you— Moses, in whom you trust. For if you believed Moses, you would believe Me; for he wrote about Me. But if you do not believe his writings, how will you believe My words?"

John 5:39–47 NKJV

*D*o you read the Bible looking for answers to your questions? Or do you read the Bible looking for God's answers to his questions? Jesus told the religious establishment that they were indeed very serious about the Bible, but that it wasn't doing them a whole lot of good. They read the Bible. They knew what it said. But the implications of God's words still escaped them. Instead of seeking the esteem of God, they cared about only the esteem of their colleagues.

The word translated *trust* and the word translated *believed* are the same in Greek, so Jesus expressed what seems to be a paradox. "You're trusting in Moses, but if you trusted in Moses, then you would trust me." And then, "Since you don't trust in Moses, then it follows that you don't trust in me." Huh?

Jesus was pointing out the contradiction in the thinking of the religious leaders. There was a gap between what they claimed to believe and how they actually lived. By pointing out their internal conflicts, Jesus wanted them to confront the contradiction, to recognize the problem in their lives, and then to change their minds. Jesus wanted the religious leaders of his people to recognize the truth. Interestingly, the book of Acts reveals that many Pharisees and priests did become believers in Jesus after his resurrection.

It's better for us to listen to Jesus and discover what matters to him rather than listen to only our own hearts and what matters to us. We don't always know what we want let alone what we need. But Jesus does. We can trust him with our lives.

BRIGHT LIGHTS

In Jerusalem, during the Feast of Tabernacles:

Jesus spoke to [the Pharisees] again: "I am the light of the world. Anyone who follows Me will never walk in the darkness but will have the light of life."

So the Pharisees said to Him, "You are testifying about Yourself. Your testimony is not valid."

"Even if I testify about Myself," Jesus replied, "My testimony is valid, because I know where I came from and where I'm going. But you don't know where I come from or where I'm going. You judge by human standards. I judge no one. And if I do judge, My judgment is true, because I am not alone, but I and the Father who sent Me judge together. Even in your law it is written that the witness of two men is valid. I am the One who testifies about Myself, and the Father who sent Me testifies about Me."

Then they asked Him, "Where is Your Father?"

"You know neither Me nor My Father," Jesus answered. "If you knew Me, you would also know My Father." He spoke these words by the treasury, while teaching in the temple complex. But no one seized Him, because His hour had not come.

John 8:12–20 HCSB

🌼

*M*any people fear the dark. Jesus offered to get rid of what we fear. At the time of creation, God created light from the darkness and provided the sun and moon to give light by day and night. Jesus claimed to be the light of the world, not in a literal, physical sense like the sun or moon, but in a metaphorical sense. By "light of life," Jesus meant that he was able to give meaning and purpose to people. He could give them the direction needed for making better decisions.

Bad things can happen to people in life through no fault of their own. But sometimes, bad things happen to people because they make poor decisions. Jesus announced that he could bring people out of such darkness. Past bad decisions did not mean a person's future would have to be dark too. The Pharisees, in the dark but not realizing it, cringed from the light that Jesus offered. Jesus told them that he and his Father together were offering them a path to life.

Because the religious leaders didn't really know God, they failed to recognize the Son, and so they continued to stumble about in the darkness. Jesus doesn't want us to stumble through life. He wants us to accept a bright path, a life full of meaning and value.

TROUBLED HEARTS

Jesus was teaching his disciples during the Last Supper, and he told them he was going to leave them:

"Do not let your heart be troubled; believe in God, believe also in Me. In My Father's house are many dwelling places; if it were not so, I would have told you; for I go to prepare a place for you. If I go and prepare a place for you, I will come again and receive you to Myself, that where I am, there you may be also. And you know the way where I am going."

Thomas said to Him, "Lord, we do not know where You are going, how do we know the way?"

Jesus said to him, "I am the way, and the truth, and the life; no one comes to the Father but through Me. If you had known Me, you would have known My Father also; from now on you know Him, and have seen Him."

John 14:1–7 NASB

❄

The disciples thought they had good reason to feel troubled. Jesus had just told them he was going to leave them. It was the last thing they expected to hear. It crushed all their hopes and left them confused. But Jesus offered them hope for their troubled hearts. He did not want them to be worried. He did not want them to be afraid for their futures. They thought he had given them bad news when in fact he was giving them the best possible news there could be.

Jesus reminded his disciples about the kingdom of God. He explained that there was a purpose for his coming crucifixion. His death would not be a defeat of their hopes. Instead, it would be the key that would open the gates of the kingdom for them. Thanks to the cross, their sins would be forgiven. Thanks to the cross, they would become the children of their Father in heaven and live with him forever.

There was plenty of room in God's "house." In Jewish thinking, although a house could be a building, it more commonly referred to a family, a household, or even a royal dynasty. By telling his disciples there was room in his Father's house, Jesus was telling them they were going to become part of his family.

The only way for us to become children of God is through Jesus. We have been adopted by God and will live with him forever, thanks to him. That's why our hearts should never be troubled.

HELP IS COMING

During the Last Supper, after Judas's departure, Jesus said:

"When the Counselor comes, whom I will send to you from the Father, the Spirit of truth who goes out from the Father, he will testify about me. And you also must testify, for you have been with me from the beginning.

"All this I have told you so that you will not go astray. They will put you out of the synagogue; in fact, a time is coming when anyone who kills you will think he is offering a service to God. They will do such things because they have not known the Father or me. I have told you this, so that when the time comes you will remember that I warned you. I did not tell you this at first because I was with you.

"Now I am going to him who sent me, yet none of you asks me, 'Where are you going?' Because I have said these things, you are filled with grief. But I tell you the truth: It is for your good that I am going away. Unless I go away, the Counselor will not come to you; but if I go, I will send him to you."

John 15:26–16:7 NIV

❧

*W*herever God is, there is his kingdom. With the coming of the Counselor—the Holy Spirit—God's kingdom would continue in the lives of the disciples, even when Jesus was gone. Jerusalem would be destroyed by the Romans within a generation, and nearly every disciple would be martyred for his faith. Despite the suffering that would come their way, the kingdom of God would endure. Thanks to their witness and the ever-growing number of Christians, the presence of the kingdom of God would grow and spread throughout the world.

Jesus let them know ahead of time how the world would turn against them so they could understand that what they faced was not something God didn't anticipate. Jesus was attempting to let his disciples see the bigger picture. He wanted them to understand that as painful as it might be, God was always with them. Jesus told his disciples that their grief was misplaced. His coming departure was actually a wonderful thing, because only through his death and resurrection could the kingdom ever come.

We don't have to face the problems of life by ourselves. Jesus is always with us, because his Spirit lives inside us. We're never separated from God's kingdom.

YOU SAID IT

The whole body of [the Sanhedrin] got up and brought [Jesus] before Pilate. And they began to accuse Him, saying, "We found this man misleading our nation and forbidding to pay taxes to Caesar, and saying that He Himself is Christ, a King."

So Pilate asked Him, saying, "Are You the King of the Jews?" And He answered him and said, "It is as you say."

Then Pilate said to the chief priests and the crowds, "I find no guilt in this man."

But they kept on insisting, saying, "He stirs up the people, teaching all over Judea, starting from Galilee even as far as this place."

When Pilate heard it, he asked whether the man was a Galilean. And when he learned that He belonged to Herod's jurisdiction, he sent Him to Herod, who himself also was in Jerusalem at that time.

Now Herod was very glad when he saw Jesus; for he had wanted to see Him for a long time, because he had been hearing about Him and was hoping to see some sign performed by Him.

Luke 23:1–8 NASB

Israel's religious establishment was attempting to get Jesus executed for being the leader of a rebellion. Hadn't Jesus just admitted his guilt by answering Pilate's question with a yes? Why, then, did Pilate conclude that he was not guilty?

Pilate could see through the accusations and understood that the disagreement between Jesus and his accusers was purely religious. And the Roman government had absolutely no interest in getting involved with religious disputes. Therefore, Pilate saw no point in entertaining the charges.

When he learned that Jesus was from Galilee, Pilate thought he might be able to solve his problem by making him someone else's problem. Herod was in charge of Galilee. Pilate, who had jurisdiction only in Judea, wasn't responsible for Galileans. But Herod just sent him back.

Pilate, like most government officials anywhere, was concerned primarily with keeping his job. The issue of Jesus could easily blow up in his face. In the end, for the sake of civil order and his job, he was willing to sacrifice Jesus.

Pilate carried out the will of Jesus' Father: Jesus was supposed to die on that Roman cross. Pilate actually made the right choice. But he did it for all the wrong reasons and in all the wrong ways. Just because we do God's will doesn't mean we're not doing the wrong thing. Our attitudes behind what we do are critically important to God. It's not just about our outward actions or the results we get.

PROTECTION

Jesus prayed in the Garden of Gethsemane:

"I am no longer in the world, but they are in the world, and I am coming to you. Holy Father, protect them in your name that you have given me, so that they may be one, as we are one. While I was with them, I protected them in your name that you have given me. I guarded them, and not one of them was lost except the one destined to be lost, so that the scripture might be fulfilled. But now I am coming to you, and I speak these things in the world so that they may have my joy made complete in themselves. I have given them your word, and the world has hated them because they do not belong to the world, just as I do not belong to the world. I am not asking you to take them out of the world, but I ask you to protect them from the evil one. They do not belong to the world, just as I do not belong to the world. Sanctify them in the truth; your word is truth. As you have sent me into the world, so I have sent them into the world. And for their sakes I sanctify myself, so that they also may be sanctified in truth."

John 17:11–19 NRSV

❧

Joy is not the same as happiness. Joy lasts longer and runs deeper. Joy is happiness multiplied. Jesus prayed that his disciples—you and I—would have the joy Jesus had. Jesus is God, Creator of the universe and its owner, who always gets his way in the end.

On the night Jesus was betrayed, he told his Father that he was no longer in the world. He knew he was about to die. So he focused on his disciples, who would remain in the world after he was gone. Jesus did not pray that they would become wealthy, have power and fame, or live in big houses. He asked for something better. He asked that they be protected, not from poverty or pain, but from the evil one. Jesus asked that they be sanctified.

Sanctified means "to be devoted to God and his purposes." Sanctification isn't just a matter of righteousness, which comes from God. Sanctification means that his disciples would do God's work and be used for God's purposes, whatever those purposes might be.

We are given over to God's purposes. We belong to God. We are his prized possession and are precious to him. We can watch with excitement the wonderful things he'll do with us and for us. We can take joy in the fact that God takes joy in us.

ARROGANCE AND HUMILITY

Arrogance is a consequence of focusing on oneself to the exclusion of others. This results from the basic flaw in our natures that we love ourselves but are afraid no one else does. Humility is the essence of focusing on others to the exclusion of oneself. Only with God's help can our arrogance be transformed into humility. In the ideal world, everyone else would be concerned only with our well-being, just as we'd be concerned only with the well-being of everyone else. Humility is at ease only when the one loved is happy. In fact, joy arises most strongly from seeing the joy of others. Humility is love, which is not self-seeking.

※

Love does not delight in evil but rejoices with
the truth. It always protects, always trusts,
always hopes, always perseveres.
1 Corinthians 13:6–7 NIV

QUESTIONS

Every year Jesus' parents went to Jerusalem for the Passover festival. When Jesus was twelve years old, they attended the festival as usual. After the celebration was over, they started home to Nazareth, but Jesus stayed behind in Jerusalem. His parents didn't miss him at first, because they assumed he was among the other travelers. But when he didn't show up that evening, they started looking for him among their relatives and friends.

When they couldn't find him, they went back to Jerusalem to search for him there. Three days later they finally discovered him in the Temple, sitting among the religious teachers, listening to them and asking questions. All who heard him were amazed at his understanding and his answers.

His parents didn't know what to think. "Son," his mother said to him, "why have you done this to us? Your father and I have been frantic, searching for you everywhere."

"But why did you need to search?" he asked. "Didn't you know that I must be in my Father's house?" But they didn't understand what he meant.

Then he returned to Nazareth with them and was obedient to them. And his mother stored all these things in her heart.

Jesus grew in wisdom and in stature and in favor with God and all the people.

Luke 2:41–52 NLT

*B*eing a parent to Jesus could not have been easy. Although he didn't misbehave, he behaved in ways that were surprising and unexpected. Religiously, Jewish boys become men during the bar-mitzvah, the coming-of-age ceremony during which a thirteen-year-old recites a series of standardized questions and answers. When Jesus stayed behind at the temple, he was only twelve. Jesus surprised the teachers in the temple with his questions and answers that went beyond those rote requirements.

His parents spent a frantic three days trying to locate him once they realized he wasn't with them anymore. They blamed him for their fear. Jesus' response was to ask them why they'd been looking for him at all, since they knew he had to be in his "Father's house."

Jesus was reminding them that he was not just an ordinary child. He was the Messiah, sent to earth for a specific purpose, and so how could he ever be at risk? Mary and Joseph, unlike normal parents, had no reason to worry.

Mary "stored all these things in her heart." That is, she thought about what Jesus had told her and tried to make sense of it all.

We have to believe that if God is involved in something, we needn't fear failure or loss.

DAY 63

❋❋❋❋❋❋❋❋❋❋❋❋❋❋❋❋❋❋❋❋❋❋❋❋❋❋❋❋❋❋❋

WATERWORKS

[John the Baptist said,] "I baptize with water those who repent of their sins and turn to God. But someone is coming soon who is greater than I am—so much greater that I'm not worthy even to be his slave and carry his sandals. He will baptize you with the Holy Spirit and with fire. He is ready to separate the chaff from the wheat with his winnowing fork. Then he will clean up the threshing area, gathering the wheat into his barn but burning the chaff with never-ending fire."

Then Jesus went from Galilee to the Jordan River to be baptized by John. But John tried to talk him out of it. "I am the one who needs to be baptized by you," he said, "so why are you coming to me?"

But Jesus said, "It should be done, for we must carry out all that God requires." So John agreed to baptize him.

After his baptism, as Jesus came up out of the water, the heavens were opened and he saw the Spirit of God descending like a dove and settling on him. And a voice from heaven said, "This is my dearly loved Son, who brings me great joy."

Matthew 3:11–17 NLT

❋

*R*eal love means always wanting and doing what is best for someone. If we really believed that God loved us like that, that his will for us was always what was best for us, we'd never resist his will. Jesus was concerned only with doing what his Father wanted. Human beings, in contrast, are generally more concerned only with doing what they want.

John knew that the Messiah was coming. John saw himself as God's servant, as a human being of limited consequence. It made no sense to him that Jesus should ask him—or any other human being—for baptism. Rather, John saw only his own need for redemption; he was aware only of his own failings. That prevented him from seeing beyond himself to what someone else might need—in this case, Jesus' need to begin his public ministry, to receive, not the baptism of repentance that John had been giving everyone else, but rather the baptism given to those who were becoming rabbis. There were many sorts of baptisms performed regularly in Judaism: for conversion, for ceremonial cleansing, and for those becoming rabbis or priests. John, because of his focus, because of his own needs, had trouble seeing beyond his own habitual patterns.

Because of our fallen nature, we tend to think of things only in terms of what's in it for us, or what we're used to. We must find ways to look at ourselves, our priorities, our habits in new ways. We should constantly be willing to re-examine who we are and what we think we are doing.

YOU NEED TO EAT

In the region of Galilee:

Jesus passed through the grainfields on the Sabbath. His disciples were hungry and began to pick and eat some heads of grain. But when the Pharisees saw it, they said to Him, "Look, Your disciples are doing what is not lawful to do on the Sabbath!"

He said to them, "Haven't you read what David did when he and those who were with him were hungry—how he entered the house of God, and they ate the sacred bread, which is not lawful for him or for those with him to eat, but only for the priests? Or haven't you read in the Law that on Sabbath days the priests in the temple violate the Sabbath and are innocent? But I tell you that something greater than the temple is here! If you had known what this means: I desire mercy and not sacrifice, you would not have condemned the innocent. For the Son of Man is Lord of the Sabbath."

Matthew 12:1–8 HCSB

米

*P*eople are the focus of God's attention, and he made rules for our benefit. He didn't create people so he could have rules. Rules are not the priority. People are the priority. God told his people to keep the Sabbath. And he told his priests what all their duties were. Sometimes the priests violated God's Sabbath and never felt guilty about it. They sometimes had to offer sacrifices on the Sabbath. And sometimes they had to perform circumcisions on the eighth day after a birth, even if that eighth day was the Sabbath.

Jesus told his critics that they had forgotten the whole purpose of the Sabbath, which was simply that people needed time off. The need to satisfy hunger took precedence over the minutiae of the law. Just as David and his men, fleeing from Saul for their lives, needed food for their journey and took what they could find, so the disciples were doing nothing wrong by eating a few grains of wheat from a field as they walked along. The prohibition of "working on the Sabbath" could not be allowed to prevent people from doing what needed to be done.

Jesus claimed to be the Lord of the Sabbath. His use of the term *Lord* didn't just mean that he was the boss. When Jews said the word *Lord*, they meant *God*. Jesus told his critics that he was God, and since he approved of what the disciples were doing, the discussion was over.

The rules aren't supposed to get in the way of our doing what's right. If we remember that our priority is to love people and to seek what is best for them, we'll use the rules only to help rather than to hinder.

NO WAY

Jesus made it clear to his disciples that it was now necessary for him to go to Jerusalem, submit to an ordeal of suffering at the hands of the religious leaders, be killed, and then on the third day be raised up alive. Peter took him in hand, protesting, "Impossible, Master! That can never be!"

But Jesus didn't swerve. "Peter, get out of my way. Satan, get lost. You have no idea how God works."

Then Jesus went to work on his disciples. "Anyone who intends to come with me has to let me lead. You're not in the driver's seat; *I* am. Don't run from suffering; embrace it. Follow me and I'll show you how. Self-help is no help at all. Self-sacrifice is the way, my way, to finding yourself, your true self. What kind of deal is it to get everything you want but lose yourself? What could you ever trade your soul for?

"Don't be in such a hurry to go into business for yourself. Before you know it the Son of Man will arrive with all the splendor of his Father, accompanied by an army of angels. You'll get everything you have coming to you, a personal gift. This isn't pie in the sky by and by. Some of you standing here are going to see it take place, see the Son of Man in kingdom glory."

Matthew 16:21–28 MSG

❀

*A*re Peter and the devil the same person? When Jesus referred to Peter as Satan, he was not making an identification of who Peter was. He didn't mean that Peter was suddenly possessed by the devil. Rather, Jesus meant that Peter's statement was the sort of thing Satan would say.

Peter, along with most Jewish people of the time, believed that the Messiah would be leading a triumphant revolt against the hated Roman occupiers. A dying Messiah didn't fit his expectations, and so Peter rejected Jesus' words. Satan's expectations of the Messiah were the same as Peter's. Satan, too, expected Jesus to lead a rebellion against the Romans. Satan, too, expected Jesus to establish the kingdom of God on earth, with the Davidic monarchy restored to all its glory. Neither Peter nor Satan knew what Jesus was actually planning to do. Peter, by his well-intentioned words, was attempting to thwart God's plan in the same way Satan hoped to thwart God's plan.

Protecting someone from death is a good thing, unless it's Jesus who is dying to save us from our sins. Sometimes the right thing feels wrong. We have to be guided by love, and we have to listen to God. We have to gain God's perspective on our lives. Sometimes it is hard to understand how painful circumstances can ever be beneficial. But then we always have Jesus' death on a Roman cross as a prime example.

WHO'S THE BOSS?

In the village of Capernaum:

The disciples came to Jesus and asked, "Who is the greatest in the kingdom of heaven?"

He called a little child and had him stand among them. And he said: "I tell you the truth, unless you change and become like little children, you will never enter the kingdom of heaven. Therefore, whoever humbles himself like this child is the greatest in the kingdom of heaven.

"And whoever welcomes a little child like this in my name welcomes me. But if anyone causes one of these little ones who believe in me to sin, it would be better for him to have a large millstone hung around his neck and to be drowned in the depths of the sea.

"Woe to the world because of the things that cause people to sin! Such things must come, but woe to the man through whom they come!"

Matthew 18:1–7 NIV

🌾

The disciples thought Jesus would answer their question, "Who is the greatest in the kingdom of heaven?" with someone's name. Perhaps they thought he would say God, or maybe name himself. In his heart, each disciple may have hoped to hear his own name.

The disciples' question rose from false presuppositions. They thought they knew what the kingdom of God was—a descendant of David sitting on an earthly throne, ruling from Jerusalem, the new world capital. They imagined something like the Roman Empire, only bigger and badder. Who would be the greatest in such an earthly kingdom? The obvious answer would be someone rich, or someone famous, someone who had performed great deeds, subdued armies. Perhaps a general. Certainly someone of significance.

Jesus challenged everyone's expectations when he brought a child over and announced, "This one."

How could that be? Children were unimportant and powerless. How could the greatest in the kingdom of heaven be like that? Like a little kid?

That's what Jesus was like. He was the *Son* of God. He arrived to do not his own will, but the will of his Father who had sent him. He accomplished only what his Father did through him. People who focused their attention on God and others, rather than on themselves, were the ones who were greatest. We are like Jesus when we do God's will. We are like Jesus when we realize that whatever good we accomplish is by God's strength rather than our own. We can do nothing, but he can do everything through us.

DIVORCE

When Jesus finished teaching, he left Galilee and went to the part of Judea that is east of the Jordan River. Large crowds followed him, and he healed their sick people.

Some Pharisees wanted to test Jesus. They came up to him and asked, "Is it right for a man to divorce his wife for just any reason?"

Jesus answered, "Don't you know that in the beginning the Creator made a man and a woman? That's why a man leaves his father and mother and gets married. He becomes like one person with his wife. Then they are no longer two people, but one. And no one should separate a couple that God has joined together."

The Pharisees asked Jesus, "Why did Moses say that a man could write out divorce papers and send his wife away?"

Jesus replied, "You are so heartless! That's why Moses allowed you to divorce your wife. But from the beginning God did not intend it to be that way. I say that if your wife has not committed some terrible sexual sin, you must not divorce her to marry someone else. If you do, you are unfaithful."

The disciples said, "If that's how it is between a man and a woman, it's better not to get married."

Jesus told them, "Only those people who have been given the gift of staying single can accept this teaching. Some people are unable to marry because of birth defects or because of what someone has done to their bodies. Others stay single in order to serve God better. Anyone who can accept this teaching should do so."

Matthew 19:1–12 CEV

❧

*Q*uestions aren't always what they seem. Why would some Pharisees quiz Jesus on whether it was right for a man to divorce his wife? There was much more to the question than just the legality of divorce. They wanted to know if divorce could be had for "any reason." Jesus said no, that divorce should never happen, except maybe for adultery. He explained that God never intended for relationships to be irrevocably breached. To do so was counter to the whole concept of love and forgiveness.

The disciples were taken aback. They decided that not being married at all was better than being "stuck" with a bad wife.

Jesus agreed with them. Whether celibacy was the consequence of circumstances beyond an individual's control, or because that person chose to commit himself to God in that way, celibacy, Jesus explained, could be considered a gift from God. Certainly it was far preferable to a bad or unhappy marriage. Both marriage and celibacy are gifts from God. We should gladly accept whichever God gives us, and thank him for it.

WHO SAID?

During Jesus' last week in Jerusalem:

When [Jesus] came into the temple, the chief priests and the elders of the people confronted Him as He was teaching, and said, "By what authority are You doing these things? And who gave You this authority?"

But Jesus answered and said to them, "I also will ask you one thing, which if you tell Me, I likewise will tell you by what authority I do these things: The baptism of John—where was it from? From heaven or from men?"

And they reasoned among themselves, saying, "If we say, 'From heaven,' He will say to us, 'Why then did you not believe him?' But if we say, 'From men,' we fear the multitude, for all count John as a prophet." So they answered Jesus and said, "We do not know."

And He said to them, "Neither will I tell you by what authority I do these things."

Matthew 21:23–27 NKJV

✺

"Don't you know who I am?" Celebrities have often been heard uttering those words when they don't believe they're being treated as well as they think their fame entitles them. The religious establishment didn't believe who Jesus was. They asked Jesus about who gave him the right to do what he was doing—coming into Jerusalem, cleansing the temple, teaching things contrary to established custom. Jesus responded with a question, the same question he asks of all who come to him, even now—the question of John the Baptist: Was John's baptism from heaven, or was it from men? That is, was it from God, or did he just make it up?

The religious establishment refused to answer Jesus' question. Instead, they pleaded ignorance. But in reality, they had already decided on an answer that they were too afraid to speak. They had decided that John was not from God. Likewise, they had already decided that Jesus was not from God. Their question was not designed to relieve their ignorance. They hoped only to get Jesus to say something that would confirm what they believed. They wound up disappointed. Jesus made it even harder for them to deny the reality of his identity.

We must face the same question that troubled the Pharisees. Jesus is either God or he is nothing but a human being. Everything depends on how we decide. If he's just a human being, then we can safely ignore him. But if he is God, then nothing about him is safe at all. We ignore him at our peril, because if he is God, he will change our lives forever.

✂✂✂✂✂✂✂✂✂✂✂✂✂✂✂✂✂✂✂✂✂✂✂✂✂✂✂✂✂✂✂

INVITATIONS

In the temple courts in Jerusalem:

Jesus spoke to [the chief priests and Pharisees] again in parables, saying,

"The kingdom of heaven may be compared to a king who gave a wedding feast for his son. And he sent out his slaves to call those who had been invited to the wedding feast, and they were unwilling to come. Again he sent out other slaves saying, 'Tell those who have been invited, "Behold, I have prepared my dinner; my oxen and my fattened livestock are all butchered and everything is ready; come to the wedding feast."'

"But they paid no attention and went their way, one to his own farm, another to his business, and the rest seized his slaves and mistreated them and killed them. But the king was enraged, and he sent his armies and destroyed those murderers and set their city on fire.

"Then he said to his slaves, 'The wedding is ready, but those who were invited were not worthy. Go therefore to the main highways, and as many as you find there, invite to the wedding feast.' Those slaves went out into the streets and gathered together all they found, both evil and good; and the wedding hall was filled with dinner guests.

"But when the king came in to look over the dinner guests, he saw a man there who was not dressed in wedding clothes, and he said to him, 'Friend, how did you come in here without wedding clothes?' And the man was speechless.

"Then the king said to the servants, 'Bind him hand and foot, and throw him into the outer darkness; in that place there will be weeping and gnashing of teeth.'

"For many are called, but few are chosen."

Matthew 22:1–14 NASB

✂

*J*esus' parables never compared the kingdom of heaven to earthly kingdoms. Most of his parables didn't even have government officials in them. Though this parable has a king in it, the story has little to do with governing. Instead, it's all about a party.

Jesus' parables all had morals. They were not allegories, where each character and event represented some person or thing. Instead, the story taken as a whole was the message. The moral was the reason for the parable.

The moral—the point—of Jesus' parable about a king who threw a party was that although everyone gets an invitation and no one is excluded, not everyone wants to come. That explains the one without wedding clothes who was speechless. The ill-dressed man, for whatever reason, had not really wanted to be there. Otherwise, he'd have worn the right clothes.

God has invited everyone into his kingdom. For those of us who want to come, there is no question that God will welcome us.

THE MOST IMPORTANT THING

Jesus was in the temple just before Passover:

When the Pharisees heard that [Jesus] had silenced the Sadducees with his reply, they met together to question him again. One of them, an expert in religious law, tried to trap him with this question: "Teacher, which is the most important commandment in the law of Moses?"

Jesus replied, "'You must love the Lord your God with all your heart, all your soul, and all your mind.' This is the first and greatest commandment. A second is equally important: 'Love your neighbor as yourself.' The entire law and all the demands of the prophets are based on these two commandments."

Then, surrounded by the Pharisees, Jesus asked them a question: "What do you think about the Messiah? Whose son is he?"

They replied, "He is the son of David."

Jesus responded, "Then why does David, speaking under the inspiration of the Spirit, call the Messiah 'my Lord'? For David said,

'The LORD said to my Lord,
Sit in the place of honor at
my right hand until I humble
your enemies beneath your
feet.'

Since David called the Messiah 'my Lord,' how can the Messiah be his son?"

No one could answer him. And after that, no one dared to ask him any more questions.

Matthew 22:34–46 NLT

❦

*J*esus answered every hard question and responded to every objection the religious establishment had for him. The Sadducees had presented Jesus with their toughest puzzle, and Jesus solved it in an instant. It was then the turn of the Pharisees, who of course would fare no better.

When they asked Jesus about the greatest commandment, their expectation was that no matter which one he picked, they'd be able to show that some other law was better. They hoped to make Jesus look foolish.

Once again, Jesus' answer avoided their trap. And before they could react, Jesus turned the tables and asked them about the issue that motivated all their attacks upon him: who they thought the Messiah was.

Jesus showed them that they had no clue about the Messiah since they had no answer for a rather obvious paradox in the scripture about him. How could he be both a descendant of David and God himself? They had never considered the incarnation—God becoming human.

We must be ready to open our minds and adapt ourselves to what the Bible says rather than insist upon what we think we already know.

WITHOUT HONOR

[Jesus] went away from [the Sea of Galilee] and came to His hometown, and His disciples followed Him. When the Sabbath came, He began to teach in the synagogue, and many who heard Him were astonished. "Where did this man get these things?" they said. "What is this wisdom given to Him, and how are these miracles performed by His hands? Isn't this the carpenter, the son of Mary, and the brother of James, Joses, Judas, and Simon? And aren't His sisters here with us?" So they were offended by Him.

Then Jesus said to them, "A prophet is not without honor except in his hometown, among his relatives, and in his household." So He was not able to do any miracles there, except that He laid His hands on a few sick people and healed them. And He was amazed at their unbelief.

Mark 6:1–6 HCSB

❀

*T*he people whom we think we know best, to whom we are closest, are the ones we are most likely to underestimate. It is easy to miss the wonder that is a neighbor, friend, or family member. When a teenage son or daughter first takes the wheel of the family car, most parents struggle to adjust to their offspring's new abilities. Our minds are filled with memories of skinned knees, of diaper changes at three in the morning, of tiny hands gripping our finger, and of our tears as he toddled off to kindergarten. It is hard to recognize our children as budding adults. When they grow up and become fighter pilots or doctors, it doesn't seem possible.

Meanwhile, children embrace from strangers what they previously rejected from the mouths of their own parents. They believe teachers rather than the ones who feed them every day and see to it that they have a roof over their heads.

Jesus pointed out the obvious to the people of his hometown, Nazareth. A famous person isn't famous at all when he's at home. He's just Dad or Mom, or that kid down the street. There is no reason to shake his hand or get his autograph. In Nazareth, Jesus was just the son of the carpenter. Everyone knew his family. Who did he think he was?

Rather than seeing his miracles, rather than seeing he was the Messiah, they saw only the person they thought they already knew. They didn't care about what he was doing. They cared only about where he had come from. Familiarity really can breed contempt. For those of us who have grown up in the church, who have heard the Bible stories countless times, it can be easy to become jaded to the true wonder of what Jesus has given us.

A SOUL'S PRICE

Jesus was near Caesarea Philippi:

[Jesus] summoned the crowd with His disciples, and said to them, "If anyone wishes to come after Me, he must deny himself, and take up his cross and follow Me. For whoever wishes to save his life will lose it, but whoever loses his life for My sake and the gospel's will save it. For what does it profit a man to gain the whole world, and forfeit his soul? For what will a man give in exchange for his soul? For whoever is ashamed of Me and My words in this adulterous and sinful generation, the Son of Man will also be ashamed of him when He comes in the glory of His Father with the holy angels."

And Jesus was saying to them, "Truly I say to you, there are some of those who are standing here who will not taste death until they see the kingdom of God after it has come with power."

Mark 8:34–9:1 NASB

The word *paradox* is used to describe what on the face of it appears contradictory. Jesus purposely used paradox in his teaching because, by juxtaposing apparently contradictory ideas, he forced his followers and the others listening to him to ponder what he had said. Like a pebble in our shoes, so Jesus' words are like grit in our brains.

How can the loss of our lives be anything other than a loss? Jesus doesn't leave us without a resolution to that paradox. Only in dying to what we think is important—but isn't—can we become fully alive to what genuinely matters. Jesus asks us to exchange an empty husk for a full basket.

The one who wants to keep on living, who wants to make his life safe and secure, will lose everything for which he strives. If all we want is in this life, then we are going to lose everything simply because we are going to die and can't take any of that with us. Nothing we can do will keep us from losing everything that matters, if all that matters is stuff. If we want to truly live, if we believe there's more to life than what we can see and touch and hold on to, we can gain true life. Everything turns to dust, even us. If we want to avoid becoming nothing more than dust, we must hold on to Jesus. He'll never let us down.

WHO'S ON FIRST

[Jesus and his disciples] went through Galilee. [Jesus] didn't want anyone to know their whereabouts, for he wanted to teach his disciples. He told them, "The Son of Man is about to be betrayed to some people who want nothing to do with God. They will murder him. Three days after his murder, he will rise, alive." They didn't know what he was talking about, but were afraid to ask him about it.

They came to Capernaum. When he was safe at home, he asked them, "What were you discussing on the road?"

The silence was deafening—they had been arguing with one another over who among them was greatest.

He sat down and summoned the Twelve. "So you want first place? Then take the last place. Be the servant of all."

He put a child in the middle of the room. Then, cradling the little one in his arms, he said, "Whoever embraces one of these children as I do embraces me, and far more than me—God who sent me."

Mark 9:30–37 MSG

$\mathscr{I}$t's the standard nightmare. You get to school, and not only are you unprepared for the test you didn't know you were having, but you suddenly realize you forgot ever to attend a class. Jesus' disciples must have felt like that sometimes.

Jesus tried to teach his disciples what his mission on earth was about. All his talk about death and resurrection made no sense to them, and they were afraid to ask for clarification. They wanted only to think about what they thought they did understand. Since Jesus was the Messiah, they knew that meant he'd be king, and they wondered what sort of position in his kingdom they, his closest confidants, would have. They focused their energy on that issue instead of on what Jesus really wanted them to know about.

Jesus pulled that distraction away. He showed them that what they thought about the kingdom of God was all wrong. Once more, even a topic they thought they understood became completely confusing.

But they didn't ask Jesus any questions about his correction either. They preferred their delusions to reality. The disciples failed to understand that their confused daydreams were pale shadows compared to the glorious reality Jesus was trying to tell them about. Clarity came to them only with the coming of the Holy Spirit. We must not fear the truth. Some people are afraid of the Bible. They fear that they might find something in it that will challenge what they believe. But we needn't fear what God has given us. All fear can do is keep us from listening to him with understanding.

DON'T STOP

Some Greeks had gone to Jerusalem to worship during Passover. Philip from Bethsaida in Galilee was there too. So they went to him and said, "Sir, we would like to meet Jesus." Philip told Andrew. Then the two of them went to Jesus and told him . . .

Some people brought their children to Jesus so that he could bless them by placing his hands on them. But his disciples told the people to stop bothering him.

When Jesus saw this, he became angry and said, "Let the children come to me! Don't try to stop them. People who are like these little children belong to the kingdom of God. I promise you that you cannot get into God's kingdom, unless you accept it the way a child does." Then Jesus took the children in his arms and blessed them by placing his hands on them.

John 12:20–22; Mark 10:13–16 CEV

*S*ome famous people have handlers. Some CEOs are hard to contact because they hide behind a wall of secretaries and assistants. Perhaps you can arrange an appointment for next year. But Jesus didn't operate like that, despite the best efforts of his disciples to protect him. Jesus opened himself to the most unexpected visitors, such as non-Jews or children.

In Judaism, children came of age at thirteen when they had their bar mitzvahs. It was then that they could be counted as full members of the synagogue, and only then did they begin to matter to society. Until that time, they had no standing. The disciples naturally assumed that a great man—certainly the Messiah and future king—had better things to do than pay attention to children.

Jesus became angry when the children were excluded, and he told his disciples to let them come. The kingdom was open to everyone, even those who seemed not to matter. In fact, the weak and lowly, those who lacked power and prestige, were most reflective of the nature of the kingdom. People entered the kingdom of God based not on who they were, where they came from, or what they could do, but based solely on what Jesus did on the cross. Jesus called the children to himself. He allowed non-Jewish people to talk to him.

Actions, ability, or connections don't matter. How much money you have doesn't matter. You're welcomed into the kingdom of God not because of who you are, but because of who the King is.

YES, WE CAN

While Jesus and his disciples made their way toward Jerusalem:

James and John, the sons of Zebedee, came up to Jesus and asked, "Teacher, will you do us a favor?"

Jesus asked them what they wanted, and they answered, "When you come into your glory, please let one of us sit at your right side and the other at your left."

Jesus told them, "You don't really know what you're asking! Are you able to drink from the cup that I must soon drink from or be baptized as I must be baptized?"

"Yes, we are!" James and John answered.

Then Jesus replied, "You certainly will drink from the cup from which I must drink. And you will be baptized just as I must! But it isn't for me to say who will sit at my right side and at my left. That is for God to decide."

When the ten other disciples heard this, they were angry with James and John. But Jesus called the disciples together and said: "You know that those foreigners who call themselves kings like to order their people around. And their great leaders have full power over the people they rule. But don't act like them. If you want to be great, you must be the servant of all the others. And if you want to be first, you must be everyone's slave. The Son of Man did not come to be a slave master, but a slave who will give his life to rescue many people."

Mark 10:35–45 CEV

❀

*T*he path to true leadership is not where most expect to find it. Jesus challenged his disciples' notions about the order of things.

The people of Jesus' day expected the Messiah to overthrow the Roman government and reestablish the Davidic monarchy, making Israel the center of a new empire. The disciples jockeyed for position in the future government, and two of them, the brothers James and John, attempted to get the plum posts.

Jesus gave them a job interview, but then pointed out that he wasn't the one to make the final decision on positions in the coming kingdom. When the other disciples found out what the brothers had done, they were furious. Jesus then used the situation to explain how much they had all misunderstood about the nature of what Jesus was doing on earth.

Jesus' explanation that humility was the path to greatness, and that even he had come to serve, rather than be boss, startled his disciples. If Jesus wasn't the boss, then no one could be. The implications of Jesus' words challenged their notions of how husbands and wives, parents and children, masters and slaves, and governors and governed, related to one another. We become more like Jesus as we learn to submit ourselves to others.

RIDDLE ME THIS

[Jesus and his disciples] came again to Jerusalem. And as [Jesus] was walking in the temple, the chief priests, the scribes, and the elders came to Him. And they said to Him, "By what authority are You doing these things? And who gave You this authority to do these things?"

But Jesus answered and said to them, "I also will ask you one question; then answer Me, and I will tell you by what authority I do these things: The baptism of John—was it from heaven or from men? Answer Me."

And they reasoned among themselves, saying, "If we say, 'From heaven,' He will say, 'Why then did you not believe him?' But if we say, 'From men'"—they feared the people, for all counted John to have been a prophet indeed. So they answered and said to Jesus, "We do not know."

And Jesus answered and said to them, "Neither will I tell you by what authority I do these things."

Mark 11:27–33 NKJV

❦

The religious leaders believed they were the boss. But Jesus acted with obvious confidence. He never asked the religious leaders for their permission. He never sought their favor. That was part of their annoyance with him. He didn't acknowledge who was boss. In fact, he acted as if he was the boss. So the chief priests, the scribes, the elders questioned Jesus' right to do what he was doing.

When they asked him who had given him his authority, they weren't really looking for an answer. They already knew they had not granted Jesus permission to do what he was doing. With their question, they were simply telling Jesus to shut up and go away.

But the religious establishment had forgotten that they were not in charge of the temple. The temple belonged to God. They served in the temple because God had placed them there. They served God, and they served the people of Israel. They were merely servants, not the bosses they imagined themselves to be. The religious establishment couldn't understand that, any more than they could understand that Jesus was the God they claimed to be working for, whom they claimed to worship, love, and care about. In that sense, Jesus was boss, not them.

"Who's the boss?" isn't even the right question. Jesus wasn't about being in charge. He was about being a servant. When we love someone, we don't think about being his boss or wonder who is in charge. Instead, we think about what we can do to help him and please him. We may even stop thinking about ourselves at all. That's the love that Jesus gives, and desires from us.

WHAT A WASTE

While [Jesus] was in Bethany at the home of Simon the leper, and reclining at the table, there came a woman with an alabaster vial of very costly perfume of pure nard; and she broke the vial and poured it over His head.

But some were indignantly remarking to one another, "Why has this perfume been wasted? For this perfume might have been sold for over three hundred denarii, and the money given to the poor." And they were scolding her.

But Jesus said, "Let her alone; why do you bother her? She has done a good deed to Me. For you always have the poor with you, and whenever you wish you can do good to them; but you do not always have Me. She has done what she could; she has anointed My body beforehand for the burial. Truly I say to you, wherever the gospel is preached in the whole world, what this woman has done will also be spoken of in memory of her."

Mark 14:3–9 NASB

❀

*W*ho matters most? In the first century, people were not supposed to enter the houses of lepers. Everyone stayed as far away from them as they possibly could. In fact, the law of Moses ordered that lepers be excluded from society.

One day, Jesus had a meal with a man named Simon, who was a leper. Then a woman, unnamed, arrived and poured some expensive perfume on Jesus' head.

The criticism of her act was directed more against Jesus than against the woman. By their criticism, the other dinner guests were suggesting that the perfume was wasted because it was used on Jesus. But perfume exists for one reason and one reason alone: to be put on people. Jesus was certainly worthy of being perfumed. Although the woman might have done other things with the perfume, nothing was wrong with her using it for the very purpose it had been created.

Pouring oil or perfume on the heads of new kings—anointing them—was a common ritual. *Messiah* is a Hebrew word that means "anointed one." The equivalent Greek word is *Christ*. Jesus explained that this unnamed woman had anointed him for his burial. His soon-coming death was the reason he had been born. Her gift would be spoken of forever because she was the one who had anointed him for his messianic role of saving the world from sin.

Kings were anointed in palaces by honored men, but Jesus was anointed by a woman in a leper's house. Women were second-class citizens. Lepers were excluded from society. But Jesus thought they were perfect for his anointing. We must be careful not to exclude people from taking part in serving God. Those we think unworthy are those whom God loves just as much as he loves us.

KEEP IT SIMPLE

In the region of Galilee:

Jesus now called the Twelve and gave them authority and power to deal with all the demons and cure diseases. He commissioned them to preach the news of God's kingdom and heal the sick. He said, "Don't load yourselves up with equipment. Keep it simple; *you* are the equipment. And no luxury inns—get a modest place and be content there until you leave. If you're not welcomed, leave town. Don't make a scene. Shrug your shoulders and move on."

Commissioned, they left. They traveled from town to town telling the latest news of God, the Message, and curing people everywhere they went.

Herod, the ruler, heard of these goings on and didn't know what to think. There were people saying John had come back from the dead, others that Elijah had appeared, still others that some prophet of long ago had shown up. Herod said, "But I killed John—took off his head. So who is this that I keep hearing about?" Curious, he looked for a chance to see him in action.

Luke 9:1–9 MSG

*M*ost people learn more by doing than by listening. Jesus understood this about human beings, and he sent some of his disciples off on a mission trip so they could put his words into action.

When Jesus sent his disciples about the countryside, he gave them the authority—that is, the ability—to do exactly what he had done. They could cure diseases and cast out demons. Along with that, they proclaimed the good news that God's kingdom had come.

Jesus said that they didn't need to worry about their expenses or about where they were going to stay while they were away. They were to go out with only the clothes on their backs and nothing more. God would provide for them.

Faith comes from experience, not from words on a page or from the mouth of a gifted speaker. We learn to rely on someone only with the passage of time and experience. The disciples, with the experience of healing and teaching like Jesus, learned to depend on God in ways they never had before.

Life is how we learn to trust God. We hear what he says to do, and then we do it. We begin to live as if his words are true. As it works out for us, as we do what he tells us, and as we witness his work in our lives, so our faith grows.

DYING WITH THE MOST TOYS

As he traveled toward Jerusalem, Jesus preached to large crowds:

A man in a crowd said to Jesus, "Teacher, tell my brother to give me my share of what our father left us when he died."

Jesus answered, "Who gave me the right to settle arguments between you and your brother?"

Then he said to the crowd, "Don't be greedy! Owning a lot of things won't make your life safe."

So Jesus told them this story: "A rich man's farm produced a big crop, and he said to himself, 'What can I do? I don't have a place large enough to store everything.'

"Later, he said, 'Now I know what I'll do. I'll tear down my barns and build bigger ones, where I can store all my grain and other goods. Then I'll say to myself, "You have stored up enough good things to last for years to come. Live it up! Eat, drink, and enjoy yourself."'

"But God said to him, 'You fool! Tonight you will die. Then who will get what you have stored up?'

"This is what happens to people who store up everything for themselves, but are poor in the sight of God."

Luke 12:13–21 CEV

❋

*P*eople think what they can see and touch is what will keep them safe and well. They think they are in control of their lives.

Becoming rich toward God comes with a shift in perspective and a re-ordering of priorities. For the rich man of Jesus' parable, building more storage facilities to protect his burgeoning crops was a good idea. In itself, there was nothing wrong with his plan. Grain left out in the rain would rot. But in his focus on barns, he'd lost sight of God. Moses had warned the ancient Israelites that when they finally came into the promised land and started reaping their crops and enjoying their prosperity, they must not forget who had given it all to them. The rich man lost sight of what Moses had warned the Israelites to remember.

Jesus' words were designed to remind his audience of what they should already have known from the Old Testament. Everything they had came from God. Since that was true, they should focus on God, not on what he had given them.

Our treasures on earth are just as transitory as our physical existence. We're reminded of that truth every time something breaks or we get sick. Eventually everything around us crumbles. Life is more than the stuff we manage to accumulate.

PUTTING ON AIRS

Near Jerusalem, Jesus was eating in the home of a prominent Pharisee:

When [Jesus] noticed how the guests picked the places of honor at the table, he told them this parable: "When someone invites you to a wedding feast, do not take the place of honor, for a person more distinguished than you may have been invited. If so, the host who invited both of you will come and say to you, 'Give this man your seat.' Then, humiliated, you will have to take the least important place. But when you are invited, take the lowest place, so that when your host comes, he will say to you, 'Friend, move up to a better place.' Then you will be honored in the presence of all your fellow guests. For everyone who exalts himself will be humbled, and he who humbles himself will be exalted."

Then Jesus said to his host, "When you give a luncheon or dinner, do not invite your friends, your brothers or relatives, or your rich neighbors; if you do, they may invite you back and so you will be repaid. But when you give a banquet, invite the poor, the crippled, the lame, the blind, and you will be blessed. Although they cannot repay you, you will be repaid at the resurrection of the righteous."

When one of those at the table with him heard this, he said to Jesus, "Blessed is the man who will eat at the feast in the kingdom of God."

Luke 14:7–15 NIV

*M*any people have insecurities. They forget that they have been created in the image of God. They try to compensate for their feelings of inadequacy by preening and doing what they can to make themselves look better than anyone else looks.

Jesus did not directly attack the human desire for honor. Rather, Jesus simply pointed out that if you really want to make yourself look better, the best strategy is humility. Humility leads to honor more surely than self-aggrandizement. Putting others first is the best way of putting yourself first.

Likewise, one's motivation for inviting guests to dinner should not be to receive an invitation in return. You should do good, not because of what you'll get out of it, but because of what you can do for someone else.

Real love is not self-centered. Focusing on your own needs and making yourself priority isn't showing yourself love at all. Loving yourself means that you love others first. If you really want what's best for you, you have to do what's best for someone else without thinking about yourself at all. Only in looking to help others can you help yourself and receive the greatest rewards of all.

UNSAVORY

On the road to Jerusalem, just before reaching Jericho:

Jesus told a story to some people who thought they were better than others and who looked down on everyone else:

"Two men went into the temple to pray. One was a Pharisee and the other a tax collector. The Pharisee stood over by himself and prayed, 'God, I thank you that I am not greedy, dishonest, and unfaithful in marriage like other people. And I am really glad that I am not like that tax collector over there. I go without eating for two days a week, and I give you one tenth of all I earn.'

"The tax collector stood off at a distance and did not think he was good enough even to look up toward heaven. He was so sorry for what he had done that he pounded his chest and prayed, 'God, have pity on me! I am such a sinner.'

Then Jesus said, "When the two men went home, it was the tax collector and not the Pharisee who was pleasing to God. If you put yourself above others, you will be put down. But if you humble yourself, you will be honored."

Luke 18:9–14 CEV

꽃

*J*udging people is easy. Loving them isn't so easy. Jesus explained that people tend to get their priorities out of whack, and what they think is good often turns out to be bad. The Pharisee believed himself to be good because of his selective comparison with the people around him. His prayer to God consisted of a list of reasons that he was better than any other people. Besides his tithing, he fasted twice a week, probably on the second and fifth days of the week. He fasted on the second day because tradition held that Moses had ascended Mount Sinai on that day to receive the stone tablets. On the fifth day of the week, Moses had descended on the news of the golden calf.

The tax collector, on the other hand, simply recognized reality. He knew he was a sinner and realized he couldn't do anything to fix it. All he could count on was the mercy of God. The Pharisee needed God's mercy just as much as the tax collector did. The tax collector recognized his need. The Pharisee saw the need of the tax collector, too, but he didn't see that he needed anything from God, except maybe a pat on the back for being so good.

We need to recognize who we really are. The best of us fall woefully short of perfection. Compared to Jesus, we're all just tax collectors and sinners whom Jesus had to rescue because we couldn't rescue ourselves.

WHAT THE LORD NEEDS

When [Jesus] approached Beth-phage and Bethany, near the mount that is called Olivet, He sent two of the disciples, saying, "Go into the village ahead of you; there, as you enter, you will find a colt tied on which no one yet has ever sat; untie it and bring it here. If anyone asks you, 'Why are you untying it?' you shall say, 'The Lord has need of it.'"

So those who were sent went away and found it just as He had told them. As they were untying the colt, its own-ers said to them, "Why are you untying the colt?"

They said, "The Lord has need of it." They brought it to Jesus, and they threw their coats on the colt and put Jesus on it. As He was going, they were spreading their coats on the road. As soon as He was approaching, near the descent of the Mount of Olives, the whole crowd of the disciples began to praise God joyfully with a loud voice for all the miracles which they had seen, shouting:

"Blessed is the King who comes in the name of the Lord; Peace in heaven and glory in the highest!"

Luke 19:29–38 NASB

❀

*W*hat does Jesus need? One might believe that Jesus doesn't need any-thing. But one day, a week before Passover, Jesus needed a colt, and he had his disciples procure it.

Why would someone allow strangers to take a colt simply by saying that the Lord needed it? The word translated *Lord* is a word that in the first century was used by Jewish people to refer to God. So when the disciples asked to bor-row the colt for the Lord, its owner would believe it was needed for a religious purpose.

Nevertheless, the story about the colt is presented as a miracle: Jesus knew beforehand what would happen, and ordinarily people do not give property to strangers who ask for it. But Jesus is God, and since God "owns the cattle on a thousand hills," the animal was his regardless. The story once again reminds us that Jesus is more than just a man. And if Jesus wants something, he will get it. Jesus had the power to heal the sick, and he had the power to borrow some-thing if he needed it, when he needed it.

God needs you. Don't imagine that he won't do with you what he needs to do with you. And since he loves you, becoming party to his plan will be a good thing for him, for you, and for everyone else.

SLAVE LEADERSHIP

During Jesus' last week in Jerusalem:

A dispute also arose among [the disciples] as to which one of them was to be regarded as the greatest. But [Jesus] said to them, "The kings of the Gentiles lord it over them; and those in authority over them are called benefactors. But not so with you; rather the greatest among you must become like the youngest, and the leader like one who serves. For who is greater, the one who is at the table or the one who serves? Is it not the one at the table? But I am among you as one who serves.

"You are those who have stood by me in my trials; and I confer on you, just as my Father has conferred on me, a kingdom, so that you may eat and drink at my table in my kingdom, and you will sit on thrones judging the twelve tribes of Israel."

Luke 22:24–30 NRSV

❈

*T*he needs of others outweigh the needs you have. This isn't because you're unworthy, however. It is because you're the most important. You can care for others, not because you despise yourself, but because you love them and think they're great too.

Jesus asked his disciples who was more important, the one sitting and eating, or the one serving the food. That is, was the most important person the servant or his master? The obvious answer was that the master was more important. But rather than acting important, rather than sitting at the table, Jesus instead chose the role of a servant. So who was the greatest, then? Jesus, the servant.

According to Jesus, serving one another was a matter of choice rather than force. He thought his disciples should choose to serve each another just as Jesus chose to serve them. And just as no one was to think of himself as the master, so no one could make someone else serve.

Nevertheless, his disciples would be among those sitting and eating at Jesus' table. They would have the same role as Jesus in the kingdom; they would even judge the twelve tribes of Israel. Jesus was still sitting at his table; he was the great one, and he was still the Master, regardless of what he was doing or whom he was serving. Serving another person does not lower you or change who you are. It does not change your actual status; it elevates the status of others. It means, simply, that you love others. By choosing to love them, you elevate them.

LIKE FATHER, LIKE SON

In Jerusalem during the Sabbath, Jesus healed a paralyzed man and told him to carry his mat:

For this reason the Jews persecuted Jesus, and sought to kill Him, because He had done these things on the Sabbath. But Jesus answered them, "My Father has been working until now, and I have been working."

Therefore the Jews sought all the more to kill Him, because He not only broke the Sabbath, but also said that God was His Father, making Himself equal with God. Then Jesus answered and said to them, "Most assuredly, I say to you, the Son can do nothing of Himself, but what He sees the Father do; for whatever He does, the Son also does in like manner. For the Father loves the Son, and shows Him all things that He Himself does; and He will show Him greater works than these, that you may marvel. For as the Father raises the dead and gives life to them, even so the Son gives life to whom He will. For the Father judges no one, but has committed all judgment to the Son, that all should honor the Son just as they honor the Father. He who does not honor the Son does not honor the Father who sent Him."

John 5:16–23 NKJV

A diplomat is described as someone who can tell you to go to hell in such a way that you look forward to the trip. Jesus was no diplomat. When the crowd got angry with him, he just added another reason for them to be outraged. Jesus justified his service to humanity on the Sabbath by pointing out that his Father didn't take the day off. The already angry crowd grew angrier still. Not only was Jesus a Sabbath-breaker, now he was also blaspheming.

By calling God his Father, the crowd understood that Jesus claimed to be God. The son of a man is, like his father, a man. But since there is but one God, God's Son must simply be God.

The crowd did not like that at all, but Jesus didn't back down. He hammered the point home. His critics were right. He was claiming equality with God. Everything Jesus knew, everything he did, he'd gotten from his Father. He also told them that if they didn't accept him as God, they were the ones guilty of the blasphemy.

Jesus was not concerned with making himself likable. He was concerned only with making sure people understood what he meant, even if they didn't like it. Jesus' words were often inflammatory. Sometimes the truth matters more than peace and quiet—or being well liked.

LAWBREAKERS

During the Festival of Tabernacles:

When it was now the midst of the feast Jesus went up into the temple, and began to teach.

The Jews then were astonished, saying, "How has this man become learned, having never been educated?"

So Jesus answered them and said, "My teaching is not Mine, but His who sent Me. If anyone is willing to do His will, he will know of the teaching, whether it is of God or whether I speak from Myself. He who speaks from himself seeks his own glory; but He who is seeking the glory of the One who sent Him, He is true, and there is no unrighteousness in Him. Did not Moses give you the Law, and yet none of you carries out the Law? Why do you seek to kill Me?"

The crowd answered, "You have a demon! Who seeks to kill You?"

Jesus answered them, "I did one deed, and you all marvel. For this reason Moses has given you circumcision (not because it is from Moses, but from the fathers), and on the Sabbath you circumcise a man. If a man receives circumcision on the Sabbath so that the Law of Moses will not be broken, are you angry with Me because I made an entire man well on the Sabbath? Do not judge according to appearance, but judge with righteous judgment."

John 7:14–24 NASB

※

*J*esus lacked the normal credentials. He was not the student of a famous rabbi. The religious leaders listening to him were struck with the contradiction. How could he know so much when he'd never had a formal education?

When the gospel writer John used the term *Jews,* he generally did not mean the ordinary people of Israel. He meant the religious establishment who had rejected Jesus. They were the educated elite. They claimed to know it all. After they questioned his credentials, Jesus questioned theirs. If they were so educated, why were they planning to violate one of the more obvious of the Ten Commandments, the one that forbade murder?

They wanted to kill him because they thought they knew how the Messiah should act, and Jesus didn't act that way.

Human beings easily believe they know everything. When that happens, it's no longer possible for them to learn anything. People don't look for answers if they believe they've already found them.

Jesus had no formal education, and he turned out just fine. The religious leaders had a lot of education, and it hadn't done them any good. True education leads to humility rather than to arrogance; it leads more to a desire to hear than to a desire to speak. We have truly become educated when we realize how little we actually know. Until then, we've learned nothing.

CHECKLIST

Some of the people who lived in Jerusalem started to ask each other, "Isn't this the man they are trying to kill? But here he is, speaking in public, and they say nothing to him. Could our leaders possibly believe that he is the Messiah? But how could he be? For we know where this man comes from. When the Messiah comes, he will simply appear; no one will know where he comes from."

While Jesus was teaching in the Temple, he called out, "Yes, you know me, and you know where I come from. But I'm not here on my own. The one who sent me is true, and you don't know him. But I know him because I come from him, and he sent me to you." Then the leaders tried to arrest him; but no one laid a hand on him, because his time had not yet come.

Many among the crowds at the Temple believed in him. "After all," they said, "would you expect the Messiah to do more miraculous signs than this man has done?"

When the Pharisees heard that the crowds were whispering such things, they and the leading priests sent Temple guards to arrest Jesus.

John 7:25–32 NLT

🎞

*S*hakespeare's Hamlet told his friend, "There are more things in heaven and earth, Horatio, than are dreamt of in your philosophy." The Pharisees thought they knew how the Messiah should act and what he should do, despite the fact that they hadn't even worked out how to reconcile all the prophecies about him.

One of the unsolved questions about the Messiah related to his origins. Some taught that the Messiah's origins were "of old," like those of Melchizedek, the king of Salem who had met Abraham and accepted his tithe, unknown and unknowable. Like those who had advised Herod at the birth of Jesus, others believed that the Messiah's point of origin was clear. He would come from Bethlehem. Jesus responded that he had come from God. That was how he could be "of old" and also be born in Bethlehem.

Meanwhile, the people continued to wonder if perhaps Jesus actually was the Messiah, despite the problems their leadership had with him. Even with the questions of his origins, there were still his miracles to resolve. Jesus was certainly different from any other human being they'd ever known.

Jesus remains the same today as he was then: different from anyone else we've ever known. It's okay if we don't have all the answers. And we should never assume we have him all figured out. The wiser we become, the more we realize how foolish it is to think that we know it all.

HIDE AND SEEK

In Jerusalem, during the Festival of Tabernacles:

[Jesus] said to them again, "I'm going away; you will look for Me, and you will die in your sin. Where I'm going, you cannot come."

So the Jews said again, "He won't kill Himself, will He, since He says, 'Where I'm going, you cannot come'?"

"You are from below," He told them, "I am from above. You are of this world; I am not of this world. Therefore I told you that you will die in your sins. For if you do not believe that I am He, you will die in your sins."

"Who are You?" they questioned.

"Precisely what I've been telling you from the very beginning," Jesus told them. "I have many things to say and to judge about you, but the One who sent Me is true, and what I have heard from Him—these things I tell the world."

They did not know He was speaking to them about the Father. So Jesus said to them, "When you lift up the Son of Man, then you will know that I am He, and that I do nothing on My own. But just as the Father taught Me, I say these things. The One who sent Me is with Me. He has not left Me alone, because I always do what pleases Him."

As He was saying these things, many believed in Him.

John 8:21–30 HCSB

The reason we don't understand some of what Jesus tells us isn't because he's not clear. It's because we can't hear him over the shouts of our own ideas. Jesus' words were often enigmatic to those who first heard him. But from our perspective, his words are perfectly clear.

Jesus told his critics that he was going to be crucified, that he would die and then return to his Father in heaven. They did not share his destiny in heaven since they, the religious leaders of Israel, had refused to believe him. Sadly, the gospel of John has been twisted by anti-Semites who attempt to blame the Jews for Jesus' death and the world's problems. John was Jewish, the disciples were Jewish, and the overwhelming majority of early Christians were Jewish. Jesus directed his criticism at the religious leadership of Israel, not the Jewish people as a whole.

Find out what matters to Jesus, not what matters to you. When you quiet your mind, lay aside the concerns and questions you have, and try to hear Jesus on his terms. You will discover his questions and his concerns and be able to make them your own.

CRAZY

During the Festival of Tabernacles in Jerusalem:

At this point the Jews [told Jesus], "Now we *know* you're crazy. Abraham died. The prophets died. And you show up saying, 'If you practice what I'm telling you, you'll never have to face death, not even a taste.' Are you greater than Abraham, who died? And the prophets died! Who do you think you are!"

Jesus said, "If I turned the spotlight on myself, it wouldn't amount to anything. But my Father, the same One you say is your Father, put me here at this time and place of splendor. You haven't recognized him in this. But I have. If I, in false modesty, said I didn't know what was going on, I would be as much of a liar as you are. But I do know, and I am doing what he says. Abraham—your 'father'—with jubilant faith looked down the corridors of history and saw my day coming. He saw it and cheered."

The Jews said, "You're not even fifty years old—and Abraham saw you?"

"Believe me," said Jesus, "*I am who I am* long before Abraham was anything."

That did it—pushed them over the edge. They picked up rocks to throw at him. But Jesus slipped away, getting out of the Temple.

John 8:52–59 MSG

※

*J*esus is not just a man.

"I am who I am," the phrase that Jesus used and applied to himself, was a quotation from Exodus 3:14. In using it, Jesus claimed to be the God who spoke to Abraham, who met Moses at the burning bush, and who led the Jewish people out of Egyptian bondage. Moses belonged to a polytheistic society where many gods were worshipped. When he asked God for a name, he did it so he could let the people of Israel know which god had sent him. God responded by saying, "I am who I am." He didn't need a name since he was the only God.

In Hebrew, the name *Yahweh* simply means "He is." God told Moses, "I am." Moses went back to the Israelites and told them, "'He is' sent me." Jewish people later decided to stop using God's name for fear of taking it in vain. In place of his name, they used the word *Lord*. When Jesus' disciples and the authors of the New Testament call Jesus *Lord*, they are identifying him as the God of the Old Testament.

The religious leaders reacted to Jesus' claim of being their God by picking up stones to kill him as a blasphemer. In their eyes, Jesus could be only a man. But we know better. Jesus is God. But the Jesus we worship is not far away, divorced from our lives and concerns. It was a mistake for the religious leadership not to accept that Jesus was God. We must be careful not to make a mistake just as big, and forget that he was also human.

THE GODS

During Hanukkah, Jesus replied to the religious leaders in the temple courts:

"In your Scriptures doesn't God say, 'You are gods'? You can't argue with the Scriptures, and God spoke to those people and called them gods. So why do you accuse me of a terrible sin for saying that I am the Son of God? After all, it is the Father who prepared me for this work. He is also the one who sent me into the world. If I don't do as my Father does, you should not believe me. But if I do what my Father does, you should believe because of that, even if you don't have faith in me. Then you will know for certain that the Father is one with me, and I am one with the Father."

Again they wanted to arrest Jesus. But he escaped and crossed the Jordan to the place where John had earlier been baptizing. While Jesus was there, many people came to him. They were saying, "John didn't work any miracles, but everything he said about Jesus is true." A lot of those people also put their faith in Jesus.

John 10:34–42 CEV

In Jesus' day, the caesar of Rome believed himself to be a god, as had many other kings throughout history. Jesus told his critics that even God called some of them "gods." Of course, when God called the kings "gods," he was being sarcastic. In Psalm 82, God referred to the kings of the earth as "gods" as he criticized them for their actions. In Ezekiel's prophecy, God addressed the king of Tyre as a god and then inquired if he'd continue to insist on his divinity in the face of those who killed him.

Jesus referenced such Old Testament usage because he knew that the religious leaders of Israel would never accuse God of blasphemy for calling monarchs gods. They understood the reason God called those men gods. Jesus suggested that they not be so quick to judge him a blasphemer. Instead, they needed to consider the miracles that Jesus was performing, miracles that went far beyond any miracles ever performed by anyone else. Unlike the kings of the world who only claimed to be God, Jesus had proof that he was.

Jesus said that he is God. He challenged those around him to believe or not, based on what he said and based on what he did. Jesus' challenge remains for those of us who hear him today.

BATH TIME

Just before Jesus' last Passover, during an evening meal:

[Jesus] came to Simon Peter, who said to him, "Lord, are you going to wash my feet?"

Jesus answered, "You do not know now what I am doing, but later you will understand."

Peter said to him, "You will never wash my feet."

Jesus answered, "Unless I wash you, you have no share with me."

Simon Peter said to him, "Lord, not my feet only but also my hands and my head!" Jesus said to him, "One who has bathed does not need to wash, except for the feet, but is entirely clean. And you are clean, though not all of you." For he knew who was to betray him; for this reason he said, "Not all of you are clean."

After he had washed their feet, had put on his robe, and had returned to the table, he said to them, "Do you know what I have done to you? You call me Teacher and Lord—and you are right, for that is what I am. So if I, your Lord and Teacher, have washed your feet, you also ought to wash one another's feet. For I have set you an example, that you also should do as I have done to you. Very truly, I tell you, servants are not greater than their master, nor are messengers greater than the one who sent them. If you know these things, you are blessed if you do them."

John 13:6–17 NRSV

*N*o one likes to get in trouble. Peter always wanted to do the right thing. In fact, one could say that his heart was always in the right place. But he was impetuous and often confused.

Foot washing was a common custom in Jesus' day. When people traveled, they usually walked. Dusty or muddy roads, combined with open-toed sandals, meant that when you entered someone's home, it was a good idea to rinse off the dirty feet rather than track the filth through the house. Such a task was usually left to the servant. Certainly one would never expect a rabbi to be washing his disciples' feet. That's why Peter at first reacted negatively to Jesus' offer.

Jesus washed his disciples' feet to make a spiritual and relational point. Jesus proclaimed himself the servant God, a God who stooped to take care of his people, who cared more for their needs than for his status. Our concern should likewise not be for our status or place in society. Rather, our concern should be about the needs of others. Just as Jesus had freely submitted to them, so we must freely submit to one another.

FRIENDS AND ENEMIES

Jesus gave everything he had when we were his enemies. We have trouble sometimes doing things for our dear friends and family. Would we even consider lifting a finger, let alone giving all we have, to someone who broke into our house to steal something and then sued us for a million dollars because they tripped over the light cord? Yet that's precisely how God treats his enemies. Jesus encouraged us always to do what was best for everyone, even those who are our enemies. Our righteousness should be independent of the righteousness of others. Enemies are best overcome by changing them into friends.

❊

If your enemy is hungry, feed him;
if he is thirsty, give him a drink.
Romans 12:20 NKJV

BAD FRUIT TASTES BAD

During his Sermon on the Mount near the Sea of Galilee, Jesus said:

"Enter through the narrow gate; for the gate is wide and the way is broad that leads to destruction, and there are many who enter through it. For the gate is small and the way is narrow that leads to life, and there are few who find it.

"Beware of the false prophets, who come to you in sheep's clothing, but inwardly are ravenous wolves. You will know them by their fruits. Grapes are not gathered from thorn bushes nor figs from thistles, are they? So every good tree bears good fruit, but the bad tree bears bad fruit. A good tree cannot produce bad fruit, nor can a bad tree produce good fruit. Every tree that does not bear good fruit is cut down and thrown into the fire. So then, you will know them by their fruits.

"Not everyone who says to Me, 'Lord, Lord,' will enter the kingdom of heaven, but he who does the will of My Father who is in heaven will enter. Many will say to Me on that day, 'Lord, Lord, did we not prophesy in Your name, and in Your name cast out demons, and in Your name perform many miracles?' And then I will declare to them, 'I never knew you; depart from Me, you who practice lawlessness.'"

Matthew 7:13–23 NASB

According to Moses, a person who claimed to bear a message from God was a true prophet only if what he said actually happened. If a prophet spoke, but his words did not come to pass, the Israelites were told they could safely ignore such a person, because that so-called prophet was just making it up.

Jesus explained that even though a person talked a good game, who they really were was going to come out—and what mattered was who they really were. The person who makes extravagant claims on his résumé, for instance, is going to be embarrassed when his prospective employer calls the reference and hears, "We have no record of his ever having worked for us."

Words are empty if they are not followed by actions. The Israelites were practical people. If someone claimed he knew how to do something, people would believe him only if they saw him doing it. If a person claimed he built his fence, he'd better not have been paying his neighbor to build it for him.

That's why the apostle James would later write that faith without works is dead. Empty words are just that; they are empty. Real faith is transformative. Real faith does the work of God. If we claim to believe in God, we should not be living our lives the same way an atheist might.

THE SICK

While Jesus was in Nazareth:

[Jesus] saw a man named Matthew sitting at the tax office, and He said to him, "Follow Me!" So he got up and followed Him.

While He was reclining at the table in the house, many tax collectors and sinners came as guests to eat with Jesus and His disciples. When the Pharisees saw this, they asked His disciples, "Why does your Teacher eat with tax collectors and sinners?"

But when He heard this, He said, "Those who are well don't need a doctor, but the sick do. Go and learn what this means: I desire mercy and not sacrifice. For I didn't come to call the righteous, but sinners."

Then John's disciples came to Him, saying, "Why do we and the Pharisees fast often, but Your disciples do not fast?"

Jesus said to them, "Can the wedding guests be sad while the groom is with them? The days will come when the groom will be taken away from them, and then they will fast. No one patches an old garment with unshrunk cloth, because the patch pulls away from the garment and makes the tear worse. And no one puts new wine into old wineskins. Otherwise, the skins burst, the wine spills out, and the skins are ruined. But they put new wine into fresh wineskins, and both are preserved."

Matthew 9:9–17 HCSB

❋

*M*ark Twain once said that the stuff in the Bible he didn't understand didn't bother him. What bothered him was the stuff in the Bible he did understand.

Jesus told the religious leaders that the sick, not the healthy, needed a physician. Jesus told John's disciples that fasting would be an odd choice at a wedding party. Then Jesus illustrated what he meant by talking of new wine in old wine flasks, and patching old clothes with unshrunk cloth. No one would be so silly. So what was Jesus' point?

Some have suggested that Jesus was referring to Judaism versus Christianity, the Old Testament versus the New Testament, but in the context, that doesn't fit. The context is the healthy versus the sick, fasting versus not fasting. Jesus continued that theme of polar opposites with old versus new. But he didn't say that one was better than the other.

Instead, Jesus' point was very simple. Do the right thing at the right time. The disciples of John and Jesus' pharisaical critics were failing to discern the times. For instance, praying to God for an hour is a wonderful thing to do— unless we were asked to just say grace before dinner. We need to be aware of our circumstances and adjust accordingly.

MERCY

In Nazareth, Jesus attended a party in Matthew's house:

As Jesus left the house, he was followed by two blind men crying out, "Mercy, Son of David! Mercy on us!" When Jesus got home, the blind men went in with him. Jesus said to them, "Do you really believe I can do this?" They said, "Why, yes, Master!"

He touched their eyes and said, "Become what you believe." It happened. They saw. Then Jesus became very stern. "Don't let a soul know how this happened." But they were hardly out the door before they started blabbing it to everyone they met.

Right after that, as the blind men were leaving, a man who had been struck speechless by an evil spirit was brought to Jesus. As soon as Jesus threw the evil tormenting spirit out, the man talked away just as if he'd been talking all his life. The people were up on their feet applauding: "There's never been anything like this in Israel!"

The Pharisees were left sputtering, "Hocus-pocus. It's nothing but hocus-pocus. He's probably made a pact with the devil."

Then Jesus made a circuit of all the towns and villages. He taught in their meeting places, reported kingdom news, and healed their diseased bodies, healed their bruised and hurt lives. When he looked out over the crowds, his heart broke. So confused and aimless they were, like sheep with no shepherd. "What a huge harvest!" he said to his disciples. "How few workers! On your knees and pray for harvest hands!"

Matthew 9:27–38 MSG

One size does not fit all. Jesus adapted how he worked with people according to their individual needs. When the two blind men asked Jesus for mercy, he questioned them about their faith. With their affirmation of faith, he healed them. Then he ordered them to keep silent.

But when Jesus saw a man who was unable to speak, he simply healed him. Those who witnessed the act were astonished. Jesus did not tell the formerly speechless man to keep silent, nor did he demand silence of the audience who witnessed it.

There isn't a cookie-cutter approach to human relationships, nor to our relationship with God. Relationships between persons are dynamic and changing. The best way to handle the same individual will change depending on circumstances and the passage of time. Jesus listened, he watched, and he acted in unique ways with each person as was necessary. What didn't change was Jesus' love and concern for those he met. We need to be able and willing to adapt the message of God's kingdom to our audience. Our goal should always be to communicate clearly and effectively.

REAL FAMILY

In the region of Galilee, after casting out a demon, Jesus was speaking to a crowd:

"[The demon] says, 'I will return to my house from which I came.' When it comes, it finds it empty, swept, and put in order. Then it goes and brings along seven other spirits more evil than itself, and they enter and live there; and the last state of that person is worse than the first. So will it be also with this evil generation."

While [Jesus] was still speaking to the crowds, his mother and his brothers were standing outside, wanting to speak to him. Someone told him, "Look, your mother and your brothers are standing outside, wanting to speak to you."

But to the one who had told him this, Jesus replied, "Who is my mother, and who are my brothers?" And pointing to his disciples, he said, "Here are my mother and my brothers! For whoever does the will of my Father in heaven is my brother and sister and mother."

Matthew 12:44–50 NRSV

*P*ermanent solutions rarely are. Jesus compared the state of the people of Israel in his generation to the state of a man who'd been freed from a demon who would get that demon back, plus an additional seven. The Jewish people of Jesus' day fit that picture because their Messiah had arrived to free them from their sins.

They could think only about being freed from the Roman Empire, however. Within fewer than forty years, the Jewish people would launch a rebellion against the Romans. But the rebellion would fail. Their situation was bad before the rebellion, and it would become far worse afterward. Jerusalem would be leveled, the temple burned to the ground, and the population scattered across the empire. They would be even more oppressed by the Roman government than they were before.

The Jewish people, like the man cleansed of a demon, could choose to turn to God. They could accept what God's kingdom actually was, God in their hearts, or they could reject that, turn to their own devices, and suffer for their poor choices. Unfortunately, they chose poorly.

Become a part of God's family. God's way doesn't always seem to be what we really want. But God knows our hearts and our needs more thoroughly than we know them ourselves. Don't be reluctant to do what God wants, since what he wants is always in our best interests.

HOW TO PAY TAXES

While [Jesus and his disciples] were staying in Galilee, Jesus said to them, "The Son of Man is about to be betrayed into the hands of men, and they will kill Him, and the third day He will be raised up." And they were exceedingly sorrowful.

When they had come to Capernaum, those who received the temple tax came to Peter and said, "Does your Teacher not pay the temple tax?"

He said, "Yes."

And when he had come into the house, Jesus anticipated him, saying, "What do you think, Simon? From whom do the kings of the earth take customs or taxes, from their sons or from strangers?"

Peter said to Him, "From strangers."

Jesus said to him, "Then the sons are free. Nevertheless, lest we offend them, go to the sea, cast in a hook, and take the fish that comes up first. And when you have opened its mouth, you will find a piece of money; take that and give it to them for Me and you."

Matthew 17:22–27 NKJV

Going fishing rarely pays the bills nowadays. But once, that's just what Jesus had Peter do. When he told Peter to go fishing to find the money to pay for the temple tax, he was not giving Peter a universal pattern on how to solve our tax or financial woes.

That doesn't mean there is no universal principle at work in the passage. We learn that when God does tell us to do something, we can be confident that it will work out. And we learn, too, that, like Peter, we are sons of the kingdom. We are not just servants. We are not just citizens of the heavenly kingdom. We are members of its royal family, with all the privileges and blessings that are a part of that.

We also learn that Jesus picked his battles. Sometimes he was happy to offend the religious establishment. But he wasn't willing to do so over this tax because of the principle of love. The temple tax supported those who worked in the temple. It paid the priests; it paid those who did maintenance; it paid small businesspeople who kept the temple supplied with ink and paper and oil. The livelihood and welfare of ordinary people were dependent upon the tax.

Though Jesus and the disciples were technically exempt, it was better to pay than not to pay. The needs of others take precedence over our own.

FISHERS OF MEN

Passing along the beach of Lake Galilee, [Jesus] saw Simon and his brother Andrew net-fishing. Fishing was their regular work. Jesus said to them, "Come with me. I'll make a new kind of fisherman out of you. I'll show you how to catch men and women instead of perch and bass." They didn't ask questions. They dropped their nets and followed.

A dozen yards or so down the beach, he saw the brothers James and John, Zebedee's sons. They were in the boat, mending their fishnets. Right off, he made the same offer. Immediately, they left their father Zebedee, the boat, and the hired hands, and followed.

Then they entered Capernaum. When the Sabbath arrived, Jesus lost no time in getting to the meeting place. He spent the day there teaching. They were surprised at his teaching—so forthright, so confident—not quibbling and quoting like the religion scholars.

Mark 1:16–22 MSG

❧

*J*esus wasn't a hypnotist. Jesus already had a relationship with those he finally called to be his disciples. His disciples had heard John the Baptist proclaim him the Messiah, and they had heard him speak. They were leaving behind their businesses, their jobs, and their livelihoods, but they believed they were making a good choice. In their minds, they believed they were joining the future king of Israel—of the world—and they were getting in on the ground floor. For them, it was a no-brainer. As fishermen, they were certainly prosperous and comfortable. But being part of the future royal house would be far better. They knew the story of David. They knew that those who had followed him early when he was still on the run from Saul later gained status and immense wealth.

They did not believe they were sacrificing anything by becoming Jesus' disciples. After pentecost and the coming of the Holy Spirit, they understood that Jesus had not come to establish the physical kingdom they had expected. But they realized that the deal they had made was even better than what they had thought. They had not joined a temporary, earthly position of authority and wealth. Instead, they had joined the household of God himself for all eternity.

Following Jesus is the best decision you can ever make. You're not sacrificing anything at all. You're gaining everything.

SCUM OF THE EARTH

Jesus went out to the lakeshore again and taught the crowds that were coming to him. As he walked along, he saw Levi son of Alphaeus sitting at his tax collector's booth. "Follow me and be my disciple," Jesus said to him. So Levi got up and followed him.

Later, Levi invited Jesus and his disciples to his home as dinner guests, along with many tax collectors and other disreputable sinners. (There were many people of this kind among Jesus' followers.) But when the teachers of religious law who were Pharisees saw him eating with tax collectors and other sinners, they asked his disciples, "Why does he eat with such scum?"

When Jesus heard this, he told them, "Healthy people don't need a doctor—sick people do. I have come to call not those who think they are righteous, but those who know they are sinners."

Mark 2:13–17 NLT

*J*esus came to do the laundry. Levi, the son of Alphaeus, is sometimes called Matthew. He was a tax collector. Tax collectors were prosperous individuals who lived well and never lacked for anything. But they were universally denounced. They were the lowest of the low. They lived high and mighty off the wages of others. Tax collectors had turned against their own people. They accepted a fortune in exchange for their souls. They sold out their homeland for money. They were collaborators and traitors. Most religious people wanted to see them dead.

But Jesus asked such a person to become one of his disciples. And then Jesus attended a party he threw, paid for by the tax collector's ill-gotten gain. The party was filled with more tax collectors and the women they kept. The Pharisees were beside themselves with righteous indignation. They wanted to know how Jesus could eat with the lowlifes of society if he really was the Messiah.

According to the expectations and understandings of the religious establishment, one of the roles of the Messiah was to cleanse the nation of sinners. Instead, Jesus was partying with them. It made no sense.

The religious establishment missed the fact that though one could get rid of dirty laundry by burning it, there was a much better way to get rid of it—just clean it. God prefers simply to clean the dirt that stains our souls rather than to destroy us. Mercy is God's first choice, not his last choice. Just as he has been merciful to us, so we can be merciful to others.

OUT OF HIS MIND

In a house near the Sea of Galilee just after Jesus had appointed his twelve apostles:

When His family heard this, they set out to restrain Him, because they said, "He's out of His mind." The scribes who had come down from Jerusalem said, "[Jesus] has Beelzebul in Him!" and, "He drives out demons by the ruler of the demons!"

So [Jesus] summoned them and spoke to them in parables: "How can Satan drive out Satan? If a kingdom is divided against itself, that kingdom cannot stand. If a house is divided against itself, that house cannot stand. And if Satan rebels against himself and is divided, he cannot stand but is finished!

"On the other hand, no one can enter a strong man's house and rob his possessions unless he first ties up the strong man. Then he will rob his house. I assure you: People will be forgiven for all sins and whatever blasphemies they may blaspheme. But whoever blasphemes against the Holy Spirit never has forgiveness, but is guilty of an eternal sin"—because they were saying, "He has an unclean spirit."

Then His mother and His brothers came, and standing outside, they sent word to Him and called Him. A crowd was sitting around Him and told Him, "Look, Your mother, Your brothers, and Your sisters are outside asking for You."

He replied to them, "Who are My mother and My brothers?" And looking about at those who were sitting in a circle around Him, He said, "Here are My mother and My brothers! Whoever does the will of God is My brother and sister and mother."

Mark 3:21–35 HCSB

*O*pposition sometimes arises from where you least expect it. When the religious establishment that didn't approve of Jesus finally tried to explain that Jesus was getting his power from the devil, it wasn't much of a shock. But Jesus' own family did not believe that he was the Messiah either. While the religious establishment was arguing that Jesus was filled with the devil, his own family concluded that Jesus was simply crazy.

For the religious establishment, their unbelief led them to blaspheme against the Holy Spirit that empowered Jesus. They argued that it was really the devil doing the miracles. Where his family's lack of belief had merely motivated them to try to rescue him, the religious establishment's lack of belief had led them to seek Jesus' death.

Doing the right thing, being a good person, and making the best choices do not guarantee that we will have a life filled with peace or prosperity. In fact, we're very likely to face persecution, just as Jesus did, and just as he warned us to expect.

GOOD NEWS

After the triumphal entry, Jesus, who was in Jerusalem with his disciples, said:

"Be on your guard! You will be taken to courts and beaten with whips in their meeting places. And because of me, you will have to stand before rulers and kings to tell about your faith. But before the end comes, the good news must be preached to all nations.

"When you are arrested, don't worry about what you will say. You will be given the right words when the time comes. But you will not really be the ones speaking. Your words will come from the Holy Spirit.

"Brothers and sisters will betray each other and have each other put to death. Parents will betray their own children, and children will turn against their parents and have them killed. Everyone will hate you because of me. But if you keep on being faithful right to the end, you will be saved."

Mark 13:9–13 CEV

*T*aking the hard road will make you happier than taking the easy road. Jesus predicted that very bad things would happen to those who became his followers. Of the twelve original disciples, only John died peacefully of old age. All the others were murdered for their faith in Jesus.

But Jesus promised that those who were faithful to the end would be saved. Our vision is usually too small. We can see only our daily problems. We worry. But we miss the bigger picture. When Jesus told his disciples what was coming, they were thinking of God's kingdom in physical terms. They expected the reestablishment of the Davidic monarchy. They understood that rebellions were hard. They remembered the stories about David when he was on the run from Saul and all the hardships both he and his men endured. The disciples knew there would be fighting and setbacks. But for them, it would be worthwhile once they sat triumphant over the world with Jesus. Any hardship is endurable when one sees the bigger picture and understands the bigger purpose. For the disciples, they saw a big picture. Only later, after Jesus' death and resurrection, did the disciples realize that their vision of a physical kingdom on earth was insignificant compared to the everlasting kingdom of heaven.

We can become overwhelmed by our problems. Current pain easily drives out our memories of past comfort and our hope for the future. But we need to remember that Jesus has reassured us that our momentary sorrow is nothing in comparison to the glories to come.

❀❀❀❀❀❀❀❀❀❀❀❀❀❀❀❀❀❀❀❀❀❀❀❀❀❀❀❀❀❀❀❀❀❀

SPIRIT POWER

Jesus returned to Galilee with the power of the Spirit. News about him spread everywhere. He taught in the Jewish meeting places, and everyone praised him.

Jesus went back to Nazareth, where he had been brought up, and as usual he went to the meeting place on the Sabbath. When he stood up to read from the Scriptures, he was given the book of Isaiah the prophet. He opened it and read,

"The Lord's Spirit has come
to me, because he has chosen
me to tell the good news to
the poor. The Lord has sent
me to announce freedom for
prisoners, to give sight to the
blind, to free everyone who
suffers, and to say, 'This is the
year the Lord has chosen.'"

Jesus closed the book, then handed it back to the man in charge and sat down. Everyone in the meeting place looked straight at Jesus.

Then Jesus said to them, "What you have just heard me read has come true today."

Luke 4:14–21 CEV

❀

*J*esus lived and acted as a good Jewish man his entire life. He followed all the teachings of Moses and the prophets because he was their fulfillment.

When Jesus finished his forty days in the wilderness being tempted by the devil, he returned home to Nazareth, a village located in the plains between the coast of the Mediterranean and the Sea of Galilee. He regularly attended the local synagogue on the Sabbath. The idea of meeting together once a week for worship and instruction in the commandments of God had developed in Israel after the people returned from exile in Babylon. God had sent them into exile for abandoning God. When their descendants returned, therefore, they were determined to avoid a repetition of that punishment. They decided that if they met together weekly to hear instruction in the Scriptures, they wouldn't be tempted to abandon God again. The first Christians were Jewish, so they adapted the synagogue pattern for the early congregations of believers.

The rabbi called upon Jesus to read the passage of the Bible selected for that week. It was from the prophet Isaiah. Upon reading the passage, Jesus announced that he was the one Isaiah was speaking about.

In his hometown, Jesus confirmed his identity to his friends and family. There's no harder group to stand before than our own family. It is hard for them to see us as anything other than the son, brother, daughter, or sister they remember. We must do God's will, no matter where the opposition comes from.

NO SATISFYING EVERYONE

In the region of Galilee Jesus was preaching and teaching, and he praised John the Baptist:

(And all the people who heard this, including the tax collectors, acknowledged the justice of God, because they had been baptized with John's baptism. But by refusing to be baptized by him, the Pharisees and the lawyers rejected God's purpose for themselves.)

"To what then will I compare the people of this generation, and what are they like? They are like children sitting in the marketplace and calling to one another,

'We played the flute for you,
and you did not dance; we
wailed, and you did not weep.'

For John the Baptist has come eating no bread and drinking no wine, and you say, 'He has a demon'; the Son of Man has come eating and drinking, and you say, 'Look, a glutton and a drunkard, a friend of tax collectors and sinners!' Nevertheless, wisdom is vindicated by all her children."

Luke 7:29–35 NRSV

Jesus compared the religious leaders of his day to children who refused to be satisfied. No matter what God did for them, no matter whom God sent their way to preach to them, they remained unmoved. Nothing was ever enough for them.

John the Baptist and Jesus both came from God. One was a hermit who lived alone in the wilderness, subsisting on whatever insects he could find as long as they were kosher. The other was surrounded by friends; he was popular and outgoing, and he was often invited to parties where he would eat the best food and drink the best drinks.

We can serve God no matter what lifestyle God has called us to live. Some serve God in poverty and deprivation, working long years without spouse or children in primitive conditions, in poor health, perhaps in far-off and strange lands. Others become wealthy, are promoted to places of power and authority, and never lack for the pleasures and joys that life can bring. Most of us fall somewhere in between.

Whatever God has asked of us, we can rejoice in it. Whatever God has asked of us, we may find some people do not understand or approve of what we're doing or how we're living. We can never please all the people all the time. But whatever God has asked of us, we can be confident that God will bless us and reward us for our obedience. God's judgment on our lives is the only one that really matters.

BABIES

On his way to Jerusalem, Jesus sent seventy disciples ahead of him:

Then the seventy [disciples Jesus had sent out to preach the gospel] returned with joy, saying, "Lord, even the demons are subject to us in Your name."

And [Jesus] said to them, "I saw Satan fall like lightning from heaven. Behold, I give you the authority to trample on serpents and scorpions, and over all the power of the enemy, and nothing shall by any means hurt you. Nevertheless do not rejoice in this, that the spirits are subject to you, but rather rejoice because your names are written in heaven."

In that hour Jesus rejoiced in the Spirit and said, "I thank You, Father, Lord of heaven and earth, that You have hidden these things from the wise and prudent and revealed them to babes. Even so, Father, for so it seemed good in Your sight. All things have been delivered to Me by My Father, and no one knows who the Son is except the Father, and who the Father is except the Son, and the one to whom the Son wills to reveal Him."

Then He turned to His disciples and said privately, "Blessed are the eyes which see the things you see; for I tell you that many prophets and kings have desired to see what you see, and have not seen it, and to hear what you hear, and have not heard it."

Luke 10:17–24 NKJV

More people than just the twelve apostles followed Jesus. Crowds of men and women followed him everywhere he went. From those followers, Jesus selected seventy for a special ministry where they not only taught Jesus' words but also performed many of the same sorts of miracles that he had. The seventy came back excited most by the fact that demons would obey them.

Jesus informed them that Satan could no longer harm them. As spectacular as a lightning strike was, so had been Satan's defeat at the hands of the seventy. Although Satan was a dangerous figure in the Bible, he was always completely subject to God and his people. He was a minor figure who rarely showed up, and then only to be beaten up by either God or God's servants. That the demons were subject to the seventy was therefore par for the course.

One of the proverbs says that we should not rejoice at the fall of our enemies (Proverbs 24:17). Jesus encouraged his followers to move past their glee over Satan's defeat. He told them they should instead focus on something far more exciting—the glorious reality that their names were written in heaven. What Jesus did for us on the cross was the biggest miracle of all. Getting to share that miracle with others is the most exciting thing we can do.

CONFLICT

On his way to Jerusalem, Jesus was teaching his followers and said:

"I have come to set the world on fire, and I wish it were already burning! I have a terrible baptism of suffering ahead of me, and I am under a heavy burden until it is accomplished. Do you think I have come to bring peace to the earth? No, I have come to divide people against each other! From now on families will be split apart, three in favor of me, and two against—or two in favor and three against.

"'Father will be divided against son and son against father; mother against daughter and daughter against mother and mother-in-law against daughter-in-law and daughter-in law against mother-in-law.'"

Then Jesus turned to the crowd and said, "When you see clouds beginning to form in the west, you say, 'Here comes a shower.' And you are right. When the south wind blows, you say, 'Today will be a scorcher.' And it is. You fools! You know how to interpret the weather signs of the earth and sky, but you don't know how to interpret the present times.

"Why can't you decide for yourselves what is right? When you are on the way to court with your accuser, try to settle the matter before you get there. Otherwise, your accuser may drag you before the judge, who will hand you over to an officer, who will throw you into prison. And if that happens, you won't be free again until you have paid the very last penny."

Luke 12:49–59 NLT

※

*J*esus did not come to bring peace to the world. Instead, he said that he came to divide it. Yes, the gospel is good news. Yes, Jesus offers us peace, not as the world gives. Yes, Jesus said that the world would know Christians were his disciples because of the love they have for one another.

Jesus offered peace to his followers. But the religious establishment and the Roman government violently opposed Jesus and his disciples and offered them anything but peace. Just as Jesus and his disciples were estranged from their own friends and families, so those of us who choose Christ may likewise find ourselves at odds with our family, our friends, our religious leaders, and our government. Peace will not always be possible or even desirable. Jesus was and continues to be a divisive figure.

There is a time for peace, and a time for conflict. What matters most to us is the truth of what Jesus did, the truth of who Jesus is, and the truth of the impact he has had on our lives. Sometimes insisting on the truth of God may mean we can't get along with some people. It may even mean that they choose to hate us. But we will always have the peace Jesus has given us.

FINANCIAL MALFEASANCE

Near Jerusalem, just before the triumphal entry:

[Jesus] also said to the disciples: "There was a rich man who received an accusation that his manager was squandering his possessions. So he called the manager in and asked, 'What is this I hear about you? Give an account of your management, because you can no longer be my manager.'

"Then the manager said to himself, 'What should I do, since my master is taking the management away from me? I'm not strong enough to dig; I'm ashamed to beg. I know what I'll do so that when I'm removed from management, people will welcome me into their homes.'

"So he summoned each one of his master's debtors. 'How much do you owe my master?' he asked the first one.

"'A hundred measures of oil,' he said.

"'Take your invoice,' he told him, 'sit down quickly, and write 50.'

"Next he asked another, 'How much do you owe?'

"'A hundred measures of wheat,' he said.

"'Take your invoice,' he told him, 'and write 80.'

"The master praised the unrighteous manager because he had acted astutely. For the sons of this age are more astute than the sons of light in dealing with their own people. And I tell you, make friends for yourselves by means of the unrighteous money so that when it fails, they may welcome you into eternal dwellings. Whoever is faithful in very little is also faithful in much, and whoever is unrighteous in very little is also unrighteous in much. So if you have not been faithful with the unrighteous money, who will trust you with what is genuine? And if you have not been faithful with what belongs to someone else, who will give you what is your own?"

Luke 16:1–12 HCSB

※

*J*esus' parable of the dishonest manager is disturbing because Jesus seems to be encouraging dishonesty. The hero of Jesus' story was a dishonest man. He squandered his employer's property. Then he had his employer's debtors alter their bills to their advantage.

But his employer praised him for his cunning. And Jesus encouraged his disciples to be just as cunning. So what's going on here? Did Jesus encourage stealing and lying?

The parable should still be taken at face value. Jesus was encouraging his disciples to be as shrewd in their work for the kingdom of God as the Pharisees were in working for the kingdom of the world. Go ahead and make money, but use it for God's kingdom. Money is worthless, except as it is used in this world to make preparation for the next.

※※※※※※※※※※※※※※※※※※※※※※※※※※※※※※※※

PAST DUE

In Jerusalem, after the triumphal entry:
[Jesus] began to tell the people this parable: "A man planted a vineyard, leased it to tenant farmers, and went away for a long time. At harvest time he sent a slave to the farmers so that they might give him some fruit from the vineyard. But the farmers beat him and sent him away empty-handed. He sent yet another slave, but they beat that one too, treated him shamefully, and sent him away empty-handed. And he sent yet a third, but they wounded this one too and threw him out.

"Then the owner of the vineyard said, 'What should I do? I will send my beloved son. Perhaps they will respect him.'

"But when the tenant farmers saw him, they discussed it among themselves and said, 'This is the heir. Let's kill him, so the inheritance will be ours!' So they threw him out of the vineyard and killed him.

"Therefore, what will the owner of the vineyard do to them? He will come and destroy those farmers and give the vineyard to others."

But when they heard this they said, "No—never!"

But He looked at them and said, "Then what is the meaning of this Scripture:

"The stone that the builders rejected—this has become the cornerstone? Everyone who falls on that stone will be broken to pieces, and if it falls on anyone, it will grind him to powder!"

Then the scribes and the chief priests looked for a way to get their hands on Him that very hour, because they knew He had told this parable against them, but they feared the people.

Luke 20:9–19 HCSB

※

*J*esus' parables were often obscure to those who heard them. In the case of his parable about the tenant farmers, Israel's religious establishment got his point immediately. And they were furious.

The religious establishment had an accommodation with the Roman government that gave those religious leaders a comfortable lifestyle, but they had turned their backs on God. By means of his parable, Jesus told those leaders that they were about to lose everything because they had rejected God's prophets, such as John the Baptist, and were now rejecting God's Son, Jesus. Within a generation, the religious establishment would encourage a rebellion against their Roman overlords. The Romans attacked with overwhelming force. The Roman army destroyed the city of Jerusalem, burned the temple to the ground, and scattered the Jewish population across the empire.

When we allow ourselves to become distracted by our circumstances, habits, and comfortable lives, we may find that Jesus' words can make us uncomfortable too. We may need to rethink our own lives and choices.

GOD'S SACRIFICE

John was [east of the Jordan River near Bethany] again with two of his disciples. When he saw Jesus passing by, he said, "Look, the Lamb of God!"

When the two disciples heard him say this, they followed Jesus. Turning around, Jesus saw them following and asked, "What do you want?"

They said, "Rabbi" (which means Teacher), "where are you staying?"

"Come," he replied, "and you will see."

So they went and saw where he was staying, and spent that day with him. It was about the tenth hour.

Andrew, Simon Peter's brother, was one of the two who heard what John had said and who had followed Jesus. The first thing Andrew did was to find his brother Simon and tell him, "We have found the Messiah" (that is, the Christ). And he brought him to Jesus.

Jesus looked at him and said, "You are Simon son of John. You will be called Cephas" (which, when translated, is Peter).

John 1:35–42 NIV

What do we want from Jesus? One of Jesus' first two disciples was identified as Andrew. The second disciple, who remained unnamed throughout John's gospel, was most likely John himself.

When Jesus asked Andrew and John what they wanted, there was more to his question than wondering about being followed. The word used for *following* indicates they had become his disciples. Jesus' question, "What do you want?" was his formal invitation for them to become disciples. They accepted his invitation by asking him where he was staying and by addressing him as *Rabbi*, an Aramaic word that meant "my teacher."

Andrew brought his brother Simon to meet Jesus. Jesus gave Simon a new name, Cephas. We see Aramaic words like *rabbi* and *Cephas* in the text because Aramaic was the language they were using. The New Testament was not written in Aramaic, however, but in Greek because Greek was the dominant language in the eastern half of the Roman Empire. The good news of the kingdom was not just for the people living in Palestine. It was for the world. *Cephas* means "rock" in English, as does the more familiar Greek form of the name, Peter.

When Jesus told them "you will see," it was not just to see where he stayed. It was an invitation to a life of wonder, a life as his disciples, where they would see more than they could imagine. Jesus offers us the same vision—a life of abundance and never-ending wonders. He offers us his Father's kingdom.

YOU CAN'T HANDLE THE TRUTH

On the Mount of Olives near Jerusalem, during the Feast of Tabernacles:

Jesus answered [the Pharisees]:

"If God were your Father, you would love me, because I came from God and only from him. He sent me. I did not come on my own. Why can't you understand what I am talking about? Can't you stand to hear what I am saying? Your father is the devil, and you do exactly what he wants. He has always been a murderer and a liar. There is nothing truthful about him. He speaks on his own, and everything he says is a lie. Not only is he a liar himself, but he is also the father of all lies.

"Everything I have told you is true, and you still refuse to have faith in me. Can any of you accuse me of sin? If you cannot, why won't you have faith in me? After all, I am telling you the truth. Anyone who belongs to God will listen to his message. But you refuse to listen, because you don't belong to God."

John 8:42–47 CEV

❁

The religious leaders of Jesus' day were not so much interested in the truth as in maintaining their position and authority. The lies they'd lived with so long were comfortable. The truth was not.

The religious establishment received the harshest criticism from Jesus of anyone with whom he'd ever come in contact. They claimed that the only Father they had was God. Jesus responded harshly by telling them that since they hated his Son, God was not their Father at all.

Jesus announced that their father was Satan rather than God. Jesus was not speaking literally. He meant that their actions and beliefs were those of Satan—they were liars and murderers.

Throughout the history of Israel, the religious establishment had been guilty of rejecting God's prophets and killing them. They were at least being consistent by conspiring to kill Jesus. As to lying, they refused to believe the truth. They chose to accept false ideas about who the Messiah was and what he was supposed to do.

Those who belong to God recognize God. They believe what God believes. By not recognizing Jesus for who he was, Israel's religious leaders demonstrated that they had nothing to do with God at all. Their claim to be faithful followers of God was demonstrably false. They were lying. But we are part of God's kingdom, and we are his children. Since his Spirit lives inside us, we recognize his voice when we hear it, whether we have strayed far away from him or not.

CHOOSE TO BELIEVE

At that time the festival of the Dedication took place in Jerusalem. It was winter, and Jesus was walking in the temple, in the portico of Solomon. So the Jews gathered around him and said to him, "How long will you keep us in suspense? If you are the Messiah, tell us plainly."

Jesus answered, "I have told you, and you do not believe. The works that I do in my Father's name testify to me; but you do not believe, because you do not belong to my sheep. My sheep hear my voice. I know them, and they follow me. I give them eternal life, and they will never perish. No one will snatch them out of my hand. What my Father has given me is greater than all else, and no one can snatch it out of the Father's hand. The Father and I are one."

The Jews took up stones again to stone him. Jesus replied, "I have shown you many good works from the Father. For which of these are you going to stone me?"

The Jews answered, "It is not for a good work that we are going to stone you, but for blasphemy, because you, though only a human being, are making yourself God."

John 10:22–33 NRSV

*T*he winter Festival of Dedication is better known as Hanukkah. It commemorated the rededication of the temple following the successful outcome of the Maccabean revolt against Antiochus Epiphanes, the king of the Seleucid Empire. Nearly two centuries before Jesus, Antiochus had killed many Jews and defiled the temple in Jerusalem by sacrificing a pig to Zeus on its altar.

After his defeat, the Jews cleansed the temple. They had enough oil to light the temple lamps for only a single day, though the cleansing and rededication ceremony took eight days. But they began with what they had, and God kept the lamps burning the full eight days.

Every year after that, the Jewish people celebrated the miracle.

During the celebration of Hanukkah in Jerusalem, religious leaders approached Jesus and demanded that he announce plainly that he was the Messiah, if indeed he was. Jesus' response was that he'd already done so, but they didn't believe him.

Sometimes we'd like to think that "if only people could see a miracle," they would believe. But it simply doesn't work that way for most people. Those who rejected Jesus had seen his miracles. They'd heard him speak with their own ears. And yet they still refused to believe. Belief is a choice. Truth does not ensure acceptance, nor does overwhelming evidence. Juries still acquit the guilty and convict the innocent. It should not surprise us when people fail to believe in Jesus.

DEATH OF A FRIEND

On the Mount of Olives near Jerusalem, during the Feast of Tabernacles:

From Bethany the sisters [of Lazarus, Martha and Mary] sent to [Jesus], saying, "Lord, behold, he whom You love is sick."

When Jesus heard that, He said, "This sickness is not unto death, but for the glory of God, that the Son of God may be glorified through it."

Now Jesus loved Martha and her sister and Lazarus. So, when He heard that he was sick, He stayed two more days in the place where He was. Then after this He said to the disciples, "Let us go to Judea again."

The disciples said to Him, "Rabbi, lately the Jews sought to stone You, and are You going there again?"

Jesus answered, "Are there not twelve hours in the day? If anyone walks in the day, he does not stumble, because he sees the light of this world. But if one walks in the night, he stumbles, because the light is not in him." These things He said, and after that He said to them, "Our friend Lazarus sleeps, but I go that I may wake him up."

Then His disciples said, "Lord, if he sleeps he will get well." However, Jesus spoke of his death, but they thought that He was speaking about taking rest in sleep.

Then Jesus said to them plainly, "Lazarus is dead. And I am glad for your sakes that I was not there, that you may believe. Nevertheless let us go to him."

Then Thomas, who is called the Twin, said to his fellow disciples, "Let us also go, that we may die with Him."

John 11:3–16 NKJV

*I*f Jesus doesn't seem to be doing anything for you now, it doesn't mean that he doesn't care or that he doesn't have a reason for it all. Jesus responded to the news that his friend Lazarus was sick by continuing to do what he was doing. He didn't stop and go visit Lazarus or his family. He let Lazarus suffer and die.

When Jesus said that Lazarus's illness was "not unto death," he didn't mean that he wouldn't die—he meant that his death wouldn't be final. When bad things happen, it is hard to see past the pain that results. From God's perspective, Lazarus's suffering and his family's grief had meaning.

That meaning came only after Lazarus was raised from the dead. The same goes for any suffering we experience. It may never make sense during our lives, but we should trust that God really does know what he is doing, always, just as Jesus knew with Lazarus. After his resurrection, Lazarus's experience made sense. It will be the same way for us.

TRIUMPH

When [Jesus and his disciples] had come near Jerusalem and had reached Bethphage, at the Mount of Olives, Jesus sent two disciples, saying to them, "Go into the village ahead of you, and immediately you will find a donkey tied, and a colt with her; untie them and bring them to me. If anyone says anything to you, just say this, 'The Lord needs them.' And he will send them immediately." This took place to fulfill what had been spoken through the prophet, saying,

"Tell the daughter of Zion,

Look, your king is coming to you, humble, and mounted on a donkey, and on a colt, the foal of a donkey."

The disciples went and did as Jesus had directed them; they brought the donkey and the colt, and put their cloaks on them, and he sat on them. A very large crowd spread their cloaks on the road, and others cut branches from the trees and spread them on the road. The crowds that went ahead of him and that followed were shouting,

"Hosanna to the Son of David!

Blessed is the one who comes in the name of the Lord!

Hosanna in the highest heaven!"

Matthew 21:1–9 NRSV

*J*esus healed the sick, cast out demons, and raised the dead. Massive crowds hung on his every word. He was God in the flesh, the Creator of the universe, and yet he was humble.

Many prophecies in the Old Testament foretold when the Messiah would come and what he would be like. The prophet Zechariah predicted that the Messiah would arrive humbly, upon a donkey. Donkeys were beasts of burden, used for carrying food and supplies. They weren't the sort of animal anyone expected to carry a conquering king. When heading off to war, kings sat on mighty steeds or in chariots behind a team of horses. The president of the United States does not pedal a bicycle across town to address Congress. But that's how Jesus rode into Jerusalem, upon the lowliest of animals used for human transportation.

By arriving in Jerusalem in such a manner, Jesus announced to the crowds that, though he was the Messiah, he was not going to conquer the world in quite the manner they might have expected. Most of the disciples missed that Jesus was God's servant, conquering the world by dying for its sins.

This same Jesus has come into our lives. The changes he will bring our way are not predictable. We must not allow our expectations to stand in the way of recognizing the wonders he has in store for us.

PREPARATIONS

In Jerusalem, just before Jesus' last Passover:

Judas Iscariot, who was one of the twelve, went to the chief priests in order to betray him to them. When they heard it, they were greatly pleased, and promised to give him money. So he began to look for an opportunity to betray him.

On the first day of Unleavened Bread, when the Passover lamb is sacrificed, his disciples said to him, "Where do you want us to go and make the preparations for you to eat the Passover?"

So he sent two of his disciples, saying to them, "Go into the city, and a man carrying a jar of water will meet you; follow him, and wherever he enters, say to the owner of the house, 'The Teacher asks, Where is my guest room where I may eat the Passover with my disciples?' He will show you a large room upstairs, furnished and ready. Make preparations for us there." So the disciples set out and went to the city, and found everything as he had told them; and they prepared the Passover meal.

Mark 14:10–16 NRSV

꽃

*F*or Jesus, the future wasn't undiscovered country. He always knew what was coming. Jesus knew where he wanted to celebrate his final Passover with his disciples, and he told his disciples how to find that place. Jesus knew what the future held, whether it was when and where a man would be carrying a jar of water, or when and where he would be betrayed. Judas looked for an opportunity to betray Jesus. But Jesus already knew the betrayal would come. As Jesus prepared for the Passover, he also prepared to become the Passover Lamb.

After three years with Jesus, the disciples had learned to do whatever Jesus said. They did not argue with him. They did not ask him how he knew there would be such a man carrying a water jar. They simply went and did just as Jesus asked. Meanwhile, Judas, who knew what the other disciples knew about Jesus, did not consider that a man who could predict the course of a man with a water jar could doubtless predict Judas's course as well. Judas acted, in his betrayal of Jesus, as if Jesus were merely a human being, an ordinary man who could be trapped by circumstance.

Eleven of the disciples believed Jesus was the Messiah and the Son of God. One had decided otherwise. They all saw what they believed. And their actions demonstrated their beliefs. How we live our lives shows what we really believe.

A TIME TO SCATTER

In the Upper Room during the Last Supper:

As they were eating, Jesus took bread, blessed and broke it, and gave it to them and said, "Take, eat; this is My body."

Then He took the cup, and when He had given thanks He gave it to them, and they all drank from it. And He said to them, "This is My blood of the new covenant, which is shed for many. Assuredly, I say to you, I will no longer drink of the fruit of the vine until that day when I drink it new in the kingdom of God."

And when they had sung a hymn, they went out to the Mount of Olives.

Then Jesus said to them, "All of you will be made to stumble because of Me this night, for it is written:

'I will strike the Shepherd,
And the sheep will be scattered.'

"But after I have been raised, I will go before you to Galilee."

Peter said to Him, "Even if all are made to stumble, yet I will not be."

Jesus said to him, "Assuredly, I say to you that today, even this night, before the rooster crows twice, you will deny Me three times."

But he spoke more vehemently, "If I have to die with You, I will not deny You!"

And they all said likewise.

Mark 14:22–31 NKJV

※

*J*esus did something new and different with the old familiar patterns of the annual ceremony that celebrated God's victory over Egypt. He took the normal *matzo*—a hard, crackerlike bread made without yeast—and said it was his body. He said the wine was his blood.

At the time, the disciples didn't understand what Jesus meant by the changes he introduced into the familiar ritual. Instead, they thought they were about to overthrow the Roman Empire. As God had overcome Egypt, so he'd overcome Rome. When Jesus told them that he would not drink wine again until the day he drank it in the kingdom of God, they would likely have thought that Jesus meant the next time they celebrated Passover, Jesus would be sitting on a throne in Jerusalem.

Peter was not alone in his willingness to die for Jesus. All the disciples believed the same. They had seen Jesus raise Lazarus from the dead. If they died in the coming war of liberation, then so what? Jesus could raise them just as easily. Why did Jesus think they would be scattered? How could Jesus believe that they would deny him?

Jesus knows who we are and what we need. He knows the problems of tomorrow, and he'll see to it that we make it through.

BETRAYAL

During the Last Supper:

[Jesus said,] "I am not speaking of all of you; I know whom I have chosen. But it is to fulfill the scripture, 'The one who ate my bread has lifted his heel against me.' I tell you this now, before it occurs, so that when it does occur, you may believe that I am he. Very truly, I tell you, whoever receives one whom I send receives me; and whoever receives me receives him who sent me."

After saying this Jesus was troubled in spirit, and declared, "Very truly, I tell you, one of you will betray me."

The disciples looked at one another, uncertain of whom he was speaking. One of his disciples—the one whom Jesus loved—was reclining next to him; Simon Peter therefore motioned to him to ask Jesus of whom he was speaking.

So while reclining next to Jesus, he asked him, "Lord, who is it?"

Jesus answered, "It is the one to whom I give this piece of bread when I have dipped it in the dish." So when he had dipped the piece of bread, he gave it to Judas son of Simon Iscariot. After he received the piece of bread, Satan entered into him. Jesus said to him, "Do quickly what you are going to do." Now no one at the table knew why he said this to him. Some thought that, because Judas had the common purse, Jesus was telling him, "Buy what we need for the festival"; or, that he should give something to the poor. So, after receiving the piece of bread, he immediately went out. And it was night.

John 13:18–30 NRSV

*J*esus always knew who would betray him. He always knew that he was going to die. On the night that it was going to happen, he gave his disciples the details.

The disciples apparently didn't grasp how events were about to unfold. The dipping of the piece of bread and the offering of it to Judas was ordinarily a gesture of honor. What Jesus dipped the bread into is impossible to say. It might have been olive oil, a meat sauce, or even a bit of the wine, since all those were available as part of the Passover meal. Jesus' point in the action was to identify the betrayer for John. But after Judas scurried away, John wrote that none of them knew why he'd left.

John and the disciples weren't unusually dense. It's simply hard for any of us to understand new ideas that contradict what we thought before. After the events, the disciples understood that Judas was not the friend they had imagined, though they would remain shocked by the betrayal. Sometimes we will be shocked by events in our own lives too. But Jesus will help us through them, help us make sense of them, and help us recover.

I AM THAT I AM

In the Sanhedrin's chambers in Jerusalem:

The high priest stood up before them all and questioned Jesus, "Don't You have an answer to what these men are testifying against You?" But He kept silent and did not answer anything. Again the high priest questioned Him, "Are You the Messiah, the Son of the Blessed One?"

"I am," said Jesus, "and all of you will see the Son of Man seated at the right hand of the Power and coming with the clouds of heaven."

Then the high priest tore his robes and said, "Why do we still need witnesses? You have heard the blasphemy! What is your decision?"

And they all condemned Him to be deserving of death. Then some began to spit on Him, to blindfold Him, and to beat Him, saying, "Prophesy!" Even the temple police took Him and slapped Him.

Mark 14:60–65 HCSB

*J*esus sometimes spoke most profoundly when he said nothing. During his trial, people lied about what Jesus said and what he did. Jesus did not respond to any of their false accusations. He kept his mouth shut and was silent.

His lack of response was in keeping with the principle of turning the other cheek and not resisting an evil person. There were prophecies about the Messiah keeping silent in the face of false accusations. Jesus' silence matched his words. Jesus spoke only to acknowledge the truth—he was the Messiah.

The idea of the Messiah as the Son of God was nothing out of the ordinary among the Jews. Nor was the Messiah's close association with God, as God's right hand, a new concept.

The high priest reacted by accusing Jesus of blasphemy because the high priest did not agree that Jesus was the Messiah. He believed Jesus was empowered by Satan. The charge of blasphemy was dependent upon their rejection of Jesus' claim as spurious. There was no objective proof against Jesus, only their subjective wish that it be so. Their confidence in the rightness of their position led them to abuse Jesus and to demand that he "prophesy."

Jesus went back to being silent, refusing to respond to his mistreatment or the additional lies of his enemies.

Jesus knew there was a time to speak, and a time to be silent. He did not mix up those times. We, too, must be prepared to speak when the opportunity arises. But we must also be wise enough to know when it would be better for us to keep our mouths shut.

KEEPING WARM

While all this was going on, Peter was down in the courtyard. One of the Chief Priest's servant girls came in and, seeing Peter warming himself there, looked hard at him and said, "You were with the Nazarene, Jesus."

He denied it: "I don't know what you're talking about." He went out on the porch. A rooster crowed.

The girl spotted him and began telling the people standing around, "He's one of them." He denied it again.

After a little while, the bystanders brought it up again. "You've got to be one of them. You've got 'Galilean' written all over you."

Now Peter got really nervous and swore, "I never laid eyes on this man you're talking about." Just then the rooster crowed a second time. Peter remembered how Jesus had said, "Before a rooster crows twice, you'll deny me three times." He collapsed in tears.

Mark 14:66–72 MSG

Only hindsight is twenty-twenty. Even if you knew what the future held, it wouldn't affect your choices. Peter knew the future, but he remembered Jesus' words and took them to heart only after he had fulfilled them. He did not remember Jesus' words the first time he denied Christ. He did not remember them the second time. He didn't even remember them after the third time! He only remembered the words of Jesus when he heard the rooster crow, after it was too late. Only when Jesus' prophecy was completely fulfilled did Peter recognize that he had somehow done just what Jesus predicted.

Prophecy does not get in the way of human freedom of choice. Peter was not a puppet being pulled along by his strings. He made every bad choice of his own free will, not once, but three times. When it was over, he did not think to himself, *I had no choice in that*, or *God made me do it*. He didn't even think, *The devil made me do it*. He knew, in the depths of his soul, that he had done it himself. He reacted accordingly, with overwhelming guilt and despair. He knew that he alone had brought himself to that place.

That God knows ahead of time what we will do and that in some sense the future has already been determined does not violate our freedom or the responsibility we bear for our actions. We must accept responsibility for our own lives, for good or ill. We have no one else to blame.

THE FIRST DAY

When Jesus rose early on the first day of the week, he appeared first to Mary Magdalene, out of whom he had driven seven demons. She went and told those who had been with him and who were mourning and weeping. When they heard that Jesus was alive and that she had seen him, they did not believe it.

Afterward Jesus appeared in a different form to two of them while they were walking in the country. These returned and reported it to the rest; but they did not believe them either.

Later Jesus appeared to the Eleven as they were eating; he rebuked them for their lack of faith and their stubborn refusal to believe those who had seen him after he had risen.

He said to them, "Go into all the world and preach the good news to all creation. Whoever believes and is baptized will be saved, but whoever does not believe will be condemned. And these signs will accompany those who believe: In my name they will drive out demons; they will speak in new tongues; they will pick up snakes with their hands; and when they drink deadly poison, it will not hurt them at all; they will place their hands on sick people, and they will get well."

Mark 16:9–18 NIV

*S*ome people change the world forever. Jesus is one of those people. So profound is his impact, that the world's history is divided by his birth—the years before Jesus was born and the years after.

There are significant textual problems with the last nine verses of the gospel of Mark, which briefly record some of Jesus' words given after the world-altering event of his resurrection. In fact, the oldest manuscripts lack these final verses of Mark's gospel altogether, while other copies have completely different endings. Just because these verses may not have been part of the original form of the gospel of Mark, however, does not mean they are not true.

Jesus told his followers to proclaim the message of the good news everywhere, and he promised to protect them. Paul survived a snakebite on the island of Malta after his shipwreck. Peter and the other apostles healed the sick and drove out demons. The gospel message began in Jerusalem and within a few generations spread out until it became the dominant faith on earth. Today, more people claim to be Christians than belong to any other religion. Jesus, accepted or not as Messiah, has changed the world and the lives of all humans, everywhere, forever. For those of us who have believed, he has changed us for eternity.

MISSING THE OBVIOUS

Jesus met two of his disciples walking on the road to Emmaus:

[Jesus] said to them, "So thick-headed! So slow-hearted! Why can't you simply believe all that the prophets said? Don't you see that these things had to happen, that the Messiah had to suffer and only then enter into his glory?" Then he started at the beginning, with the Books of Moses, and went on through all the Prophets, pointing out everything in the Scriptures that referred to him.

They came to the edge of the village where they were headed. He acted as if he were going on but they pressed him: "Stay and have supper with us. It's nearly evening; the day is done." So he went in with them. And here is what happened: He sat down at the table with them. Taking the bread, he blessed and broke and gave it to them. At that moment, open-eyed, wide-eyed, they recognized him. And then he disappeared.

Back and forth they talked. "Didn't we feel on fire as he conversed with us on the road, as he opened up the Scriptures for us?"

Luke 24:25–32 MSG

Sometimes the elephant in the room really is impossible to see. When Jesus rose from the dead, his disciples were as slow to recognize him as they had been slow to understand his predictions regarding his death in the first place.

When we see the sun sink beneath the horizon at sunset, we know that in fact we are witnessing the earth rotating on its axis rather than watching the motion of the sun. But before Copernicus, most people took what they saw and interpreted it as the sun's moving instead of the earth's moving. The people of Jesus' day could read the words of the Bible as easily as we can today. But they interpreted them in a different way. That affected how they saw the events of Jesus' life before his resurrection. After his resurrection, Jesus explained the familiar words of Scripture in brand-new ways for them, helping them to understand that what had happened to Jesus was not a defeat but was in fact what the Bible had foretold all along for the Messiah. Only after Jesus had retrained them could they see the world as it actually was. At that moment, they suddenly recognized Jesus was there, alive, just as he'd predicted all along.

We see what we believe, and it took Jesus' words to help the early Christians believe the truth so that they could see indeed. It's like finding the hidden object in a painting. It sometimes is hard for us to see the truth. We may struggle to make sense of it. But after we finally understand, we'll wonder how we could ever have missed something so obvious.

BLINDNESS

Saul was uttering threats with every breath and was eager to kill the Lord's followers. So he went to the high priest. He requested letters addressed to the synagogues in Damascus, asking for their cooperation in the arrest of any followers of the Way he found there. He wanted to bring them—both men and women—back to Jerusalem in chains.

As he was approaching Damascus on this mission, a light from heaven suddenly shone down around him. He fell to the ground and heard a voice saying to him, "Saul! Saul! Why are you persecuting me?"

"Who are you, lord?" Saul asked.

And the voice replied, "I am Jesus, the one you are persecuting! Now get up and go into the city, and you will be told what you must do."

The men with Saul stood speechless, for they heard the sound of someone's voice but saw no one! Saul picked himself up off the ground, but when he opened his eyes he was blind. So his companions led him by the hand to Damascus. He remained there blind for three days and did not eat or drink.

Acts 9:1–9 NLT

※

*E*vil triumphs when good men stand by and do nothing. Sometimes it appears to triumph even when *bad* men stand by. Saul was his Hebrew name; Paul was his Greek name. They were used interchangeably, depending on the language he was using. Saul had stood by and watched the execution of Stephen with approval. He then did everything he could to exterminate Christianity.

When Jesus confronted Paul on his way to Damascus, he did not ask Paul why he was persecuting Christians. Instead, Jesus asked Paul why he was persecuting him. The church is called the body of Christ. It is also called the bride of Christ. Jesus loves us as much as he loves his own body because we are one with him.

When Paul asked his own question, he demonstrated that he already knew its answer. He called Jesus "Lord." Paul wasn't being polite. When a Jew said "Lord," it could mean one thing only—God.

Paul knew he was talking to God. And soon he learned that God also went by the name Jesus. Paul immediately repented of his entire life. Everything before that bright shining moment in Jesus' presence became meaningless to him. Thanks to the Holy Spirit, every Christian's life has been just as radically transformed by the presence of Jesus as Paul's was in that instant. We have become new creatures, the old ways have passed, and everything has become new. It's as if we went to bed sick, only to awaken completely healed, or as if we had no money, only to stumble upon a forgotten treasure.

LOVE OVERCOMES FEAR

In Damascus there was a disciple named Ananias. And the Lord said to him in a vision, "Ananias!"

"Here I am, Lord!" he said.

"Get up and go to the street called Straight," the Lord said to him, "to the house of Judas, and ask for a man from Tarsus named Saul, since he is praying there. In a vision he has seen a man named Ananias coming in and placing his hands on him so he may regain his sight."

"Lord," Ananias answered, "I have heard from many people about this man, how much harm he has done to Your saints in Jerusalem. And he has authority here from the chief priests to arrest all who call on Your name."

But the Lord said to him, "Go! For this man is My chosen instrument to carry My name before Gentiles, kings, and the sons of Israel. I will certainly show him how much he must suffer for My name!"

So Ananias left and entered the house. Then he placed his hands on him and said, "Brother Saul, the Lord Jesus, who appeared to you on the road you were traveling, has sent me so you may regain your sight and be filled with the Holy Spirit."

Acts 9:10–17 HCSB

✖

*J*esus brings down all the walls that separate people from one another, even the walls that seem necessary. God told Ananias to do something that seemed to him like a bad idea.

Ananias was a disciple living in Damascus. (He is not to be confused with the man married to Sephira, who dropped dead because he had lied to the Holy Spirit about some property he'd sold.) When Jesus told Ananias to cure Paul's blindness, Ananias couldn't avoid expressing his fear about Paul. Paul was well known as a persecutor. But Jesus explained how things had changed in Paul's life. Ananias was the first Christian to learn of Paul's conversion, and he learned what Paul's ministry from that moment on was going to be, even before Paul learned it.

In a couple of sentences, Jesus summarized the remainder of the book of Acts and the future course of Paul's life. Paul started by being set apart by the Holy Spirit to take the gospel to the Gentiles. Then Paul was arrested and suffered and spent time proclaiming the gospel to kings such as Agrippa.

From the beginning, God knew what Paul was becoming and who he would be. God had a plan for Paul. God has a wonderful plan for all of us, and our lives will help God achieve his ultimate purposes. We are all part of God's plans.

IT'S KOSHER NOW

The Roman centurion Cornelius sent three messengers—one of Cornelius's soldiers and two of his servants—to Peter in Joppa:

As the three travelers were approaching the town, Peter went out on the balcony to pray. It was about noon. Peter got hungry and started thinking about lunch. While lunch was being prepared, he fell into a trance. He saw the skies open up. Something that looked like a huge blanket lowered by ropes at its four corners settled on the ground. Every kind of animal and reptile and bird you could think of was on it. Then a voice came: "Go to it, Peter—kill and eat."

Peter said, "Oh, no, Lord. I've never so much as tasted food that was not kosher."

The voice came a second time: "If God says it's okay, it's okay."

This happened three times, and then the blanket was pulled back up into the skies.

As Peter, puzzled, sat there trying to figure out what it all meant, the men sent by Cornelius showed up at Simon's front door. They called in, asking if there was a Simon, also called Peter, staying there. Peter, lost in thought, didn't hear them, so the Spirit whispered to him, "Three men are knocking at the door looking for you. Get down there and go with them. Don't ask any questions. I sent them to get you."

Peter went down and said to the men, "I think I'm the man you're looking for. What's up?"

They said, "Captain Cornelius, a God-fearing man well-known for his fair play—ask any Jew in this part of the country—was commanded by a holy angel to get you and bring you to his house so he could hear what you had to say." Peter invited them in and made them feel at home.

Acts 10:9–23 MSG

✳

*J*esus sometimes spoke in parables, because a good story, like a picture, is worth a thousand words.

Jesus appeared to Peter while he was waiting for his lunch. Unsurprisingly, perhaps, Peter had a dream about food. But it was non-Kosher food. Jesus told him to eat it anyhow, not once but three times.

Jesus was not trying to give Peter new regulations about what was kosher. Like most Jewish people, Peter believed that Gentiles were excluded from the love of God, just as pigs were excluded from his plate. When Jesus told his disciples to take the gospel to the whole world, they thought he meant taking it to the Jewish people scattered throughout the Roman Empire.

Peter's vision helped him and the rest of the church realize that the gospel message was for all humanity, not just for the Jews. Peter and the other apostles listened to God, who opened the way so that all of us could believe.

PERSECUTOR

After his arrest in Jerusalem, Paul addressed the angry mob that wanted to kill him:

[Paul said,] "Brothers and fathers, listen now to my defense."

When [the angry crowd in Jerusalem] heard him speak to them in Aramaic, they became very quiet.

Then Paul said: "I am a Jew, born in Tarsus of Cilicia, but brought up in this city. Under Gamaliel I was thoroughly trained in the law of our fathers and was just as zealous for God as any of you are today. I persecuted the followers of this Way to their death, arresting both men and women and throwing them into prison, as also the high priest and all the Council can testify. I even obtained letters from them to their brothers in Damascus, and went there to bring these people as prisoners to Jerusalem to be punished.

"About noon as I came near Damascus, suddenly a bright light from heaven flashed around me. I fell to the ground and heard a voice say to me, 'Saul! Saul! Why do you persecute me?'

"'Who are you, Lord?' I asked.

"'I am Jesus of Nazareth, whom you are persecuting,' he replied. My companions saw the light, but they did not understand the voice of him who was speaking to me."

Acts 22:1–9 NIV

When you control a conversation, what's the first thing you're most likely to talk about? Life's latest challenges? Paul's first conversation with Jesus meant more to him than anything else in his life. Whenever he had the chance, he told people all about it.

Arrested in Jerusalem, Paul addressed the angry mob in their local language, Aramaic. Aramaic was the language that the people in Israel had been speaking ever since their return from their Babylonian exile. When Jesus first met Paul, he was a Pharisee. He had trained under Gamaliel, the best-known rabbi of the day. Gamaliel had once told the other members of the Sanhedrin to be slow about condemning the Christians since several false messiahs had arisen in the past. He believed the new Christian movement was likely to die out, too, if it were merely human in its origin. But if not, then to resist it would be to resist God.

Paul had resisted God his whole life until he met him on the road to Damascus.

After that, Paul chose to talk only about Jesus, even though he could have complained about his confinement, griped about the prison food, or begged for his freedom. We can choose to focus on our own concerns, or, like Paul, we can choose to focus on Jesus and his concerns.

TAKE A LETTER

I am John, a follower together with all of you. We suffer because Jesus is our king, but he gives us the strength to endure. I was sent to Patmos Island, because I had preached God's message and had told about Jesus. On the Lord's day the Spirit took control of me, and behind me I heard a loud voice that sounded like a trumpet. The voice said, "Write in a book what you see. Then send it to the seven churches in Ephesus, Smyrna, Pergamum, Thyatira, Sardis, Philadelphia, and Laodicea."

When I turned to see who was speaking to me, I saw seven gold lampstands. There with the lampstands was someone who seemed to be the Son of Man. He was wearing a robe that reached down to his feet, and a gold cloth was wrapped around his chest. His head and his hair were white as wool or snow, and his eyes looked like flames of fire. His feet were glowing like bronze being heated in a furnace, and his voice sounded like the roar of a waterfall.

Revelation 1:9–15 CEV

When everything goes wrong in your life, wouldn't it be nice if Jesus came and told you why? The apostle John had that rare and wonderful experience. Jesus had been John's closest and best friend, but more than fifty years had passed since he'd last seen him. As an old man, John was exiled for his faith to the island of Patmos, not far from what is today the nation of Turkey. Of all the apostles, he alone survived. The rest had been murdered. Christians everywhere were dying. The Romans had destroyed Jerusalem and burned the temple to the ground. Things did not appear to be going well, not for him or for any of God's people.

Then, unexpectedly, Jesus met him in a vision, not as John remembered him, but in all his glory as God. Jesus was finally back, and he told John to write down everything that he was about to say—and to share it with seven churches.

The book of Revelation, the result of John's wonderful visions from Jesus, has ever after been a source of comfort to Christians suffering severe persecution for their faith. Jesus' revelation was a comfort not only to John but to all believers everywhere. Every day, Christians somewhere suffer for what they believe. We may or may not be among them, but we can pray for those who are.

TRUE WEALTH

Jesus' letter to the church in Smyrna:

This is what you must write to the angel of the church in Smyrna:

I am the first and the last. I died, but now I am alive! Listen to what I say.

I know how much you suffer and how poor you are, but you are rich. I also know the cruel things being said about you by people who claim to be God's people. But they are really not. They are a group that belongs to Satan. Don't worry about what you will suffer. The devil will throw some of you into jail, and you will be tested and made to suffer for ten days. But if you are faithful until you die, I will reward you with a glorious life.

If you have ears, listen to what the Spirit says to the churches. Whoever wins the victory will not be hurt by the second death.

Revelation 2:8–11 CEV

✻

God's perspective is hard to come by and hard to keep in our heads. Smyrna is on the west coast of what is today the nation of Turkey. At the end of a major east-west road, it had a good harbor, along with a major temple dedicated to the worship of Rome and its emperor. Unsurprisingly, the city was loyal to the Roman Empire. The Christian community in Smyrna was in conflict with the Jewish people there, or at least with its leaders. The Jewish religious leaders regularly accused the Christians of crimes, and they repeatedly brought all their legal disagreements before the city's government.

In the letter that Jesus dictated to John, Jesus told the suffering Christians that the religious leaders who were persecuting them, though they claimed to belong to God, actually didn't. Instead, the religious establishment aligned against them in Smyrna belonged to Satan.

Jesus comforted his people in Smyrna with the fact that though they would suffer, it would be only temporarily. The "ten days" meant that they would suffer for a short time, just as Daniel and his three companions suffered. They were tested for ten days by having to eat nothing but vegetables and having to drink nothing but water. But when the time of testing ended, they not only survived but they prospered. Likewise, God struck Egypt with ten plagues, but as a result, Israel gained its freedom.

God is as concerned with our moments of pain and sorrow as we are. When we hurt, he hurts. But bad times are not permanent. Our comfort can come in gaining God's perspective on our lives. Eternity with Jesus will make all our suffering, no matter how severe, seem like nothing in the end. It will be a fading memory, like a bad dream that evaporates in the bright sunshine of a new morning.

SATAN'S HOME

Jesus dictated a letter to the church in Pergamum:

"To the angel of the church in Pergamum write: These are the words of him who has the sharp two-edged sword:

"I know where you are living, where Satan's throne is. Yet you are holding fast to my name, and you did not deny your faith in me even in the days of Antipas my witness, my faithful one, who was killed among you, where Satan lives. But I have a few things against you: you have some there who hold to the teaching of Balaam, who taught Balak to put a stumbling block before the people of Israel, so that they would eat food sacrificed to idols and practice fornication. So you also have some who hold to the teaching of the Nicolaitans. Repent then. If not, I will come to you soon and make war against them with the sword of my mouth. Let anyone who has an ear listen to what the Spirit is saying to the churches. To everyone who conquers I will give some of the hidden manna, and I will give a white stone, and on the white stone is written a new name that no one knows except the one who receives it."

Revelation 2:12–17 NRSV

❈

*G*od's Word is a sword that cuts both ways. When Jesus had John write to the Christians in Pergamum, it seemed as if Satan had taken up residence there because of the persecution and the fact that the Roman governor regularly held court there. Pergamum was also the oldest and most prominent center for emperor worship in the area. Worst of all, sin had crept into the church.

The Nicolaitans are mentioned nowhere else in the Bible. They may have been Gnostics who taught that the material and spiritual realms were entirely separate. They believed they could indulge their flesh with no spiritual repercussions.

Hidden manna referred to the manna in the ark of the covenant. According to legend, after the Babylonians destroyed the ark, the prophet Jeremiah hid the manna in a cave on Mount Nebo, where it was to remain until the time of the Messiah, when God would once again feed his people with it.

The white stone might be an invitation to attend the messianic banquet. The new name on it might then be the name of Christ, the name of God, or most likely, the name of the invited person, enabling him to take part in the messianic banquet. God can bring judgment, but he can also bring healing. When God punishes us, he does it for our long-term benefit. We will be better off because of the hand of God in our lives.

BELIEF AND DISBELIEF

We doubt God, we doubt ourselves, and we doubt our friends and family. But faith dwells in the shadow of doubt. The other side of disbelief is belief. Belief grows out of disbelief. Skepticism gives way to faith. Jesus told the father of a demon-possessed boy that "everything is possible for him who believes." Then the father told Jesus, "I do believe; help me overcome my unbelief!" (Mark 9:23–24 NIV). Belief comes from seeing results. It grows from the soil of despair watered by the repeated rain of mercy. It comes from recognizing the character and reliability of the one in whom we learn to believe. That's why love always trusts.

※

All things are possible to him who believes.
Mark 9:23 NKJV

✳✳✳✳✳✳✳✳✳✳✳✳✳✳✳✳✳✳✳✳✳✳✳✳✳✳✳✳✳✳✳✳✳

AMAZING FAITH

When Jesus had entered Capernaum, a centurion came to Him, pleading with Him, saying, "Lord, my servant is lying at home paralyzed, dreadfully tormented."

And Jesus said to him, "I will come and heal him."

The centurion answered and said, "Lord, I am not worthy that You should come under my roof. But only speak a word, and my servant will be healed. For I also am a man under authority, having soldiers under me. And I say to this one, 'Go,' and he goes; and to another, 'Come,' and he comes; and to my servant, 'Do this,' and he does it."

When Jesus heard it, He marveled, and said to those who followed, "Assuredly, I say to you, I have not found such great faith, not even in Israel! And I say to you that many will come from east and west, and sit down with Abraham, Isaac, and Jacob in the kingdom of heaven. But the sons of the kingdom will be cast out into outer darkness. There will be weeping and gnashing of teeth." Then Jesus said to the centurion, "Go your way; and as you have believed, so let it be done for you." And his servant was healed that same hour.

Matthew 8:5–13 NKJV

✳

*W*e trust what we can hold, what we can see, what we can taste. Food on our plate today is worth more to us than the promise of food on tomorrow's plate. That's why idolatry is so common. People like to see whom they are praying to. But one day, a person raised in idolatry and only lately come to God approached Jesus about his sick servant.

The centurion's faith, according to Jesus, was greater than the faith of anyone else he had ever found, because he believed without seeing. He believed, even though his idolatrous culture was based on sight. The Roman centurion was able to step beyond the confines of his upbringing and the norms of his society. He marched beyond his cultural horizon.

The Jewish people had the law and the prophets. They had long experience with God's power, like a rich man with a lot of money in the bank. The centurion, like a pauper begging in the street, had nothing. The context of the centurion's belief—the sort of man he was and where he'd come from—made his faith striking. How big our faith is depends on who we are and what we experience. The longer we live with God, the more we will see him at work in our lives and the more faith we will have. The more we get to know him, the more we learn to trust him.

THE GHOST

Immediately after [feeding the five thousand], Jesus insisted that his disciples get back into the boat and cross to the other side of the lake, while he sent the people home. After sending them home, he went up into the hills by himself to pray. Night fell while he was there alone.

Meanwhile, the disciples were in trouble far away from land, for a strong wind had risen, and they were fighting heavy waves. About three o'clock in the morning Jesus came toward them, walking on the water. When the disciples saw him walking on the water, they were terrified. In their fear, they cried out, "It's a ghost!"

But Jesus spoke to them at once. "Don't be afraid," he said. "Take courage. I am here!"

Then Peter called to him, "Lord, if it's really you, tell me to come to you, walking on the water."

"Yes, come," Jesus said.

So Peter went over the side of the boat and walked on the water toward Jesus. But when he saw the strong wind and the waves, he was terrified and began to sink. "Save me, Lord!" he shouted.

Jesus immediately reached out and grabbed him. "You have so little faith," Jesus said. "Why did you doubt me?"

When they climbed back into the boat, the wind stopped. Then the disciples worshiped him. "You really are the Son of God!" they exclaimed.

Matthew 14:22–33 NLT

*J*esus won't necessarily try to fix all the wrong notions that are in our heads. He picks his battles. After a long day of preaching, after feeding the five thousand, Jesus sent his disciples across the Sea of Galilee for some rest and relaxation while he went off to pray for a while. The wind was against them, and they made slow progress in their trip to the far side of the lake. Late at night, tired and exhausted, they thought they saw a ghost.

Thanks to the influence of Greek culture, by Jesus' time belief in ghosts was widespread among the Jewish people. But Jesus did not launch into a theological or philosophical treatise against the notion of ghosts. He merely reassured them that he wasn't one. Jesus' concern at that moment was not their false belief in ghosts, which was merely a symptom of something far more damaging—their fear that they were all alone against the world.

We may believe many silly things today. But just as he did with his disciples, Jesus doesn't berate us for those silly beliefs. Instead, he simply tells us to take courage and not be afraid, because he is there with us.

TERRIFIED

Near the Sea of Galilee:

Six days [after Jesus promised his disciples that some of them would see Jesus coming into his kingdom before they died,] Jesus took Peter and the two brothers, James and John, and led them up a high mountain to be alone. As the men watched, Jesus' appearance was transformed so that his face shone like the sun, and his clothes became as white as light. Suddenly, Moses and Elijah appeared and began talking with Jesus.

Peter exclaimed, "Lord, it's wonderful for us to be here! If you want, I'll make three shelters as memorials—one for you, one for Moses, and one for Elijah."

But even as he spoke, a bright cloud overshadowed them, and a voice from the cloud said, "This is my dearly loved Son, who brings me great joy. Listen to him." The disciples were terrified and fell face down on the ground.

Then Jesus came over and touched them. "Get up," he said. "Don't be afraid." And when they looked up, Moses and Elijah were gone, and they saw only Jesus.

Matthew 17:1–8 NLT

*J*esus can be frightening. When God or his angels appeared before people in the Bible, usually the first thing they had to say was, "Don't be afraid." When Jesus became brighter than normal, when the glowing cloud engulfed the disciples, and when God spoke from that cloud, the disciples experienced fear. Simply hearing God's voice was more than they could handle. They didn't experience reverential awe. They were terrified.

Terror is the sort of feeling a human being gets in the face of death. When a robber sticks a gun in someone's face and demands his money, the victim is terrified. When an aircraft crash-lands in a river, the passengers are terrified.

Why is God so scary for human beings? It comes from the deep, gut-level realization of just who and what God is. Standing before God is like facing a life-threatening illness, a tornado, or an earthquake. A person realizes instinctively his fragility and mortality. Human beings before God stand on the brink.

As fearful, as terrifying, as God is, believers are told, "Fear not." The Bible explains that being afraid of God is the beginning of wisdom. Afterward, Jesus enlightened his disciples. No matter what we face in life, no matter what comes, we can "fear not." Fear is the beginning, not the end, of our relationship with God. Fear is vanquished by knowledge, by the profound realization that God loves us. God's love casts out our fear. As our relationship with God matures, we'll come to understand just how much we mean to him—and how much he means to us.

HOW LITTLE IS LITTLE?

Near the Sea of Galilee after his transfiguration:

When [Jesus and his disciples] reached the crowd, a man approached and knelt down before Him. "Lord," he said, "have mercy on my son, because he has seizures and suffers severely. He often falls into the fire and often into the water. I brought him to Your disciples, but they couldn't heal him."

Jesus replied, "You unbelieving and rebellious generation! How long will I be with you? How long must I put up with you? Bring him here to Me." Then Jesus rebuked the demon, and it came out of him, and from that moment the boy was healed.

Then the disciples approached Jesus privately and said, "Why couldn't we drive it out?"

"Because of your little faith," He told them. "For I assure you: If you have faith the size of a mustard seed, you will tell this mountain, 'Move from here to there,' and it will move. Nothing will be impossible for you. However, this kind does not come out except by prayer and fasting."

Matthew 17:14–21 HCSB

❧

*T*here's a lot less to faith than we imagine. A mustard seed is a rather tiny thing, barely an eighth of an inch around. But a mustard plant grows to become anywhere from two to nearly five feet tall; it is huge compared to crops like wheat or barley. Jesus told his disciples that if they had faith as small as a mustard seed, they could even tell a mountain to relocate itself.

Before he said that, however, he had berated his disciples because they had "little faith." Jesus said you don't need much, but it apparently was possible to have less than enough. How tiny must the disciple's faith have been, then?

Faith is simple trust. You trust your living room couch because it's always worked up until now. It doesn't take much to trust your couch. You don't agonize over it; you just sit.

Beginning with Abraham, God had taken care of his people for thousands of years. Jesus' disciples had witnessed him perform some rather amazing things. And yet their trust just wasn't there. They didn't approach the removal of the demon from the child in the same way they would approach sitting down in a chair. They entertained the thought that it might not work. That's how tiny their faith was. It was so tiny that it wasn't there at all.

By "little" faith, Jesus meant any faith at all, or at least an admittance that we don't really believe. Confession works, too, and is itself a kind of faith. Faith cannot be manufactured. We develop faith as we pay attention to what God does for us. We learn to trust him by our repeated exposure to God at work in our lives every day.

LEAFY DEATH

After the triumphal entry, Jesus and his disciples spent the night in Bethany:

Early the next morning Jesus was returning to the city [of Jerusalem]. He was hungry. Seeing a lone fig tree alongside the road, he approached it anticipating a breakfast of figs. When he got to the tree, there was nothing but fig leaves. He said, "No more figs from this tree—ever!" The fig tree withered on the spot, a dry stick. The disciples saw it happen. They rubbed their eyes, saying, "Did we really see this? A leafy tree one minute, a dry stick the next?"

But Jesus was matter-of-fact: "Yes—and if you embrace this kingdom life and don't doubt God, you'll not only do minor feats like I did to the fig tree, but also triumph over huge obstacles. This mountain, for instance, you'll tell, 'Go jump in the lake,' and it will jump. Absolutely everything, ranging from small to large, as you make it a part of your believing prayer, gets included as you lay hold of God."

Matthew 21:18–22 MSG

※

*J*esus was hungry, and the fig tree failed to give him what a fig tree was supposed to give him. Fig trees, by definition, should produce figs. It was the right time of year for figs, so there was no reason for Jesus not to expect to find them on that tree.

That this particular tree hadn't produced figs meant that the tree had failed to fulfill its purpose. So Jesus told the fig tree what to do next. It obeyed him, since Jesus was its Creator. Jesus had no doubt about what would happen to the fig tree. And he used what happened to the fig tree as an opportunity to teach his disciples a lesson about faith. Faith is the expectation and certitude that events will turn out a certain way. Faith is taking something for granted. In the case of one of God's promises, faith is simply believing that he will do what he said—he loves us, he has the power to do it, and so he will do it.

We can't fake faith. We can't pretend we have it. Either we have it or we don't. Little faith is still faith, still the expectation that what God has promised will happen. God will never disappoint us. He won't fail us. A neighbor or friend might forget a promise. The water might not be hot when we turn the knob. But God will always do just what he promised us. We can count on God, always.

NO REST FOR THE WEARY

In the country of the Gerasenes, by the shore of the Sea of Galilee:

As [Jesus] was getting into the boat, the man who had been demon-possessed kept begging [Jesus] to be with Him. But [Jesus] would not let him; instead, He told him, "Go back home to your own people, and report to them how much the Lord has done for you and how He has had mercy on you." So he went out and began to proclaim in the Decapolis how much Jesus had done for him, and they were all amazed.

When Jesus had crossed over again by boat to the other side, a large crowd gathered around Him while He was by the sea. One of the synagogue leaders, named Jairus, came, and when he saw Jesus, he fell at His feet and kept begging Him, "My little daughter is at death's door. Come and lay Your hands on her so she can get well and live."

So Jesus went with him, and a large crowd was following and pressing against Him.

Mark 5:18–24 HCSB

Not everyone gets to sit on the front row. Jesus had many followers besides the twelve apostles. Both men and women followed him all over the countryside. Crowds gathered everywhere he went. There were the seventy that Jesus sent out to proclaim the good news of the kingdom. After his resurrection, 120 gathered at the time of pentecost. More than one person could take the place of Judas; many people had been with Jesus from the time of John's baptism until his resurrection.

But when Jesus healed a man filled with demons who called themselves Legion, Jesus refused to let him come with him, no matter how hard he pleaded. Why, was Jesus' boat overloaded? Not at all. Jesus had a job only that man could do. Jesus told him to return home and tell the people he knew what Jesus had done for him. Like the seventy, Jesus was sending this man off to proclaim the news of the kingdom.

Jesus has many jobs for his people. Some will go to foreign lands as missionaries. Some will become pastors in small churches. Some will be husbands, some will be wives, some will work in factories, and some will be firefighters, doctors, nurses, clerks, bankers, or soldiers. God has a role for you that only you can fulfill. And when people hear what Jesus has done for you, they will be amazed.

DESPERATE WOMAN

Near the Sea of Galilee as Jesus was on his way to heal the daughter of Jairus:

A woman who had suffered a condition of hemorrhaging for twelve years—a long succession of physicians had treated her, and treated her badly, taking all her money and leaving her worse off than before—had heard about Jesus. She slipped in from behind and touched his robe. She was thinking to herself, "If I can put a finger on his robe, I can get well." The moment she did it, the flow of blood dried up. She could feel the change and knew her plague was over and done with.

At the same moment, Jesus felt energy discharging from him. He turned around to the crowd and asked, "Who touched my robe?"

His disciples said, "What are you talking about? With this crowd pushing and jostling you, you're asking, 'Who touched me?' Dozens have touched you!"

But he went on asking, looking around to see who had done it. The woman, knowing what had happened, knowing she was the one, stepped up in fear and trembling, knelt before him, and gave him the whole story.

Jesus said to her, "Daughter, you took a risk of faith, and now you're healed and whole. Live well, live blessed! Be healed of your plague."

Mark 5:25–34 MSG

❁

*W*e don't need to make an appointment in order to see Jesus. Jesus will let us come whenever we want. All that matters is that we come.

When the hemorrhaging woman heard about Jesus, she decided that he would be able to help her. We don't know what the basis was for her belief that touching the fabric of his robe would fix her problem. We know of no similar healings. There are no stories in the Old Testament about such matters. But the hemorrhaging woman knew Jesus had the power to heal.

According to ceremonial law, if he touched her or anything that belonged to her, he would be ceremonially unclean until sunset. And he might not want to become defiled like that. But if she merely touched the hem of his garment, then he could be spared such ceremonial defilement.

In fact, she believed that in the press of the crowd, he would never even have to know anything had happened. But when Jesus stopped and made a search for who had touched him, she feared the worst, even though she had been healed. But Jesus didn't want to humiliate her publicly. Instead, he wanted to let everyone know publicly about her faith.

Jesus cherishes human faith. Trusting Jesus proves that we know who he is and that he loves us. We know he will always do what is in our best interests.

IT'S NEVER TOO LATE

Near the Sea of Galilee:

While Jesus was still speaking, some men came from the house of Jairus, the synagogue ruler. "Your daughter is dead," they said. "Why bother the teacher any more?"

Ignoring what they said, Jesus told the synagogue ruler, "Don't be afraid; just believe."

He did not let anyone follow him except Peter, James and John the brother of James. When they came to the home of the synagogue ruler, Jesus saw a commotion, with people crying and wailing loudly. He went in and said to them, "Why all this commotion and wailing? The child is not dead but asleep." But they laughed at him.

After he put them all out, he took the child's father and mother and the disciples who were with him, and went in where the child was. He took her by the hand and said to her, *"Talitha koum!"* (which means, "Little girl, I say to you, get up!"). Immediately the girl stood up and walked around (she was twelve years old). At this they were completely astonished. He gave strict orders not to let anyone know about this, and told them to give her something to eat.

Mark 5:35–43 NIV

*J*esus created the universe. He breathed life into lifeless dirt. Restoring life to a little girl was not so hard. The ruler or president of a synagogue was a layperson who had the responsibility for conducting worship and instruction.

Not all the religious leaders in Israel opposed Jesus. But when his daughter died, Jairus and those around him thought it was too late for Jesus to help them. Jesus, however, told Jairus not to worry.

Jesus allowed only Jairus and his wife, along with three of his closest disciples, to witness the raising of the little girl back to life. Her name is never given. When Jesus brought her back to life, he didn't use her name to call her back to the land of the living. He simply called her "little girl." That was enough. Jesus spoke in Aramaic; in fact, all the conversations and words spoken by Jesus and the disciples were in Aramaic. The New Testament was written in Greek for the sake of the Jews and Gentiles who did not live in Israel.

Jesus told the family not to publicize what he had done. Jesus didn't help people for the publicity. He helped because he loved them. Jesus didn't do his good works for the praise of people any more than we should be doing our good works for that reason. If Jesus wasn't about being noticed for his miracles, then we shouldn't be about getting noticed for our good deeds either.

SHAKING OFF THE DUST

Somewhere near Nazareth:

Jesus taught in all the neighboring villages. Then he called together his twelve apostles and sent them out two by two with power over evil spirits. He told them, "You may take along a walking stick. But don't carry food or a traveling bag or any money. It's all right to wear sandals, but don't take along a change of clothes. When you are welcomed into a home, stay there until you leave that town. If any place won't welcome you or listen to your message, leave and shake the dust from your feet as a warning to them."

The apostles left and started telling everyone to turn to God. They forced out many demons and healed a lot of sick people by putting olive oil on them.

Jesus became so well-known that Herod the ruler heard about him. Some people thought he was John the Baptist, who had come back to life with the power to work miracles. Others thought he was Elijah or some other prophet who had lived long ago. But when Herod heard about Jesus, he said, "This must be John! I had his head cut off, and now he has come back to life."

Mark 6:6–16 CEV

❧

*W*e can have anything we want when what we want is God's will. Jesus spent most of his time preaching and teaching in the region around the Sea of Galilee in northern Israel. He sent his apostles out to increase the impact of his teaching. An apostle—or ambassador—does not speak for himself. The ambassador of a nation, for instance, is a stand-in for the government who sent him. He has the same authority as the government. Thus, Jesus' twelve apostles had the same power over disease and evil spirits that Jesus himself did. When they spoke, they were speaking "in Jesus' name," not by invoking the phrase as if it were an incantation, but simply as an ambassador does by nature of being an ambassador. When Jesus' ambassadors shook the dust from their feet, it was not a judgment, but rather a warning of possible judgment to come if no repentance was forthcoming.

Just as an ambassador is not about his will, so we are not about our will, but the will of Jesus, who has called us by his name. When we act as his ambassadors, we have the same authority, the same power, as Jesus himself because we are concerned with his will rather than our own and can say, "Not my will, but your will be done."

MIRACLES NEVER CEASE

Jesus fed five thousand near the Sea of Galilee:

As soon as the meal was finished, Jesus insisted that the disciples get in the boat and go on ahead across to Bethsaida while he dismissed the congregation. After sending them off, he climbed a mountain to pray.

Late at night, the boat was far out at sea; Jesus was still by himself on land. He could see his men struggling with the oars, the wind having come up against them. At about four o'clock in the morning, Jesus came toward them, walking on the sea. He intended to go right by them. But when they saw him walking on the sea, they thought it was a ghost and screamed, scared out of their wits.

Jesus was quick to comfort them: "Courage! It's me. Don't be afraid." As soon as he climbed into the boat, the wind died down. They were stunned, shaking their heads, wondering what was going on. They didn't understand what he had done at the supper. None of this had yet penetrated their hearts.

They beached the boat at Gennesaret and tied up at the landing. As soon as they got out of the boat, word got around fast. People ran this way and that, bringing their sick on stretchers to where they heard he was. Wherever he went, village or town or country crossroads, they brought their sick to the marketplace and begged him to let them touch the edge of his coat—that's all. And whoever touched him became well.

Mark 6:45–56 MSG

✽

*J*esus doesn't want us to be afraid. When the disciples were rowing against the wind, while they were stuck trying to cross the lake that Jesus had told them to cross, they got scared by the unexpected appearance of Jesus. Rather than assuming that Jesus would be with them in their hard struggle, they were more willing to believe in ghosts. Mark commented that the implications of the feeding of the five thousand hadn't yet penetrated the disciples' hearts. What was the implication of those miraculous loaves and fishes? Just as God had fed the Israelites in the wilderness with bread from heaven, so had Jesus fed the multitude in Galilee. That meant that Jesus was God come down to earth in human form.

Jesus' disciples should have understood that they could never be in danger. They were certain to arrive on the other side of the lake because Jesus told them to go. But like the disciples, we often find it easier to trust our circumstances —that is, to believe what our eyes show us—than to trust the one who is Lord over our circumstances. Jesus told his disciples not to fear, because he was with them. Likewise, Jesus is always with us.

CONFUSED DISCIPLES

Near the Sea of Galilee:

Jesus took Peter, James, and John, and led them up a high mountain to be alone. As the men watched, Jesus' appearance was transformed, and his clothes became dazzling white, far whiter than any earthly bleach could ever make them. Then Elijah and Moses appeared and began talking with Jesus.

Peter exclaimed, "Rabbi, it's wonderful for us to be here! Let's make three shelters as memorials—one for you, one for Moses, and one for Elijah." He said this because he didn't really know what else to say, for they were all terrified.

Then a cloud overshadowed them, and a voice from the cloud said, "This is my dearly loved Son. Listen to him." Suddenly, when they looked around, Moses and Elijah were gone, and they saw only Jesus with them.

As they went back down the mountain, he told them not to tell anyone what they had seen until the Son of Man had risen from the dead. So they kept it to themselves, but they often asked each other what he meant by "rising from the dead."

Then they asked him, "Why do the teachers of religious law insist that Elijah must return before the Messiah comes?"

Jesus responded, "Elijah is indeed coming first to get everything ready. Yet why do the Scriptures say that the Son of Man must suffer greatly and be treated with utter contempt? But I tell you, Elijah has already come, and they chose to abuse him, just as the Scriptures predicted."

Mark 9:2–13 NLT

*T*rusting God comes from knowing God. On the mountain, Jesus became glorious. But Jesus told his disciples to keep it quiet until after his resurrection. They understood about keeping quiet, but the part about "rising from the dead" was a puzzler for them. That is why they then asked Jesus about Elijah coming "first." They wanted to know if maybe Elijah had something to do with that "rising" Jesus had told them about. John the Baptist had just been executed by Herod. They knew that John the Baptist was the Elijah who had been predicted. They wondered if he was coming back.

Then Jesus asked them a probing question: If Elijah was supposed to restore all things, why did Jesus have to suffer and be rejected? Jesus wanted them to understand that his death and resurrection would solve the problem of sin; it would restore the broken relationship that existed between God and humanity.

The disciples often didn't understand Jesus. But they still trusted him. We don't trust God because we've had all our questions answered; we trust God because we know him. Trust is built on a relationship, not answers to questions.

I KIND OF BELIEVE, MAYBE

After Jesus' transfiguration, near the Sea of Galilee:

[Jesus] answered [the father of the demon-possessed boy] and said, "O faithless generation, how long shall I be with you? How long shall I bear with you? Bring him to Me." Then they brought him to Him. And when he saw Him, immediately the spirit convulsed him, and he fell on the ground and wallowed, foaming at the mouth.

So He asked his father, "How long has this been happening to him?"

And he said, "From childhood. And often he has thrown him both into the fire and into the water to destroy him. But if You can do anything, have compassion on us and help us."

Jesus said to him, "If you can believe, all things are possible to him who believes."

Immediately the father of the child cried out and said with tears, "Lord, I believe; help my unbelief!"

When Jesus saw that the people came running together, He rebuked the unclean spirit, saying to it, "Deaf and dumb spirit, I command you, come out of him and enter him no more!" Then the spirit cried out, convulsed him greatly, and came out of him. And he became as one dead, so that many said, "He is dead." But Jesus took him by the hand and lifted him up, and he arose.

And when He had come into the house, His disciples asked Him privately, "Why could we not cast it out?"

So He said to them, "This kind can come out by nothing but prayer and fasting."

Mark 9:19–29 NKJV

※

Belief can grow from unbelief. The boy's father, the disciples, and the people witnessing the boy's convulsions all had a problem—they suffered from unbelief. Jesus saw the problem for what it was and marveled at it. Had they forgotten who their God was? Were the words of their prophets and their rescue from Egypt that far in the past?

Demon possession appears only in the Gospels and the book of Acts. No stories of demons inhabiting people appear in the Old Testament or elsewhere in the New. The symptoms of demon possession vary widely, ranging from intensified strength to deafness and to fortune-telling. In this passage, the demon had taken the child's speech and seemed intent on causing him physical harm.

Facing his child's suffering, the father of the boy finally asked Jesus for help. He believed that Jesus could help him believe. Even Jesus' disciples lacked faith. But unlike the disciples, the father asked Jesus to help him overcome his unbelief, thereby acknowledging that Jesus could cure even a lack of faith.

Jesus healed the boy and removed the demon plaguing him. But more important, God restored faith to a father who had lost it but wanted it back desperately.

FORGIVENESS

After the triumphal entry, during Jesus' last week in Jerusalem:

When evening came, [Jesus and the disciples] would go out of the city. As they were passing by in the morning, they saw the fig tree withered from the roots up. Being reminded, Peter said to Him, "Rabbi, look, the fig tree which You cursed has withered."

And Jesus answered saying to them, "Have faith in God. Truly I say to you, whoever says to this mountain, 'Be taken up and cast into the sea,' and does not doubt in his heart, but believes that what he says is going to happen, it will be granted him. Therefore I say to you, all things for which you pray and ask, believe that you have received them, and they will be granted you. Whenever you stand praying, forgive, if you have anything against anyone, so that your Father who is in heaven will also forgive you your transgressions. But if you do not forgive, neither will your Father who is in heaven forgive your transgressions."

Mark 11:19–26 NASB

✳

*G*od's will is always accomplished, so if you want guaranteed success, then discover God's will first. After the triumphal entry into Jerusalem, Jesus and his disciples left and went to the nearby village of Bethany. As they approached, Jesus saw a fig tree and thought to get some figs from it. There were none. So Jesus cursed the tree to permanent fruitlessness.

The next day, the disciples discovered that the tree had died. Jesus took the opportunity to teach them something about faith, perhaps part of his reason for cursing the tree in the first place. Jesus never did anything by accident.

During his lesson on faith, Jesus suggested that God will give us anything we want if we have enough faith. Did Jesus mean that the only thing standing between a new sports car and us is our doubt? Not exactly. We first have to know it is God's will.

Forgiving other people is an example of something that we know is God's will. Jesus told us to forgive other people, and so we can do that without doubt. If God asked us to order a mountain into the sea, then we would know that was God's will and could ask for it free of doubt. But praying for forgiveness is actually bigger than tossing a real mountain into the sea. The prophet Micah wrote, "You will again have compassion on us; you will tread our sins underfoot and hurl all our iniquities into the depths of the sea" (Micah 7:19 NIV). *That's* the mountain Jesus was talking about.

DON'T BELIEVE IT

In Jerusalem, during the week before Jesus' final Passover, he said:

"So when you see the 'abomination of desolation,' spoken of by Daniel the prophet, standing where it ought not" (let the reader understand), "then let those who are in Judea flee to the mountains. Let him who is on the housetop not go down into the house, nor enter to take anything out of his house. And let him who is in the field not go back to get his clothes. But woe to those who are pregnant and to those who are nursing babies in those days! And pray that your flight may not be in winter. For in those days there will be tribulation, such as has not been since the beginning of the creation which God created until this time, nor ever shall be. And unless the Lord had shortened those days, no flesh would be saved; but for the elect's sake, whom He chose, He shortened the days.

"Then if anyone says to you, 'Look, here is the Christ!' or, 'Look, He is there!' do not believe it. For false christs and false prophets will rise and show signs and wonders to deceive, if possible, even the elect. But take heed; see, I have told you all things beforehand."

Mark 13:14–23 NKJV

❀

*T*here is a time to believe, and a time to disbelieve. Belief is not a good thing if you believe a lie. One thing Jesus warned his disciples against shortly before his crucifixion was, in fact, a problem the disciples were already aware of—the appearance of false messiahs. In the decades before and after Jesus, many false messiahs appeared, all announcing the same message: the world is a mess, the time of God's judgment has arrived, and we need to make war against the Romans. When the bad times come, there will always be those who claim that only they can solve the problems. Jesus told his followers not to believe those bearers of false hope.

Moses warned the ancient Israelites not to believe a prophet—even if he performed wonders and even if what he said came true—if that prophet asked them to believe in other gods (Deuteronomy 13:1–5). Likewise, Jesus warned his disciples against believing in any messiahs other than him. No one can take the place of Jesus in the lives of his followers. No one else is necessary, and no one else can do the job. Jesus is the only Savior. God wants us to recognize the difference between the truth and a lie, and to believe only the truth.

A LEPER'S TALE

Near the Sea of Galilee:

While [Jesus] was in one of the towns, a man was there who had a serious skin disease all over him. He saw Jesus, fell facedown, and begged Him: "Lord, if You are willing, You can make me clean."

Reaching out His hand, He touched him, saying, "I am willing; be made clean," and immediately the disease left him. Then He ordered him to tell no one: "But go and show yourself to the priest, and offer what Moses prescribed for your cleansing as a testimony to them."

But the news about Him spread even more, and large crowds would come together to hear Him and to be healed of their sicknesses. Yet He often withdrew to deserted places and prayed. On one of those days while He was teaching, Pharisees and teachers of the law were sitting there who had come from every village of Galilee and Judea, and also from Jerusalem.

Luke 5:12–17 HCSB

※

Sometimes we say, "I wouldn't touch that with a ten-foot pole," but Jesus never let poles come between him and the people who needed him. In India, those of the lowest class were called the "untouchables." The upper classes would have nothing to do with them. In ancient Israel, lepers were the "untouchables." People avoided them out of fear of becoming lepers themselves. To be a leper meant losing your friends, your family, and everything that mattered to you. You were, for all practical purposes, dead.

But when an unnamed leper begged Jesus for healing, Jesus wasn't afraid. Jesus touched him. He reached out to a man whom no one else would reach out to. And then he healed him of his affliction.

As was so common, Jesus told the man to tell no one what had happened but to follow the law of Moses, which prescribed how a leper who had been healed could have that healing certified by the religious leaders. Once his healing was certified, he could rejoin the society from which he'd been excluded. He could have his life back.

Jesus is not afraid to touch us, no matter who we are or how worthy we may think we are of being forever excluded. No matter how big a mess we think we've made of our lives, Jesus is ready to reach out to help us clean it up.

DON'T GO TO ANY TROUBLE

When [Jesus] had concluded all His sayings in the hearing of the people, He entered Capernaum. A centurion's slave, who was highly valued by him, was sick and about to die. When the centurion heard about Jesus, he sent some Jewish elders to Him, requesting Him to come and save the life of his slave. When they reached Jesus, they pleaded with Him earnestly, saying, "He is worthy for You to grant this, because he loves our nation and has built us a synagogue." Jesus went with them, and when He was not far from the house, the centurion sent friends to tell Him, "Lord, don't trouble Yourself, since I am not worthy to have You come under my roof. That is why I didn't even consider myself worthy to come to You. But say the word, and my servant will be cured. For I too am a man placed under authority, having soldiers under my command. I say to this one, 'Go!' and he goes; and to another, 'Come!' and he comes; and to my slave, 'Do this!' and he does it."

Jesus heard this and was amazed at him, and turning to the crowd following Him, He said, "I tell you, I have not found so great a faith even in Israel!" When those who had been sent returned to the house, they found the slave in good health.

Luke 7:1–10 HCSB

*N*othing ventured; nothing gained. The centurion didn't feel deserving, but he asked anyway. In Luke's presentation of the story of the centurion with the sick slave, some elders encouraged Jesus to go to the centurion based on what a good man he was.

Jesus didn't heal the centurion because the soldier was a good man. Jesus didn't heal people based on their goodness. It was only after he healed them that he told them to "sin no more."

The centurion told Jesus that a word from Jesus would be enough; Jesus didn't even have to go to him. In Luke's telling of the tale, Jesus didn't even announce the healing. Instead, we get only Jesus' reaction to the centurion's great faith, followed by the news that the slave was healed.

The centurion didn't believe himself worthy of Jesus' presence, but Jesus marveled at his faith. The centurion, though the builder of a synagogue, remained a Gentile. He had not converted to Judaism. The centurion's faith, and Jesus' healing of his slave, demonstrated that the grace of God is available to the entire human race. The Messiah who was supposed to destroy the Romans healed the slave of a leader in their armed forces.

Jesus will do more than we expect. Jesus reaches beyond where we think he would, could, or should go. He is not bound by what binds us.

❊❊❊❊❊❊❊❊❊❊❊❊❊❊❊❊❊❊❊❊❊❊❊❊❊❊❊❊❊❊❊❊❊

FINDING TRUST

Not far from the Sea of Galilee:

[Jesus'] mother and brothers showed up but couldn't get through to him because of the crowd. He was given the message, "Your mother and brothers are standing outside wanting to see you."

He replied, "My mother and brothers are the ones who hear and do God's Word. Obedience is thicker than blood."

One day he and his disciples got in a boat. "Let's cross the lake," he said. And off they went. It was smooth sailing, and he fell asleep. A terrific storm came up suddenly on the lake. Water poured in, and they were about to capsize. They woke Jesus: "Master, Master, we're going to drown!"

Getting to his feet, he told the wind, "Silence!" and the waves, "Quiet down!" They did it. The lake became smooth as glass.

Then he said to his disciples, "Why can't you trust me?"

They were in absolute awe, staggered and stammering, "Who is this, anyway? He calls out to the winds and sea, and they do what he tells them!"

Luke 8:19–25 MSG

❊

*W*ithout trust, there can be no obedience. Jesus' mother and brothers didn't believe him to be the Messiah. They looked at Jesus' lifestyle, and all they could see was a problem. They believed that Jesus was behaving in an irrational way. They were concerned for his health and welfare. Jesus used their concern for him to point out that belief involved hearing and then doing God's word.

His disciples were no better than his family at doing God's word. Although they were obedient when it came to getting in the boat and heading across the lake, when a problem came up, they were quick to doubt him. Neither Jesus' family nor his disciples trusted him. Hearing God's words and doing them depend upon trusting them.

When the disciples awakened Jesus, they had no thought about any way out. Instead, they merely informed him that they were doomed to drown. Their situation overwhelmed their ability to see who Jesus was. Of course, their inability to see past their situation did not prevent Jesus from doing what had to be done. Jesus' ability to save is not dependent upon our ability to believe that he can do it. Jesus does what is necessary regardless of our panic.

FEAR IN THE WAY

After healing a demon-possessed man, Jesus crossed the Sea of Galilee:

[As] Jesus returned, the people welcomed Him, for they had all been waiting for Him. And there came a man named Jairus, and he was an official of the synagogue; and he fell at Jesus' feet, and began to implore Him to come to his house; for he had an only daughter, about twelve years old, and she was dying. But as He went, the crowds were pressing against Him.

And a woman who had a hemorrhage for twelve years, and could not be healed by anyone, came up behind Him and touched the fringe of His cloak, and immediately her hemorrhage stopped.

And Jesus said, "Who is the one who touched Me?" And while they were all denying it, Peter said, "Master, the people are crowding and pressing in on You."

But Jesus said, "Someone did touch Me, for I was aware that power had gone out of Me."

When the woman saw that she had not escaped notice, she came trembling and fell down before Him, and declared in the presence of all the people the reason why she had touched Him, and how she had been immediately healed.

And He said to her, "Daughter, your faith has made you well; go in peace."

Luke 8:40–48 NASB

*W*hy do we always assume the worst? The unnamed woman with the hemorrhage appears in three of the four gospel accounts. When Jesus asked who had touched him, the woman responded with fear, despite the fact that the bleeding she had been afflicted with for twelve long years had stopped. She received from Jesus just what she wanted.

She was afraid of Jesus because the default setting on human beings is distrust of God and his intentions. In the garden of Eden, the Serpent planted a foul lie in the mind of Eve, the mother of us all, that God did not have the best of intentions for her. She came to believe that God was withholding something wonderful in the fruit that he'd forbidden. Ever since, human beings have believed that God's intentions may not always be good. The woman feared that Jesus would take away the gift she had snatched from him. She thought that perhaps he hadn't really been willing to give her that healing.

But God doesn't take away the gifts that he gives to his children. God's gifts are irrevocable. Jesus reassured that woman, as he reassures us today, that she could go in peace. We need always to assume the best from God. We need to trust God's character and good intentions.

JUST ASLEEP

In a Galilean town:

While Jesus was still speaking, someone came from the house of Jairus, the synagogue ruler. "Your daughter is dead," he said. "Don't bother the teacher any more."

Hearing this, Jesus said to Jairus, "Don't be afraid; just believe, and she will be healed."

When he arrived at the house of Jairus, he did not let anyone go in with him except Peter, John and James, and the child's father and mother. Meanwhile, all the people were wailing and mourning for her. "Stop wailing," Jesus said. "She is not dead but asleep."

They laughed at him, knowing that she was dead. But he took her by the hand and said, "My child, get up!" Her spirit returned, and at once she stood up. Then Jesus told them to give her something to eat. Her parents were astonished, but he ordered them not to tell anyone what had happened.

Luke 8:49–56 NIV

*B*ecause Jesus is with us, we don't have to be afraid anymore. Luke repeated the story of Jairus the synagogue ruler, but as usual, Luke put his own unique spin on things. Writing to a non-Jewish audience, Luke didn't bother to insert any of the Aramaic wording that appeared in Mark's rendition. When Jesus told Jairus not to be afraid, we discover from Luke that Jesus told Jairus why he didn't need to be afraid—Jesus promised to heal his daughter.

Jairus had experience with sick people getting well, but when people were dead, it was too late. Jesus brought something new into the world. As the prophet Isaiah said of Jesus, "by his wounds we are healed" (Isaiah 53:5 NIV). What more profound illness do people face than the illness of death?

Jesus told Jairus to keep the miracle to himself because Jesus hadn't done it for praise or fame. He'd done it out of compassion. Besides, we don't get excited by the everyday miracles of life. On the first day manna appeared in the time of Moses, people saw it as a miracle. After thirty years of eating it every day, it was no more miraculous than a sunrise—which tells us something about our perception of sunrises. Jesus hoped we would realize that as unusual as a dead girl coming back to life was, it was no more special or difficult than the daily miracles of God that we take for granted.

LOSING IS WINNING

Near Bethsaida, after Peter proclaimed that Jesus was the Messiah:

[Jesus] strictly warned and commanded them to tell this to no one, saying, "The Son of Man must suffer many things, and be rejected by the elders and chief priests and scribes, and be killed, and be raised the third day."

Then He said to them all, "If anyone desires to come after Me, let him deny himself, and take up his cross daily, and follow Me. For whoever desires to save his life will lose it, but whoever loses his life for My sake will save it. For what profit is it to a man if he gains the whole world, and is himself destroyed or lost? For whoever is ashamed of Me and My words, of him the Son of Man will be ashamed when He comes in His own glory, and in His Father's, and of the holy angels."

Luke 9:21–26 NKJV

✽

*W*hat we think we already know can get in the way of recognizing the truth. Look at what it did to the disciples. They were still surprised by Jesus' execution even after he had warned them about it so often. Whatever didn't fit their beliefs about the Messiah—that he would restore the kingdom to Israel—they failed to hear. In common with all human beings, they paid attention only to what reinforced what they already believed. They were like people who notice the misbehavior of people they despise because it proves their point about them.

Those who were to be crucified were forced to bear their own crosses to the place where they would die. They were made participants in their own executions. Jesus told his disciples that he was going to die such a death and that those who followed him would have to suffer that same fate.

Many of his disciples did indeed follow Jesus in dying violently at the hands of the Roman government. More profoundly, however, Jesus tried to explain to them the significance of his coming death. He wanted them to understand that by being his disciples they were going to participate in his suffering. Because of their faith, Jesus' death on the cross would save their souls.

Listening to Jesus means that we have to stop listening to ourselves and to all other voices demanding our attention. We must let go of our concerns and instead listen to the concerns of Jesus. Only then can our deepest concerns, concerns we might not even know we have, find resolution.

WHAT'S YOUR PROBLEM?

Just after Jesus' transfiguration near the Sea of Galilee:

Jesus and his three disciples came down from the mountain and were met by a large crowd. Just then someone in the crowd shouted, "Teacher, please do something for my son! He is my only child! A demon often attacks him and makes him scream. It shakes him until he foams at the mouth, and it won't leave him until it has completely worn the boy out. I begged your disciples to force out the demon, but they couldn't do it."

Jesus said to them, "You people are stubborn and don't have any faith! How much longer must I be with you? Why do I have to put up with you?"

Then Jesus said to the man, "Bring your son to me." While the boy was being brought, the demon attacked him and made him shake all over. Jesus ordered the demon to stop. Then he healed the boy and gave him back to his father.

Luke 9:37–42 CEV

❋

*B*ecause he loves us, Jesus never gives up on us. Jesus' words to his disciples may seem harsh. In the face of the boy's suffering, Jesus berated them for being "stubborn" and having "no faith." He then wondered aloud about how long he was going to have to stay with them and put up with it all.

Where was Jesus' compassion? Why was he suddenly so cross with them? The context explains it. Jesus had sent his disciples two by two to preach about the kingdom, with Jesus' authority to heal and cast out demons. He had fed the five thousand. Peter had declared that Jesus was the Messiah, and Jesus had predicted his own death and resurrection. Three of Jesus' closest disciples witnessed his transfiguration on the mountain, saw Moses and Elijah, and heard the voice of the Father. Jesus blew up at his disciples when they failed to help just one poor man and his son after all that. Nevertheless, Jesus solved the problem, despite the stubbornness and faithlessness around him. He healed the boy from the demon and restored a son to his father.

Jesus may be disappointed by our failures, just as he was with his disciples', but he'll keep working with us, as he kept working with them. He put up with his disciples for the rest of their lives and for all eternity. In fact, Jesus more than just puts up with us. He loves us and will be with us always.

MORE TOLERABLE FOR SODOM

On his way to Jerusalem for the last time, Jesus said:

"Whenever you enter a town and they do not welcome you, go out into its streets and say, 'Even the dust of your town that clings to our feet, we wipe off in protest against you. Yet know this: the kingdom of God has come near.' I tell you, on that day it will be more tolerable for Sodom than for that town.

"Woe to you, Chorazin! Woe to you, Bethsaida! For if the deeds of power done in you had been done in Tyre and Sidon, they would have repented long ago, sitting in sackcloth and ashes. But at the judgment it will be more tolerable for Tyre and Sidon than for you. And you, Capernaum, will you be exalted to heaven?

"No, you will be brought down to Hades.

"Whoever listens to you listens to me, and whoever rejects you rejects me, and whoever rejects me rejects the one who sent me."

Luke 10:10–16 NRSV

What does it take to get people to believe? It depends on whether people want to believe. Jesus did most of his teaching and miracles in the region around the Sea of Galilee. Chorazin was a town about two miles north of Capernaum. Bethsaida was located at the northeast corner of the Sea of Galilee where the Jordan River flows into it. Both cities had witnessed Jesus' teaching and his miracles, but most of the inhabitants had not been convinced. Jesus condemned them by suggesting that Tyre and Sidon would have repented if they'd seen such marvels.

If Tyre and Sidon had repented, and had the miracles that were done in Chorazin and Bethsaida been done in them, why didn't God do such miracles for them? We know it is God's will that no one should perish. If there was a way of saving those cities, God surely would have saved them.

By condemning Chorazin and Bethsaida, Jesus was not suggesting that there had been hope for those wicked cities of the past. Jesus' point was simply that Chorazin and Bethsaida were without excuse. Jesus had done enough for them. They should have believed. Now that they had rejected Jesus, their blood would be on their own hands. Those ancient, evil cities had only God's prophets in their midst, men like Isaiah and Ezekiel. Chorazin and Bethsaida had God himself in their midst, in the person of Jesus Christ. To whom much was given, much would be required. Like the ancient people, we have God's prophets in our midst—we can read their words every day in the Scriptures. And we have the words of Jesus himself. It is easy for us to believe.

SAMARITAN FAITH

It happened as [Jesus] went to Jerusalem that He passed through the midst of Samaria and Galilee. Then as He entered a certain village, there met Him ten men who were lepers, who stood afar off. And they lifted up their voices and said, "Jesus, Master, have mercy on us!"

So when He saw them, He said to them, "Go, show yourselves to the priests." And so it was that as they went, they were cleansed.

And one of them, when he saw that he was healed, returned, and with a loud voice glorified God, and fell down on his face at His feet, giving Him thanks. And he was a Samaritan. So Jesus answered and said, "Were there not ten cleansed? But where are the nine? Were there not any found who returned to give glory to God except this foreigner?" And He said to him, "Arise, go your way. Your faith has made you well."

Luke 17:11–19 NKJV

Jesus made a habit of going to all the wrong places and hanging out with all the wrong people. Not only did he go to Samaria, but he also met up with its lepers. According to the law, they had to stand apart from others and call out "unclean" so that people would know to avoid them. When the ten lepers wanted Jesus to heal them, they didn't come near. Instead, they begged for mercy from a distance. Jesus' response was simply to tell them to go show themselves to the priests. A leper had to go through a lot in order to gain official recognition of his cleansing. Leviticus 14 lays out all the details. He had to be ceremonially washed. He had to shave hair off his body. And he had to perform a series of sacrifices.

As those ten men started on the journey to present themselves to the priests, their disease left them. Nine of the men continued on their way. But one of them, a Samaritan, turned back to glorify God. Jesus thought it was strange that only one, the one who wasn't even an Israelite, expressed thanks. Jesus told the man that his faith had healed him.

Notice, however, that the other nine remained healed. Jesus did not take back his blessing from the other nine lepers who failed to thank him. Jesus intervenes in our lives because of his mercy. But he still appreciates being thanked. We, too, have been cleansed, and so we have much for which we can give thanks to God every day.

LET ME SEE

[Jesus] took the twelve aside and said to them, "See, we are going up to Jerusalem, and everything that is written about the Son of Man by the prophets will be accomplished. For he will be handed over to the Gentiles; and he will be mocked and insulted and spat upon. After they have flogged him, they will kill him, and on the third day he will rise again." But they understood nothing about all these things; in fact, what he said was hidden from them, and they did not grasp what was said.

As he approached Jericho, a blind man was sitting by the roadside begging. When he heard a crowd going by, he asked what was happening. They told him, "Jesus of Nazareth is passing by." Then he shouted, "Jesus, Son of David, have mercy on me!" Those who were in front sternly ordered him to be quiet; but he shouted even more loudly, "Son of David, have mercy on me!" Jesus stood still and ordered the man to be brought to him; and when he came near, he asked him, "What do you want me to do for you?" He said, "Lord, let me see again." Jesus said to him, "Receive your sight; your faith has saved you."

Luke 18:31–42 NRSV

We can be more blind sometimes than the blindest man Jesus ever healed. Luke's juxtaposition of the blindness of his disciples and the healing of a blind man was not accidental. Luke wanted to make a point about how sight—understanding—is a gift of God. Jesus could not have been clearer with his disciples concerning what was about to happen to him when they got to Jerusalem. Still the disciples didn't get it. They thought the Messiah would kill the Romans, not be killed by them.

They were blind because they thought they already knew what was going on. They were convinced that they could see, when they couldn't see at all.

The blind man knew he was blind. Jesus healed him and told him that his faith had saved him. His faith made him seek out Jesus. His only expectation for what the Messiah would do was to end his blindness. No other expectation clouded his mind.

In contrast, Jesus' disciples were blinded by what they thought they could see, by what they thought they knew of the Messiah. The blind man understood better. We can understand Jesus' message best when we approach it with humility and openness.

❀❀❀❀❀❀❀❀❀❀❀❀❀❀❀❀❀❀❀❀❀❀❀❀❀❀❀❀❀❀❀❀❀❀❀

NONE OF YOUR BUSINESS

One day, Jesus was teaching in the temple and telling the good news. So the chief priests, the teachers, and the nation's leaders asked him, "What right do you have to do these things? Who gave you this authority?"

Jesus replied, "I want to ask you a question. Who gave John the right to baptize? Was it God in heaven or merely some human being?"

They talked this over and said to each other, "We can't say that God gave John this right. Jesus will ask us why we didn't believe John. And we can't say that it was merely some human who gave John the right to baptize. The crowd will stone us to death, because they think John was a prophet."

So they told Jesus, "We don't know who gave John the right to baptize."

Jesus replied, "Then I won't tell you who gave me the right to do what I do."

Luke 20:1–8 CEV

❀

*I*t's good news when the hometown wins, unless you were rooting for the other side. That the religious establishment reacted with anger to Jesus preaching good news tells us something about the religious establishment.

After Jesus drove the moneylenders from the temple and while he was preaching, the religious leaders approached Jesus and asked him about the source of his authority. Jesus used his popularity and the popularity of his cousin, John the Baptist, against the religious leaders. They did not believe Jesus was authorized to do what he was doing. They did not believe John the Baptist was a prophet of God. But they were well aware of what most of the people in the crowd believed. When Jesus asked them about John's message, they realized they couldn't say anything without getting themselves in serious trouble.

When the religious leaders refused to answer Jesus, Jesus likewise refused to answer them. Jesus' point was that they didn't believe John came from God, so there was no reason for them to believe Jesus when he told them he came from God and had God's authority for his actions. Their question was not an honest one. He knew it, and they knew it. They wouldn't accept the truth, so what was the point in giving it to them?

When someone has already made up his mind, giving him the facts is not going to change it. We need to be careful about how fast we make up our minds. A made-up mind can too often become a fortress against the truth. Pray that God's grace will change things.

BEDAZZLED

[Jesus] was back in Cana of Galilee, the place where he made the water into wine. Meanwhile in Capernaum, there was a certain official from the king's court whose son was sick. When he heard that Jesus had come from Judea to Galilee, he went and asked that he come down and heal his son, who was on the brink of death. Jesus put him off: "Unless you people are dazzled by a miracle, you refuse to believe."

But the court official wouldn't be put off. "Come down! It's life or death for my son."

Jesus simply replied, "Go home. Your son lives."

The man believed the bare word Jesus spoke and headed home. On his way back, his servants intercepted him and announced, "Your son lives!"

He asked them what time he began to get better. They said, "The fever broke yesterday afternoon at one o'clock." The father knew that that was the very moment Jesus had said, "Your son lives."

That clinched it. Not only he but his entire household believed. This was now the second sign Jesus gave after having come from Judea into Galilee.

John 4:46–54 MSG

True faith doesn't require much evidence, since faith is a gift from God and not something we create in ourselves. Herod the Tetrarch was the ruler in Galilee. One of his officials had a son who was sick and on the brink of death.

Jesus criticized the people around him for needing miracles in order to believe. John the Baptist had announced Jesus was the Messiah, and Jesus had begun preaching his message, but he hadn't performed any other miracles. Jesus' only miracle up until then had been turning water into wine at a wedding. But this official in Herod's court believed that Jesus' status as the Messiah was enough. If Jesus was the Messiah, then healing people was part of the package. When Jesus told him his son lived, he believed it and headed back home. Not only did this official believe that Jesus was the Messiah, but soon the other members of his household did too. They were dazzled, and so they believed. For some people, a miracle was enough. But the father believed simply because he knew the Messiah could take care of his boy. He had believed before any miracle.

For others, like the religious leadership in Israel, even Jesus' many miracles would not be enough for them to believe. Jesus' promises are certain because of who he is. We don't need dazzling miracles. If we doubt, the doubt arises irrationally from ourselves alone and not because Jesus hasn't done enough for us yet.

THE BREAD OF LIFE

[After Jesus fed a crowd of 5,000, some of them followed him around the Sea of Galilee and] asked him, "What miraculous sign then will you give that we may see it and believe you? What will you do? Our forefathers ate the manna in the desert; as it is written: 'He gave them bread from heaven to eat.'"

Jesus said to them, "I tell you the truth, it is not Moses who has given you the bread from heaven, but it is my Father who gives you the true bread from heaven. For the bread of God is he who comes down from heaven and gives life to the world."

"Sir," they said, "from now on give us this bread."

Then Jesus declared, "I am the bread of life. He who comes to me will never go hungry, and he who believes in me will never be thirsty. But as I told you, you have seen me and still you do not believe. All that the Father gives me will come to me, and whoever comes to me I will never drive away. For I have come down from heaven not to do my will but to do the will of him who sent me. And this is the will of him who sent me, that I shall lose none of all that he has given me, but raise them up at the last day. For my Father's will is that everyone who looks to the Son and believes in him shall have eternal life, and I will raise him up at the last day."

John 6:30–40 NIV

Human beings are never satisfied. Jesus fed five thousand people in a miraculous way. Their response was not to believe Jesus but to wonder what he could do to make them believe; they pointed out what Moses had done in the wilderness. Jesus corrected them. Moses hadn't fed the ancient Israelites. God had. Jesus wasn't just another Moses; he was like the manna that had come down from heaven.

But the crowd didn't understand. They were fixated on getting a free meal, while he was trying to tell them about the meal they really needed to eat. Jesus compared himself to bread and to being eaten because in order for us to continue living, something else must die. Even a vegetarian kills plants in order to stay alive. So in order for us to have eternal life, Jesus had to die. Our eternal life cost us nothing, but it cost Jesus everything.

SECRET MESSIAH

Jesus decided to leave Judea and to start going through Galilee because the leaders of the people wanted to kill him. It was almost time for the Festival of Shelters, and Jesus' brothers said to him, "Why don't you go to Judea? Then your disciples can see what you are doing. No one does anything in secret, if they want others to know about them. So let the world know what you are doing!" Even Jesus' own brothers had not yet become his followers.

Jesus answered, "My time hasn't yet come, but your time is always here. The people of this world cannot hate you. They hate me, because I tell them that they do evil things. Go on to the festival. My time hasn't yet come, and I am not going." Jesus said this and stayed on in Galilee.

After Jesus' brothers had gone to the festival, he went secretly, without telling anyone.

During the festival the leaders looked for Jesus and asked, "Where is he?" The crowds even got into an argument about him. Some were saying, "Jesus is a good man," while others were saying, "He is lying to everyone." But the people were afraid of their leaders, and none of them talked in public about him.

When the festival was about half over, Jesus went into the temple and started teaching. The leaders were surprised and said, "How does this man know so much? He has never been taught!"

John 7:1–15 CEV

*W*as Jesus a liar? His brothers, who didn't believe he was the Messiah, told him that if he wanted to become a public figure, he had to appear in public, so why not go to the Festival of Shelters? Jesus told them it wasn't his time, but then he went there without telling anyone.

Deception is not always a lie. When a quarterback fakes a punt and then passes, has he lied to the opposing team? When a general pretends he is invading by land and then comes in by the sea, has he lied to his enemy? No, we'd say they were both using good strategy. Jesus' behavior must be understood as a strategic move. Jesus' brothers did not yet believe. That means they were still playing for the other side.

Jesus had a specific plan in mind for the feast, a plan that did not involve his brothers or their expectations. By misleading his brothers, he ensured that he would be able to get to Jerusalem to preach the gospel while avoiding arrest by the religious establishment. It was not yet time for Jesus to die.

Jesus' critics, like the Pharisees, were quick to find fault with his behavior. We must be careful not to start thinking like the Pharisees. Only when we realize that we need to learn can God successfully start to teach us.

EXPELLED

On a Sabbath in Jerusalem, Jesus healed a man born blind:

The man [Jesus had healed of blindness] answered [the Jewish leaders], "Here is an astonishing thing! You do not know where he comes from, and yet he opened my eyes. We know that God does not listen to sinners, but he does listen to one who worships him and obeys his will. Never since the world began has it been heard that anyone opened the eyes of a person born blind. If this man were not from God, he could do nothing."

They answered him, "You were born entirely in sins, and are you trying to teach us?" And they drove him out.

Jesus heard that they had driven him out, and when he found him, he said, "Do you believe in the Son of Man?"

He answered, "And who is he, sir? Tell me, so that I may believe in him."

Jesus said to him, "You have seen him, and the one speaking with you is he."

He said, "Lord, I believe." And he worshiped him.

John 9:30–38 NRSV

❀

$\mathcal{W}$e want a place to belong, where everyone knows our name. Many of the people whom Jesus spent time with and healed remain unnamed in the New Testament. The man born blind, whom Jesus healed, was "driven" out of his synagogue. Even his parents hadn't been ready to stand up for him. It can be dangerous to disagree with people in authority. Speaking "truth to power" sometimes results, as it did for that poor man, in that power simply smashing one down.

The man born blind refused to be silenced, even by the threat of losing his place in society. Perhaps the fact that he'd spent most of his life scratching out a living by begging on the periphery of society anyway meant that he didn't feel invested in that society to begin with. More likely, the startling reality of the truth was so powerful for him that he cared for nothing but that truth. His life was so profoundly changed that he could not deny reality, no matter how strongly the people around him wanted to force him to deny it.

Jesus went to him in his abandoned state. Jesus showed him that he wasn't alone after all. When you have the truth, the only ones you lose are the liars. When Jesus revealed himself to a man of truth, that man recognized Jesus for who he was and worshipped him. Thanks to Jesus, we have a place to belong, and he knows our names.

DO YOU SEE ME NOW?

Still in Jerusalem, Jesus spoke to the critical Pharisees:

"I came into the world to bring everything into the clear light of day, making all the distinctions clear, so that those who have never seen will see, and those who have made a great pretense of seeing will be exposed as blind."

Some Pharisees overheard him and said, "Does that mean you're calling us blind?"

Jesus said, "If you were really blind, you would be blameless, but since you claim to see everything so well, you're accountable for every fault and failure.

"Let me set this before you as plainly as I can. If a person climbs over or through the fence of a sheep pen instead of going through the gate, you know he's up to no good—a sheep rustler! The shepherd walks right up to the gate. The gatekeeper opens the gate to him and the sheep recognize his voice. He calls his own sheep by name and leads them out. When he gets them all out, he leads them and they follow because they are familiar with his voice. They won't follow a stranger's voice but will scatter because they aren't used to the sound of it."

John 9:39–10:5 MSG

※

*J*esus forsook diplomacy when it came to his relationship with the Pharisees. After healing a man born blind, Jesus told them that he wasn't trying to be obscure with his teaching. Instead, he was trying to make everything as clear as possible so that those who didn't understand would come to understand, while those who claimed to know it all would be shown for what they were—clueless.

The Pharisees were clued in enough to realize that Jesus was insulting them when he called them blind. Jesus gave them an illustration to further make his point. He told the Pharisees that they were up to no good, like robbers sneaking into a sheepfold. The sheep—God's people—would not listen to them. But they would listen to Jesus because he was speaking with a familiar voice, the voice of God that all God's people recognized if they really understood the Scriptures and really loved him.

God loves sinners. With the tax collectors, his love was gentle. With the Pharisees, it was harsh. In both cases, Jesus wanted repentance.

God's people usually recognize God. But mistakes are always possible. The Pharisees thought they were God's people, but they didn't recognize Jesus. We may want to be more careful and exercise greater humility than they did.

DON'T GIVE UP

Jesus finally reached Bethany, where his friend Lazarus had recently died:

[Martha] went away and called Mary her sister, saying secretly, "The Teacher is here and is calling for you."

And when she heard it, she got up quickly and was coming to Him.

Now Jesus had not yet come into the village, but was still in the place where Martha met Him.

Then the Jews who were with her in the house, and consoling her, when they saw that Mary got up quickly and went out, they followed her, supposing that she was going to the tomb to weep there.

Therefore, when Mary came where Jesus was, she saw Him, and fell at His feet, saying to Him, "Lord, if You had been here, my brother would not have died."

When Jesus therefore saw her weeping, and the Jews who came with her also weeping, He was deeply moved in spirit and was troubled, and said, "Where have you laid him?" They said to Him, "Lord, come and see."

Jesus wept.

So the Jews were saying, "See how He loved him!"

But some of them said, "Could not this man, who opened the eyes of the blind man, have kept this man also from dying?"

John 11:28–37 NASB

The best thing for you may turn out to be unpleasant. Jesus' will for Lazarus was that he get sick and die. Jesus' will for his friends and relatives was that they experience grief to bring glory to God when Jesus raised Lazarus from the dead. Even if it is all for the best, though, the pain is no less intense.

After Jesus learned where Lazarus had been placed, in the shortest verse of the Bible, we learn that he cried. Jesus cried over the death of Lazarus when he knew Lazarus would be alive soon because Jesus felt the same grief that all humans feel over the death of a loved one.

Christians find it easy to think of Jesus as God. Too often, we have trouble accepting the fact that he was also human. Jesus laughed and Jesus cried, feeling the same joys and pains that any human being has ever experienced.

The death of Lazarus and Jesus' interactions with the mourners give us added insight into the heart of Jesus. We get to know Jesus not just in the words he spoke, but also in his tears, which were no different from the ones we shed in our darkest hours. Like Jesus, we know that the resurrection is coming. But like Jesus, we still will cry.

DRAW A MAP

During the Last Supper, Jesus talked with his disciples about his destiny:

"No, we don't know, Lord," Thomas said. "We have no idea where you are going, so how can we know the way?"

Jesus told him, "I am the way, the truth, and the life. No one can come to the Father except through me. If you had really known me, you would know who my Father is. From now on, you do know him and have seen him!"

Philip said, "Lord, show us the Father, and we will be satisfied."

Jesus replied, "Have I been with you all this time, Philip, and yet you still don't know who I am? Anyone who has seen me has seen the Father! So why are you asking me to show him to you? Don't you believe that I am in the Father and the Father is in me? The words I speak are not my own, but my Father who lives in me does his work through me. Just believe that I am in the Father and the Father is in me. Or at least believe because of the work you have seen me do.

"I tell you the truth, anyone who believes in me will do the same works I have done, and even greater works, because I am going to be with the Father. You can ask for anything in my name, and I will do it, so that the Son can bring glory to the Father. Yes, ask me for anything in my name, and I will do it!"

John 14:5–14 NLT

What is the greatest work we could ever be involved with? The apostle Thomas asked two questions: Where was Jesus going, and how could they follow him? Philip just wanted to see the Father. Jesus responded with three points.

First, Jesus said that he was going to the Father and that Jesus was the only way to get to the Father. Second, if you know Jesus, then you know the Father. Third, those who believe in Jesus will be able to do more and better works than Jesus ever did.

How can that be? Just as Jesus told parables to make his words more easily understood, so he painted pictures with his miracles. Healing the blind and deaf, raising the dead—those were dynamic metaphors for what Jesus came to do spiritually. In his life, Jesus reached but a handful of human beings. Since his resurrection and the coming of the Holy Spirit, untold millions have been brought from spiritual death to spiritual life through the message of the gospel. That's how we've performed works greater than Jesus had. There are no greater works for us to do than to remove spiritual blindness, deafness, and death.

SIMPLE TRUTH

Jesus gave final instructions to his disciples at the Last Supper:

"Ah!" His disciples said. "Now You're speaking plainly and not using any figurative language. Now we know that You know everything and don't need anyone to question You. By this we believe that You came from God."

Jesus responded to them, "Do you now believe? Look: An hour is coming, and has come, when each of you will be scattered to his own home, and you will leave Me alone. Yet I am not alone, because the Father is with Me. I have told you these things so that in Me you may have peace. You will have suffering in this world. Be courageous! I have conquered the world."

Jesus spoke these things, looked up to heaven, and said:

"Father, the hour has come. Glorify Your Son so that the Son may glorify You, for You gave Him authority over all flesh; so He may give eternal life to all You have given Him.

"This is eternal life: that they may know You, the only true God, and the One You have sent—Jesus Christ.

"I have glorified You on the earth by completing the work You gave Me to do.

"Now, Father, glorify Me in Your presence with that glory I had with You before the world existed."

John 16:29–17:5 HCSB

❋

God can overcome our failures. He stays with us even when we make the wrong choices. Jesus gave his disciples his reassurance even as he told them that they would fail him. He promised them peace and victory through suffering, even as he promised they would abandon him in his hour of greatest need. Knowing their coming betrayal, Jesus prayed for them nevertheless.

Jesus did not come into existence in Bethlehem. He always was and always will be. He is the Creator of heaven and earth. He is God Almighty. He became human for but a brief eye blink in the never-ending span of eternity. Remembering how it had been and how it would be gave Jesus the strength to face the cross. Nevertheless, he was a human being. He had the same human revulsion and fear of death, the same distaste for the physical pain he would have to experience.

In the same way he could endure his cross, so we can endure ours. We, too, have been granted eternal life. We, too, will live with God in glory forever. And for us as well as for Jesus, all our suffering and all our problems are but eye blinks in the never-ending story of eternity. Just as tears fade with the passing of time, so will all our pains.

DYING LIKE A MAN

At the sixth hour darkness came over the whole land until the ninth hour. And at the ninth hour Jesus cried out in a loud voice, *"Eloi, Eloi, lama sabachthani?"*—which means, "My God, my God, why have you forsaken me?"

When some of those standing near heard this, they said, "Listen, he's calling Elijah."

One man ran, filled a sponge with wine vinegar, put it on a stick, and offered it to Jesus to drink. "Now leave him alone. Let's see if Elijah comes to take him down," he said.

With a loud cry, Jesus breathed his last.

The curtain of the temple was torn in two from top to bottom. And when the centurion, who stood there in front of Jesus, heard his cry and saw how he died, he said, "Surely this man was the Son of God!"

Some women were watching from a distance. Among them were Mary Magdalene, Mary the mother of James the younger and of Joses, and Salome. In Galilee these women had followed him and cared for his needs. Many other women who had come up with him to Jerusalem were also there.

Mark 15:33–41 NIV

*J*esus didn't enjoy doing his Father's will all the time. When Jesus was dying, he cried out, "My God, my God, why have you forsaken me?" Why did Jesus say that? Some have suggested that when God put all the sins of the world on Jesus, for the first time ever Jesus experienced separation from his Father.

But that explanation forgets that Jesus was a man. He had been betrayed by one of his closest friends. Most of the rest of his followers had run away. He died as a man on the cross, in agony and alone. He felt abandoned as he died on the cross because he had the same feelings and needs that all humans do.

Jesus loved life, and he experienced its full range of emotions. Human beings were created in God's image, and as God he already knew those feelings. Feelings simply are, like the blue in the sky or the wet in water. Some people seem bothered by Jesus' cry of despair when he died. Rather, we should be bothered only if he hadn't cried out.

God understands the pain of being human, the sometimes desperation of it. He knows. He's been there. Sometimes there is reason to feel despair. It is not a sin to feel devastated, any more than it is to feel encouraged. Like Jesus, we can rejoice when times are good and cry when times are bad.

❀❀❀❀❀❀❀❀❀❀❀❀❀❀❀❀❀❀❀❀❀❀❀❀❀❀❀❀❀❀❀❀

ANOTHER DAY IN PARADISE

The soldiers also mocked [Jesus], coming up to Him, offering Him sour wine, and saying, "If You are the King of the Jews, save Yourself!"

Now there was also an inscription above Him, "THIS IS THE KING OF THE JEWS."

One of the criminals who were hanged there was hurling abuse at Him, saying, "Are You not the Christ? Save Yourself and us!"

But the other answered, and rebuking him said, "Do you not even fear God, since you are under the same sentence of condemnation? And we indeed are suffering justly, for we are receiving what we deserve for our deeds; but this man has done nothing wrong."

And he was saying, "Jesus, remember me when You come in Your kingdom!"

And He said to him, "Truly I say to you, today you shall be with Me in Paradise."

Luke 23:36–43 NASB

❀

*J*esus knows what it's like to be mocked. He knows what it's like to be bullied. And he knows what it is to suffer. But he didn't let even extreme circumstances stop him from doing what he needed to do or focusing on the needs of someone else instead of himself. Two criminals hung on crosses alongside Jesus; one joined in mocking him, and the other accepted his fate and rebuked the mockery.

The thief on Jesus' right did not have the time or opportunity to do any good works, to make restitution for the crimes for which he'd been condemned. He couldn't join a church, tithe, or be baptized. He didn't even express repentance. He did not call Jesus Lord. All he did was call Jesus by name and ask him to remember him when he came into his kingdom. He had simple faith, and he made a simple request.

On the basis of those few words, Jesus told the criminal—who remains unnamed—that he would join Jesus in paradise that very day. The word *paradise* that Jesus used had originated with the Persians. It referred to the pleasure gardens belonging to the Persian king. Jesus said "today" because before the sun went down that evening, both the criminal and Jesus would be dead.

All human beings are like that criminal on the cross, unable to save ourselves or do anything to improve our situations. Jesus did everything and gave everything so that we who are unable to save ourselves can join him in paradise.

FEAR NOT!

The Sabbath was over, and it was almost daybreak on Sunday when Mary Magdalene and the other Mary went to see the tomb. Suddenly a strong earthquake struck, and the Lord's angel came down from heaven. He rolled away the stone and sat on it. The angel looked as bright as lightning, and his clothes were white as snow. The guards shook from fear and fell down, as though they were dead.

The angel said to the women, "Don't be afraid! I know you are looking for Jesus, who was nailed to a cross. He isn't here! God has raised him to life, just as Jesus said he would. Come, see the place where his body was lying. Now hurry! Tell his disciples that he has been raised to life and is on his way to Galilee. Go there, and you will see him. That is what I came to tell you."

The women were frightened and yet very happy, as they hurried from the tomb and ran to tell his disciples. Suddenly Jesus met them and greeted them. They went near him, held on to his feet, and worshiped him. Then Jesus said, "Don't be afraid! Tell my followers to go to Galilee. They will see me there."

Matthew 28:1–10 CEV

*T*he first person to know that Jesus was the Messiah was a woman. Likewise, the first person to know Jesus had been resurrected was a woman. That women were the first witnesses to Jesus' resurrection is significant. Had the gospel writers been just making up the stories, they would never have chosen women as the first witnesses. In the first century, in both Greek and Hebrew society, women were not regarded as reliable witnesses. No man would have picked them as the leading characters in the foundational event of Christianity.

It makes sense that the first words from the angel to the two women were, "Don't be afraid." Everything the women thought they knew had been overthrown. They'd just experienced an earthquake that had shaken the land, but the resurrection of Jesus was an earthquake in their souls.

The women left the angel happy but still frightened. That was when Jesus met them. Suddenly they had not just the words of an angel, but also the words of Jesus himself. Any doubts they might have still harbored were gone.

When Jesus came, the women's fear went away for good. Jesus can take away what scares us because he is with us always now. We don't face life alone.

SISTERHOOD

The Lord and his disciples were traveling along and came to [Bethany]. When they got there, a woman named Martha welcomed him into her home. She had a sister named Mary, who sat down in front of the Lord and was listening to what he said. Martha was worried about all that had to be done. Finally, she went to Jesus and said, "Lord, doesn't it bother you that my sister has left me to do all the work by myself? Tell her to come and help me!"

The Lord answered, "Martha, Martha! You are worried and upset about so many things, but only one thing is necessary. Mary has chosen what is best, and it will not be taken away from her."

Luke 10:38–42 CEV

Once we know what Jesus want us to do, we shouldn't worry about what our neighbor might be doing. Our sole concern is to do whatever it is that Jesus asks from us. We can leave our neighbor alone to do whatever Jesus asks of him.

Mary and Martha, with their brother, Lazarus, lived in Bethany, a village on the slope of the Mount of Olives, barely two miles east of Jerusalem. They became good friends with Jesus.

Martha made at least three mistakes in her relationship with her sister. First, if she wanted something of her sister, she should have talked to her sister. Why go to someone else? Second, Jesus may have been a man, but he was not Mary's brother, father, or any other male relative. Based on the prevailing custom of the time, Jesus had no authority over Mary's behavior. And third, Martha was the one who believed that work needed to get done around the house. Well and good, but why should Mary have to have the same concerns as Martha?

The guest was more important than whatever Martha was doing for the guest. Martha forgot that Jesus was more important than the preparations. Mary, in contrast, had chosen to focus her attentions on the guest, rather than on preparations for the guest.

While people might appreciate the meal and a clean place in which to visit, what they really appreciate is the time they spend with us. People matter more than anything else.

WHAT'S UP?

Two of Jesus' followers were walking to the village of Emmaus, seven miles from Jerusalem. As they walked along they were talking about everything that had happened. As they talked and discussed these things, Jesus himself suddenly came and began walking with them. But God kept them from recognizing him.

He asked them, "What are you discussing so intently as you walk along?"

They stopped short, sadness written across their faces. Then one of them, Cleopas, replied, "You must be the only person in Jerusalem who hasn't heard about all the things that have happened there the last few days."

"What things?" Jesus asked.

"The things that happened to Jesus, the man from Nazareth," they said. "He was a prophet who did powerful miracles, and he was a mighty teacher in the eyes of God and all the people. But our leading priests and other religious leaders handed him over to be condemned to death, and they crucified him. We had hoped he was the Messiah who had come to rescue Israel. This all happened three days ago.

"Then some women from our group of his followers were at his tomb early this morning, and they came back with an amazing report. They said his body was missing, and they had seen angels who told them Jesus is alive! Some of our men ran out to see, and sure enough, his body was gone, just as the women had said."

Luke 24:13–24 NLT

✻

*T*here are none so blind as those who will not see. Blindness was a common problem throughout the gospel stories, both literally and figuratively. Cleopas and the other disciple failed to recognize Jesus on the road to Emmaus because the disciples didn't really know Jesus at all—as Jesus' question demonstrated.

Of course, Jesus already knew what they were discussing. Because of his miracles, they believed that Jesus was a prophet and a mighty teacher. They had hoped that he was the Messiah who would rescue Israel from the Romans. When the Romans killed Jesus, those hopes had been dashed. The odd reports that Jesus' body had vanished only added to their confusion.

With their confusion and blindness exposed, Jesus could turn his attention to enlightening them. He spent the journey healing their blindness. When their faulty beliefs had been removed, they suddenly had the clarity of mind to recognize Jesus.

We often don't even know enough to ask the right questions. Without Jesus' question to his disciples, those disciples wouldn't have been able to see Jesus. Only when we realize our eyes are closed can Jesus help us open them.

DAY 163

COULD USE A BITE

That very hour [the two disciples who had seen Jesus on the road to Emmaus] got up and returned to Jerusalem. They found the Eleven and those with them gathered together, who said, "The Lord has certainly been raised, and has appeared to Simon!" Then they began to describe what had happened on the road and how He was made known to them in the breaking of the bread.

And as they were saying these things, He Himself stood among them. He said to them, "Peace to you!" But they were startled and terrified and thought they were seeing a ghost. "Why are you troubled?" He asked them. "And why do doubts arise in your hearts? Look at My hands and My feet, that it is I Myself! Touch Me and see, because a ghost does not have flesh and bones as you can see I have." Having said this, He showed them His hands and feet. But while they still could not believe because of their joy and were amazed, He asked them, "Do you have anything here to eat?" So they gave Him a piece of a broiled fish, and He took it and ate in their presence.

Luke 24:33–43 HCSB

The afterlife is physical. We don't become ghosts or spirits. There had been many witnesses to Jesus' resurrection—the two disciples on the road to Emmaus, several women, and even Peter. But when Jesus appeared suddenly in the room with the disciples, they were terrified and their first thought—their automatic reaction—was to think it was a ghost.

Human beings are funny things. Sometimes we are slow to accept reality.

Jesus told them a ghost does not have "flesh and bones," a standard idiom indicating that he was solid and real, proven when he ate some of their food. The many people whom Jesus had raised from the dead should have prepared his disciples for Jesus' resurrection. The fact that they had already seen him before should have prepared them. But it is hard to take a man's coming back from the dead for granted.

Jesus' resurrection demonstrates that our own resurrection is going to happen. That he was physical and ate food tells us our resurrection bodies will be much like our current bodies. That they recognized him—eventually—tells us that our bodies will be recognizably ours. He still had the scars of his ordeal, but they had been healed. We, too, may bear scars from our lives here, but like Jesus' scars, they will heal.

DOUBTING THOMAS

Thomas, sometimes called the Twin, one of the Twelve, was not with them when Jesus came. The other disciples told him, "We saw the Master."

But he said, "Unless I see the nail holes in his hands, put my finger in the nail holes, and stick my hand in his side, I won't believe it."

Eight days later, his disciples were again in the room. This time Thomas was with them. Jesus came through the locked doors, stood among them, and said, "Peace to you."

Then he focused his attention on Thomas. "Take your finger and examine my hands. Take your hand and stick it in my side. Don't be unbelieving. Believe."

Thomas said, "My Master! My God!"

Jesus said, "So, you believe because you've seen with your own eyes. Even better blessings are in store for those who believe without seeing."

Jesus provided far more God-revealing signs than are written down in this book. These are written down so you will believe that Jesus is the Messiah, the Son of God, and in the act of believing, have real and eternal life in the way he personally revealed it.

John 20:24–31 MSG

ealthy skepticism can easily become pathological. After all the people Jesus had raised back to life, after all Jesus' promises, and after everyone he knew affirmed it, Thomas's skepticism seems somewhat extreme. He saw Jesus die, but he refused to accept his resurrection unless he saw the proof for himself.

When Jesus appeared before Thomas, he said, "Peace be with you!" That was merely the standard Jewish greeting, "Shalom alekem," the equivalent of "Hi!" The simplicity of the greeting and the ordinariness of the situation stand in stark contrast to the significance of the moment for Thomas.

In the midst of the shock of Jesus' suddenly showing up, Jesus offered Thomas exactly what he asked for. Thomas wasn't expecting actually to touch Jesus' nail holes in order to believe. He simply had been expressing his frustration and his need to see Jesus for himself.

When we believe that Jesus lives without the opportunity to see him or touch him, we experience the rewards of faith. We can relax in the face of adversity, even when we don't see a way out, because we have learned to trust God for what is unseen. Blessings and happiness are ours.

SPIRIT BAPTISM

Peter had to explain his actions toward the Gentiles to the other disciples:

"Right then three men who had been sent to me from Caesarea stopped at the house where I was staying. The Spirit told me to have no hesitation about going with them. These six brothers also went with me, and we entered the man's house. He told us how he had seen an angel appear in his house and say, 'Send to Joppa for Simon who is called Peter. He will bring you a message through which you and all your household will be saved.'

"As I began to speak, the Holy Spirit came on them as he had come on us at the beginning. Then I remembered what the Lord had said: 'John baptized with water, but you will be baptized with the Holy Spirit.' So if God gave them the same gift as he gave us, who believed in the Lord Jesus Christ, who was I to think that I could oppose God?"

When they heard this, they had no further objections and praised God, saying, "So then, God has granted even the Gentiles repentance unto life."

Acts 11:11–18 NIV

❋

*T*he universe can change for us overnight. What's old can become unexpectedly new again. When Peter saw Gentiles filled with the Holy Spirit, Peter remembered Jesus' words. And it changed his perception of their meaning. When Jesus left, he promised that he would send the Holy Spirit on the day of pentecost. Peter knew what the Spirit's arrival had done to him. The Spirit's arrival had made him a fearless preacher of the gospel instead of the man who denied Christ three times.

When Peter witnessed the same thing happen to Gentiles that had happened to him at pentecost, he realized Jesus' words meant far more than he had imagined. Peter suddenly realized that his prejudices against Gentiles and his beliefs about the nature of God had been wrong. He realized that as much as Jesus' words predicting the coming Spirit had been directed to him and the other disciples, Jesus' promise was also for the entire human race. Peter suddenly reinterpreted what Jesus had said. He saw Jesus' words in a new light.

Jesus' words had not changed. What Jesus meant by his words had not changed. But what Peter understood about them did. What we think we know of God and the Bible may on occasion turn out to be completely wrong or incomplete. Like Peter, we need to be ready to listen to Jesus all over again.

NOT TO WORRY

Paul left Athens and went to Corinth, where he met Aquila, a Jewish man from Pontus. Not long before this, Aquila had come from Italy with his wife Priscilla, because Emperor Claudius had ordered the Jewish people to leave Rome. Paul went to see Aquila and Priscilla and found out that they were tent makers. Paul was a tent maker too. So he stayed with them, and they worked together.

Every Sabbath, Paul went to the Jewish meeting place. He spoke to Jews and Gentiles and tried to win them over. But after Silas and Timothy came from Macedonia, he spent all his time preaching to the Jews about Jesus the Messiah. Finally, they turned against him and insulted him. So he shook the dust from his clothes and told them, "Whatever happens to you will be your own fault! I am not to blame. From now on I am going to preach to the Gentiles."

Paul then moved into the house of a man named Titius Justus, who worshiped God and lived next door to the meeting place. Crispus was the leader of the meeting place. He and everyone in his family put their faith in the Lord. Many others in Corinth also heard the message, and all the people who had faith in the Lord were baptized.

One night, Paul had a vision, and in it the Lord said, "Don't be afraid to keep on preaching. Don't stop! I am with you, and you won't be harmed. Many people in this city belong to me." Paul stayed on in Corinth for a year and a half, teaching God's message to the people.

Acts 18:1–11 CEV

*I*t's easy to tell someone not to be afraid. It's harder to be free of fear. When Paul reached Corinth, he supported himself by making tents. Paul soon faced serious trouble and opposition in Corinth. Paul was human and, just like any of us, it was easy for him to become discouraged, to wonder whether things would work out, to second-guess himself, or even to think perhaps he'd made a mistake. But Jesus appeared to Paul and told him not to be afraid, and to keep doing what he was doing.

Just as God spoke to Elijah when he despaired that he was the last prophet, so Jesus told Paul that the city of Corinth was filled with many of God's people. Jesus knew that Paul needed the comfort only other people could give.

When we get discouraged, not only should we pray to God, we should also make a point to spend time with other believers so we can share with them our burdens. We'll feel better when we're not by ourselves. Jesus knows we need other people.

PATIENCE AND IMPATIENCE

Love is patient and perseveres, and it always looks out for the best in people and in situations. But we human beings are poor at judging what is actually in our best interests. We become overwhelmed by the gratification of our pleasures today and fail to reckon with whether it's really in our best interests tomorrow. We grow impatient, and so we eat the cake now and regret the weight gain later. Patience is the ability to recognize what is actually in our best interests. Patience comes from realizing that waiting is not a punishment and that what we endure now will benefit us later.

❋

We must be determined to run the race that is ahead of us. We must keep our eyes on Jesus, who leads us and makes our faith complete. He endured the shame of being nailed to a cross, because he knew that later on he would be glad he did. Now he is seated at the right side of God's throne!
Hebrews 12:1–2 CEV

ARE WE THERE YET?

During the Sermon on the Mount, Jesus said:

"I say to you, do not worry about your life, what you will eat or what you will drink; nor about your body, what you will put on. Is not life more than food and the body more than clothing? Look at the birds of the air, for they neither sow nor reap nor gather into barns; yet your heavenly Father feeds them. Are you not of more value than they? Which of you by worrying can add one cubit to his stature?

"So why do you worry about clothing? Consider the lilies of the field, how they grow: they neither toil nor spin; and yet I say to you that even Solomon in all his glory was not arrayed like one of these. Now if God so clothes the grass of the field, which today is, and tomorrow is thrown into the oven, will He not much more clothe you, O you of little faith?

"Therefore do not worry, saying, 'What shall we eat?' or 'What shall we drink?' or 'What shall we wear?' For after all these things the Gentiles seek. For your heavenly Father knows that you need all these things. But seek first the kingdom of God and His righteousness, and all these things shall be added to you. Therefore do not worry about tomorrow, for tomorrow will worry about its own things. Sufficient for the day is its own trouble."

Matthew 6:25–34 NKJV

❋

*S*ome people live their whole lives in the future. The triumphs and tribulations of today slip away without notice, so concerned are they with tomorrow.

God has given us the strength we need for today. When we expend that strength on tomorrow, we wear ourselves out for today. And we have no reason to assume that tomorrow will be a problem. If we have to think about tomorrow, then at least we should have positive thoughts about it.

We can have positive thoughts that God will take care of us. God knows our needs as much as we do. He cares about us as much as we care about ourselves.

We shouldn't keep asking whether we're there yet like some child on a trip with her parents. Instead, we can simply enjoy the time with our parents: we can focus on God with us now and trust God to take care of what we need when we need it. We don't even have to think about it. We can use our minds for more important things, such as enjoying God today, this very moment, in this bright shining instant.

FIRM FOUNDATION

At the end of the Sermon on the Mount, Jesus said:

"Everyone who hears these words of Mine and acts on them, may be compared to a wise man who built his house on the rock. And the rain fell, and the floods came, and the winds blew and slammed against that house; and yet it did not fall, for it had been founded on the rock. Everyone who hears these words of Mine and does not act on them, will be like a foolish man who built his house on the sand. The rain fell, and the floods came, and the winds blew and slammed against that house; and it fell—and great was its fall."

When Jesus had finished these words, the crowds were amazed at His teaching; for He was teaching them as one having authority, and not as their scribes.

When Jesus came down from the mountain, large crowds followed Him. And a leper came to Him and bowed down before Him, and said, "Lord, if You are willing, You can make me clean."

Jesus stretched out His hand and touched him, saying, "I am willing; be cleansed." And immediately his leprosy was cleansed. And Jesus said to him, "See that you tell no one; but go, show yourself to the priest and present the offering that Moses commanded, as a testimony to them."

Matthew 7:24–8:4 NASB

❧

*W*hen Jesus said that we should act on his words, which words did he mean? Jesus had just given the Beatitudes, spoken about what it really meant to love others, and he had warned against worrying. A life could be built on those words.

Jesus spoke as the prophets of old had, "thus says the Lord." He backed up his words with miracles seen only in the lives of those prophets. Just as the prophet Elisha had cleansed Naaman of leprosy, so Jesus cleansed a man of leprosy. Jesus' authority made him stand out from the scribes and other religious leaders.

Horrible things happen in the storms of life—your baby dies, you face terminal illness, you stand on the brink of financial ruin. If you have built your life on the truth of the gospel rather than on the lies of wishful thinking, you will stand secure, knowing that whatever happens, you are not alone and God will see you through. If you can stand to lose everything, if you can give up your life for Christ and not feel cheated, if you believe God loves you even when the world crashes around your ears, you have built your life on Jesus' words. And for those who have not, it is never too late while you're living.

ENCOURAGEMENT

In the vicinity of the Sea of Galilee:

When Jesus had finished giving these instructions to his twelve disciples, he went out to teach and preach in towns throughout the region.

John the Baptist, who was in prison, heard about all the things the Messiah was doing. So he sent his disciples to ask Jesus, "Are you the Messiah we've been expecting, or should we keep looking for someone else?"

Jesus told them, "Go back to John and tell him what you have heard and seen—the blind see, the lame walk, the lepers are cured, the deaf hear, the dead are raised to life, and the Good News is being preached to the poor. And tell him, 'God blesses those who do not turn away because of me.' "

As John's disciples were leaving, Jesus began talking about him to the crowds. "What kind of man did you go into the wilderness to see? Was he a weak reed, swayed by every breath of wind? Or were you expecting to see a man dressed in expensive clothes? No, people with expensive clothes live in palaces. Were you looking for a prophet? Yes, and he is more than a prophet. John is the man to whom the Scriptures refer when they say, 'Look, I am sending my messenger ahead of you, and he will prepare your way before you.' "

Matthew 11:1–9 NLT

✻

*D*id any prophet prosper? Was any prophet widely praised in his own lifetime? John the Baptist proclaimed that Jesus was the Messiah. Jesus proclaimed that John the Baptist was the Elijah everyone had been hoping would usher in the Messiah's coming.

John was in prison awaiting his inevitable execution. Did he begin to wonder if perhaps he'd made a mistake? John was a man, no different from any other human being. It is only natural to imagine that problems might be God's way of telling us that we're going the wrong way.

But Jesus reassured John, as he reassures us. We need to look at the bigger picture, beyond today's trials. Did we hear from God? Is God at work? Did God's people, doing God's work, ever have an easy time of it? Can we tell from trouble or its lack that God is in this trial? John had done precisely what God had wanted him to do. He was in the center of God's will. And yet he was in prison and would soon die for a frivolous reason. God's will is more than the sum of our own experiences, and it is not just about us. We are a part of God's grand design, a grand design that will benefit everyone who calls on the name of the Lord.

DAY 170

ELIJAH'S ROLE

Near the Sea of Galilee, Jesus continued talking about John the Baptist:

"This is he of whom it is written: 'Behold, I send My messenger before Your face, who will prepare Your way before You.'

"Assuredly, I say to you, among those born of women there has not risen one greater than John the Baptist; but he who is least in the kingdom of heaven is greater than he. And from the days of John the Baptist until now the kingdom of heaven suffers violence, and the violent take it by force. For all the prophets and the law prophesied until John. And if you are willing to receive it, he is Elijah who is to come. He who has ears to hear, let him hear!

"But to what shall I liken this generation? It is like children sitting in the marketplaces and calling to their companions, and saying:

'We played the flute for you,
And you did not dance;
We mourned to you,
And you did not lament.'

"For John came neither eating nor drinking, and they say, 'He has a demon.' The Son of Man came eating and drinking, and they say, 'Look, a glutton and a winebibber, a friend of tax collectors and sinners!' But wisdom is justified by her children."

Matthew 11:10–18 NKJV

---

*Y*ou can't satisfy all the people all the time. Elijah was a great prophet who nevertheless faced discouragement. He wondered at times whether what he was doing was really worth it. He ran in terror when his life was threatened. And yet he was God's man in God's time. John the Baptist's role was just like that of Elijah. Elijah stood up to Ahab, and John stood up to Herod. Elijah was taken to heaven in a fiery chariot, and John went to heaven by dying.

The religious leaders rejected John the Baptist as demon-possessed. He lived in the wilderness, ate the worst possible food, and never touched wine. Meanwhile, the religious leaders condemned Jesus as a gluttonous drunk since he spent time in people's homes eating their food and drinking their wine.

Jesus responded to both criticisms by claiming that "wisdom is justified by her children." What does that mean? It means that wisdom—specifically, the wisdom of God—is proved right by its results. If we're of God, Jesus argued, then that will become obvious soon enough.

According to the old cliché, the best vengeance is to live well. The message begun by John and finished by Jesus has lasted for nearly two thousand years. The truth shall overcome. What we do for God will endure forever.

A YEAR WITH JESUS

THISTLES

In a town by the Sea of Galilee:

Jesus dismissed the congregation and went into the house. His disciples came in and said, "Explain to us that story of the thistles in the field."

So he explained. "The farmer who sows the pure seed is the Son of Man. The field is the world, the pure seeds are subjects of the kingdom, the thistles are subjects of the Devil, and the enemy who sows them is the Devil. The harvest is the end of the age, the curtain of history. The harvest hands are angels.

"The picture of thistles pulled up and burned is a scene from the final act. The Son of Man will send his angels, weed out the thistles from his kingdom, pitch them in the trash, and be done with them. They are going to complain to high heaven, but nobody is going to listen. At the same time, ripe, holy lives will mature and adorn the kingdom of their Father.

"Are you listening to this? Really listening?

"God's kingdom is like a treasure hidden in a field for years and then accidentally found by a trespasser. The finder is ecstatic—what a find!—and proceeds to sell everything he owns to raise money and buy that field."

Matthew 13:36–44 MSG

What's the price of your life? The kingdom of God is worth far more. The kingdom of God isn't like any worldly government. Jesus said that it's like wheat seeds among weeds, which are separated only at the harvest. Then he said that it's a hidden treasure buried in a field and the one who finds that treasure happily sells everything he has in exchange for it.

Jesus' two parables, told one after the other, teach us that the kingdom is not just about tomorrow. The kingdom of God is also now. The seeds planted in the field belong to God's kingdom now, not just at the harvest. And the kingdom of God has such a high value that the one who gives up everything for it doesn't feel as if he's given up anything.

We are friends of the king, his brothers and sisters, reigning with him. We lose sight of reality if we forget we belong to God now. We are children of the king, not tomorrow but today, and our treasure is not here but with our king.

MAKING A POINT

In a house in Capernaum, Jesus taught his disciples:

"If your hand or your foot causes you to stumble, cut it off and throw it away; it is better for you to enter life maimed or lame than to have two hands or two feet and to be thrown into the eternal fire. And if your eye causes you to stumble, tear it out and throw it away; it is better for you to enter life with one eye than to have two eyes and to be thrown into the hell of fire.

"Take care that you do not despise one of these little ones; for, I tell you, in heaven their angels continually see the face of my Father in heaven. What do you think? If a shepherd has a hundred sheep, and one of them has gone astray, does he not leave the ninety-nine on the mountains and go in search of the one that went astray? And if he finds it, truly I tell you, he rejoices over it more than over the ninety-nine that never went astray. So it is not the will of your Father in heaven that one of these little ones should be lost."

Matthew 18:8–14 NRSV

*D*oes Jesus want his followers to procure small guillotines to get rid of offensive body parts? Certainly not. Jesus used a literary technique called *hyperbole* —he exaggerated in order to make his point. His point was that if something is standing between us and the kingdom, then we'd do well to get rid of it. Better that than to lose our way or to stumble to our destruction. Which is better, to lose something precious and live, or to keep it and die? Like those trapped in rubble forced to choose amputation or death, life always takes precedence. We are willing to give up anything in order to save our lives.

The question is, do we really understand what is at stake? Do we really understand what we have with the kingdom of God? If so, then it's a no-brainer to seek first God's kingdom and his righteousness. We wouldn't think of eating grass and drinking polluted water when we could be feasting in a fine restaurant on our favorite food. We'd never sleep under a rainy sky on a cold rock when we have a house and a warm bed. In gaining the kingdom of God, we give up nothing but sadness, pain, and death.

A TIME FOR TEARING DOWN

During Jesus' last week in Jerusalem:

Jesus went out and departed from the temple, and His disciples came up to show Him the buildings of the temple. And Jesus said to them, "Do you not see all these things? Assuredly, I say to you, not one stone shall be left here upon another, that shall not be thrown down."

Now as He sat on the Mount of Olives, the disciples came to Him privately, saying, "Tell us, when will these things be? And what will be the sign of Your coming, and of the end of the age?"

And Jesus answered and said to them: "Take heed that no one deceives you. For many will come in My name, saying, 'I am the Christ,' and will deceive many. And you will hear of wars and rumors of wars. See that you are not troubled; for all these things must come to pass, but the end is not yet. For nation will rise against nation, and kingdom against kingdom. And there will be famines, pestilences, and earthquakes in various places. All these are the beginning of sorrows."

Matthew 24:1–8 NKJV

*T*he world always has trouble. The disciples asked Jesus three questions. First, they wanted to know what Jesus meant by the destruction of the temple. Second, they asked about the sign of his "coming." Finally, they asked about the end of the age.

The disciples weren't thinking about the second coming of Jesus. When they asked about his "coming," they were wondering when he'd come into his kingdom and take the throne of David. When they wondered about the end of the age, they wanted to know when the age of Roman domination over Israel would end.

The disciples were a bit puzzled by Jesus' answers. Jesus began by explaining about his "coming." He warned of false messiahs offering false hope. He warned that the disasters of war and earthquake were merely the beginning of sorrows.

Since Jesus spoke those words to his disciples in the last week before his crucifixion, the pattern of the world he described has continued without end. The endless wars and endless natural disasters have merely been the beginning of our sorrows. Life has problems in it. Such ordinary problems—even big things like wars and earthquakes—do not mean that God is about to end the world. Life continues despite disasters, and God is in control. Jesus told us not to be troubled by any of it.

GREAT TRIBULATION

Near the temple in Jerusalem, Jesus said:

"Staying with it—that's what God requires. Stay with it to the end. You won't be sorry, and you'll be saved. All during this time, the good news— the Message of the kingdom—will be preached all over the world, a witness staked out in every country. And then the end will come.

"But be ready to run for it when you see the monster of desecration set up in the Temple sanctuary. The prophet Daniel described this. If you've read Daniel, you'll know what I'm talking about. If you're living in Judea at the time, run for the hills; if you're working in the yard, don't return to the house to get anything; if you're out in the field, don't go back and get your coat. Pregnant and nursing mothers will have it especially hard. Hope and pray this won't happen during the winter or on a Sabbath.

"This is going to be trouble on a scale beyond what the world has ever seen, or will see again. If these days of trouble were left to run their course, nobody would make it. But on account of God's chosen people, the trouble will be cut short."

Matthew 24:13–22 MSG

*W*inston Churchill once gave an address that included this well-known phrase: "Never give in." That thought had kept him going during the darkest days of the Second World War. Jesus offered similar encouragement to his people facing even darker times. The destruction of Jerusalem and its temple by the Romans was one of the major turning points in history.

In AD 66, the Jewish people revolted against Rome, established a revolutionary government, and kicked the Romans out of Jerusalem. In AD 70, the Romans returned in force. When the Roman army arrived in Jerusalem bearing the banners and standards of Caesar—idols of the emperor—Christians made the connection to Daniel's prophecy about a "monster of desecration." Because Jesus warned his followers to flee, all the Christians ran away from Jerusalem.

Thankfully, the events Jesus foretold did not happen in the winter, and the Romans did not attack on a Sabbath. But thousands of people were slaughtered, and those who survived were scattered. Persecutions arose against Christians with increasing ferocity. But the church grew in the face of that persecution; so much so that within a couple of hundred years, Christianity became the official religion of the Roman Empire that had once persecuted it. Jesus had told his followers to never give up, and in the end they triumphed. It's the same for us today. Sticking with it, regardless of what we face, is all Jesus asks.

VULTURES

Beside the temple during the week before Passover, Jesus warned his disciples:

"Then if anyone says to you, 'Look, here is the Christ!' or 'There!' do not believe it. For false christs and false prophets will rise and show great signs and wonders to deceive, if possible, even the elect. See, I have told you beforehand.

"Therefore if they say to you, 'Look, He is in the desert!' do not go out; or 'Look, He is in the inner rooms!' do not believe it. For as the lightning comes from the east and flashes to the west, so also will the coming of the Son of Man be. For wherever the carcass is, there the eagles will be gathered together.

"Immediately after the tribulation of those days the sun will be darkened, and the moon will not give its light; the stars will fall from heaven, and the powers of the heavens will be shaken."

Matthew 24:23–29 NKJV

*W*hen Jesus comes into his kingdom, it will be as obvious as a lightning flash. No one will have to call us or whisper in our ears. Just as vultures circling a carcass in a field are visible for miles, it will be just as apparent when Jesus comes.

Jesus' phrases about the sun and the moon being darkened were taken from the words of the prophets in the Old Testament who had used them to describe the destruction of God's enemies. When a city was attacked and burned, the rising smoke of its destruction obscured the sky, blackening sun and moon. Certainly, those who saw Jerusalem burned by the Romans witnessed such changes in the sky.

Ever since the time of Christ, many false messiahs and false prophets have arisen to offer people earthly solutions to their earthly problems. For instance, between AD 132 and 136, more than sixty years after the destruction of Jerusalem, a man named Bar Kokhba was proclaimed the messiah by the religious establishment, and he led a second Jewish revolt against the Roman Empire. Like the one that had caused the temple's destruction, this revolt, too, was crushed. Eventually, every false prophet, every false messiah dies and comes to ruin.

We should never look to humans for our salvation. We must never imagine that some individual has a closer relationship to God than we do. We must not give in to the lie that some human being has solutions to all the problems in our personal lives or all the problems in the world at large.

SECOND COMING

Two days before the Last Supper, Jesus said:

"The sign of the Son of Man will appear in heaven, and then all the tribes of the earth will mourn, and they will see the Son of Man coming on the clouds of heaven with power and great glory. And He will send His angels with a great sound of a trumpet, and they will gather together His elect from the four winds, from one end of heaven to the other.

"Now learn this parable from the fig tree: When its branch has already become tender and puts forth leaves, you know that summer is near. So you also, when you see all these things, know that it is near—at the doors! Assuredly, I say to you, this generation will by no means pass away till all these things take place. Heaven and earth will pass away, but My words will by no means pass away."

Matthew 24:30–35 NKJV

Jesus didn't tell his disciples everything they wanted to know, because what they wanted to know more about sometimes wasn't reality. They wanted to know about a physical kingdom when Jesus was speaking about a spiritual one. For the disciples who were looking for Jesus to establish his rule in Jerusalem as Israel's rightful king, what Jesus described about his coming would have seemed to them exactly what they were expecting. When Jesus spoke about "the tribes of the earth," they thought he meant that he at last was going to raise an army and defeat the Romans. When Jesus said that the angels would gather the elect, his disciples thought all the Jewish people were going to be brought back to Israel from wherever they had been scattered across the world. And the timeframe they heard from Jesus was just what they had hoped—it would all happen within their lifetimes.

Of course, their interpretation of what Jesus was saying wasn't quite right. Their misunderstanding illustrates the problem we sometimes face in interpreting anything that someone says. Sometimes we miss the context, and sometimes we impose our own expectations upon their words, much as a person with a crush can misinterpret the actions and statements of the one he or she is attracted to.

So what did Jesus mean? Within Christianity, there are nearly as many interpretations as there are churches. When it comes to figuring out the future, we should consider the difficulty that the disciples had understanding what Jesus was doing during his first appearance on earth. That should serve as a warning that when it comes to Jesus' second coming, there is a lot left for us to learn.

LOTS TO DO

In Capernaum:

After Jesus left the synagogue with James and John, they went to Simon and Andrew's home. Now Simon's mother-in-law was sick in bed with a high fever. They told Jesus about her right away. So he went to her bedside, took her by the hand, and helped her sit up. Then the fever left her, and she prepared a meal for them.

That evening after sunset, many sick and demon-possessed people were brought to Jesus. The whole town gathered at the door to watch. So Jesus healed many people who were sick with various diseases, and he cast out many demons. But because the demons knew who he was, he did not allow them to speak.

Before daybreak the next morning, Jesus got up and went out to an isolated place to pray. Later Simon and the others went out to find him. When they found him, they said, "Everyone is looking for you."

But Jesus replied, "We must go on to other towns as well, and I will preach to them, too. That is why I came." So he traveled throughout the region of Galilee, preaching in the synagogues and casting out demons.

Mark 1:29–39 NLT

*J*esus made people feel wonderful. Look at Peter's mother-in-law in Capernaum. Jesus simply went to where she was, took her by the hand, and helped her sit up—and she wasn't sick anymore. No one had asked for her healing. Not even she had made the request. But she was healed nevertheless. God does not wait to take care of us only when we ask, which is good, since we may not always know what we need.

After Peter's mother-in-law was healed, she prepared a meal for Jesus and the disciples. That may seem an odd response to being healed, but it reveals just how thoroughly healed she was. She was able to do once again what she normally did—care for those around her. It is akin to the lame man's not only walking, but also picking up his mat and carrying it. It demonstrated the completeness of the healing.

Capernaum was a small town. Soon, every sick person, everyone who knew a sick person, and everyone who just wanted to watch descended upon the house where Jesus was. He was kept busy for hours. When Jesus changes our lives, he does more than just transform *our* lives. His work in us soon spreads to everyone we know. Jesus' work in a life can never stay a secret.

SURPRISING OBEDIENCE

On the shore of the Sea of Galilee:

On that day, when evening had come, [Jesus] told [his disciples], "Let's cross over to the other side of the lake." So they left the crowd and took Him along since He was already in the boat. And other boats were with Him. A fierce windstorm arose, and the waves were breaking over the boat, so that the boat was already being swamped. But He was in the stern, sleeping on the cushion. So they woke Him up and said to Him, "Teacher! Don't you care that we're going to die?"

He got up, rebuked the wind, and said to the sea, "Silence! Be still!" The wind ceased, and there was a great calm. Then He said to them, "Why are you fearful? Do you still have no faith?"

And they were terrified and asked one another, "Who then is this? Even the wind and the sea obey Him!"

Mark 4:35–41 HCSB

The disciples went from being afraid of a storm to being afraid of Jesus. After leaving a crowd of people, Jesus and his disciples got in a boat and headed across the Sea of Galilee. The Sea of Galilee is a harp-shaped, freshwater lake in the northern part of Israel about seven hundred feet below sea level. Thirteen miles long, it is surrounded by hills more than a thousand feet high. Because of them, abrupt temperature shifts occur, leading to sudden and violent storms on the lake. Just such a storm blew up when Jesus and his disciples were attempting to cross the water.

The storm scared the disciples. They were experienced fishermen who had spent their lives on the lake, and they knew that many men had perished in its deep waters. But when they awakened Jesus, rather than joining their panic, he simply made the storm stop.

Where they had been terrified of the storm, they suddenly became terrified by Jesus. The disciples knew from the Old Testament that only the Creator of the world had the ability to start and stop storms. For the disciples, it was their first realization that Jesus was more than human. Jesus wondered at their lack of faith. The disciples realized with his spectacular miracle that Jesus had good reason for his wondering. Faith comes from understanding and knowing in whom or in what we are putting our faith. Fear was the beginning of such knowledge for Jesus' disciples. The longer they were with Jesus, the more their faith would grow. The same will happen to us too.

DOGS

Jesus set out for the vicinity of Tyre. He entered a house there where he didn't think he would be found, but he couldn't escape notice. He was barely inside when a woman who had a disturbed daughter heard where he was. She came and knelt at his feet, begging for help. The woman was Greek, Syro-Phoenician by birth. She asked him to cure her daughter.

He said, "Stand in line and take your turn. The children get fed first. If there's any left over, the dogs get it."

She said, "Of course, Master. But don't dogs under the table get scraps dropped by the children?"

Jesus was impressed. "You're right! On your way! Your daughter is no longer disturbed. The demonic affliction is gone." She went home and found her daughter relaxed on the bed, the torment gone for good.

Mark 7:24–30 MSG

❋

*T*here was no pattern to how Jesus relieved people of demon possession. He gave no special ritual to be performed in expelling a demon. The only thing that all the demon expulsions of the New Testament have in common is the involvement of Jesus. The method of expelling demons, however, varied from situation to situation. Sometimes we see Jesus talking to the demon, getting its name. Other times we see him rebuking the demon. But with the Greek woman from Tyre, Jesus never even saw the little girl who was possessed, nor did he talk to the demon. All his attention was directed toward the little girl's mother, with whom he had a discussion about whether he should even bother to help her at all.

He made no gestures; he uttered no words of rebuke to the demon. He simply granted the mother's request. Jesus told her that the demon was gone and that her daughter was fine.

God is not limited in how he solves the problems facing people. He can do it with a word or with no words. The reality is that Jesus can do whatever he wants to do. He isn't limited by his location or by his proximity to the problem. There is no formula for solving the problems. Jesus has no need to wait for us to utter a certain phrase before he acts. He has no need for us to get to a special place or to do or not do a special thing. When Jesus agrees—or more accurately, when we agree with Jesus—then he will simply do what he wills.

GOODNESS GRACIOUS

Jesus was east of the Jordan River, intending to go to Jerusalem:

As Jesus started on his way, a man ran up to him and fell on his knees before him. "Good teacher," he asked, "what must I do to inherit eternal life?"

"Why do you call me good?" Jesus answered. "No one is good—except God alone. You know the commandments: 'Do not murder, do not commit adultery, do not steal, do not give false testimony, do not defraud, honor your father and mother.'"

"Teacher," he declared, "all these I have kept since I was a boy."

Jesus looked at him and loved him. "One thing you lack," he said. "Go, sell everything you have and give to the poor, and you will have treasure in heaven. Then come, follow me."

At this the man's face fell. He went away sad, because he had great wealth.

Jesus looked around and said to his disciples, "How hard it is for the rich to enter the kingdom of God!"

The disciples were amazed at his words. But Jesus said again, "Children, how hard it is?? to enter the kingdom of God! It is easier for a camel to go through the eye of a needle than for a rich man to enter the kingdom of God."

The disciples were even more amazed, and said to each other, "Who then can be saved?"

Jesus looked at them and said, "With man this is impossible, but not with God; all things are possible with God."

Mark 10:17–27 NIV

*J*esus sometimes made it easy for some people. But for others, he made it impossible.

A man approached Jesus one day and wanted to know how he could live forever. Jesus told him God had given commandments, and he listed six out of the ten, which the man affirmed that he had kept. Then Jesus asked him to sell everything he had and give to the poor.

What Jesus showed the man was that there was nothing he could do to gain eternal life. Jesus found the one thing to ask that the man couldn't bring himself to do.

That's the critical surprise of the story—that young man wasn't alone. None of us can fulfill all the commandments. None of us can do anything to gain everlasting life. The young man asked what he could do. Jesus gave him an answer he didn't want, that no one wants. We can do nothing to gain eternal life.

What is impossible for human beings is possible for God. Eternal life belongs to us not because of what we do but because of what Jesus did on the cross.

PERSISTENCE OF VISION

Jesus and his disciples went to Jericho. And as they were leaving, they were followed by a large crowd. A blind beggar by the name of Bartimaeus son of Timaeus was sitting beside the road. When he heard that it was Jesus from Nazareth, he shouted, "Jesus, Son of David, have pity on me!" Many people told the man to stop, but he shouted even louder, "Son of David, have pity on me!"

Jesus stopped and said, "Call him over!"

They called out to the blind man and said, "Don't be afraid! Come on! He is calling for you." The man threw off his coat as he jumped up and ran to Jesus.

Jesus asked, "What do you want me to do for you?"

The blind man answered, "Master, I want to see!"

Jesus told him, "You may go. Your eyes are healed because of your faith."

Right away the man could see, and he went down the road with Jesus.

Mark 10:46–52 CEV

꽃

*I*t's easier to heal a blind man than to transform a heart. But Jesus did both. Jericho served as a gateway to Jerusalem. On its outskirts was a blind man known as Bartimaeus. When he learned that Jesus was coming by, he started doing what he always did with everyone who came by. He lifted his voice and begged, mouthing the words that such a beggar would always mouth: "Have pity on me."

By addressing Jesus as "son of David," the blind man was acknowledging that Jesus was the Messiah and the rightful King of Israel. When Jesus asked the beggar what he wanted, Jesus already knew what it was. But he wanted him to say aloud what was hidden in his heart.

Bartimaeus knew that Jesus could give him something more than mere coins. So he asked Jesus for what he knew he could spare. Bartimaeus's reaction to gaining his sight was to go "down the road" with Jesus. The Greek word implies more than simply walking a ways with Jesus. The word is used of those who become disciples. It meant that from that moment on, Bartimaeus became one of Jesus' followers. Bartimaeus was with Jesus for the rest of his life.

Today, we who claim Jesus as our Savior go "down the road" with him. We are rightfully amazed when a blind man can see. But we should be even more amazed when a man decides to become a follower of Jesus, because spiritual blindness is the harder thing to cure.

POOR AND HAPPY

Near the Sea of Galilee, Jesus had just chosen his twelve apostles:

When they came down from the mountain, the disciples stood with Jesus on a large, level area, surrounded by many of his followers and by the crowds. There were people from all over Judea and from Jerusalem and from as far north as the seacoasts of Tyre and Sidon. They had come to hear him and to be healed of their diseases; and those troubled by evil spirits were healed. Everyone tried to touch him, because healing power went out from him, and he healed everyone.

Then Jesus turned to his disciples and said,

"God blesses you who are poor, for the Kingdom of God is yours. God blesses you who are hungry now, for you will be satisfied. God blesses you who weep now, for in due time you will laugh.

"What blessings await you when people hate you and exclude you and mock you and curse you as evil because you follow the Son of Man. When that happens, be happy! Yes, leap for joy! For a great reward awaits you in heaven. And remember, their ancestors treated the ancient prophets that same way."

Luke 6:17–23 NLT

❊

*J*esus often said things contrary to common sense. The last people in the world anyone might think of as blessed were the very people Jesus addressed. The word translated as *blessed* simply means "happy." Jesus said that the poor—those who were hungry and weeping—were happy, which was certainly not the obvious conclusion.

Jesus said such people were happy because they were the ones closest to God. They were the ones God paid the most attention to, and they were the ones to whom the kingdom of God belonged.

Jesus spoke to crowds everywhere he went, and he taught much the same thing to everyone. The words that we find in the Sermon on the Mount were reused in other times and at other places. In Luke's gospel, the words that were part of that Sermon on the Mount in the other gospels were repeated on a plain near the shores of the Sea of Galilee.

In a world that, like ours, defined happiness by how much wealth you had, how big your house was, and how much power you wielded, Jesus' words were a startling breath of fresh air. The kingdom of God was something the poor in spirit possessed by virtue of their relationship with God. We can experience God's kingdom now, thanks to God's presence in our lives. When we have God, Jesus said, we have everything we need.

HAVING EARS TO HEAR

In the region of Galilee:

[Jesus] was traveling from one town and village to another, preaching and telling the good news of the kingdom of God. The Twelve were with Him, and also some women who had been healed of evil spirits and sicknesses: Mary, called Magdalene (seven demons had come out of her); Joanna the wife of Chuza, Herod's steward; Susanna; and many others who were supporting them from their possessions.

As a large crowd was gathering, and people were flocking to Him from every town, He said in a parable: "A sower went out to sow his seed. As he was sowing, some fell along the path; it was trampled on, and the birds of the sky ate it up. Other seed fell on the rock; when it sprang up, it withered, since it lacked moisture. Other seed fell among thorns; the thorns sprang up with it and choked it. Still other seed fell on good ground; when it sprang up, it produced a crop: 100 times what was sown." As He said this, He called out, "Anyone who has ears to hear should listen!"

Luke 8:1–8 HCSB

When you think you're doomed, it's good news to find out you're not. When a farmer sowed grain, the overwhelming majority of that grain sprang up and grew. Little seed was wasted. No farmer stood on a road when he scattered his seeds. He always stood in his plowed field. Only the smallest handful of grain ever missed the rich dirt, was snatched away by birds, or fell to thorns.

The seeds Jesus scattered—his words about the kingdom—were mostly effective. Jesus was telling those listening to him that the kingdom would grow and become abundant. Crop yields of a hundred times what was sown were stupendous. Agronomists consider a yield of three grains of wheat for each grain planted the minimum necessary to sustain human life. To have a hundred-fold increase—a hundred grains for each planted—meant no more worry about anything for the farmer because he had enough to sustain himself and his family —and an abundance to sell on the open market.

Famine was always a fear in the ancient world. So Jesus' story would have resonated strongly with those who heard him. Jesus wanted us to know that God's kingdom will grow, and that it will grow spectacularly well. Evangelism—sharing our faith with those around us—yields mostly rich rewards.

THE KINGDOM CAN'T WAIT

When it came close to the time for his Ascension, [Jesus] gathered up his courage and steeled himself for the journey to Jerusalem. He sent messengers on ahead. They came to a Samaritan village to make arrangements for his hospitality. But when the Samaritans learned that his destination was Jerusalem, they refused hospitality. When the disciples James and John learned of it, they said, "Master, do you want us to call a bolt of lightning down out of the sky and incinerate them?"

Jesus turned on them: "Of course not!" And they traveled on to another village.

On the road someone asked if he could go along. "I'll go with you, wherever," he said.

Jesus was curt: "Are you ready to rough it? We're not staying in the best inns, you know."

Jesus said to another, "Follow me."

He said, "Certainly, but first excuse me for a couple of days, please. I have to make arrangements for my father's funeral."

Jesus refused. "First things first. Your business is life, not death. And life is urgent: Announce God's kingdom!"

Then another said, "I'm ready to follow you, Master, but first excuse me while I get things straightened out at home."

Jesus said, "No procrastination. No backward looks. You can't put God's kingdom off till tomorrow. Seize the day."

Luke 9:51–62 MSG

When the Samaritans learned Jesus was on his way to Jerusalem, they became inhospitable. A big argument between Jews and Samaritans was over the question of where to worship God. Jews insisted that Jerusalem was the only right place, while the Samaritans believed that only Mount Gerazim would do.

James and John suggested Jesus simply wipe the Samaritans from the earth. They didn't like Samaritans anyway. They believed they were headed to Jerusalem so Jesus could lead armies against the enemies of God. They wondered why they couldn't get rid of those troublesome, rude Samaritans.

Jesus told them no. They didn't understand Jesus' purpose at all, any more than the people along the way who indicated a willingness to join Jesus but wanted to wait awhile. Those who were giving Jesus excuses were doing so because they wanted to wait to see how things turned out. Was he really the Messiah? Would he really bring in the kingdom? They did not understand Jesus' real purpose any more than John and James did.

The Christian message is called "good news" for a reason. Jesus didn't come to raise armies; he came to bring the kingdom of God to us. He offers us far more than any earthly kingdom. He offers us eternity.

DON'T WORRY, BE HAPPY

Jesus said to his disciples: "Therefore I tell you, do not worry about your life, what you will eat; or about your body, what you will wear. Life is more than food, and the body more than clothes. Consider the ravens: They do not sow or reap, they have no storeroom or barn; yet God feeds them. And how much more valuable you are than birds! Who of you by worrying can add a single hour to his life? Since you cannot do this very little thing, why do you worry about the rest?

"Consider how the lilies grow. They do not labor or spin. Yet I tell you, not even Solomon in all his splendor was dressed like one of these. If that is how God clothes the grass of the field, which is here today, and tomorrow is thrown into the fire, how much more will he clothe you, O you of little faith! And do not set your heart on what you will eat or drink; do not worry about it. For the pagan world runs after all such things, and your Father knows that you need them. But seek his kingdom, and these things will be given to you as well."

Luke 12:22–31 NIV

❧

*L*ife has all sorts of problems. Jesus never said it didn't. But during a sermon by the Sea of Galilee, Jesus told us not to worry. His prohibition on worry was practical. Do birds worry? Do flowers worry? The world is full of what they need, and God takes care of them. Birds weren't particularly valuable. In the sacrificial system, the sort of animal to be sacrificed depended upon a person's wealth. Birds were what the poorest people presented as for their sin offerings. Birds were common. Like flowers, they were everywhere.

Jesus' point was simple: If God takes care of birds and flowers, what do we have to worry about? Do we think we matter less to God than birds and flowers? God knows what we need, and he'll take care of it. We should find something else for our brains to do. We have no reason to focus on the mundane things of day-to-day life. Food and clothing are givens, like a sunrise or the wind in Chicago. We need to find something else to think about, like the kingdom of God. If we focus our energies on God, we'll be happier, and that's more productive. Worrying never did anyone a bit of good or changed anything.

HURRY UP AND WAIT

Near Jerusalem for the last time, Jesus reassured his disciples:

"Do not be afraid, little flock, for it is your Father's good pleasure to give you the kingdom. Sell your possessions, and give alms. Make purses for yourselves that do not wear out, an unfailing treasure in heaven, where no thief comes near and no moth destroys. For where your treasure is, there your heart will be also.

"Be dressed for action and have your lamps lit; be like those who are waiting for their master to return from the wedding banquet, so that they may open the door for him as soon as he comes and knocks. Blessed are those slaves whom the master finds alert when he comes; truly I tell you, he will fasten his belt and have them sit down to eat, and he will come and serve them. If he comes during the middle of the night, or near dawn, and finds them so, blessed are those slaves.

"But know this: if the owner of the house had known at what hour the thief was coming, he would not have let his house be broken into. You also must be ready, for the Son of Man is coming at an unexpected hour."

Luke 12:32–40 NRSV

Jesus promised his disciples that he would come unexpectedly. To illustrate what he meant, he compared his future arrival to that of Jewish wedding customs of the time. The groom did not tell his bride when he would show up to get her. It was a surprise and part of the fun of getting married. So the bride, her family, the guests, and everyone else involved had to simply wait in anticipation and make certain that they were always ready. Jesus' story then takes an odd turn. In a real banquet, the servants were the ones who would serve their master. But Jesus had the master serving the servants, a hint about the nature of Jesus' kingdom.

To drive the point home in a way that perhaps is clearer for modern readers of the Bible, Jesus said his arrival would also be like the coming of a thief. No one knows about a burglary before it happens. That his disciples should await his coming prepared, no matter how long the delay, was so important that Jesus explained it to them in more than one way.

We should live our lives each day in anticipation of Jesus' coming. We never know when he may come for us, whether in the clouds or in our dying breath. Each day should be lived to the fullest, with hopeful expectation.

WISDOM

Shortly before Passover, near Jerusalem, Jesus asked his disciples:

"Who are faithful and wise servants? Who are the ones the master will put in charge of giving the other servants their food supplies at the proper time? Servants are fortunate if their master comes and finds them doing their job. A servant who is always faithful will surely be put in charge of everything the master owns.

"But suppose one of the servants thinks that the master won't return until late. Suppose that servant starts beating all the other servants and eats and drinks and gets drunk. If that happens, the master will come on a day and at a time when the servant least expects him. That servant will then be punished and thrown out with the servants who cannot be trusted.

"If servants are not ready or willing to do what their master wants them to do, they will be beaten hard. But servants who don't know what their master wants them to do will not be beaten so hard for doing wrong. If God has been generous with you, he will expect you to serve him well. But if he has been more than generous, he will expect you to serve him even better."

Luke 12:42–48 CEV

🌼

*T*he Pharisees and religious leaders fancied themselves in the service of God. In fact, however, they were mostly just serving themselves. Jesus warned his disciples about them repeatedly, in many different ways and at many different times. The parable about a bad servant was one such warning.

The purpose of servants was to do the jobs their master needed to have done but preferred not to do. Ideally, the master shouldn't have to think about it. The servants should just do their jobs. In our modern world, our servants are things like our cars, the electricity in our homes, or the plumbing. We don't think about our cars unless they break down. We flick a switch and expect the light to come on. We turn a knob and expect the water to be hot in the shower. We become angry when any of our modern servants fail us.

Jesus' point about the parable of the servants that he gave his disciples was that he didn't want his disciples to turn out as the Pharisees had. He wanted them to be different. He wanted them to serve God and one another. That's what Jesus wants of us too.

KEEP ON KEEPING ON

Jesus told them a story showing that it was necessary for them to pray consistently and never quit. He said, "There was once a judge in some city who never gave God a thought and cared nothing for people. A widow in that city kept after him: 'My rights are being violated. Protect me!'

"He never gave her the time of day. But after this went on and on he said to himself, 'I care nothing what God thinks, even less what people think. But because this widow won't quit badgering me, I'd better do something and see that she gets justice—otherwise I'm going to end up beaten black-and-blue by her pounding.'"

Then the Master said, "Do you hear what that judge, corrupt as he is, is saying? So what makes you think God won't step in and work justice for his chosen people, who continue to cry out for help? Won't he stick up for them? I assure you, he will. He will not drag his feet. But how much of that kind of persistent faith will the Son of Man find on the earth when he returns?"

Luke 18:1–8 MSG

People in general are impatient. Jesus used the parable of the unjust judge to make the point that praying to God is never a waste of time. Even a horrible judge who doesn't properly do his job will do it if he is nagged enough. God, who is not a negligent judge, will certainly bring justice for his chosen people. Jesus was making a point about God. God isn't lazy, he isn't too busy, and he isn't distracted. He isn't dragging his feet. He is doing what needs to be done as quickly as it needs to be done.

Some have looked at the Holocaust and wondered where God was. The question would be a reasonable one had the Germans won the war. But they didn't. They lost. So where was God? He was using the Allied nations to fight the Axis powers. After Germany's defeat, he divided it and used the Soviets to enslave half of it for a generation. As a result of what the Jewish people suffered, the world decided to restore Israel as a nation. And it all happened considerably faster than the four hundred years of slavery endured by the Israelites in Egypt before God liberated them.

God does take care of his people. He does bring justice to them. And he'll do it as quickly as possible. Count on it.

KILL THEM

In Jericho, Jesus told a parable to his disciples:

"Another [servant] came, saying, 'Master, here is your mina, which I have kept put away in a handkerchief. For I feared you, because you are an austere man. You collect what you did not deposit, and reap what you did not sow.' And he said to him, 'Out of your own mouth I will judge you, you wicked servant. You knew that I was an austere man, collecting what I did not deposit and reaping what I did not sow. Why then did you not put my money in the bank, that at my coming I might have collected it with interest?'

"And he said to those who stood by, 'Take the mina from him, and give it to him who has ten minas.' (But they said to him, 'Master, he has ten minas.') 'For I say to you, that to everyone who has will be given; and from him who does not have, even what he has will be taken away from him. But bring here those enemies of mine, who did not want me to reign over them, and slay them before me.'"

Luke 19:20–27 NKJV

※

*J*esus and his disciples were on their way to Jerusalem. His disciples thought Jesus was about to become the new king over Israel. The purpose of Jesus' parable was to correct their erroneous thought.

Jesus told a parable about a man of noble birth who went to a distant country to have himself appointed king and then to return. Though most of the man's servants were wise, one made poor choices and lost everything as a result, joining the fate of those who had rejected him as their king. Jesus' story might have reminded his disciples about Herod and his descendants, who ruled the people of Israel because Rome had given the throne to them. After Herod the Great died in 4 BC, for instance, his son Archelaus went to Rome to have his father's will confirmed so he could become king in his place. A group of Jewish leaders followed him to Rome to protest his appointment.

Jesus knew Judas would betray him, the religion leadership of Israel would reject him, and he would die at the hands of the Romans. Judas would lose his place, and the religious leaders would lose their place when Jerusalem and the temple were destroyed within a generation. Meanwhile, Jesus' disciples would be left behind to work without him. He wanted them—and us—to work in confidence, knowing that he will come back again. And when he finally returns, he'll bring us our reward.

CAN'T KEEP QUIET

As soon as [Jesus] was approaching, near the descent of the Mount of Olives, the whole crowd of the disciples began to praise God joyfully with a loud voice for all the miracles which they had seen, shouting:

"Blessed is the King who comes in the name of the Lord; Peace in heaven and glory in the highest!"

Some of the Pharisees in the crowd said to Him, "Teacher, rebuke Your disciples."

But Jesus answered, "I tell you, if these become silent, the stones will cry out!"

When He approached Jerusalem, He saw the city and wept over it, saying, "If you had known in this day, even you, the things which make for peace! But now they have been hidden from your eyes. For the days will come upon you when your enemies will throw up a barricade against you, and surround you and hem you in on every side, and they will level you to the ground and your children within you, and they will not leave in you one stone upon another, because you did not recognize the time of your visitation."

Luke 19:37–44 NASB

The Pharisees were like the grumpy neighbor who always complains that the music is too loud. They did not believe Jesus was the Messiah, and they were upset because Jesus was allowing his followers to proclaim that he was.

The Pharisees feared that Jesus was leading the people of Israel astray, filling them with false hope, and starting a rebellion that would bring the Romans to destroy the Jewish people. But within forty years, the Pharisees and other religious leaders would lead that rebellion themselves, all because they failed to recognize when God had actually come to live with them. They refused to see that the kingdom of God had actually arrived. The Pharisees were looking for God and the kingdom in all the wrong places and in all the wrong ways. If they had known, if they had accepted God's kingdom, they wouldn't have kept striving for a physical, earthly kingdom that would lead to their city's destruction not many years later. For that reason, Jesus wept over Jerusalem.

God wants to bless us. In fact, he has blessed us. But it is easy to become so absorbed by our own expectations and desires that we completely miss seeing his blessing by forgetting the joys of what we take for granted. Each day we should consider how blessed we really are.

WHERE YOUR HEART IS

Jesus was teaching his followers in the temple by telling them a parable:

"Look at the fig tree and all the trees; as soon as they sprout leaves you can see for yourselves and know that summer is already near. So also, when you see these things taking place, you know that the kingdom of God is near. Truly I tell you, this generation will not pass away until all things have taken place. Heaven and earth will pass away, but my words will not pass away.

"Be on guard so that your hearts are not weighed down with dissipation and drunkenness and the worries of this life, and that day does not catch you unexpectedly, like a trap. For it will come upon all who live on the face of the whole earth. Be alert at all times, praying that you may have the strength to escape all these things that will take place, and to stand before the Son of Man."

Every day he was teaching in the temple, and at night he would go out and spend the night on the Mount of Olives, as it was called. And all the people would get up early in the morning to listen to him in the temple.

Luke 21:29–37 NRSV

A dog recognizes the sound of his owner's footsteps on the front porch. His tail reacts immediately, long before the front door actually opens. Jesus used similar images so that his disciples would understand that the kingdom of God was near. Not long before he was crucified, Jesus announced to his disciples that God's kingdom would arrive before their generation had passed away.

Where is the kingdom of God that Jesus promised his disciples? Was Jesus wrong? Are we misunderstanding something? Repeatedly, Jesus told his disciples that the kingdom of God was near. Repeatedly, he told parables to describe what the kingdom of God was like. Never once did his description sound like a political entity.

Like the disciples, we tend to misunderstand what the kingdom of God is. The kingdom is about God taking up residence and ruling in the hearts of his people. With the coming of God's Holy Spirit at pentecost, and then with the destruction of the Jerusalem temple, the church became something separate from the old earthly nation of Israel. The church became a kingdom of priests, worshipping God in Spirit and truth. Our worship was no longer—and could never again—be conducted in an earthly temple. The kingdom of God began when Jesus came, and it has been expanding ever since. It will continue to do so until Jesus returns as he promised. Even now, we are citizens of God's kingdom and serve as its ambassadors to a needy world.

THE DEAD WILL RISE

Jesus was in Jerusalem with his disciples for a religious festival, and he addressed the religious leaders who were criticizing him for healing on the Sabbath:

"It's urgent that you listen carefully to this: Anyone here who believes what I am saying right now and aligns himself with the Father, who has in fact put me in charge, has at this very moment the real, lasting life and is no longer condemned to be an outsider. This person has taken a giant step from the world of the dead to the world of the living.

"It's urgent that you get this right: The time has arrived—I mean right now!—when dead men and women will hear the voice of the Son of God and, hearing, will come alive. Just as the Father has life in himself, he has conferred on the Son life in himself. And he has given him the authority, simply because he is the Son of Man, to decide and carry out matters of Judgment.

"Don't act so surprised at all this. The time is coming when everyone dead and buried will hear his voice. Those who have lived the right way will walk out into a resurrection Life; those who have lived the wrong way, into a resurrection Judgment.

"I can't do a solitary thing on my own: I listen, then I decide. You can trust my decision because I'm not out to get my own way but only to carry out orders."

John 5:24–30 MSG

We have eternal life, but we will one day die. Jesus promised eternal life to those who believed in him, and yet he spoke of a coming resurrection sometime in the distant future. We can have eternal life now, even though we have to await a future resurrection, because we are alive in God now.

The sins that severed our connection to God have been removed, thanks to Jesus. Jesus said that those who have believed have crossed over from death to life. The bridge that spans the gap between God and us has been restored, and this time we're connected forever to the eternal God. He has put his Spirit—his very life that can never end—into us. Since our lives are now everlasting, that means he will never take it back. We live forever in him, and he lives in us. Our existence will not end, even when our bodies cease to be, because God will never cease to be, and we're forever a part of him.

We long for the coming resurrection when our bodies will be restored. We look forward to it in hope and expectation. We look forward to seeing the ones we love who have passed on before us. Yet we live forever with him even now.

GROWING GRAPES

Jesus taught his disciples during the Last Supper:

"I am the true grapevine, and my Father is the gardener. He cuts off every branch of mine that doesn't produce fruit, and he prunes the branches that do bear fruit so they will produce even more. You have already been pruned and purified by the message I have given you. Remain in me, and I will remain in you. For a branch cannot produce fruit if it is severed from the vine, and you cannot be fruitful unless you remain in me.

"Yes, I am the vine; you are the branches. Those who remain in me, and I in them, will produce much fruit. For apart from me you can do nothing. Anyone who does not remain in me is thrown away like a useless branch and withers. Such branches are gathered into a pile to be burned. But if you remain in me and my words remain in you, you may ask for anything you want, and it will be granted! When you produce much fruit, you are my true disciples. This brings great glory to my Father."

John 15:1–8 NLT

❄

The vine was an emblem of peace and prosperity for the ancient Israelites. The Old Testament prophets used the vine as a metaphor for the nation of Israel. Jesus claimed to be the true Vine, as compared to ancient Israel, which had been an unproductive vine, thanks to the people's idolatry and their failure to treat one another with love.

The purpose of any grapevine is to produce grapes. In order to get the best crop, the branches need to be pruned, with the dead and worthless ones being removed entirely. Jesus gave this analogy while his disciples were at the Last Supper, after Judas had left. Judas was an example of a branch that was removed, that had not stayed dependent upon Jesus.

Jesus emphasized the importance of abiding in him. That means we are joined with Jesus. We have become an intimate part of him. Those who belong to Jesus, who are connected to Jesus as a vine is connected to its branches, will bear fruit—not because of their own efforts, but simply because they belong to Jesus. If we are in Jesus, anything we want will be granted, because all we want is what the Vine wants—fruit. Fruit is everything that Jesus ever did while he walked on earth. We Christians strive to do what Jesus did.

WEAKNESS

Following the Last Supper:

After singing a hymn, [Jesus and His disciples] went out to the Mount of Olives.

Then Jesus said to them, "You will all fall away because of Me this night, for it is written, 'I will strike down the shepherd, and the sheep of the flock shall be scattered.'

"But after I have been raised, I will go ahead of you to Galilee."

But Peter said to Him, "Even though all may fall away because of You, I will never fall away."

Jesus said to him, "Truly I say to you that this very night, before a rooster crows, you will deny Me three times."

Peter said to Him, "Even if I have to die with You, I will not deny You." All the disciples said the same thing too.

Then Jesus came with them to a place called Gethsemane, and said to His disciples, "Sit here while I go over there and pray."

Matthew 26:30–36 NASB

꧁

*Y*ou will fail me." That's what Jesus told his disciples, but Jesus never gave up on them. After the Last Supper, Jesus and his disciples went to the Garden of Gethsemane to pray. Rather, Jesus went to pray. The disciples went to sleep. Jesus warned his disciples that they would all desert him. Likewise, he reassured them that he'd meet up with them again in Galilee after his resurrection.

Peter insisted that he would never deny Jesus, and he affirmed a willingness to die for him. All the disciples insisted the same, and all of them missed the words of comfort Jesus offered. The disciples expected to fight for Jesus against the Romans. They did not expect Jesus to surrender and die meekly. Unable to die for him gloriously in battle as they had imagined, they fled. Though all the disciples ran, Peter was singled out with a prophecy. He stands out as the representative for all their bad behavior.

The disciples missed the promise of Jesus' resurrection, and they spent three days in unnecessary misery before the reality of his resurrection forced them to joy. Jesus was not surprised by their reaction. He planned for it. He fixed it. God knows us. He knows how we'll react to our lives. He isn't at a loss, and he won't give up on us, no matter how often we give up on him, or worse, ourselves. Jesus always goes ahead of us to meet up with us again.

WAKE UP

They came to a place which was named Gethsemane; and [Jesus] said to His disciples, "Sit here while I pray." And He took Peter, James, and John with Him, and He began to be troubled and deeply distressed. Then He said to them, "My soul is exceedingly sorrowful, even to death. Stay here and watch."

He went a little farther, and fell on the ground, and prayed that if it were possible, the hour might pass from Him. And He said, "Abba, Father, all things are possible for You. Take this cup away from Me; nevertheless, not what I will, but what You will."

Then He came and found them sleeping, and said to Peter, "Simon, are you sleeping? Could you not watch one hour? Watch and pray, lest you enter into temptation. The spirit indeed is willing, but the flesh is weak."

Again He went away and prayed, and spoke the same words. And when He returned, He found them asleep again, for their eyes were heavy; and they did not know what to answer Him.

Then He came the third time and said to them, "Are you still sleeping and resting? It is enough! The hour has come; behold, the Son of Man is being betrayed into the hands of sinners. Rise, let us be going. See, My betrayer is at hand."

Mark 14:32–42 NKJV

❈

*S*leeping on your job will get you fired. But three times Jesus found his disciples sleeping. He tried to awaken them three times. The first two times he tried to awaken them to join him in prayer. The last time he tried to awaken them so they could witness his betrayal.

Jesus had told his disciples what was going on all along. And all along, the disciples just didn't get it. Had they understood the necessity of praying that night, had they known that in only a short hour their Master would be arrested and taken away to be crucified, they would have doubtless acted differently. But how many times had they been with Jesus when he went off to pray? Jesus prayed all the time. How was that night different from all the others? That very question was probably on their minds, since every Passover a child was supposed to ask that question.

How was that night different from all others? Jesus changed the meaning of the bread and wine, the meaning of prayer, and the meaning of the concept of the Messiah. The world would never be the same after Jesus fulfilled his destiny. Jesus' disciples weren't his employees. They weren't his servants. They were his brothers and his friends. We don't work for Jesus; we're part of his family.

SILENCE IS LOUD

Early in the morning the chief priests with the elders and scribes and the whole Council, immediately held a consultation; and binding Jesus, they led Him away and delivered Him to Pilate.

Pilate questioned Him, "Are You the King of the Jews?" And He answered him, "It is as you say."

The chief priests began to accuse Him harshly.

Then Pilate questioned Him again, saying, "Do You not answer? See how many charges they bring against You!"

But Jesus made no further answer; so Pilate was amazed.

Now at the feast he used to release for them any one prisoner whom they requested. The man named Barabbas had been imprisoned with the insurrectionists who had committed murder in the insurrection. The crowd went up and began asking him to do as he had been accustomed to do for them.

Pilate answered them, saying, "Do you want me to release for you the King of the Jews?" For he was aware that the chief priests had handed Him over because of envy. But the chief priests stirred up the crowd to ask him to release Barabbas for them instead.

Answering again, Pilate said to them, "Then what shall I do with Him whom you call the King of the Jews?"

They shouted back, "Crucify Him!"

But Pilate said to them, "Why, what evil has He done?" But they shouted all the more, "Crucify Him!" Wishing to satisfy the crowd, Pilate released Barabbas for them, and after having Jesus scourged, he handed Him over to be crucified.

Mark 15:1–15 NASB

Jesus merely agreed with the truth; he never sought to defend himself or to argue a point. Pilate was amazed by the silence of Jesus. He had seen numberless criminals, and he knew criminals were quick to claim innocence.

Jesus was different. He acknowledged that he was the King of the Jews. In a world where only Rome decided who was king and who was not, that made Jesus guilty as charged. But Pilate wasn't buying it. Jesus didn't act like some pretender to the throne. He didn't strut; he didn't offer excuses.

Pilate decided that Jesus really was innocent, but he had to pander to what the mob wanted in order to keep the crowd from turning against him and destroying his career.

It isn't easy to do the right thing, even when you know what the right thing is and you want to do it. When faced with the choice of doing the right thing or keeping his job, Pilate chose to keep his job. Most people today will do the same thing; they will just follow orders and procedure. But Jesus asks us to follow him.

MOVE ALONG

After [Jesus] had suffered, He also presented Himself alive to them by many convincing proofs, appearing to them during 40 days and speaking about the kingdom of God.

While He was together with them, He commanded them not to leave Jerusalem, but to wait for the Father's promise. "This," He said, "is what you heard from Me; for John baptized with water, but you will be baptized with the Holy Spirit not many days from now."

So when they had come together, they asked Him, "Lord, at this time are You restoring the kingdom to Israel?"

He said to them, "It is not for you to know times or periods that the Father has set by His own authority. But you will receive power when the Holy Spirit has come upon you, and you will be My witnesses in Jerusalem, in all Judea and Samaria, and to the ends of the earth."

After He had said this, He was taken up as they were watching, and a cloud received Him out of their sight. While He was going, they were gazing into heaven, and suddenly two men in white clothes stood by them. They said, "Men of Galilee, why do you stand looking up into heaven? This Jesus, who has been taken from you into heaven, will come in the same way that you have seen Him going into heaven."

Acts 1:3–11 HCSB

❈

Jesus had died and been resurrected. He'd spent years telling his disciples about the kingdom of God. But just before he ascended back to his Father, the disciples, with their one question, demonstrated that they were nearly as confused about the kingdom as they had been the first day Jesus called them to join him along the shores of Galilee.

The disciples were still looking for a physical kingdom. Did Jesus remind them of any of his previous lessons to them? No. He just told them to be his witnesses throughout the world. If we want to see the kingdom of God, we need to get to work spreading the good news. That's how the kingdom will come—one heart at a time.

After Jesus left, angels appeared and asked the disciples why they were still standing there, staring at the sky. Staring at the sky where Jesus had gone was certainly a normal reaction, but the Holy Spirit was coming, and the disciples had work to do. What matters is not staring at the sky, waiting for Jesus to come back. What matters is for us to do what Jesus asked his disciples to do—spread the good news of the kingdom.

ALL WILL BE WELL

Paul faced the Sanhedrin in Jerusalem:

Paul, knowing some of the council was made up of Sadducees and others of Pharisees and how they hated each other, decided to exploit their antagonism: "Friends, I am a stalwart Pharisee from a long line of Pharisees. It's because of my Pharisee convictions—the hope and resurrection of the dead—that I've been hauled into this court."

The moment he said this, the council split right down the middle, Pharisees and Sadducees going at each other in heated argument. Sadducees have nothing to do with a resurrection or angels or even a spirit. If they can't see it, they don't believe it. Pharisees believe it all. And so a huge and noisy quarrel broke out. Then some of the religion scholars on the Pharisee side shouted down the others: "We don't find anything wrong with this man!

And what if a spirit has spoken to him? Or maybe an angel? What if it turns out we're fighting against God?"

That was fuel on the fire. The quarrel flamed up and became so violent the captain was afraid they would tear Paul apart, limb from limb. He ordered the soldiers to get him out of there and escort him back to the safety of the barracks.

That night the Master appeared to Paul: "It's going to be all right. Everything is going to turn out for the best. You've been a good witness for me here in Jerusalem. Now you're going to be my witness in Rome!"

Acts 23:6–11 MSG

꒰꒱

*P*essimism has no place in the lives of Christians. Once Paul returned to Jerusalem, he went to the temple. While there, he nearly caused a riot and got himself arrested. When the Roman authorities realized he was a Roman citizen, they released him to appear before the Sanhedrin. He was soon under arrest again.

Ever since Paul went to Jerusalem, things had gone badly for him. And they were getting worse. In the darkness of the evening, alone in jail, Jesus offered Paul encouragement. He told Paul that he was going to Rome to continue being a missionary. Paul wanted nothing more than to tell others about Jesus.

Paul was still in jail and would stay there a long time. But knowing what God's will was for him and then doing it was the best way for him to stay encouraged. Part of God's will for us, like Paul, is to testify about Jesus, wherever we happen to be. Along our way, God will always take care of us.

ENDURANCE

Jesus dictated a letter to the church in Ephesus:

"These are the words of him who holds the seven stars in his right hand and walks among the seven golden lampstands: I know your deeds, your hard work and your perseverance. I know that you cannot tolerate wicked men, that you have tested those who claim to be apostles but are not, and have found them false. You have persevered and have endured hardships for my name, and have not grown weary.

"Yet I hold this against you: You have forsaken your first love. Remember the height from which you have fallen!

Repent and do the things you did at first. If you do not repent, I will come to you and remove your lampstand from its place. But you have this in your favor: You hate the practices of the Nicolaitans, which I also hate.

"He who has an ear, let him hear what the Spirit says to the churches. To him who overcomes, I will give the right to eat from the tree of life, which is in the paradise of God."

Revelation 2:1–7 NIV

❋

The urgent needs of the moment can distract us from what really matters. Often there is a gap between what we want to accomplish and what we actually wind up spending all our time on. Jesus warned the Ephesians about getting distracted. Ephesus was a prosperous port city along the Aegean Sea on Turkey's west coast. The first of the seven letters that Jesus dictated to John was addressed to the church there. The seven lampstands represented the seven churches of Asia Minor, and the stars in Jesus' hands represented the members of those churches.

Jesus once told his disciples that people would know they were his disciples because they loved one another. When hatred for sin changed into hatred for those who sin, Jesus told the Ephesians that they had lost their first love. They had become distracted from their true purpose. Jesus came to rescue people from sin, not to condemn them. Jesus warned the church in Ephesus that should they not change, he would remove their lampstand. That is, they would cease to be a church. Where hatred replaces love, the unity of the body will crumble and members will scatter. Churches die when hate replaces love. We need to remember to offer redemption rather than condemnation to those who need Jesus.

KEEP YOUR CLOTHES ON

The apostle John had visions on the island of Patmos:

I saw three unclean spirits like frogs coming out of the mouth of the dragon, out of the mouth of the beast, and out of the mouth of the false prophet. For they are spirits of demons, performing signs, which go out to the kings of the earth and of the whole world, to gather them to the battle of that great day of God Almighty.

"Behold, I am coming as a thief. Blessed is he who watches, and keeps his garments, lest he walk naked and they see his shame."

And they gathered them together to the place called in Hebrew, Armageddon.

Then the seventh angel poured out his bowl into the air, and a loud voice came out of the temple of heaven, from the throne, saying, "It is done!"

And there were noises and thunderings and lightnings; and there was a great earthquake, such a mighty and great earthquake as had not occurred since men were on the earth. Now the great city was divided into three parts, and the cities of the nations fell. And great Babylon was remembered before God, to give her the cup of the wine of the fierceness of His wrath. Then every island fled away, and the mountains were not found. And great hail from heaven fell upon men, each hailstone about the weight of a talent. Men blasphemed God because of the plague of the hail, since that plague was exceedingly great.

Revelation 16:13–21 NKJV

✻

What if you knew Jesus was coming back today? Martin Luther was hoeing weeds in his garden when a member of his church asked him that very question. Martin Luther responded quickly, "I'd be hoeing weeds."

In the middle of John's visions about the future, Jesus announced that he was going to return without warning. He said that those who were watching and prepared for his arrival wouldn't be caught as some person rousted from bed naked in the middle of the night to confront a problem. In that part of the world, it was warm and humid most of the year, so people regularly slept unclothed. But if you knew there was going to be an earthquake, or if you knew there was going to be a burglary, or if you knew your best friend were going to drop by, then you'd make a point of wearing some clothing so you could confront the problem without embarrassment and without wasting the time dressing in the darkness.

Jesus' point was that he wanted his people always to be doing his will, whatever that might be, whether it's hoeing weeds or preaching the gospel.

DESERVED AND UNDESERVED

Workers receive wages for their work, and so do sinners. They both get what they deserve. The wages of sin are death. In contrast, a gift is never earned: it is undeservered. Forgiveness, everlasting life, and the kingdom of heaven are gifts from God, regardless of actions good or bad, and are completely undeserved.

✺

God demonstrates His own love toward us, in that
while we were still sinners, Christ died for us.
Much more then, having now been justified
by His blood, we shall be saved from wrath
through Him. For if when we were enemies we
were reconciled to God through the death of
His Son, much more, having been reconciled,
we shall be saved by His life.
Romans 5:8–10 NKJV

GOING TO THE PIGS

After Jesus had crossed the lake, he came to shore near the town of Gadara and started down the road. Two men with demons in them came to him from the tombs. They were so fierce that no one could travel that way. Suddenly they shouted, "Jesus, Son of God, what do you want with us? Have you come to punish us before our time?"

Not far from there a large herd of pigs was feeding. So the demons begged Jesus, "If you force us out, please send us into those pigs!" Jesus told them to go, and they went out of the men and into the pigs. All at once the pigs rushed down the steep bank into the lake and drowned.

The people taking care of the pigs ran to the town and told everything, especially what had happened to the two men. Everyone in town came out to meet Jesus. When they saw him, they begged him to leave their part of the country.

Matthew 8:28–34 CEV

⁂

*A*re we as obedient as the demons? When Jesus told the demons to go somewhere, that's where they went. Demons were limited in what they could and could not do. Though they did not care what people thought or what people wanted, whenever Jesus spoke, they did exactly what he said. Did they lack free will? Weren't they evil? Didn't they, by definition, usually disobey God?

Demons in the Bible appeared to take Jesus' words more seriously than many human beings did. They knew who Jesus was, they knew that he was God, and they knew they'd better obey him or else. Certainly, the demons were free to do whatever they wanted to do. But they knew better than to ever disobey Jesus. They knew that disobeying Jesus would be disastrous for them. Of course, entering the pigs did not turn out so well for them. The man they had possessed was freed of them, and the pigs were dead. But that was their idea. They had asked for it. Jesus had them go into the pigs because he knew what the outcome would be. The demons thought they would escape. Jesus knew it would bring about their destruction.

Demons are the definition of evil, and yet they still obeyed Jesus' commands and asked for his permission. Jesus controlled them. Unlike demons, we will sometimes resist doing what Jesus wants us to do. Like demons, we sometimes come up with our own ideas. Instead, we can choose to seek only to discover Jesus' will and to carry it out.

BLASPHEMY

After getting into a boat [Jesus] crossed the sea and came to his own town.

And just then some people were carrying a paralyzed man lying on a bed. When Jesus saw their faith, he said to the paralytic, "Take heart, son; your sins are forgiven."

Then some of the scribes said to themselves, "This man is blaspheming."

But Jesus, perceiving their thoughts, said, "Why do you think evil in your hearts? For which is easier, to say, 'Your sins are forgiven,' or to say, 'Stand up and walk'? But so that you may know that the Son of Man has authority on earth to forgive sins"—he then said to the paralytic—"Stand up, take your bed and go to your home." And he stood up and went to his home. When the crowds saw it, they were filled with awe, and they glorified God, who had given such authority to human beings.

Matthew 9:1–8 NRSV

The biggest miracles are the hardest ones to recognize. When a paralyzed man was brought to Jesus, he didn't tell him that he was healed. Instead, Jesus told him to be encouraged! And why should he be encouraged? Because his paralysis was gone? No, he should be encouraged because his sins were forgiven.

His sins weren't the reason he was paralyzed. He didn't go to Jesus for what seemed his most obvious need. The reason he went to Jesus and the reason his friends cut a hole in the roof to make sure he could get to him had nothing to do with being healed physically. Instead, the paralyzed man went to Jesus for spiritual healing. He went in order to be forgiven. Jesus saw his faith and the faith of his friends, and because of that faith, Jesus forgave the man.

What happened to the man after he was forgiven was secondary. And it didn't happen for the sake of the paralyzed man who already believed in Jesus and who already knew that Jesus was in fact God himself. The paralyzed man was relieved of his paralysis for the sake of those who had witnessed his being forgiven but still didn't have a clue about who Jesus was.

Getting healed is great, but what matters most of all is being forgiven for our sins. Jesus gave us the greatest gift we could ever want! Having our sins forgiven and being granted eternal life is the biggest miracle of all.

RAISING THE DEAD

Jesus was in Nazareth when John's disciples asked him about fasting:

As [Jesus] finished saying this, a local official appeared, bowed politely, and said, "My daughter has just now died. If you come and touch her, she will live." Jesus got up and went with him, his disciples following along.

Just then a woman who had hemorrhaged for twelve years slipped in from behind and lightly touched his robe. She was thinking to herself, "If I can just put a finger on his robe, I'll get well." Jesus turned—caught her at it. Then he reassured her: "Courage, daughter. You took a risk of faith, and now you're well." The woman was well from then on.

By now they had arrived at the house of the town official, and pushed their way through the gossips looking for a story and the neighbors bringing in casseroles. Jesus was abrupt: "Clear out! This girl isn't dead. She's sleeping." They told him he didn't know what he was talking about. But when Jesus had gotten rid of the crowd, he went in, took the girl's hand, and pulled her to her feet—alive. The news was soon out, and traveled throughout the region.

Matthew 9:18–26 MSG

*J*esus made it all look easy. When Jesus healed someone, there were no explosions, no sparkles in the air, no waving of wands or muttering of spells. He didn't flap his hands about. When the woman who had suffered a hemorrhage for twelve years needed healing, she was the one doing all the physical effort by attempting to sneak up and touch him. Her belief and her touch were enough for her to become well. When the local official's daughter was dead, all Jesus did was walk up to where she was lying. Then he grabbed her hand and helped her get out of the bed. She was simply alive.

The miraculous became mundane in Jesus. It was no more spectacular, seemingly no more out of the ordinary, than the work he had done as a carpenter. In fact, it was usually less time consuming and less labor intensive. Jesus, like any carpenter, could take some wood and, with a bit of diligent effort, turn it into a table or a chair. With the sick or the dead, Jesus transformed them even more easily.

The miraculous is God's normal. In fact, if resurrections were as common as sunrises, we'd stop paying attention to them. This says, perhaps, that we might want to pay more attention to sunrises. God performs miracles all the time. Resolve today to not take them for granted.

TO THE JEWS FIRST

In the region of Galilee:

When [Jesus] had called His twelve disciples to Him, He gave them power over unclean spirits, to cast them out, and to heal all kinds of sickness and all kinds of disease. Now the names of the twelve apostles are these: first, Simon, who is called Peter, and Andrew his brother; James the son of Zebedee, and John his brother; Philip and Bartholomew; Thomas and Matthew the tax collector; James the son of Alphaeus, and Lebbaeus, whose surname was Thaddaeus; Simon the Cananite, and Judas Iscariot, who also betrayed Him.

These twelve Jesus sent out and commanded them, saying: "Do not go into the way of the Gentiles, and do not enter a city of the Samaritans. But go rather to the lost sheep of the house of Israel. And as you go, preach, saying, 'The kingdom of heaven is at hand.' Heal the sick, cleanse the lepers, raise the dead, cast out demons. Freely you have received, freely give. Provide neither gold nor silver nor copper in your money belts, nor bag for your journey, nor two tunics, nor sandals, nor staffs; for a worker is worthy of his food."

Matthew 10:1–11 NKJV

*N*othing builds faith better than experience. Jesus sent his twelve disciples out into the region around the Sea of Galilee, to all the villages and towns in it, to proclaim that God's kingdom was near. To demonstrate the truth of their words, Jesus gave his disciples the ability to perform all the miracles he had been performing—they healed the sick, they cleansed the lepers, they raised the dead, and they cast out demons. None of the gospel writers give details about their activities, where precisely they went, or how many people were raised from the dead.

When the disciples discovered they could raise the dead and heal the sick, the disciples stopped worrying about their rather precarious financial situation. Jesus hadn't let them take any money or extra clothes. They were forced to be dependent upon God and those they served.

When one miracle happened, and then another, and as they found their needs provided for at each step of the way, their confidence inevitably grew. Jesus was training his disciples for the time when he would be gone, when the men would be on their own with only the Spirit to guide them. We, as followers of Jesus today, have been sent out into the world with no less than those first twelve disciples.

PREY AND PREDATORS

In Galilee, Jesus instructed his disciples:

"Behold, I send you out as sheep in the midst of wolves. Therefore be wise as serpents and harmless as doves. But beware of men, for they will deliver you up to councils and scourge you in their synagogues. You will be brought before governors and kings for My sake, as a testimony to them and to the Gentiles. But when they deliver you up, do not worry about how or what you should speak. For it will be given to you in that hour what you should speak; for it is not you who speak, but the Spirit of your Father who speaks in you.

"Now brother will deliver up brother to death, and a father his child; and children will rise up against parents and cause them to be put to death. And you will be hated by all for My name's sake. But he who endures to the end will be saved. When they persecute you in this city, flee to another. For assuredly, I say to you, you will not have gone through the cities of Israel before the Son of Man comes."

Matthew 10:16–23 NKJV

*W*e're going to suffer. Jesus expects us to. When Jesus sent his disciples out into the world to proclaim the good news and to heal people, he warned them that they were defenseless.

What Jesus described to them was, and ever has been, the experience of the Christian church. Without end, portions of the body of Christ have always experienced persecution, from the time of the Romans until the modern era. Usually that opposition came from the outside, but sometimes it came from inside Christians' families. Jesus suggested his followers respond to persecution by enduring it if necessary and by fleeing from it if possible.

Jesus told his disciples that they would not pass through all the cities of Israel before "the son of Man comes." Although some take Jesus' words as a prophecy regarding the Second Coming, the context seems to suggest something else. The Twelve went among several villages in Galilee. Then Jesus and his disciples went to Jerusalem, and Jesus was crucified. Jesus' crucifixion and the resurrection were the "coming" Jesus was speaking of, the redemption of humanity, the beginning of the kingdom of God in the hearts of people everywhere. Since Jesus endured the cross and lives with us today, we can endure anything.

THE DETAILS

Jesus continued teaching his disciples in Galilee:

"A disciple is not above his teacher, nor a servant above his master. It is enough for a disciple that he be like his teacher, and a servant like his master. If they have called the master of the house Beelzebub, how much more will they call those of his household! Therefore do not fear them. For there is nothing covered that will not be revealed, and hidden that will not be known.

"Whatever I tell you in the dark, speak in the light; and what you hear in the ear, preach on the housetops. And do not fear those who kill the body but cannot kill the soul. But rather fear Him who is able to destroy both soul and body in hell. Are not two sparrows sold for a copper coin? And not one of them falls to the ground apart from your Father's will. But the very hairs of your head are all numbered. Do not fear therefore; you are of more value than many sparrows.

"Therefore whoever confesses Me before men, him I will also confess before My Father who is in heaven. But whoever denies Me before men, him I will also deny before My Father who is in heaven."

Matthew 10:24–33 NKJV

No matter how bad a mess we make, Jesus will help us clean it up. In the context of Jesus' sending his disciples out to proclaim the eminent coming of the kingdom of God, Jesus gave them a warning: don't be afraid of people; be afraid of God.

Jesus told his disciples that those who denied him before men, he would deny before his Father in heaven. But consider that Peter denied Jesus not once, but three times before a rooster crowed.

Did Jesus deny Peter before his Father? And if so, what does that mean? Since Peter was forgiven and restored after his denial, denial can be forgiven. It isn't a one-way ticket to hell. Just because we didn't stand up for Jesus today, doesn't mean we can't do it tomorrow. What Peter did in a moment of terror didn't make him unfit for eternity. Our fear of someone who threatens our life may sometimes overwhelm our fear of God, who could do far worse to us. Jesus knew that, and so he warned his disciples. Being human, they were able to keep their perspective better at some times than at others. But Jesus was quick to forgive them when they lost perspective about whom to fear. For all their faults, the disciples still turned the world upside down. God has already forgiven us, thanks to Jesus' work on the cross. Like the disciples, we, too, can change the world.

A TIME FOR WAR

In Galilee, Jesus had more words for his disciples:

"Do not think that I came to bring peace on earth. I did not come to bring peace but a sword. For I have come to 'set a man against his father, a daughter against her mother, and a daughter-in-law against her mother-in-law'; and 'a man's enemies will be those of his own household.' He who loves father or mother more than Me is not worthy of Me. And he who loves son or daughter more than Me is not worthy of Me. And he who does not take his cross and follow after Me is not worthy of Me. He who finds his life will lose it, and he who loses his life for My sake will find it.

"He who receives you receives Me, and he who receives Me receives Him who sent Me. He who receives a prophet in the name of a prophet shall receive a prophet's reward. And he who receives a righteous man in the name of a righteous man shall receive a righteous man's reward. And whoever gives one of these little ones only a cup of cold water in the name of a disciple, assuredly, I say to you, he shall by no means lose his reward."

Matthew 10:34–42 NKJV

The angels declared, "On earth peace, goodwill toward men" (Luke 2:14 NKJV), and their words are repeated frequently during the Christmas season. But Jesus also affirmed that he did not come to bring peace on earth. Instead, he came to bring war.

Jesus divides people. He breaks up families and friends. Followers of Jesus have suffered persecution, even death. Jesus' demands are paradoxical: If you love your parents more than you love Jesus, then you're not worthy of Jesus. If you find your life, you'll lose it; but if you lose it for Jesus, then you'll find it.

This sounds extreme in a comfortable society that tolerates and even encourages Christian commitment, but what Jesus said remains literally relevant. In some parts of the world, if you decide to become a Christian, you're deciding to be cut off from your family, to have your husband or wife divorce you, to lose your friends, and quite possibly to lose your life. In a comfortable, tolerant, Western civilization, we don't have to make such choices. But what Jesus asked remains relevant even for us. What are our priorities? What matters most to us? How far will we go for Jesus? We still must decide.

SIGNS AND WONDERS

In Galilee, right after Jesus healed a blind and mute demon-possessed man:

Some of the Pharisees and teachers of the law said to [Jesus], "Teacher, we want to see a miraculous sign from you."

He answered, "A wicked and adulterous generation asks for a miraculous sign! But none will be given it except the sign of the prophet Jonah. For as Jonah was three days and three nights in the belly of a huge fish, so the Son of Man will be three days and three nights in the heart of the earth. The men of Nineveh will stand up at the judgment with this generation and condemn it; for they repented at the preaching of Jonah, and now one greater than Jonah is here. The Queen of the South will rise at the judgment with this generation and condemn it; for she came from the ends of the earth to listen to Solomon's wisdom, and now one greater than Solomon is here.

"When an evil spirit comes out of a man, it goes through arid places seeking rest and does not find it."

Matthew 12:38–43 NIV

*D*oes God give us signs? The desire of the Pharisees and the teachers of the law to see a sign from Jesus seems odd in the context. Jesus and his disciples healed the sick, raised the dead, and drove out demons on a regular basis. How could the Pharisees ask for more?

The phrase "wicked and adulterous generation" that Jesus used in his response reiterated the condemnation of the Old Testament prophets, who told Israel that she was like a wife who was unfaithful to her husband. The Israelites had abandoned God for idols. Like ancient Israel, the Pharisees had turned from God. They were rejecting Jesus, and so they were acting unfaithfully with the God they claimed to love. Jesus told them that there was but one sign left for them: his death, burial, and resurrection. The pagan people of Nineveh and the queen of Sheba had repented in the face of Jonah and Solomon. But the religious establishment, confronted by Jesus, who was God himself, couldn't be convinced.

Jesus knew that nothing more could be done for the religious establishment. He knew that another miracle wouldn't change them. Miracles do not convert unbelievers into believers. Instead, unbelievers needed to repent, just as Nineveh and the queen of Sheba had. Like the Pharisees, we don't need signs. We've already received plenty of them.

KEEP THEM GUESSING

On the shore of the Sea of Galilee:

The disciples came and asked [Jesus], "Why do you speak to them in parables?"

He answered, "To you it has been given to know the secrets of the kingdom of heaven, but to them it has not been given. For to those who have, more will be given, and they will have an abundance; but from those who have nothing, even what they have will be taken away. The reason I speak to them in parables is that 'seeing they do not perceive, and hearing they do not listen, nor do they understand.' With them indeed is fulfilled the prophecy of Isaiah that says:

"'You will indeed listen, but never understand, and you will indeed look, but never perceive. For this people's heart has grown dull, and their ears are hard of hearing, and they have shut their eyes; so that they might not look with their eyes, and listen with their ears, and understand with their heart and turn—and I would heal them.'

"But blessed are your eyes, for they see, and your ears, for they hear. Truly I tell you, many prophets and righteous people longed to see what you see, but did not see it, and to hear what you hear, but did not hear it."

Matthew 13:10–17 NRSV

❀

*W*ouldn't it be great to ask Jesus a question and get an immediate response? In a way, we can. The disciples wondered why Jesus told parables. Jesus responded by telling them that they were especially blessed, even if they didn't always get the parables right away. They were getting information that people in the generations before them could only dream of.

They were like Galileo. For untold millennia, people looked at the sky and wondered about the moon and the planets. Then Galileo pointed his telescope at the sky and for the first time saw the stars for what they were.

Like a child passing from one grade to another, gradually learning how to count, how to add and subtract, and how to multiply and divide until he moves on at last to algebra, geometry, and calculus, so God revealed his secrets to the human race gradually. At last, during the time of Jesus, he gave his disciples the final revelations. They were able to know for certain what those before them had only been able to guess at. They spoke and ate with God for years as his closest friends.

Today, we stand on the shoulders of those apostles, privileged to know what they knew. Our most important questions have been answered.

WEALTHY PROBLEM

On the shore of the Sea of Galilee, Jesus taught his disciples:

"Hear the parable of the sower: When anyone hears the word of the kingdom, and does not understand it, then the wicked one comes and snatches away what was sown in his heart. This is he who received seed by the wayside. But he who received the seed on stony places, this is he who hears the word and immediately receives it with joy; yet he has no root in himself, but endures only for a while. For when tribulation or persecution arises because of the word, immediately he stumbles. Now he who received seed among the thorns is he who hears the word, and the cares of this world and the deceitfulness of riches choke the word, and he becomes unfruitful. But he who received seed on the good ground is he who hears the word and understands it, who indeed bears fruit and produces: some a hundredfold, some sixty, some thirty."

Matthew 13:18–23 NKJV

༄

*W*hy do some people not endure in Christianity? Two of the saddest situations are people described as being like "stony ground" and as being among the "thorns." Jesus explained that people who give up because of problems or persecution are like seeds in stony ground. Likewise, the person among thorns is the one who initially seems interested in the gospel, but soon gets distracted by the affairs of life—the pursuit of wealth, the day-to-day grind, and the need to survive.

In a modern, Western society, the greatest threats to faithfulness are the comfort and ease of life, the many distractions that our world can offer us. Our ground is thorny. In other parts of the world, the problem tends to be persecution, the "stony ground." Both things are equally destructive and equally distracting. People will fall away in either case. But the problem isn't the external distraction; rather, the problem is the individual's heart and the choices that he or she makes. Jesus pointed out an important reality in his parable. Some people respond well to the things that life gives them, and others don't. Some people in the church, when they face tragedy, pull away and leave. Others grow stronger and more committed. Some people when they gain wealth fall away; others become more committed and use their wealth to benefit others.

How we respond to life is up to us. Jesus planted the same seed in all of us. He expects us to be good soil for God's kingdom.

FIVE THOUSAND

In Galilee, after John the Baptist had been executed by Herod:

When Jesus heard about John, He withdrew from there in a boat to a secluded place by Himself; and when the people heard of this, they followed Him on foot from the cities. When He went ashore, He saw a large crowd, and felt compassion for them and healed their sick.

When it was evening, the disciples came to Him and said, "This place is desolate and the hour is already late; so send the crowds away, that they may go into the villages and buy food for themselves."

But Jesus said to them, "They do not need to go away; you give them something to eat!"

They said to Him, "We have here only five loaves and two fish."

And He said, "Bring them here to Me."

Ordering the people to sit down on the grass, He took the five loaves and the two fish, and looking up toward heaven, He blessed the food, and breaking the loaves He gave them to the disciples, and the disciples gave them to the crowds, and they all ate and were satisfied. They picked up what was left over of the broken pieces, twelve full baskets. There were about five thousand men who ate, besides women and children.

Matthew 14:13–21 NASB

*W*ere the five thousand Jesus fed late one afternoon better people than those for whom he hadn't provided such a meal? Those who received a miracle from him were simply those who had come to him. When people came, Jesus never drove them off without providing for their needs. He healed the sick, he cast out demons, and he raised the dead.

Five thousand were fed that evening. It was a miracle. But when those people woke from their slumber the next day, what did they have? Their bellies were empty once again. Those whom Jesus healed eventually became ill from something else. Sooner or later, they all died. Those whom he raised from the dead eventually ended up in a cemetery; we can't travel to Israel and have tea with Lazarus.

Why did Jesus perform miracles that lasted such a short time—satisfying hunger for a few hours, or relieving pain and death for a few years? What was the point since none of that lasted?

Relieving someone's suffering, easing a burden, wiping a tear, binding a wound, offering a drink, giving a gift—certainly none of those things lasts for long. Yet each momentary blessing is still a blessing.

FOUR THOUSAND

Jesus returned to the Sea of Galilee and climbed a hill and sat down. A vast crowd brought to him people who were lame, blind, crippled, those who couldn't speak, and many others. They laid them before Jesus, and he healed them all. The crowd was amazed! Those who hadn't been able to speak were talking, the crippled were made well, the lame were walking, and the blind could see again! And they praised the God of Israel.

Then Jesus called his disciples and told them, "I feel sorry for these people. They have been here with me for three days, and they have nothing left to eat. I don't want to send them away hungry, or they will faint along the way."

The disciples replied, "Where would we get enough food here in the wilderness for such a huge crowd?"

Jesus asked, "How much bread do you have?"

They replied, "Seven loaves, and a few small fish."

So Jesus told all the people to sit down on the ground. Then he took the seven loaves and the fish, thanked God for them, and broke them into pieces. He gave them to the disciples, who distributed the food to the crowd.

They all ate as much as they wanted. Afterward, the disciples picked up seven large baskets of leftover food. There were 4,000 men who were fed that day, in addition to all the women and children. Then Jesus sent the people home, and he got into a boat and crossed over to the region of Magadan.

Matthew 15:29–39 NLT

*D*on't get bored! The story of feeding the four thousand sounds very much like the story of feeding the five thousand—so much so that we might be tempted to think it's the same story. What purpose do two very similar stories serve?

After Jesus healed the first blind man, people were amazed. After the hundredth, it probably didn't feel so remarkable anymore. How many demon expulsions happened before the disciples started yawning?

God fed the huge crowd of Israelites in the wilderness every day for forty years. What Jesus did with four thousand was much the same. The Jewish people of Jesus' day expected the Messiah to feed the masses, so that's what he did. It took willful hardheadedness for the religious establishment to conclude, in the face of all Jesus did, that he was not, in fact, the Messiah.

It is easy for us to grow so familiar with Jesus that we lose sight of how marvelous he is. Every day, lives are saved, homes restored, sins forgiven, relationships mended. One person's miracle is much like another. The blessings of God surround us. Don't lose sight of them!

BINDING ARBITRATION

Jesus talked to his disciples in Capernaum:

"If your brother sins against you, go and show him his fault, just between the two of you. If he listens to you, you have won your brother over. But if he will not listen, take one or two others along, so that 'every matter may be established by the testimony of two or three witnesses.' If he refuses to listen to them, tell it to the church; and if he refuses to listen even to the church, treat him as you would a pagan or a tax collector.

"I tell you the truth, whatever you bind on earth will be bound in heaven, and whatever you loose on earth will be loosed in heaven.

"Again, I tell you that if two of you on earth agree about anything you ask for, it will be done for you by my Father in heaven. For where two or three come together in my name, there am I with them."

Matthew 18:15–20 NIV

Gossip isn't an effective way of solving the problems that exist between people. Gossip usually makes things worse. Yet we all too often still give in to its seductive temptation. Jesus' words serve as a corrective to gossip. Instead of talking *about* the person we're upset with, Jesus argued that we should talk *to* that person.

Only if talking to that person doesn't fix the problem should we consider bringing more people into the situation. Jesus set no time limits on the efforts at reconciliation. Only when a person demonstrated a lack of interest in repentance by refusing even to listen to those in the entire assembly did Jesus recommend that individual be treated as a pagan or a tax collector. But Jesus sought to redeem pagans and tax collectors. He went out of his way to talk to them, to share his love with them. Rather than cutting off the people caught in sin, Jesus suggested that those who insisted on continuing in their rebellion against God should be treated as targets for evangelism. We can hope for them to come back to us some day, much as a father might look for the return of his prodigal son.

The goal in all our interactions with the people around us should be reconciliation. People are more important than issues. Jesus wants us to restore those who are taken by sin. He wants to break down the barriers that separate us from one another and from God.

FOUR HUNDRED NINETY TIMES

While Jesus was in Capernaum, just before leaving for Jerusalem:

Peter came and said to Him, "Lord, how often shall my brother sin against me and I forgive him? Up to seven times?"

Jesus said to him, "I do not say to you, up to seven times, but up to seventy times seven.

"For this reason the kingdom of heaven may be compared to a king who wished to settle accounts with his slaves. When he had begun to settle them, one who owed him ten thousand talents was brought to him. But since he did not have the means to repay, his lord commanded him to be sold, along with his wife and children and all that he had, and repayment to be made.

"So the slave fell to the ground and prostrated himself before him, saying, 'Have patience with me and I will repay you everything.' And the lord of that slave felt compassion and released him and forgave him the debt.

"But that slave went out and found one of his fellow slaves who owed him a hundred denarii; and he seized him and began to choke him, saying, 'Pay back what you owe.'

"So his fellow slave fell to the ground and began to plead with him, saying, 'Have patience with me and I will repay you.'

"But he was unwilling and went and threw him in prison until he should pay back what was owed. So when his fellow slaves saw what had happened, they were deeply grieved and came and reported to their lord all that had happened.

"Then summoning him, his lord said to him, 'You wicked slave, I forgave you all that debt because you pleaded with me. 'Should you not also have had mercy on your fellow slave, in the same way that I had mercy on you?'"

Matthew 18:21–33 NASB

*W*henever someone bumped into him, one man would mutter as a joke, "That's four hundred eighty-nine." Peter was looking for a number like that. Just how often did he have to forgive someone?

Jesus took Peter's suggestion of seven times and multiplied it beyond reason. Jesus meant that forgiveness is never-ending. But is that practical? If your spouse beats you today and begs forgiveness tomorrow, do you have to keep forgiving him? Do you give the convicted embezzler another job in the bank? Jesus told a parable to illustrate his point about the seventy times seven. In the parable, the debtor was forgiven, but he wasn't given the opportunity to repeat the offense.

Jesus' point about forgiveness was simple. Since God has forgiven us, why can't we forgive one another? Forgiveness means giving the other person what we would want him to give us if our circumstances were reversed.

HOW TO LIVE FOREVER

When Jesus was leaving for Jerusalem, while he was east of the Jordan River:

Someone came up and asked Him, "Teacher, what good must I do to have eternal life?"

"Why do you ask Me about what is good?" He said to him. "There is only One who is good. If you want to enter into life, keep the commandments."

"Which ones?" he asked Him.

Jesus answered,

Do not murder;
do not commit adultery;
do not steal;
do not bear false witness;
honor your father and your mother;
and love your neighbor as yourself.

"I have kept all these," the young man told Him. "What do I still lack?"

"If you want to be perfect," Jesus said to him, "go, sell your belongings and give to the poor, and you will have treasure in heaven. Then come, follow Me."

When the young man heard that command, he went away grieving, because he had many possessions.

Matthew 19:16–22 HCSB

What do you really want? There are differences between Matthew's telling the story of the rich young ruler and Mark's telling of the incident. The list of commandments differs slightly. Matthew also makes explicit what Mark only implies, that if the young man wanted to live forever, then to do so he needed to keep the Ten Commandments. The list that Jesus gave was in response to the young man's question about which commandments he should follow. The young man believed he had done all of them, but he realized he still lacked something. So Jesus told him what that was. It was something that made the young man walk away in tears.

The young man walked away because of his skewed priorities. He rejected the reality Jesus revealed. He thought that Jesus' request to give up all his wealth was a sacrifice. He could see only what he would lose. He forgot all about what he had wanted to gain—eternal life.

If you really could live forever, and it cost only every cent you had, wouldn't that be a bargain? But perhaps the young man didn't really want to live forever. That, perhaps, may be the saddest implication of the story. Since the kingdom of God is of infinite worth, we give up nothing in comparison to it. What we gain from God outweighs what we think we're losing.

NOT EARNING IT

While Jesus was on his final journey to Jerusalem, he said:

"The Kingdom of Heaven is like the landowner who went out early one morning to hire workers for his vineyard. He agreed to pay the normal daily wage and sent them out to work.

"At nine o'clock in the morning he was passing through the marketplace and saw some people standing around doing nothing. So he hired them, telling them he would pay them whatever was right at the end of the day. So they went to work in the vineyard. At noon and again at three o'clock he did the same thing.

"At five o'clock that afternoon he was in town again and saw some more people standing around. He asked them, 'Why haven't you been working today?'

"They replied, 'Because no one hired us.'

"The landowner told them, 'Then go out and join the others in my vineyard.'

"That evening he told the foreman to call the workers in and pay them, beginning with the last workers first. When those hired at five o'clock were paid, each received a full day's wage. When those hired first came to get their pay, they assumed they would receive more. But they, too, were paid a day's wage. When they received their pay, they protested to the owner, 'Those people worked only one hour, and yet you've paid them just as much as you paid us who worked all day in the scorching heat.'

"He answered one of them, 'Friend, I haven't been unfair! Didn't you agree to work all day for the usual wage? Take your money and go. I wanted to pay this last worker the same as you. Is it against the law for me to do what I want with my money? Should you be jealous because I am kind to others?'"

Matthew 20:1–15 NLT

❋

*D*o we want what's fair? Or do we want what's merciful? In Jesus' parable, all the workers, no matter how long they worked, received the same pay. In the real world, the first hired were always the first paid. But for a parable, the conflict and resolution wouldn't have been as clear, so Jesus told it the way he did to make his point about the kingdom of God. God doesn't treat people the way a real farmer would treat his workers. In the kingdom of the world, we are paid according to how long and hard we work. In the kingdom of heaven, we are paid based on the generosity of God.

Our place in the kingdom is not dependent upon what we do. The kingdom of heaven isn't about justice. The kingdom of heaven isn't about playing fair. The kingdom of heaven is about generosity, mercy, and receiving undeserved gifts from God.

❉❉❉❉❉❉❉❉❉❉❉❉❉❉❉❉❉❉❉❉❉❉❉❉❉❉❉❉❉❉

ROBBER BARONS

Right after the triumphal entry:

Jesus went into the temple complex and drove out all those buying and selling in the temple. He overturned the money changers' tables and the chairs of those selling doves. And He said to them, "It is written, My house will be called a house of prayer. But you are making it a den of thieves!"

The blind and the lame came to Him in the temple complex, and He healed them. When the chief priests and the scribes saw the wonders that He did and the children in the temple complex cheering, "*Hosanna* to the Son of David!" they were indignant and said to Him, "Do You hear what these children are saying?"

"Yes," Jesus told them. "Have you never read:

You have prepared praise
from the mouths of children
and nursing infants"?

Then He left them, went out of the city to Bethany, and spent the night there.

Matthew 21:12–17 HCSB

❉

*W*as Jesus against commerce in a religious setting? Was he against profit? Did he dislike business? The religious leaders had decided that ordinary money could not be used in the temple area and insisted that it first be exchanged for special temple money. Only the special money could be used to buy the animals that the religious establishment allowed for sacrifice—and the religious leaders took a cut of the profits. Jesus' words alluded to what Jeremiah had written: "Will you steal and murder, commit adultery and perjury, burn incense to Baal and follow other gods you have not known, and then come and stand before me in this house, which bears my Name, and say, 'We are safe'—safe to do all these detestable things? Has this house, which bears my Name, become a den of robbers to you? But I have been watching!" (Jeremiah 7:9–11 NIV).

When the religious authorities criticized Jesus for letting the children cheer and call him the son of David, he quoted a section of Psalm 8 that had to do with praising God. The religious authorities were upset because of the messianic implications of what Jesus had just done in the temple and what was being said by the children. So Jesus responded by telling them their criticism was misplaced. Not only was Jesus the Messiah, but he was also God.

There is nothing wrong with profit and doing business. A worker, as Jesus said, was worthy of his hire. But if profit stands between a person and God, then it has to go.

THE OWNER

Jesus was in Jerusalem teaching during his final week:

The Pharisees plotted a way to trap [Jesus] into saying something damaging. They sent their disciples, with a few of Herod's followers mixed in, to ask, "Teacher, we know you have integrity, teach the way of God accurately, are indifferent to popular opinion, and don't pander to your students. So tell us honestly: Is it right to pay taxes to Caesar or not?"

Jesus knew they were up to no good. He said, "Why are you playing these games with me? Why are you trying to trap me? Do you have a coin? Let me see it." They handed him a silver piece.

"This engraving—who does it look like? And whose name is on it?"

They said, "Caesar."

"Then give Caesar what is his, and give God what is his."

The Pharisees were speechless. They went off shaking their heads.

Matthew 22:15–22 MSG

*J*esus always got the better of his critics. The tax in question in this verse was the Roman poll tax. The Jewish people despised it. A couple of decades before Jesus was asked about it, a popular leader from the Galilee area named Judas had led a major revolt against the Romans. For the Zealots, Judas and his revolt still inspired them to fight against Rome, and so the question was dangerous. Supporting the tax meant siding with the Romans; opposing the tax would open up Jesus to the charge of sedition. No matter how he answered, the Pharisees figured they could get Jesus into serious trouble.

When Jesus asked them to show him a denarius, Jesus revealed their hypocrisy. If they really were the good, patriotic Jews they pretended to be, then how could they carry a coin with an idolatrous portrait of Caesar carrying an inscription that described him as the "son of God"? With his answer, Jesus distanced himself from the Zealots and indicated that loyalty to a pagan government was not incompatible with loyalty to God.

What Jesus told the Pharisees took the wind out of their sails. But notice that Jesus' answer contradicted what his disciples would have expected of the Messiah. Even though not everyone was a Zealot, most Jewish people believed in Zealot goals, and they all expected the Messiah to overthrow the occupiers.

The kingdom of God and the kingdom of man are two different and sometimes mutually exclusive things. Jesus thinks we can honor both God and whatever nation we live in.

INVESTMENTS

Just outside the temple during the week before Passover, Jesus gave an illustration about what the kingdom of God would be like:

"Again, it will be like a man going on a journey, who called his servants and entrusted his property to them. To one he gave five talents of money, to another two talents, and to another one talent, each according to his ability. Then he went on his journey. The man who had received the five talents went at once and put his money to work and gained five more. So also, the one with the two talents gained two more. But the man who had received the one talent went off, dug a hole in the ground and hid his master's money.

"After a long time the master of those servants returned and settled accounts with them. The man who had received the five talents brought the other five. 'Master,' he said, 'you entrusted me with five talents. See, I have gained five more.'

"His master replied, 'Well done, good and faithful servant! You have been faithful with a few things; I will put you in charge of many things. Come and share your master's happiness!'

"The man with the two talents also came. 'Master,' he said, 'you entrusted me with two talents; see, I have gained two more.'

"His master replied, 'Well done, good and faithful servant! You have been faithful with a few things; I will put you in charge of many things. Come and share your master's happiness!'"

Matthew 25:14–23 NIV

❧

Can Jesus trust us? The kingdom of God was compared to the faithfulness of a wealthy man's servants who handled his investments while he was away. The gospel of Luke presents a similar parable, but the purpose of the trip, the amounts of money, and the number of servants differ from what Matthew described. But Jesus' point remains the same in both versions, perhaps told in different times and circumstances.

In Matthew, Jesus posited that the servants were given "talents" of money. A talent was sixty times larger than what the servants in Luke were given. A *talent* was the equivalent of nearly one hundred pounds of silver. It would have represented what a day laborer might have earned in twenty years of hard labor. It was a huge amount of money.

God has entrusted us with a huge responsibility; he has given us the wealth of his kingdom. He has left to us the choice of what to do with it. His hope is that we will invest it wisely and use it to advance his kingdom. We can do that by spending it on the lives of everyone we meet.

GOOD FOR NOTHING

Just a few days before Passover, Jesus continued his parable of the talents:

"The one also who had received the one talent came up and said, 'Master, I knew you to be a hard man, reaping where you did not sow and gathering where you scattered no seed. And I was afraid, and went away and hid your talent in the ground. See, you have what is yours.'

"But his master answered and said to him, 'You wicked, lazy slave, you knew that I reap where I did not sow and gather where I scattered no seed. Then you ought to have put my money in the bank, and on my arrival I would have received my money back with interest. Therefore take away the talent from him, and give it to the one who has the ten talents.'

"For to everyone who has, more shall be given, and he will have an abundance; but from the one who does not have, even what he does have shall be taken away. Throw out the worthless slave into the outer darkness; in that place there will be weeping and gnashing of teeth."

Matthew 25:24–30 NASB

※

Jesus didn't ask us to play it safe. He wants us to risk it all. The poet Rudyard Kipling wrote a famous poem called "If" in which he described what it meant to be an adult. One part of being an adult was the willingness to take risks and accept failure. In concluding the parable of the servants that were given talents, Jesus ended with the one who, given the least (of a still large sum of money), chose to do nothing with it. He claimed fear as his excuse, fear of losing what he'd been given.

The master didn't accept fear as the real reason for the servant's behavior. Unlike the servant in Luke's parable, the servant in Matthew's story not only had the single talent taken away, but he also was cast into "outer darkness." The weeping and gnashing of teeth were indicative of the regret the lazy servant suffered—his too-late recognition of his bad behavior.

Jesus' parable describes the kingdom of God. Its wealth is distributed unevenly, and the results are uneven. We can multiply only if we have something with which to multiply. We can't multiply by zero and get anything. An unproductive servant is no servant at all.

Jesus doesn't want us to play it safe or to think only about what is best for us. Jesus wants us to risk everything for him, remembering that all we have, all we risk, is what we got from him in the first place.

JESUS IS ONE OF US

During Jesus' last week in Jerusalem, he was teaching his disciples:

"[The King] will also say to those on the left, 'Depart from Me, you who are cursed, into the eternal fire prepared for the Devil and his angels!

For I was hungry and you gave Me nothing to eat;
I was thirsty and you gave Me nothing to drink;
I was a stranger and you didn't take Me in;
I was naked and you didn't clothe Me,
I was sick and in prison and you didn't take care of Me.'

"Then they too will answer, 'Lord, when did we see You hungry, or thirsty, or a stranger, or without clothes, or sick, or in prison, and not help You?'

"Then He will answer them, 'I assure you: Whatever you did not do for one of the least of these, you did not do for Me either.'

"And they will go away into eternal punishment, but the righteous into eternal life."

Matthew 25:41–46 HCSB

※

*J*esus is God, and he became one of us.

Those who do not take care of strangers and do not provide for the poor, sick, and imprisoned are not taking care of Jesus himself. Such people who ignore Jesus' suffering are destined for the eternal fire that God prepared for Satan and his angels. The apostle John, in one of his letters, wrote that if we claim to love God but hate our neighbor, then we don't actually love God. John was basing what he wrote on what Jesus said.

Jesus condemned the Pharisees and religious leaders who believed that the Messiah would come to destroy the wicked, such as the Gentiles, the prostitutes, and the tax collectors. The rich and powerful Sadducees and Pharisees were the ones who mistreated the poor, took the homes of widows, put debtors in prison, and burdened men with rules they wouldn't keep themselves.

This tells us something about God's priorities. Just as God's prophets in the Old Testament condemned those ancient religious rulers for worshipping other gods and mistreating the poor and the powerless, so Jesus condemned the leaders of his day for the same things. Those who belong to Jesus become part of Jesus. How we treat others is how we treat Jesus.

WASTE OF MONEY

Jesus was in the town of Bethany, eating at the home of Simon, who had leprosy. A woman came in with a bottle of expensive perfume and poured it on Jesus' head. But when his disciples saw this, they became angry and complained, "Why such a waste? We could have sold this perfume for a lot of money and given it to the poor."

Jesus knew what they were thinking, and he said: "Why are you bothering this woman? She has done a beautiful thing for me. You will always have the poor with you, but you won't always have me. She has poured perfume on my body to prepare it for burial. You may be sure that wherever the good news is told all over the world, people will remember what she has done. And they will tell others."

Matthew 26:6–13 CEV

✳

$\mathcal{W}$e shouldn't insist that God's will for our lives is necessarily God's will for everyone else. In the same town where his friends Lazarus, Mary, and Martha lived, Jesus had a meal with Simon the leper. A woman poured expensive perfume on him.

Jesus' disciples were upset because this woman had wasted money that could have been given to the poor. Jesus pointed out something that could seem very discouraging: "You will always have the poor with you." Does that mean all efforts to alleviate poverty will fail? Did Jesus suggest that the real waste of the perfume would have been to do with it what the disciples suggested?

Jesus' point was not about the everlasting nature of poverty but rather that his disciples wouldn't always have him. Yes, the Holy Spirit would indwell them; yes, Jesus lives forever at the right hand of the Father. Yes, Jesus promised to "be" with them until the end of the world. But there was a vast difference between Jesus' enjoying a meal with his disciples and being with them "in spirit." Jesus knew he would soon be dying on the cross. It was a poignant time for him, but his disciples did not understand. Soon they would.

It is never a waste to do something special for those whom we love. Life is more than just giving to the poor or whatever other "good thing" our neighbor may believe we need to do.

GET OUT OF HERE

Jesus was teaching in a synagogue in Capernaum:

Suddenly, while still in the meeting place, [Jesus] was interrupted by a man who was deeply disturbed and yelling out, "What business do you have here with us, Jesus? Nazarene! I know what you're up to! You're the Holy One of God, and you've come to destroy us!"

Jesus shut him up: "Quiet! Get out of him!" The afflicting spirit threw the man into spasms, protesting loudly—and got out.

Everyone there was incredulous, buzzing with curiosity. "What's going on here? A new teaching that does what it says? He shuts up defiling, demonic spirits and sends them packing!" News of this traveled fast and was soon all over Galilee.

Directly on leaving the meeting place, they came to Simon and Andrew's house, accompanied by James and John. Simon's mother-in-law was sick in bed, burning up with fever. They told Jesus. He went to her, took her hand, and raised her up. No sooner had the fever left than she was up fixing dinner for them.

That evening, after the sun was down, they brought sick and evil-afflicted people to him, the whole city lined up at his door!

Mark 1:23–33 MSG

When Jesus began his public ministry, the first miracle that got widespread attention occurred when he told a demon to leave a possessed man and the demon left. The response of witnesses was incredulity. They said that Jesus gave "a new teaching." Since demon exorcism was already practiced by the religious leaders (Matthew 12:27), Jesus' exorcism alone was not what was new. The difference was that Jesus' words were backed by actions. Jesus did more than just make speeches. He did something new and startling. Before Jesus arrived, casting out demons was a complex process fraught with difficulty and ritual. Jesus simply told the demon to leave—no theatrics, no formulas, and no ritual. Jesus had a power unlike any of the other teachers they'd known until then.

Jesus said to the demon, "Quiet!" The only other place in Mark's gospel account where Jesus used that particular Greek verb was when he shut down a storm on the Sea of Galilee. Demons obeyed Jesus the same way the inanimate forces of nature obeyed him, or as a well-trained animal might obey its owner. Demons, like storms, were dangerous and powerful. For Jesus, they were nothing at all. Nothing is difficult for Jesus. Jesus doesn't just offer us mere words. He offers us genuine solutions. He will move in and disrupt our lives—not merely give us advice.

THE PROOF IS IN THE PUDDING

When Jesus again entered Capernaum, the people heard that he had come home. So many gathered that there was no room left, not even outside the door, and he preached the word to them. Some men came, bringing to him a paralytic, carried by four of them. Since they could not get him to Jesus because of the crowd, they made an opening in the roof above Jesus and, after digging through it, lowered the mat the paralyzed man was lying on. When Jesus saw their faith, he said to the paralytic, "Son, your sins are forgiven."

Now some teachers of the law were sitting there, thinking to themselves, "Why does this fellow talk like that? He's blaspheming! Who can forgive sins but God alone?"

Immediately Jesus knew in his spirit that this was what they were thinking in their hearts, and he said to them, "Why are you thinking these things? Which is easier: to say to the paralytic, 'Your sins are forgiven,' or to say, 'Get up, take your mat and walk'? But that you may know that the Son of Man has authority on earth to forgive sins. . . ." He said to the paralytic, "I tell you, get up, take your mat and go home." He got up, took his mat and walked out in full view of them all. This amazed everyone and they praised God, saying, "We have never seen anything like this!"

Mark 2:1–12 NIV

"The proof is in the pudding" is a shortened form of the old proverb that "the proof of the pudding is in the eating of it." The proof of Jesus was in the healing of the man.

To open a hole in the roof of a house in ancient Israel was not as labor intensive as opening a hole in a modern roof. Nevertheless, it was still destructive, messy, and noisy. Bits of roof material would have fallen on Jesus and those around him.

When Jesus told the paralyzed man that his sins were forgiven, the teachers of the law thought Jesus was guilty of blasphemy. Obviously, it's easy to tell someone his sins are forgiven. The forgiven person doesn't change color or shape. Forgiving sins, though easier to say, was harder to do in fact. Jesus demonstrated by the visible healing that he had the power to do invisible healing. People got well all the time. But what about people having their sins forgiven? The teachers of the law were right. Only God could do that. And Jesus still has the power to forgive our sins. That is the reason he came to us.

GOD GIVES THE INCREASE

By the Sea of Galilee, when he was alone with his disciples:

Jesus also said: "You don't light a lamp and put it under a clay pot or under a bed. Don't you put a lamp on a lampstand? There is nothing hidden that will not be made public. There is no secret that will not be well known. If you have ears, pay attention!

"Listen carefully to what you hear! The way you treat others will be the way you will be treated—and even worse. Everyone who has something will be given more. But people who don't have anything will lose what little they have."

Again Jesus said: "God's kingdom is like what happens when a farmer scatters seed in a field. The farmer sleeps at night and is up and around during the day. Yet the seeds keep sprouting and growing, and he doesn't understand how. It is the ground that makes the seeds sprout and grow into plants that produce grain. Then when harvest season comes and the grain is ripe, the farmer cuts it with a sickle."

Mark 4:21–29 CEV

※

God's kingdom is obvious and inevitable. Jesus had been teaching crowds using parables. At the end of a long day, while Jesus was alone with his disciples, they asked him about the parables. He explained that although most of the people in the crowds didn't understand about the kingdom, he did not intend for the good news to remain hidden. Instead, the kingdom of God is like a lamp that would bring light to all of them, everywhere.

Jesus warned his disciples to consider carefully what he told them. They might gain insight from his words, or they might become even more confused. For a time, all the disciples were mostly confused about what Jesus was actually saying and doing. But only one of them, Judas, would never understand and would finally lose everything. Even the little he gained from his time with Jesus was taken from him in the end.

And so, what is the kingdom of God like? Jesus said that it grows all by itself in our hearts. We don't have to be anxious about it. We don't have to exercise to make it happen. It just grows, like the grain in a farmer's field. The farmer plants, but he doesn't send the rain, bring the sun, or make seeds sprout. Likewise, we will become what we are and do what God intends by his power.

THEIR FAITH

[Jesus] returned from the region of Tyre, and went by way of Sidon towards the Sea of Galilee, in the region of the Decapolis. They brought to him a deaf man who had an impediment in his speech; and they begged him to lay his hand on him. He took him aside in private, away from the crowd, and put his fingers into his ears, and he spat and touched his tongue. Then looking up to heaven, he sighed and said to him, "Ephphatha," that is, "Be opened." And immediately his ears were opened, his tongue was released, and he spoke plainly. Then Jesus ordered them to tell no one; but the more he ordered them, the more zealously they proclaimed it.

They were astounded beyond measure, saying, "He has done everything well; he even makes the deaf to hear and the mute to speak."

Mark 7:31–37 NRSV

The Decapolis was a federation of ten cities in the area east of Samaria and Galilee, including the cities of Damascus and Philadelphia. The area had a culture that was more Greek than Hebrew, and many non-Jewish people lived there. After Jesus healed the daughter of the Gentile woman in Tyre, he traveled on to visit the region.

While there, some of the people brought him a man who was deaf. He had an "impediment in his speech," which likely meant he had become deaf later in life rather than having been born deaf. Since he could no longer hear himself talk, the clarity of his speech was affected.

Unlike so many of his healings, this time Jesus made a ritual of the process. He spat, touched the man's tongue, stuck his fingers into the man's ears, and uttered an Aramaic word that the man couldn't have heard and probably wouldn't have understood, given that they were in a Greek-speaking region. The man's friends wanted Jesus to "lay his hand" on him. Jesus accommodated their expectations. Jesus works with us where we are. He comes to us in our situation, and from there takes us to where we need to be. He does not insist on our changing before he changes us. This man and his friends needed the special handling. Jesus gives us what we need.

WHAT DO YOU SEE?

Jesus and his disciples were crossing the Sea of Galilee:

The disciples had forgotten to bring any bread; and they had only one loaf with them in the boat. And [Jesus] cautioned them, saying, "Watch out— beware of the yeast of the Pharisees and the yeast of Herod."

They said to one another, "It is because we have no bread."

And becoming aware of it, Jesus said to them, "Why are you talking about having no bread? Do you still not perceive or understand? Are your hearts hardened? Do you have eyes, and fail to see? Do you have ears, and fail to hear? And do you not remember? When I broke the five loaves for the five thousand, how many baskets full of broken pieces did you collect?"

They said to him, "Twelve."

"And the seven for the four thousand, how many baskets full of broken pieces did you collect?"

And they said to him, "Seven." Then he said to them, "Do you not yet understand?"

They came to Bethsaida. Some people brought a blind man to him and begged him to touch him. He took the blind man by the hand and led him out of the village; and when he had put saliva on his eyes and laid his hands on him, he asked him, "Can you see anything?"

And the man looked up and said, "I can see people, but they look like trees, walking."

Then Jesus laid his hands on his eyes again; and he looked intently and his sight was restored, and he saw everything clearly. Then he sent him away to his home, saying, "Do not even go into the village."

Mark 8:14–26 NRSV

After warning his disciples about the Pharisees' yeast, Jesus healed a blind man. In this story, Jesus asked his disciples if they were blind. Then he reminded them about how he had twice fed large crowds. The healing of the blind man illustrated Jesus' point.

Of all the healings recorded in the Bible, this is the only one where the healing occurred in stages. Jesus put spit on the blind man's eyes, asked him how he was doing, and then touched his eyes a second time before he was completely healed.

Twice Jesus fed thousands. Twice Jesus worked to heal the blind man. Jesus' disciples, like that blind man, were slow to perceive. They understood his words the way the blind man first saw people as trees. Only later did he see clearly. Only later did the disciples understand.

If God needs us to understand something, he'll do whatever is necessary to enlighten us. He'll never give up either. He's a patient teacher.

IMMORTAL WORMS

While Jesus was in Capernaum teaching his disciples, he said:

"Whoever causes one of these little ones who believe in Me to stumble, it would be better for him if a millstone were hung around his neck, and he were thrown into the sea.

"If your hand causes you to sin, cut it off. It is better for you to enter into life maimed, rather than having two hands, to go to hell, into the fire that shall never be quenched—

"where
'Their worm does not die,
And the fire is not quenched.'

"And if your foot causes you to sin, cut it off. It is better for you to enter life lame, rather than having two feet, to be cast into hell, into the fire that shall never be quenched—

"where
'Their worm does not die
And the fire is not quenched.'

"And if your eye causes you to sin, pluck it out. It is better for you to enter the kingdom of God with one eye, rather than having two eyes, to be cast into hell fire—

"where
'Their worm does not die,
And the fire is not quenched.'

"For everyone will be seasoned with fire, and every sacrifice will be seasoned with salt. Salt is good, but if the salt loses its flavor, how will you season it? Have salt in yourselves, and have peace with one another."

Mark 9:42–50 NKJV

Jesus used hell to warn believers, not to condemn sinners. Of course, Jesus didn't think it was a good idea for his followers to maim themselves. They understood his point as easily as a modern reader understands the phrase "raining cats and dogs." Literalizing a metaphor is as big a mistake as allegorizing something that should be taken at face value.

Jesus' point was that the kingdom of God was so wonderful that missing an eye or a foot was far better than the alternative of hell. Jesus quoted odd phrases such as, "Their worm does not die" and, "Their fire is not quenched" from the very end of the book of Isaiah. The word translated *hell* came into Greek from a Hebrew phrase that meant "the Valley of Hinnon." Located just outside Jerusalem, the Valley of Hinnon was where King Ahaz worshipped Molech by sacrificing his children as burnt offerings. Afterward, it became an ever-burning garbage dump. The picture of worms and fire is one of perpetual uncleanness. It stands in sharp contrast to the wonders of God's kingdom. Our choice is stark and therefore not hard to make.

RULES OF ENGAGEMENT

In Jerusalem, after the triumphal entry:

Jesus was approached by some Sadducees—religious leaders who say there is no resurrection from the dead. They posed this question: "Teacher, Moses gave us a law that if a man dies, leaving a wife without children, his brother should marry the widow and have a child who will carry on the brother's name. Well, suppose there were seven brothers. The oldest one married and then died without children. So the second brother married the widow, but he also died without children. Then the third brother married her. This continued with all seven of them, and still there were no children. Last of all, the woman also died. So tell us, whose wife will she be in the resurrection? For all seven were married to her."

Jesus replied, "Your mistake is that you don't know the Scriptures, and you don't know the power of God. For when the dead rise, they will neither marry nor be given in marriage. In this respect they will be like the angels in heaven.

"But now, as to whether the dead will be raised—haven't you ever read about this in the writings of Moses, in the story of the burning bush? Long after Abraham, Isaac, and Jacob had died, God said to Moses, 'I am the God of Abraham, the God of Isaac, and the God of Jacob.' So he is the God of the living, not the dead. You have made a serious error."

Mark 12:18–27 NLT

*J*esus told the Sadducees that their ignorance was showing. The Sadducees did not believe in the resurrection because they believed only the first five books of the Bible, Genesis through Deuteronomy, and could find nothing in those books about an afterlife. They did not believe that the rest of the books of the Old Testament were authoritative Scripture. According to the law of Moses, if a man died childless, his brother was required to marry the widow. The first child born from the union would then carry on the name and take the inheritance of the dead man. The purpose of this law was to keep property in the dead man's family.

To prove the existence of the resurrection, Jesus quoted from what the Sadducees accepted as Scripture. Besides their not understanding Scripture, Jesus told them that they were blinded by their own culture. They were wrong to assume that the social relationships they knew in the present day would endure in the kingdom of God. The post-resurrection future with God would be nothing like the world. We can see the future only dimly; it will surprise us.

BE ALERT

In Jerusalem during Jesus' final week, he was teaching his disciples near the temple:

"In those days, after that tribulation: The sun will be darkened, and the moon will not shed its light; the stars will be falling from the sky, and the celestial powers will be shaken.

"Then they will see the Son of Man coming in clouds with great power and glory. He will send out the angels and gather His elect from the four winds, from the end of the earth to the end of the sky.

"Learn this parable from the fig tree: As soon as its branch becomes tender and sprouts leaves, you know that summer is near. In the same way, when you see these things happening, know that He is near—at the door! I assure you: This generation will certainly not pass away until all these things take place. Heaven and earth will pass away, but My words will never pass away until all these things take place. Heaven and earth will pass away, but My words will never pass away.

"Now concerning that day or hour no one knows—neither the angels in heaven nor the Son—except the Father. Watch! Be alert! For you don't know when the time is coming. It is like a man on a journey, who left his house, gave authority to his slaves, gave each one his work, and commanded the doorkeeper to be alert. Therefore be alert, since you don't know when the master of the house is coming—whether in the evening or at midnight or at the crowing of the rooster or early in the morning. Otherwise, he might come suddenly and find you sleeping. And what I say to you, I say to everyone: Be alert!"

Mark 13:24–37 HCSB

🎴

*J*esus quoted the book of Isaiah to describe the destruction that the Romans would bring against Jerusalem and its temple forty years later. Isaiah had described what it was like when the Babylonians came.

Since Rome was a new Babylon for the Jewish people, Jesus' disciples would have understood his words as a prediction of a Roman invasion of their homeland. When Jesus told them that they would see him coming "in clouds with great power and glory," they thought he meant that unlike the Israelites when the Babylonians invaded, the Messiah would prevail against the Romans.

Jesus' disciples misunderstood Jesus. Until they were enlightened by the Spirit at pentecost, they looked for only a physical kingdom. They didn't understand that Jesus spoke of a spiritual kingdom in the hearts of believers everywhere. Someday Jesus will come back and rule the earth physically, but that time was not then and it is not yet. We can comfort ourselves with the knowledge that with God in our hearts today, we already experience that kingdom of God.

THE PROPHET AT HOME

In his home synagogue in Nazareth, Jesus read the Scripture for that week:

He rolled up the scroll, handed it back to the assistant, and sat down. Every eye in the place was on him, intent. Then he started in, "You've just heard Scripture make history. It came true just now in this place."

All who were there, watching and listening, were surprised at how well he spoke. But they also said, "Isn't this Joseph's son, the one we've known since he was a youngster?"

He answered, "I suppose you're going to quote the proverb, 'Doctor, go heal yourself. Do here in your hometown what we heard you did in Capernaum.' Well, let me tell you something: No prophet is ever welcomed in his hometown. Isn't it a fact that there were many widows in Israel at the time of Elijah during that three and a half years of drought when famine devastated the land, but the only widow to whom Elijah was sent was in Sarepta in Sidon? And there were many lepers in Israel at the time of the prophet Elisha but the only one cleansed was Naaman the Syrian."

That set everyone in the meeting place seething with anger. They threw him out, banishing him from the village, then took him to a mountain cliff at the edge of the village to throw him to his doom, but he gave them the slip and was on his way.

Luke 4:20–30 MSG

✺

*J*esus told his hometown friends and family there was nothing new under the sun. Their rejection of him, thanks to their inability to see past their familiarity with him, was nothing new. No prophet had ever been accepted by his hometown crowds.

Jesus illustrated his point about prophets' being unacceptable to their own people by mentioning two stories from the Old Testament about Elijah and Elisha that infuriated everyone. Those great prophets had not healed Israelites or cared for the needs of Israelites. Instead, they had provided for Gentiles.

Most of the Jewish people despised Gentiles and believed them to be beyond God's love. Though they attended synagogue regularly and thought themselves committed to Scripture, when confronted with its actual words, they wanted nothing to do with it or with the one who had preached it to them.

Jesus wasn't the only prophet without honor in his hometown. The Bible itself is often without honor as well. It's one thing for us to say that the Bible has an honored place in our lives. It's another thing to spend time with it, listen to its words, and take those words to heart.

WORTHY OF HIS HIRE

One day as Jesus was preaching on the shore of the Sea of Galilee, great crowds pressed in on him to listen to the word of God. He noticed two empty boats at the water's edge, for the fishermen had left them and were washing their nets. Stepping into one of the boats, Jesus asked Simon, its owner, to push it out into the water. So he sat in the boat and taught the crowds from there.

When he had finished speaking, he said to Simon, "Now go out where it is deeper, and let down your nets to catch some fish."

"Master," Simon replied, "we worked hard all last night and didn't catch a thing. But if you say so, I'll let the nets down again."

And this time their nets were so full of fish they began to tear! A shout for help brought their partners in the other boat, and soon both boats were filled with fish and on the verge of sinking.

When Simon Peter realized what had happened, he fell to his knees before Jesus and said, "Oh, Lord, please leave me—I'm too much of a sinner to be around you." For he was awestruck by the number of fish they had caught, as were the others with him. His partners, James and John, the sons of Zebedee, were also amazed.

Jesus replied to Simon, "Don't be afraid! From now on you'll be fishing for people!" And as soon as they landed, they left everything and followed Jesus.

Luke 5:1–11 NLT

*W*hen Jesus borrowed one of Peter's boats as a platform for speaking to the crowd, he wasn't keeping Peter from doing his job. Fishermen did not fish during the daylight hours—they went out at night, when the fish were easier to catch. During the day, they sorted through the previous night's catch, and they cleaned and repaired their nets. Sitting in Peter's boat to teach the crowd, Jesus didn't interfere with Peter's livelihood.

Nevertheless, Jesus had "hired" Peter's boat and so paid for it by telling Peter to go fishing. In response, Peter addressed him as *Master*. The Greek word was merely an honorific. But after the fish had been caught, Peter used a different word. *Lord* was used exclusively of God by the Jewish people of that era. With a huge catch of fish in his nets, Peter responded to Jesus with fear, bowing before the Almighty.

Jesus compensated Peter generously for the boat. But then he went beyond that and offered him a better job—a position in the kingdom of God. When we give our lives to Jesus, he gives us himself and all that he has.

DAY 233

REMODELING

God had given Jesus the power to heal the sick, and some people came carrying a crippled man on a mat. They tried to take him inside the house and put him in front of Jesus. But because of the crowd, they could not get him to Jesus. So they went up on the roof, where they removed some tiles and let the mat down in the middle of the room.

When Jesus saw how much faith they had, he said to the crippled man, "My friend, your sins are forgiven."

The Pharisees and the experts began arguing, "Jesus must think he is God! Only God can forgive sins."

Jesus knew what they were thinking, and he said, "Why are you thinking that? Is it easier for me to tell this crippled man that his sins are forgiven or to tell him to get up and walk? But now you will see that the Son of Man has the right to forgive sins here on earth." Jesus then said to the man, "Get up! Pick up your mat and walk home."

At once the man stood up in front of everyone. He picked up his mat and went home, giving thanks to God. Everyone was amazed and praised God. What they saw surprised them, and they said, "We have seen a great miracle today!"

Luke 5:17–26 CEV

Sometimes Jesus asks us to do the impossible. Three times the gospel writers described the healing of the paralyzed man whose friends remodeled a house so they could reach Jesus.

After forgiving his sins, Jesus told the paralyzed man to get up and go home. The man didn't think Jesus' command was unreasonable or impossible. He didn't argue with Jesus or give him a list of excuses. He didn't tell Jesus that he'd rather stay and listen to the rest of Jesus' message that his friends had so rudely interrupted. Instead, he just got up. He took his mat, rolled it up, and headed home. And he praised God as he went.

Sometimes we might think that God has asked us to do something impossible. Walking was certainly impossible for that paralyzed man just before Jesus told him to walk. But with the command, Jesus provided the means. If Jesus asks us to do something, no matter how beyond us it seems, there's no question that we can do it. He'll always provide the way. And like the paralyzed man, we'll be praising God as we go.

NO CONDEMNATION

Near the Sea of Galilee, Jesus taught a large group on a plain:

"Do not judge, and you will not be judged; do not condemn, and you will not be condemned. Forgive, and you will be forgiven; give, and it will be given to you. A good measure, pressed down, shaken together, running over, will be put into your lap; for the measure you give will be the measure you get back."

He also told them a parable: "Can a blind person guide a blind person? Will not both fall into a pit? A disciple is not above the teacher, but everyone who is fully qualified will be like the teacher. Why do you see the speck in your neighbor's eye, but do not notice the log in your own eye? Or how can you say to your neighbor, 'Friend, let me take out the speck in your eye,' when you yourself do not see the log in your own eye? You hypocrite, first take the log out of your own eye, and then you will see clearly to take the speck out of your neighbor's eye."

Luke 6:37–42 NRSV

❋

*I*f we can't judge, then what are we supposed to do with sinners? Jesus thought we should forgive them. Not long after he picked his twelve apostles, as they sat on a plain near the Sea of Galilee, Jesus told them to stop judging one another.

To illustrate his point, Jesus told a series of extended metaphors about blind people, teachers, and logs. Rather than worrying about the behavior of the people around us, rather than concerning ourselves with our neighbors' faults, Jesus thought we'd be better off focusing on our own imperfections. After all, how much good does it do to point out how awful our neighbor is? Will he thank us for our insight? Does he take our words to heart? Have we fixed him? Since we're blind ourselves, and since we have our own set of problems, how well can we even see his needs? Jesus thought we'd do far better to focus our criticisms on ourselves and just be kind to our neighbors. Kindness tends to be responded to with kindness. And that's what we'd like them to be doing to us anyway.

We'd all like to be given the benefit of the doubt. We'd all like to be given a second chance. We'd all like to be forgiven. So Jesus encouraged his disciples —and us—to treat others just the way we'd like to be treated.

DAY 235

WIPING AWAY TEARS

[Jesus] was on His way to a town called Nain. His disciples and a large crowd were traveling with Him. Just as He neared the gate of the town, a dead man was being carried out. He was his mother's only son, and she was a widow. A large crowd from the city was also with her. When the Lord saw her, He had compassion on her and said, "Don't cry." Then He came up and touched the open coffin, and the pallbearers stopped. And He said, "Young man, I tell you, get up!"

The dead man sat up and began to speak, and Jesus gave him to his mother. Then fear came over everyone, and they glorified God, saying, "A great prophet has risen among us," and "God has visited His people." This report about Him went throughout Judea and all the vicinity.

Luke 7:11–17 HCSB

✻

*J*esus didn't just feel the pain of others. He solved it. Jesus visited a small village called Nain, about six miles southeast of Nazareth, and it isn't mentioned anywhere else in the Bible. A widow was there, weeping over her only son who had just died. As a widow, the woman's only source of support and protection would have been her son. In ancient Israel's patriarchal society, without a male relative, she would be reduced to begging. Like Naomi and Ruth upon their return to Bethlehem, her only hope was to find fields in which to glean. On top of her grief, she was facing hard times.

In the middle of a funeral procession, Jesus' words that she should "stop crying" would have been disconcertingly inappropriate. As if that weren't bad enough, he touched the casket and forced the pallbearers to stop walking. One can imagine the shock and disbelief of the crowd as they watched what Jesus was doing.

Then he told the dead man to get up.

The initial reaction of the crowd was terror. Once they realized fully what had happened, the funeral became a celebration. Their pain became joy. They decided Jesus must be a great prophet because only Elijah and Elisha had ever raised people from the dead (1 Kings 17:17–24; 2 Kings 4:18–37).

Jesus doesn't ask us just to keep a stiff upper lip; he doesn't want us simply to suck it up. Jesus can wipe our tears away by taking the reason for our tears away.

KISSING JESUS

Jesus was eating in the home of Simon the Pharisee when a woman poured perfume on him:

He turned toward the woman and said to Simon, "Do you see this woman? I came into your house. You did not give me any water for my feet, but she wet my feet with her tears and wiped them with her hair. You did not give me a kiss, but this woman, from the time I entered, has not stopped kissing my feet. You did not put oil on my head, but she has poured perfume on my feet. Therefore, I tell you, her many sins have been forgiven—for she loved much. But he who has been forgiven little loves little."

Then Jesus said to her, "Your sins are forgiven."

The other guests began to say among themselves, "Who is this who even forgives sins?"

Jesus said to the woman, "Your faith has saved you; go in peace."

Luke 7:44–50 NIV

A Pharisee named Simon invited Jesus to have dinner with him. While Jesus was reclining, a woman brought a bottle of perfume in an alabaster jar, began weeping on Jesus' feet, and then wiped his feet with her hair. Although aspects of the story resemble what Mary of Bethany did when she poured perfume on Jesus' head shortly before his crucifixion, the differences indicate Mary and this woman are not the same person and that this is a different event.

The Pharisee was offended that Jesus accepted the woman's attentions. She was described as having lived a "sinful life." Although the word is a generic word for a *sinner*, it was commonly used for prostitutes. But Jesus understood why she was behaving so strangely with him.

Jesus told the woman that her sins were forgiven and that she'd been saved by her faith. She had not asked Jesus for forgiveness. In fact, never once are we told that she said anything. But her bizarre actions indicated that something in her life had changed and that it was because of Jesus. Perhaps she had been in one of the crowds earlier in the day, listening to his preaching. His words changed her life. She believed and decided to show her gratitude to him.

Repentance is not a formula, and it is more than simply saying the right words. Repentance is a change in our attitudes, which makes us change the direction of our lives. True repentance leads us to do whatever it takes to make amends, to fix whatever we have broken.

NOT POSSIBLE

Near the town of Bethsaida, Jesus taught a large crowd:

As the day declined, the Twelve said, "Dismiss the crowd so they can go to the farms or villages around here and get a room for the night and a bite to eat. We're out in the middle of nowhere."

"You feed them," Jesus said.

They said, "We couldn't scrape up more than five loaves of bread and a couple of fish—unless, of course, you want us to go to town ourselves and buy food for everybody." (There were more than five thousand people in the crowd.)

But he went ahead and directed his disciples, "Sit them down in groups of about fifty." They did what he said, and soon had everyone seated. He took the five loaves and two fish, lifted his face to heaven in prayer, blessed, broke, and gave the bread and fish to the disciples to hand out to the crowd. After the people had all eaten their fill, twelve baskets of leftovers were gathered up.

Luke 9:12–17 MSG

※

*W*hat does abundance look like? Twelve baskets of leftovers! Jesus gave extravagantly. He didn't meet only the needs of a hungry crowd; he gave them more than they needed. They ate until they were filled—until they were satisfied, until they couldn't take anymore.

As God, Jesus could easily have made just enough food, not too much and not too little. That he had the disciples gather the leftovers was not to teach them about littering or about proper stewardship. He had them gather up the leftovers so they could see just how generous he had been—how he could make their "cup overflow" (see Psalm 23:5). Jesus wanted his disciples to understand that he was not interested in giving only the bare necessities. When the Israelites, fresh from Egypt, began building the tabernacle and its associated objects, Moses asked them to donate the necessary materials. It wasn't long before Moses had to tell them to stop because they had given too much. That's the way Jesus is with people. He gives us so much that we can't take another bite. As Paul wrote, God is able to do "immeasurably more than all we ask or imagine, according to his power that is at work within us" (Ephesians 3:20 NIV).

Thanks to his work on the cross, Jesus gave us his Father's kingdom. All our sins are forgiven. We have eternal life in God's kingdom, not only as Jesus' friends, but also as his brothers and sisters.

THE KINGDOM IS AT HAND

Jesus prepared to travel to Jerusalem:

The Lord appointed seventy-two others and sent them two by two ahead of him to every town and place where he was about to go. He told them, "The harvest is plentiful, but the workers are few. Ask the Lord of the harvest, therefore, to send out workers into his harvest field. Go! I am sending you out like lambs among wolves. Do not take a purse or bag or sandals; and do not greet anyone on the road.

"When you enter a house, first say, 'Peace to this house.' If a man of peace is there, your peace will rest on him; if not, it will return to you. Stay in that house, eating and drinking whatever they give you, for the worker deserves his wages. Do not move around from house to house.

"When you enter a town and are welcomed, eat what is set before you. Heal the sick who are there and tell them, 'The kingdom of God is near you.'"

Luke 10:1–9 NIV

❋

*J*esus sent seventy-two followers into the cities that he was about to visit himself. Their message was the same as his in both word and deed. Perhaps he chose seventy-two to match the number of elders on whom the Spirit descended in the wilderness to help Moses govern. The mission of the seventy-two was short and temporary in contrast to the worldwide and permanent mission of the twelve apostles whom Jesus sent at another time. After a single missionary tour, the seventy-two followers weren't mentioned again in the New Testament.

What did Jesus mean about peace resting on a man of peace? The standard greeting in Israel, as throughout the Middle East, was, "Peace to you." Jesus merely told them that if their greeting was accepted and they received an invitation to stay, then they should accept that home's hospitality. If their greeting was not accepted—that is, if they didn't receive an invitation to stay—they should move on to someone else. Jesus gave them instructions about how they would know where they could stay while they worked.

Jesus was proposing something new for those who worked full-time for him. Before Jesus, the rabbis in charge of the synagogues received no payment from the synagogue. They had to have a trade in order to make a living. Jesus argued that those who worked for the kingdom of God deserved to be supported by those to whom they ministered. That's why in most churches today pastors are paid a salary by the congregation they serve.

GOD IS NOT A GRUMPY FATHER

Near Jerusalem, Jesus taught his disciples:

"Suppose one of you goes to a friend in the middle of the night and says, 'Let me borrow three loaves of bread. A friend of mine has dropped in, and I don't have a thing for him to eat.' And suppose your friend answers, 'Don't bother me! The door is bolted, and my children and I are in bed. I cannot get up to give you something.'

"He may not get up and give you the bread, just because you are his friend. But he will get up and give you as much as you need, simply because you are not ashamed to keep on asking.

"So I tell you to ask and you will receive, search and you will find, knock and the door will be opened for you. Everyone who asks will receive, everyone who searches will find, and the door will be opened for everyone who knocks. Which one of you fathers would give your hungry child a snake if the child asked for a fish? Which one of you would give your child a scorpion if the child asked for an egg? As bad as you are, you still know how to give good gifts to your children. But your heavenly Father is even more ready to give the Holy Spirit to anyone who asks."

Luke 11:5–13 CEV

※

*C*hildren don't need ponies. Men don't need sports cars. But God always gives us what we need. Our trouble comes in not being able to distinguish clearly between our needs and our wants. In the time of Jesus, people usually slept together in one room in one bed. They did this not because they liked the togetherness but because their houses were small and cramped, often with only one room.

It took a lot of effort for a man to rise in the middle of the night, crawl over his entire family, and find his way to his front door in the dark. On top of that, three loaves of bread for someone else's guest in the middle of the night wasn't even a reasonable request! But even so silly an appeal could get results if one was persistent enough. It is hard to sleep with someone pounding on the door.

Sometimes we give in to our children just because we get tired of listening to them whine. But God is never in bed; he's never broke; he's never had a bad day at work. He's happy to give because he loves us. Since even grumpy neighbors and tired parents will respond to our requests, how much more then will our Father in heaven take care of giving us what we really need!

DEMONOLOGY

Near Jerusalem, Jesus healed a demon-possessed man and said:

"When a strong man, fully armed, guards his castle, his property is safe. But when one stronger than he attacks him and overpowers him, he takes away his armor in which he trusted and divides his plunder. Whoever is not with me is against me, and whoever does not gather with me scatters.

"When the unclean spirit has gone out of a person, it wanders through waterless regions looking for a resting place, but not finding any, it says, 'I will return to my house from which I came.' When it comes, it finds it swept and put in order. Then it goes and brings seven other spirits more evil than itself, and they enter and live there; and the last state of that person is worse than the first."

While he was saying this, a woman in the crowd raised her voice and said to him, "Blessed is the womb that bore you and the breasts that nursed you!"

But he said, "Blessed rather are those who hear the word of God and obey it!"

Luke 11:21–28 NRSV

❋

It's easy to miss the forest for the trees. While Jesus was talking about the behavior of demons, a woman in the crowd made a statement that seemed odd and out of place, almost as if she wasn't even listening to him. Her words don't seem to fit the context of Jesus' discussion.

She offered a blessing on Jesus' mother. What did she mean by that? Apparently, she thought that Jesus was wonderful because he was a teacher and because he had power over demons. So she wished that she could have a son just like him so she could be just as happy as Jesus' mother must be.

Jesus responded by telling her that the real happiness was not in having power over demons. It was not in having a son like Jesus. Instead, Jesus said that real happiness came from having a relationship with God, listening to what he said, and then doing what he asked. What does God want of us? He wants us to love him and the people around us. He wants us to help make the lives of those we know better. We become distracted by what we want in life, and we forget to focus on what God wants. The woman in the crowd thought happiness came from circumstances, but Jesus wanted her—and us—to understand that happiness really comes from having a vibrant relationship with God.

COMPULSION

Near Jerusalem, Jesus ate in the home of a prominent Pharisee:

When one of those who sat at the table with [Jesus] heard these things, he said to Him, "Blessed is he who shall eat bread in the kingdom of God!"

Then He said to him, "A certain man gave a great supper and invited many, and sent his servant at supper time to say to those who were invited, 'Come, for all things are now ready.' But they all with one accord began to make excuses. The first said to him, 'I have bought a piece of ground, and I must go and see it. I ask you to have me excused.' And another said, 'I have bought five yoke of oxen, and I am going to test them. I ask you to have me excused.' Still another said, 'I have married a wife, and therefore I cannot come.' So that servant came and reported these things to his master. Then the master of the house, being angry, said to his servant, 'Go out quickly into the streets and lanes of the city, and bring in here the poor and the maimed and the lame and the blind.' And the servant said, 'Master, it is done as you commanded, and still there is room.' Then the master said to the servant, 'Go out into the highways and hedges, and compel them to come in, that my house may be filled. For I say to you that none of those men who were invited shall taste my supper.'"

Luke 14:15–24 NKJV

While Jesus was at a fancy dinner in the home of a prominent Pharisee, Jesus told him that when he invited people to a meal, he shouldn't invite them based on what sort of meal he thought he'd someday get from them in return. Instead of thinking about payback from his guests, he should be thinking about how he'd be repaid by God. Then one of the dinner guests proclaimed how happy the people would be who shared in the banquet in God's kingdom.

Jesus taught a parable about who would be invited to share in God's future banquet. Jesus perhaps adapted an ancient Jewish tale about an ambitious tax collector who tried to gain social standing with the aristocrats by inviting them to dinner. But they rebuffed his offer. In order that the dinner not go to waste, the tax collector invited all the poor instead. Jesus wanted his audience to understand that God offered everyone a seat at his great banquet. God is not concerned with the status of those who come, only that they come. Those who miss out have no one but themselves to blame.

Jesus wants us to understand how easy it is for us to get into God's banquet because of how hard he's worked to get us there. We have no good excuse for not showing up.

HATRED

Jesus approached Jerusalem for the last time:

Large crowds were going along with Him; and He turned and said to them, "If anyone comes to Me, and does not hate his own father and mother and wife and children and brothers and sisters, yes, and even his own life, he cannot be My disciple. Whoever does not carry his own cross and come after Me cannot be My disciple. For which one of you, when he wants to build a tower, does not first sit down and calculate the cost to see if he has enough to complete it? Otherwise, when he has laid a foundation and is not able to finish, all who observe it begin to ridicule him, saying, 'This man began to build and was not able to finish.'

"Or what king, when he sets out to meet another king in battle, will not first sit down and consider whether he is strong enough with ten thousand men to encounter the one coming against him with twenty thousand? Or else, while the other is still far away, he sends a delegation and asks for terms of peace.

"So then, none of you can be My disciple who does not give up all his own possessions.

"Therefore, salt is good; but if even salt has become tasteless, with what will it be seasoned? It is useless either for the soil or for the manure pile; it is thrown out. He who has ears to hear, let him hear."

Luke 14:25–35 NASB

How much does it cost to be one of Jesus' disciples? As much as you have. Jesus said that following him required a willingness to place Jesus' demands above those of our families and ourselves. Disciples need to be willing to be ready for martyrdom.

"Carrying your own cross," is a powerful image. Those condemned to crucifixion had to carry their own crosses to the place of execution. A person carrying his cross was a person who had lost everything; he was stripped naked and was exhausted. He had no possessions or family. He was hungry and thirsty. And all he had ahead of him was a torturous and brutal death.

When we join with Jesus, we give up all that we were and are transformed into new creatures. Our old lives and our old ways are undone in Jesus.

THE FLAMES OF HELL

Near Jerusalem, Jesus addressed the Pharisees:

"There was once a rich man who wore expensive clothes and every day ate the best food. But a poor beggar named Lazarus was brought to the gate of the rich man's house. He was happy just to eat the scraps that fell from the rich man's table. His body was covered with sores, and dogs kept coming up to lick them. The poor man died, and angels took him to the place of honor next to Abraham.

"The rich man also died and was buried. He went to hell and was suffering terribly. When he looked up and saw Abraham far off and Lazarus at his side, he said to Abraham, 'Have pity on me! Send Lazarus to dip his finger in water and touch my tongue. I'm suffering terribly in this fire.'

"Abraham answered, 'My friend, remember that while you lived, you had everything good, and Lazarus had everything bad. Now he is happy, and you are in pain. And besides, there is a deep ditch between us, and no one from either side can cross over.'

"But the rich man said, 'Abraham, then please send Lazarus to my father's home. Let him warn my five brothers, so they won't come to this horrible place.'

"Abraham answered, 'Your brothers can read what Moses and the prophets wrote. They should pay attention to that.'

"Then the rich man said, 'No, that's not enough! If only someone from the dead would go to them, they would listen and turn to God.'

"So Abraham said, 'If they won't pay attention to Moses and the prophets, they won't listen even to someone who comes back from the dead.'"

Luke 16:19–31 CEV

Although the story of Lazarus and the rich man may give us some information about the nature of hell, it was not the primary point of the story. Jesus was trying to teach the Pharisees and Sadducees a lesson. They believed that because they were rich and powerful, they were blessed by God. They believed the poor and weak were that way because God was punishing them for their sins.

Jesus wanted the Pharisees and Sadducees to understand that external circumstances revealed nothing about how sinful a person might be. Abraham's warning that even a resurrection wouldn't convince those who wouldn't listen to Scripture was directed at the Pharisees and Sadducees. Jesus had already raised several people from the dead. Soon Jesus himself would rise from the dead. But all the miracles Jesus did weren't enough to convince the Pharisees and Sadducees who rejected him. God has given us his words and the words of his Son, Jesus Christ. Because of those words, we can believe.

JUST LIKE NOAH

Near Jerusalem, Jesus responded to the Pharisees' question about the kingdom of God:

"Just as it was in the days of Noah, so it will be in the days of the Son of Man: people went on eating, drinking, marrying and giving in marriage until the day Noah boarded the ark, and the flood came and destroyed them all. It will be the same as it was in the days of Lot: people went on eating, drinking, buying, selling, planting, building. But on the day Lot left Sodom, fire and sulfur rained from heaven and destroyed them all. It will be like that on the day the Son of Man is revealed. On that day, a man on the housetop, whose belongings are in the house, must not come down to get them. Likewise the man who is in the field must not turn back. Remember Lot's wife! Whoever tries to make his life secure will lose it, and whoever loses his life will preserve it. I tell you, on that night two will be in one bed: one will be taken and the other will be left. Two women will be grinding grain together: one will be taken and the other left. Two will be in a field: one will be taken, and the other will be left."

"Where, Lord?" they asked Him.

He said to them, "Where the corpse is, there also the vultures will be gathered."

Luke 17:26–37 HCSB

The rain was already falling, and they didn't have an umbrella. The Pharisees had wondered when the kingdom of God would arrive. Jesus told his disciples that its arrival would be unexpected. When the Flood arrived in the time of Noah and destroyed the world, when burning sulfur rained down on Sodom and consumed it, there were no warning signs other than the prophets. The events were sudden and utterly unexpected catastrophes. People were just living their lives until the moment they died. When Jesus comes back again, it will be no different from what occurred in those ancient times.

Jesus wants us to conduct ourselves differently from the people in those ancient disaster areas. He wants us to live with God's kingdom in mind. In fact, he wants us to live as if we're a part of his kingdom now because we are, thanks to the Spirit of God inside us.

We should be thankful that Jesus didn't give his disciples a date for his second coming. We can live each day with anticipation, knowing that he could come back at any moment, instead of thinking that it can't be today.

PERCENTAGES

Jesus was in the temple courts after the triumphal entry:

He looked up and saw the rich dropping their offerings into the temple treasury. He also saw a poor widow dropping in two tiny coins. "I tell you the truth," He said. "This poor widow has put in more than all of them. For all these people have put in gifts out of their surplus, but she out of her poverty has put in all she had to live on."

As some were talking about the temple complex, how it was adorned with beautiful stones and gifts dedicated to God, He said, "These things that you see—the days will come when not one stone will be left on another that will not be thrown down!"

"Teacher," they asked Him, "so when will these things be? And what will be the sign when these things are about to take place?"

Then He said, "Watch out that you are not deceived. For many will come in My name, saying, 'I am He,' and, 'The time is near.' Don't follow them. When you hear of wars and rebellions, don't be alarmed. Indeed, these things must take place first, but the end won't come right away."

Luke 21:1–9 HCSB

God sees the heart, while people can see only the surface. In the last week that Jesus was on earth, he and his disciples were in the temple complex. One woman, a widow, dropped two small coins into the temple treasury. Jesus made sure his disciples saw what happened, and then explained to them what they couldn't see. He revealed the heart behind the giver.

For God, the amount given is not what mattered; rather, the attitude behind the gift is what mattered. No one but Jesus knew that this lonely widow had given away all the money she had. No one but Jesus knew that she left the temple destitute.

More than likely, she did it because she believed God wanted her to. Because she believed that giving away all her money was God's will for her, she trusted God to take care of her needs. When God has us do something for him, he always provides the way for us to do it. On the human level, it may be impossible. But if God is involved, it will happen.

How did it work out for this widow? Did she starve? Did she prosper? What we know for certain is that God was with her and carried her through whatever she faced. In the same way, God will give us the ability to handle whatever he brings our way.

SIGNS OF THE TIMES

Near the temple, just before the Last Supper, Jesus talked to his disciples:

"When you see Jerusalem being surrounded by armies, you will know that its desolation is near. Then let those who are in Judea flee to the mountains, let those in the city get out, and let those in the country not enter the city. For this is the time of punishment in fulfillment of all that has been written. How dreadful it will be in those days for pregnant women and nursing mothers! There will be great distress in the land and wrath against this people. They will fall by the sword and will be taken as prisoners to all the nations. Jerusalem will be trampled on by the Gentiles until the times of the Gentiles are fulfilled.

"There will be signs in the sun, moon and stars. On the earth, nations will be in anguish and perplexity at the roaring and tossing of the sea. Men will faint from terror, apprehensive of what is coming on the world, for the heavenly bodies will be shaken. At that time they will see the Son of Man coming in a cloud with power and great glory. When these things begin to take place, stand up and lift up your heads, because your redemption is drawing near."

Luke 21:20–28 NIV

*E*nemies to the left. Enemies to the right. But God is in his heaven, so all is right with the world. Matthew and Mark both described a time when armies would surround the city of Jerusalem. Luke, too, reported Jesus' words, given in answer to his disciples' questions about the fate of the temple. But in Luke's recounting, an additional bit of significant data shows up. Where Matthew and Mark conclude the destruction of Jerusalem and its temple with the news of the Second Coming, Luke added that after Jerusalem fell, the people of Israel would be taken away as prisoners to all nations, while Jerusalem would suffer until the time of the Gentiles was fulfilled. Only after all that would Jesus come back.

The extra information from Jesus in Luke leads many scholars to conclude that the bulk of what Jesus predicted about Jerusalem happened when the Romans destroyed it in AD 70. The only part of Jesus' prophecy that remains in our future is his second coming.

Jesus frequently indicated that there were no signs for when he'd return. Instead, he'll come like a thief in the night. That's wonderful news for us, because it means that he could come back again to take us to our eternal home at any moment. We don't have to wait for something else to happen first.

BORN AGAIN

While Jesus was in Jerusalem for the Passover:

There was a man named Nicodemus who was a Pharisee and a Jewish leader. One night he went to Jesus and said, "Sir, we know that God has sent you to teach us. You could not work these miracles, unless God were with you."

Jesus replied, "I tell you for certain that you must be born from above before you can see God's kingdom!"

Nicodemus asked, "How can a grown man ever be born a second time?"

Jesus answered: "I tell you for certain that before you can get into God's kingdom, you must be born not only by water, but by the Spirit. Humans give life to their children. Yet only God's Spirit can change you into a child of God. Don't be surprised when I say that you must be born from above. Only God's Spirit gives new life. The Spirit is like the wind that blows wherever it wants to. You can hear the wind, but you don't know where it comes from or where it is going."

John 3:1–8 CEV

*W*hat if we could live our lives all over again? In a way, that's exactly what Jesus offers us. One night, early during Jesus' ministry, one of the members of the Jewish ruling council, the Sanhedrin, approached Jesus to find out firsthand who he was and what he was about. Unlike so many of those in leadership positions, Nicodemus genuinely wanted the truth.

The first thing that Jesus told him confused him: in order to see God's kingdom, he had to be born again. Then Jesus explained it to him. The first birth was the physical birth, when a baby came in a gush of amniotic fluid from its mother's womb. The second time was a spiritual birth.

Why did Jesus imagine that Nicodemus would understand what he meant by a spiritual birth? The prophet Joel had prophesied that in the last days, God would send his Spirit on his people. Jeremiah had predicted there would be a new covenant written on the hearts of his people to take the place of the stone tablets. When the Messiah came, the kingdom would enter the hearts of God's people, and they would never be the same. They would become an entirely new people, utterly transformed.

Being born again means that we have received the Spirit of God in place of our own spirit. God's laws are inside us now. We've been given a second chance and a brand-new life.

SPRING OF LIFE

Jesus and his disciples were traveling through Samaria and stopped at a well in Sychar:

A woman, a Samaritan, came to draw water. Jesus said, "Would you give me a drink of water?" (His disciples had gone to the village to buy food for lunch.)

The Samaritan woman, taken aback, asked, "How come you, a Jew, are asking me, a Samaritan woman, for a drink?" (Jews in those days wouldn't be caught dead talking to Samaritans.)

Jesus answered, "If you knew the generosity of God and who I am, you would be asking me for a drink, and I would give you fresh, living water."

The woman said, "Sir, you don't even have a bucket to draw with, and this well is deep. So how are you going to get this 'living water'? Are you a better man than our ancestor Jacob, who dug this well and drank from it, he and his sons and livestock, and passed it down to us?"

Jesus said, "Everyone who drinks this water will get thirsty again and again. Anyone who drinks the water I give will never thirst—not ever. The water I give will be an artesian spring within, gushing fountains of endless life."

John 4:7–14 MSG

❀

*J*esus and his disciples stopped in Samaria on their way to Jerusalem. While his disciples went to get food, Jesus sat down by a well. Soon a Samaritan woman arrived, focused on her need for water. There was no faucet for her to turn. Instead, she had to lower a bucket down a deep hole and then pull it back out. It was heavy. It took a lot of time. Then Jesus interrupted by asking her for a drink of water.

Thirst is a universal human experience. Jesus' request was simple and easily fulfilled. But Jesus was able to take something incredibly mundane and transform it into something incredibly profound.

The woman's interest grew with each word that Jesus spoke. Finally, Jesus offered her living water so that she would never thirst. The Old Testament repeatedly linked God's promises with water and made a connection between water and the Spirit. Even the rabbis taught that the Torah—the five books of Moses—were living water.

Jesus broke down the barriers of race, religion, and gender. His message of hope is available for everyone. Our longings, our sense that there is more to life than just the daily grind, can find fulfillment in Jesus. Jesus can fill up the emptiness inside us that nothing else can.

HARVESTTIME

Jesus talked to his disciples after the Samaritan woman left:

His disciples urged him, "Rabbi, eat something."

But he said to them, "I have food to eat that you know nothing about."

Then his disciples said to each other, "Could someone have brought him food?"

"My food," said Jesus, "is to do the will of him who sent me and to finish his work. Do you not say, 'Four months more and then the harvest'? I tell you, open your eyes and look at the fields! They are ripe for harvest. Even now the reaper draws his wages, even now he harvests the crop for eternal life, so that the sower and the reaper may be glad together. Thus the saying 'One sows and another reaps' is true. I sent you to reap what you have not worked for. Others have done the hard work, and you have reaped the benefits of their labor."

John 4:31–38 NIV

here is more than one kind of hunger. After Jesus' encounter with the Samaritan woman, Jesus' disciples returned with food. They were puzzled by what they found Jesus doing. When they encouraged Jesus to eat, he used their fixation on food as an opportunity to teach them, just as he had used the thirst of the Samaritan woman as an opportunity to teach her. And just as the Samaritan woman had first thought of literal water, so the disciples were stuck for a while on literal food.

Jesus clarified for them that he wasn't talking about physical food or satisfying physical hunger. He meant that he had found satisfaction in his hunger to do the job that his Father had sent him to earth to do, to proclaim the good news to people and to see them become part of God's kingdom as a consequence. The Samaritan woman joyfully believed him. Her transformed life satisfied Jesus more deeply than any of the food the disciples had brought him. The coming harvest of grain but four months in the future was nothing compared to the harvest of souls happening in that Samaritan village at that very moment.

Working for a living can be draining. We need rest and food. Paradoxically, working for the kingdom doesn't drain us spiritually. Instead, it fills us up! The lives we change, the hope we bring, and the souls we see come to Jesus can satisfy us more than the food we eat.

DO THIS

The people who had stayed on the east side of the lake knew that only one boat had been there. They also knew that Jesus had not left in it with his disciples. But the next day some boats from Tiberias sailed near the place where the crowd had eaten the bread for which the Lord had given thanks. They saw that Jesus and his disciples had left. Then they got into the boats and went to Capernaum to look for Jesus.

They found him on the west side of the lake and asked, "Rabbi, when did you get here?"

Jesus answered, "I tell you for certain that you are not looking for me because you saw the miracles, but because you ate all the food you wanted. Don't work for food that spoils. Work for food that gives eternal life. The Son of Man will give you this food, because God the Father has given him the right to do so."

"What exactly does God want us to do?" the people asked.

Jesus answered, "God wants you to have faith in the one he sent."

John 6:22–29 CEV

*I*t is hard for people to see past the obstacles in front of them. What excited the crowds was not what Jesus said. What moved them was not the healings or the exorcisms. What really got their attention was his feeding them for free.

Jesus compared the food that he had given them—food that could spoil—to the food that they should really want—the bread that could give them eternal life. Jesus then promised to give them that food. They could have it for free too.

Their response was to wonder what they had to do to get it.

We advance in school because we do our homework and pass our tests. We are paid because we do our jobs. We obey the traffic laws to avoid tickets. In life, we receive rewards or avoid punishments because of our behavior. It was only natural that the people, when Jesus berated them for coming to him only because of the free food, would think, *Ah, there's something he wants us to do. Something that he thinks God requires.*

All Jesus asked them to do, however, was to trust him. And that's all Jesus asks of us today. We don't have to perform a mighty deed. We don't have to answer a difficult riddle. We don't have to follow a list of rules. All Jesus needs us to do is to trust him.

❄❄❄❄❄❄❄❄❄❄❄❄❄❄❄❄❄❄❄❄❄❄❄❄❄❄❄❄❄❄❄❄

BUT SHE'S GUILTY!

Jesus went to the Mount of Olives.

At dawn He went to the temple complex again, and all the people were coming to Him. He sat down and began to teach them.

Then the scribes and the Pharisees brought a woman caught in adultery, making her stand in the center. "Teacher," they said to Him, "this woman was caught in the act of committing adultery. In the law Moses commanded us to stone such women. So what do You say?" They asked this to trap Him, in order that they might have evidence to accuse Him.

Jesus stooped down and started writing on the ground with His finger. When they persisted in questioning Him, He stood up and said to them,

"The one without sin among you should be the first to throw a stone at her."

Then He stooped down again and continued writing on the ground. When they heard this, they left one by one, starting with the older men. Only He was left, with the woman in the center. When Jesus stood up, He said to her, "Woman, where are they? Has no one condemned you?"

"No one, Lord," she answered.

"Neither do I condemn you," said Jesus. "Go, and from now on do not sin any more."

John 8:1–11 HCSB

❄

*J*esus didn't judge. He forgave. Although this story does not appear in the earliest manuscripts of John's gospel, it is so contrary to normal expectations that it must be a genuine episode from Jesus' life.

The guilt of the woman was not in question. It is intriguing to notice that her accusers brought her alone, without the man with whom she committed adultery, despite the fact that she was "caught in the act." In a case of adultery, according to the law of Moses, both the man and the woman were equally at fault and equally destined for death by stoning.

What Jesus might have written on the ground is not disclosed. There has been endless speculation, but such speculation often becomes a distraction from the story's disturbing point. Jesus did not condemn the woman, though she deserved it. But grace, by its nature, is unjust. The woman had betrayed her marriage vows. She had hurt someone deeply. And she was going to get away with it.

Jesus forgave her without an expression of regret or promise of reform from her at all. Jesus merely told her not to do it again. Forgiveness doesn't make the sin okay. Sin is never okay. What forgiveness does is make it as if the sin never happened in the first place.

WHO SINNED?

Jesus and his disciples were in Jerusalem:

As [Jesus] walked along, he saw a man blind from birth. His disciples asked him, "Rabbi, who sinned, this man or his parents, that he was born blind?"

Jesus answered, "Neither this man nor his parents sinned; he was born blind so that God's works might be revealed in him. We must work the works of him who sent me while it is day; night is coming when no one can work. As long as I am in the world, I am the light of the world." When he had said this, he spat on the ground and made mud with the saliva and spread the mud on the man's eyes, saying to him, "Go, wash in the pool of Siloam" (which means Sent).

Then he went and washed and came back able to see. The neighbors and those who had seen him before as a beggar began to ask, "Is this not the man who used to sit and beg?" Some were saying, "It is he." Others were saying, "No, but it is someone like him." He kept saying, "I am the man." But they kept asking him, "Then how were your eyes opened?" He answered, "The man called Jesus made mud, spread it on my eyes, and said to me, 'Go to Siloam and wash.' Then I went and washed and received my sight." They said to him, "Where is he?" He said, "I do not know."

John 9:1–12 NRSV

When the disciples saw the blind man, their question wasn't one of compassion or concern; it was a question of blame. According to the prevailing theology of the time, if you were suffering, there were only two possible reasons for it—you'd done something wrong or your parents had.

Jesus' response to the disciples' question was not what they expected at all. The blind man's lifetime of suffering was not because he had sinned or his parents had sinned. It was so that God could perform a miracle, which Jesus then proceeded to do by putting mud in the man's eyes that he then washed out in the pool near one of the walls of Jerusalem.

Bad things sometimes happen to good people. We won't always know why. But we can always be confident that God has his reasons.

HOSANNA

As [Jesus and his disciples] approached Jerusalem, at Bethphage and Bethany, near the Mount of Olives, [Jesus] sent two of His disciples, and said to them, "Go into the village opposite you, and immediately as you enter it, you will find a colt tied there, on which no one yet has ever sat; untie it and bring it here. If anyone says to you, 'Why are you doing this?' you say, 'The Lord has need of it'; and immediately he will send it back here."

They went away and found a colt tied at the door, outside in the street; and they untied it. Some of the bystanders were saying to them, "What are you doing, untying the colt?"

They spoke to them just as Jesus had told them, and they gave them permission.

They brought the colt to Jesus and put their coats on it; and He sat on it.

And many spread their coats in the road, and others spread leafy branches which they had cut from the fields. Those who went in front and those who followed were shouting:

"Hosanna!
Blessed is He who comes in
the name of the LORD;
Blessed is the coming kingdom of our father David;
Hosanna in the highest!"

Jesus entered Jerusalem and came into the temple; and after looking around at everything, He left for Bethany with the twelve, since it was already late.

Mark 11:1–11 NASB

✳

The crowd went wild! They knew their world was about to change—they just didn't know how much. The prophet Zechariah had prophesied that Israel's king would arrive on a donkey's colt. The Hebrew word *hosanna* means "Save, now" or "Save, I pray." It came from Psalm 118, which was a psalm of triumph and praise to God. The Hebrew word for *save* is related to the name Jesus. Jesus received his name specifically because he would save his people. When he rode into Jerusalem, the shouting crowd supposed he was their political savior. They expected him to save them from the Romans by raising an army and fighting against them. But Jesus was coming to save them from something far more serious—their sins. To do that, he would surrender to the Romans and die at their hands. Then he would rise to life and return to his Father.

True salvation does not come from overthrowing a government. It comes by surrendering. Salvation comes from the one who saved us from our sins. If we want change, we need to change things the way Jesus changed things—one heart at a time.

DARK DEEDS

In the Garden of Gethsemane, Jesus prayed with his disciples:

Now the betrayer had given [those who had come to arrest Jesus] a sign, saying, "The one I will kiss is the man; arrest him and lead him away under guard." So when he came, he went up to him at once and said, "Rabbi!" and kissed him. Then they laid hands on him and arrested him. But one of those who stood near drew his sword and struck the slave of the high priest, cutting off his ear.

Then Jesus said to them, "Have you come out with swords and clubs to arrest me as though I were a bandit? Day after day I was with you in the temple teaching, and you did not arrest me. But let the scriptures be fulfilled." All of them deserted him and fled.

A certain young man was following him, wearing nothing but a linen cloth. They caught hold of him, but he left the linen cloth and ran off naked.

Mark 14:44–52 NRSV

People sneak when they know they're being bad. Under cover of darkness, those who had conspired to destroy Jesus arrived. It was necessary for Judas to identify Jesus for the soldiers and leaders of the Sanhedrin even though Jesus was a public figure and was well known. Those sent out to arrest him had probably never actually seen him in the flesh. They had no pictures to guide them. They'd only heard about him. On top of that, they were trying to arrest him in the dark. Having someone to identify Jesus was critical to their success.

Judas's only purpose was to identify Jesus. To help make the arrest work, Judas tried to minimize suspicion by greeting him in an ordinary way, with a kiss, so that the other disciples wouldn't suspect Judas of doing something despicable. That way Jesus could be arrested before anyone was able to put up a fight. In Luke's gospel, the disciples asked if they could fight and Jesus told them no.

Here, Mark left those words out, since it was clear enough that Jesus wasn't going to fight back, even though he wasn't alone and even though one of the disciples drew blood. Jesus wanted the Scriptures to be fulfilled. He knew what had to happen and was willing to do God's will. He surrendered peacefully while his disciples fled in panic.

God's will is sometimes difficult. Sometimes we'll have to do it alone. Sometimes those we thought we could count on will vanish. Sometimes they might even be working against us. Jesus knows how hard it can be from personal experience, and he is always ready to be a source of encouragement for us.

SLAPPED AROUND

Jesus was arrested and in custody in the home of the high priest:

The men in charge of Jesus began poking fun at him, slapping him around. They put a blindfold on him and taunted, "Who hit you that time?" They were having a grand time with him.

When it was morning, the religious leaders of the people and the high priests and scholars all got together and brought him before their High Council. They said, "Are you the Messiah?"

He answered, "If I said yes, you wouldn't believe me. If I asked what you meant by your question, you wouldn't answer me. So here's what I have to say: From here on the Son of Man takes his place at God's right hand, the place of power."

They all said, "So you admit your claim to be the Son of God?"

"You're the ones who keep saying it," he said.

But they had made up their minds, "Why do we need any more evidence? We've all heard him as good as say it himself."

Luke 22:63–71 MSG

❧

They didn't just touch the face of God; they slapped it. After Jesus was arrested, he was mistreated and abused. In the morning, he faced the Sanhedrin, the high council, to be interrogated.

The religious establishment had already decided that Jesus couldn't be the Messiah. They didn't care what he said. They didn't care what he did. Their minds were made up. The whole interrogation was a mockery of justice, a betrayal of its supposed purpose to establish the truth of any question. For the Sanhedrin, Jesus' words merely convinced them of the lies they already believed, that he was a false Messiah and a danger to the Jewish nation who needed to be destroyed.

We can learn from Jesus' response during his trial and the behavior of those who stood opposed to Jesus. Jesus did not try to defend himself. He did not try to convince those who had already made up their minds. Instead, he merely affirmed what he knew to be true, and he acknowledged the truth when he heard it from his accusers. Like Jesus, we don't need to justify ourselves to those who hate us. We don't have to counter their lies. We don't need to defend ourselves beyond insisting and standing on the truth. In the end, those who slapped Jesus will regret it. In the end, the truth will triumph. In the end, justice will be done. God will fight for us. We don't need to fight alone.

KING OF THE JEWS

Jesus stood before the governor, and the governor asked him, "Are you the king of the Jews?"

"Yes, it is as you say," Jesus replied.

When he was accused by the chief priests and the elders, he gave no answer. Then Pilate asked him, "Don't you hear the testimony they are bringing against you?" But Jesus made no reply, not even to a single charge—to the great amazement of the governor.

Now it was the governor's custom at the Feast to release a prisoner chosen by the crowd. At that time they had a notorious prisoner, called Barabbas. So when the crowd had gathered, Pilate asked them, "Which one do you want me to release to you: Barabbas, or Jesus who is called Christ?" For he knew it was out of envy that they had handed Jesus over to him.

While Pilate was sitting on the judge's seat, his wife sent him this message: "Don't have anything to do with that innocent man, for I have suffered a great deal today in a dream because of him."

But the chief priests and the elders persuaded the crowd to ask for Barabbas and to have Jesus executed.

Matthew 27:11–20 NIV

*J*esus told Pilate that he was the King of the Jews. He was the descendant of David and the rightful heir to the throne. Jesus' genealogies in the gospels of Matthew and Luke demonstrate that. But there was more to Jesus' kingship than simply being a descendant of David. Jesus wasn't just a man. Jesus was God.

When the prophet Samuel grew old, the people of Israel became dissatisfied with the political direction of their nation. They liked Samuel, but they had no confidence in his children. They asked him to select someone to reign over them as their king. They had decided that they wanted to have a king just as all the other nations had.

Samuel was disturbed, but God told him to go along with their request. "The LORD told him: 'Listen to all that the people are saying to you; it is not you they have rejected, but they have rejected me as their king'" (1 Samuel 8:7 NIV). Jesus was God. Just as the people in Samuel's day had rejected him as king, so they rejected him once again.

Acknowledged or unacknowledged, Jesus is King, both of the Jews—as Pilate accepted—and of the world. He is our God, and he is our King. He rules over our lives for our benefit.

GONE FISHING

After his resurrection, Jesus met with his disciples by the Sea of Galilee:

Jesus said to them, "Children, you have no fish, have you?"

They answered him, "No."

He said to them, "Cast the net to the right side of the boat, and you will find some." So they cast it, and now they were not able to haul it in because there were so many fish.

That disciple whom Jesus loved said to Peter, "It is the Lord!" When Simon Peter heard that it was the Lord, he put on some clothes, for he was naked, and jumped into the sea. But the other disciples came in the boat, dragging the net full of fish, for they were not far from the land, only about a hundred yards off.

When they had gone ashore, they saw a charcoal fire there, with fish on it, and bread. Jesus said to them, "Bring some of the fish that you have just caught." So Simon Peter went aboard and hauled the net ashore, full of large fish, a hundred fifty-three of them; and though there were so many, the net was not torn. Jesus said to them, "Come and have breakfast."

Now none of the disciples dared to ask him, "Who are you?" because they knew it was the Lord. Jesus came and took the bread and gave it to them, and did the same with the fish. This was now the third time that Jesus appeared to the disciples after he was raised from the dead.

John 21:5–13 NRSV

❦

*A*fter his resurrection, Jesus told his disciples that he would meet them in Galilee, and so the disciples returned home, back to the Sea of Galilee, and back to their old lives.

Early one morning after a fruitless and frustrating night of fishing, Jesus appeared on the shore. Jesus invited them to bring some of the fish they'd just caught, thanks to him, and to join him in the breakfast he was already cooking for himself. Three years earlier Jesus had called his disciples to become fishers of men near that very spot. A new day was about to begin. Within weeks, the Holy Spirit would come, and they would start building the church of God.

But that day was just a quiet morning on the shore of a lake and a breakfast among friends. Jesus resurrected was the Jesus they had always known. This picture tells us today that Jesus is always happy to spend time with us. It doesn't take a crisis. He'll be with us during a quiet meal after a long day, or early in the morning before anything happens.

KICKING AGAINST THE GOADS

In Caesarea, Paul gave his defense to King Agrippa and his sister Bernice:

[Paul said,] "I am standing trial for the hope of the promise made by God to our fathers; the promise to which our twelve tribes hope to attain, as they earnestly serve God night and day. And for this hope, O King, I am being accused by Jews. Why is it considered incredible among you people if God does raise the dead?

"So then, I thought to myself that I had to do many things hostile to the name of Jesus of Nazareth. And this is just what I did in Jerusalem; not only did I lock up many of the saints in prisons, having received authority from the chief priests, but also when they were being put to death I cast my vote against them. And as I punished them often in all the synagogues, I tried to force them to blaspheme; and being furiously enraged at them, I kept pursuing them even to foreign cities. While so engaged as I was journeying to Damascus with the authority and commission of the chief priests, at midday, O King, I saw on the way a light from heaven, brighter than the sun, shining all around me and those who were journeying with me. And when we had all fallen to the ground, I heard a voice saying to me in the Hebrew dialect, 'Saul, Saul, why are you persecuting Me? It is hard for you to kick against the goads.'"

Acts 26:6–14 NASB

❋

*P*aul never preached to the choir. When King Agrippa and his sister Bernice arrived in Caesarea to pay their respects to the new Roman governor, Porcius Festus, Agrippa asked if he could listen to Paul. Paul told the king about how he had been a persecutor of Christians until Jesus had appeared to him and changed the course of his life.

What did Jesus mean when he told Paul that "it is hard for you to kick against the goads"? In Greek literature, to fight against the goads meant to resist one's destiny and to do battle against the "will of the gods." By persecuting Christians, Paul had been fighting God's will for his life since, as Paul later told the Galatians, God had set him apart from birth to preach the gospel message (Galatians 1:15). So when Jesus told Paul he was kicking against the goads, he was simply telling Paul that he was fighting God's will for his life—not an easy thing to do. In fact, resisting God's will is ultimately futile, because God always gets his way. Since we're going to do God's will anyway, it is better for us to give in sooner rather than later. It will hurt less.

GRACE

In his letter to the church in Corinth, Paul wrote that he didn't like to boast:

"That experience is worth boasting about, but I'm not going to do it. I will boast only about my weaknesses. If I wanted to boast, I would be no fool in doing so, because I would be telling the truth. But I won't do it, because I don't want anyone to give me credit beyond what they can see in my life or hear in my message, even though I have received such wonderful revelations from God. So to keep me from becoming proud, I was given a thorn in my flesh, a messenger from Satan to torment me and keep me from becoming proud.

"Three different times I begged the Lord to take it away. Each time he said, 'My grace is all you need. My power works best in weakness.' So now I am glad to boast about my weaknesses, so that the power of Christ can work through me. That's why I take pleasure in my weaknesses, and in the insults, hardships, persecutions, and troubles that I suffer for Christ. For when I am weak, then I am strong.

"You have made me act like a fool—boasting like this. You ought to be writing commendations for me, for I am not at all inferior to these 'super apostles,' even though I am nothing at all."

2 Corinthians 12:5–11 NLT

When all you have left is Jesus, you'll realize Jesus is enough. What was Paul's "thorn in the flesh"? Paul often used the word *flesh* to mean the sinful nature. So perhaps Paul was referring to some sin in his life that he could never overcome—like a bad temper, perhaps.

Jesus refused to remove Paul's thorn, whatever it was. Instead, Jesus told Paul that his "grace" was enough. *Grace* is an "undeserved gift." Jesus told Paul that his undeserved gift was God's forgiveness. Jesus died for all our sins. Whether we keep on having a bad temper or not, thanks to what Jesus did on the cross, God has already forgiven us.

There was no reason for Paul to worry about his thorn, whatever it might have been. Jesus' power works best in our weakness. Only when we realize how weak we are can we be amazed by the power of God—because only then do we recognize that God's power is at work in our lives rather than our own power.

THE BEGINNING AND THE END

To the seven churches in the province of Asia.

Grace and peace to you from the One who is, who was, and who is coming; from the seven spirits before His throne; and from Jesus Christ, the faithful witness, the firstborn from the dead and the ruler of the kings of the earth.

To Him who loves us and has set us free from our sins by His blood, and made us a kingdom, priests to His God and Father—to Him be the glory and dominion forever and ever. Amen.

Look! He is coming with the clouds, and every eye will see Him, including those who pierced Him. And all the families of the earth will mourn over Him. This is certain. Amen.

"I am the Alpha and the Omega," says the Lord God, "the One who is, who was, and who is coming, the Almighty."

Revelation 1:4–8 HCSB

*J*esus will make the whole world weep. Jesus told John to write letters to seven churches in the province of Asia, what today is the country of Turkey. John began by pointing out that when Jesus returns someday with the clouds, "all the families of the earth will mourn over Him." It is an allusion to the prophecy in Zechariah 12:10.

John then quoted these words: "I am the Alpha and the Omega, the One who is, who was, and who is coming, the Almighty." The "Lord God" spoke those words. John affirmed that Jesus, who lived on earth as a man and died on a cross, is none other than the Creator of the universe, the God of the Old Testament, and Yahweh himself. Most modern English translations that have a red-letter edition print Jesus' words in red.

Jesus is not just a good man. He is not just a prophet. Jesus is God himself. *Alpha* is the first letter of the Greek alphabet, and *Omega* is the last. By calling himself the Alpha and the Omega, and then repeating that he is "the beginning and the end," Jesus affirmed that he rules from the instant of creation until the very last moment in time. Jesus' words were a great comfort to John and the other Christians who were facing severe persecution at the hands of the Roman authorities. They should comfort us in whatever problems or persecutions we may face today.

LUKEWARM

Jesus' letter to Laodicea:

Write to Laodicea, to the Angel of the church. God's Yes, the Faithful and Accurate Witness, the First of God's creation, says:

"I know you inside and out, and find little to my liking. You're not cold, you're not hot—far better to be either cold or hot! You're stale. You're stagnant. You make me want to vomit. You brag, 'I'm rich, I've got it made, I need nothing from anyone,' oblivious that in fact you're a pitiful, blind beggar, threadbare and homeless.

"Here's what I want you to do: Buy your gold from me, gold that's been through the refiner's fire. Then you'll be rich. Buy your clothes from me, clothes designed in Heaven. You've gone around half-naked long enough. And buy medicine for your eyes from me so you can see, *really* see.

"The people I love, I call to account—prod and correct and guide so that they'll live at their best. Up on your feet, then! About face! Run after God!

"Look at me. I stand at the door. I knock. If you hear me call and open the door, I'll come right in and sit down to supper with you. Conquerors will sit alongside me at the head table, just as I, having conquered, took the place of honor at the side of my Father. That's my gift to the conquerors!

"Are your ears awake? Listen. Listen to the Wind Words, the Spirit blowing through the churches."

Revelation 3:14–22 MSG

※

*L*aodicea was a prosperous commercial city in northwest Asia Minor, not too far from the city of Colossae. Its church had pushed Jesus away. They had allowed the deceitfulness of riches to make them forget the Lord they loved.

Jesus told them it was easy to let him back into their lives. In fact, he told the Christians in Laodicea that he was just outside their door knocking, waiting for them to let him return. And even centuries later, a child stared at a painting of Jesus standing beside a door, knocking. His Sunday school teacher read the words Jesus spoke to the Laodicean Christians, and those words were enough to convince the child to let Jesus come into his life.

Jesus' words can be effective, even when we misapply them or are too young or limited to understand them fully. God does not wait for us to understand clearly before he changes us forever. Jesus is waiting for us to let him come in.

COMING ATTRACTIONS

As a very old man, John had visions on the island of Patmos:

[The angel] said to me, "These words are faithful and true." And the Lord God of the holy prophets sent His angel to show His servants the things which must shortly take place.

"Behold, I am coming quickly! Blessed is he who keeps the words of the prophecy of this book."

Now I, John, saw and heard these things. And when I heard and saw, I fell down to worship before the feet of the angel who showed me these things.

Then he said to me, "See that you do not do that. For I am your fellow servant, and of your brethren the prophets, and of those who keep the words of this book. Worship God." And he said to me, "Do not seal the words of the prophecy of this book, for the time is at hand. He who is unjust, let him be unjust still; he who is filthy, let him be filthy still; he who is righteous, let him be righteous still; he who is holy, let him be holy still."

Revelation 22:6–11 NKJV

*W*hen John received the visions that made up the book of Revelation, he was living in exile on the tiny island of Patmos in the Mediterranean Sea. Christians of the Roman Empire were suffering severe persecution from the Roman government. In the midst of this suffering, Jesus offered the hope that he was "coming quickly."

Nearly two thousand years later, we might wonder about Jesus' definition of "quickly." Many lives have come and gone since John recorded Jesus' words. But perhaps we're missing part of what Jesus meant when he said that he would come "quickly." While we rightfully look forward to Jesus returning someday in the clouds, he also is with us every day. In fact, he lives within our hearts. He walks beside us and suffers with us. When we hurt, he hurts.

Jesus also told us that those who keep the words of John's prophecy would be "blessed." That is, they would be happy! We can keep the words of John's prophecy by reading them and believing them. They tell us that Jesus will be victorious over the kingdoms of the world and that his kingdom, the kingdom of God, will ultimately triumph.

Jesus urges us to recognize that we belong to the kingdom of God now. And the kingdom of God is near—so near that Jesus comes quickly whenever we call for him.

THE MORNING STAR

Jesus comforted John during his exile on the island of Patmos:

"Behold, I am coming quickly, and My reward is with Me, to render to every man according to what he has done. I am the Alpha and the Omega, the first and the last, the beginning and the end."

Blessed are those who wash their robes, so that they may have the right to the tree of life, and may enter by the gates into the city. Outside are the dogs and the sorcerers and the immoral persons and the murderers and the idolaters, and everyone who loves and practices lying.

"I, Jesus, have sent My angel to testify to you these things for the churches. I am the root and the descendant of David, the bright morning star."

The Spirit and the bride say, "Come." And let the one who hears say, "Come." And let the one who is thirsty come; let the one who wishes take the water of life without cost.

I testify to everyone who hears the words of the prophecy of this book: if anyone adds to them, God will add to him the plagues which are written in this book; and if anyone takes away from the words of the book of this prophecy, God will take away his part from the tree of life and from the holy city, which are written in this book.

He who testifies to these things says, "Yes, I am coming quickly." Amen. Come, Lord Jesus.

Revelation 22:12–20 NASB

※

*J*esus will come back soon. He is coming with a reward for everyone, "according to what he has done." But Moses, David, and Paul took part in murder. The thief on the cross never performed any good deeds. And what about the woman caught in adultery, or the prostitute who bathed Jesus' feet with her tears? Will they all be locked out of the city?

Jesus' words allude to those of the prophet Isaiah, who announced that God would come to his people Israel with his reward (Isaiah 40:10; 62:11). That "reward" was not based on anything that Israel deserved. The reward referred to God's work of bestowing the blessings of salvation on his faithful people. That work is actually God's work of forgiveness (Isaiah 40:2).

Only the Lamb was "worthy" to be accepted by God (Revelation 5:12), while "those who washed their robes and made them white by the blood of the lamb" (Revelation 7:14) are to be saved. We will be rewarded by Jesus when he returns for us and we are saved not just from our sins, but also from their effects. Our reward is the inheritance we have in God's kingdom as his forgiven and adopted children.

GOOD AND EVIL

Love delights in good, not in evil. But too often, good seems hard to come by, while evil is always in stock. Most people understand that when Adam and Eve found out about sin from eating fruit off the Tree of Knowledge of Good and Evil that they had done a "bad" thing. But the tree with the forbidden fruit was not just the tree of knowledge of *evil*. It was the Tree of Knowledge of *Good* and Evil. God never wanted us to know about evil. He wanted us to know only good without realizing there could be anything else.

❀

Do not be overcome by evil,
but overcome evil with good.
Romans 12:21 NIV

REPENTANCE

When Jesus heard that John had been put in prison, he went to Galilee. But instead of staying in Nazareth, Jesus moved to Capernaum. This town was beside Lake Galilee in the territory of Zebulun and Naphtali. So God's promise came true, just as the prophet Isaiah had said,

"Listen, lands of Zebulun and Naphtali, lands along the road to the sea and east of the Jordan! Listen Galilee, land of the Gentiles! Although your people live in darkness, they will see a bright light. Although they live in the shadow of death, a light will shine on them."

Then Jesus started preaching, "Turn back to God! The kingdom of heaven will soon be here."

While Jesus was walking along the shore of Lake Galilee, he saw two brothers. One was Simon, also known as Peter, and the other was Andrew. They were fishermen, and they were casting their net into the lake. Jesus said to them, "Come with me! I will teach you how to bring in people instead of fish." Right then the two brothers dropped their nets and went with him.

Jesus walked on until he saw James and John, the sons of Zebedee. They were in a boat with their father, mending their nets. Jesus asked them to come with him too. Right away they left the boat and their father and went with Jesus.

Matthew 4:12–22 CEV

When Jesus asked his disciples to come with him, they dropped everything and followed. The disciples had already spent time with Jesus, talked to him, perhaps even witnessed a miracle before Jesus asked them to follow. They were convinced that Jesus was the Messiah. They thought that meant he was going to reestablish the monarchy, become king, defeat the Romans, and rule the world. The chance to join the Messiah's team was an opportunity not to be missed.

Over time, they discovered that they had misunderstood just what he was offering them. What he offered them was infinitely better than a petty earthly kingdom with physical prosperity and power. He offered them the chance to become the brothers of the Creator of the universe, to join in God's eternal kingdom forever.

When we understand clearly what it is we have been given in our relationship with Jesus, the problems and trials of life become vanishingly small. It doesn't seem odd at all that Peter, Andrew, James, and John would leave behind all their physical belongings, their businesses, everything they had, in order to join with Jesus. In Christ, we get not just the opportunity of a lifetime, but also the opportunity of all eternity.

BLESSED ALL OVER, DESPITE THE BILLS

Near the shore of the Sea of Galilee:

When Jesus saw the crowds, he went up the mountain; and after he sat down, his disciples came to him. Then he began to speak, and taught them, saying:

"Blessed are the poor in spirit, for theirs is the kingdom of heaven.

"Blessed are those who mourn, for they will be comforted.

"Blessed are the meek, for they will inherit the earth.

"Blessed are those who hunger and thirst for righteousness, for they will be filled.

"Blessed are the merciful, for they will receive mercy.

"Blessed are the pure in heart, for they will see God.

"Blessed are the peacemakers, for they will be called children of God.

"Blessed are those who are persecuted for righteousness' sake, for theirs is the kingdom of heaven.

"Blessed are you when people revile you and persecute you and utter all kinds of evil against you falsely on my account. Rejoice and be glad, for your reward is great in heaven, for in the same way they persecuted the prophets who were before you."

Matthew 5:1–12 NRSV

※

*M*any believe good things come to the good and bad things go to the bad. But Jesus challenged that lie. When Jesus gave his Sermon on the Mount, he explained to his disciples and the crowd that those they would least expect to be the recipients of God's good favor were in fact the ones God would bless most of all. The word *blessed* simply means "happy"—happiness in this instance given to them by God. Jesus wanted his listeners to discover that having money or power was not the basis of a happy life. Happiness could come when they recognized that their life belonged to God. God loved them, and his love for them served as the basis for their happiness.

Too often we believe that the reason we are not happy is that we've done something wrong or that we haven't found the right prayer, church, or program. We need only to realize that because God loves us and we love others, we already have joy, satisfaction, and success no matter the immediate circumstances of our lives. We are God's children. He walks with us every day, and he will always be with us. We have all eternity to live with him and those we love. We couldn't possibly be more blessed.

HIGH STANDARDS

Jesus continued his Sermon on the Mount:

"You have heard that it was said to those of ancient times, 'You shall not murder'; and 'whoever murders shall be liable to judgment.' But I say to you that if you are angry with a brother or sister, you will be liable to judgment; and if you insult a brother or sister, you will be liable to the council; and if you say, 'You fool,' you will be liable to the hell of fire. So when you are offering your gift at the altar, if you remember that your brother or sister has something against you, leave your gift there before the altar and go; first be reconciled to your brother or sister, and then come and offer your gift. Come to terms quickly with your accuser while you are on the way to court with him, or your accuser may hand you over to the judge, and the judge to the guard, and you will be thrown into prison. Truly I tell you, you will never get out until you have paid the last penny."

Matthew 5:21–26 NRSV

🌺

*T*he Pharisees had thought long and hard about who deserved to go to hell. They had come up with an obvious list of crimes—murder, for instance.

But Jesus indicated that it wasn't a question of who deserved judgment. The question was, is there anyone who *doesn't* deserve judgment? Jesus explained that even the best people still deserved God's condemnation. Everyone has been angry with someone. We've all called people "fools" or worse. The word rendered *fool* simply means "empty-headed." Calling someone "stupid" or "idiot" is not okay just because we didn't call them "fool." Jesus' point was that it is wrong to insult people at all.

Then Jesus turned up the heat. Even if we're not angry with someone, there might be someone who is angry with us, so we're still in trouble with God. We're simply never free of guilt.

Jesus wants us to understand that we all deserve God's judgment. No matter how well behaved we are, we still fall short of perfection, and there is nothing we can do about it. But God has a solution. He came up with a way for us to avoid his judgment. He punished someone else in our place, Jesus Christ, his Son. Thanks to Jesus, God forgives us of all our bad deeds and even our bad thoughts, which are legion.

SEX AND LIES

Jesus' Sermon on the Mount:

"You have heard that it was said to those of old, 'You shall not commit adultery.' But I say to you that whoever looks at a woman to lust for her has already committed adultery with her in his heart. If your right eye causes you to sin, pluck it out and cast it from you; for it is more profitable for you that one of your members perish, than for your whole body to be cast into hell. And if your right hand causes you to sin, cut it off and cast it from you; for it is more profitable for you that one of your members perish, than for your whole body to be cast into hell.

"Furthermore it has been said, 'Whoever divorces his wife, let him give her a certificate of divorce.' But I say to you that whoever divorces his wife for any reason except sexual immorality causes her to commit adultery; and whoever marries a woman who is divorced commits adultery.

"Again you have heard that it was said to those of old, 'You shall not swear falsely, but shall perform your oaths to the Lord.' But I say to you, do not swear at all: neither by heaven, for it is God's throne; nor by the earth, for it is His footstool; nor by Jerusalem, for it is the city of the great King. Nor shall you swear by your head, because you cannot make one hair white or black. But let your 'Yes' be 'Yes,' and your 'No,' 'No.' For whatever is more than these is from the evil one."

Matthew 5:27–37 NKJV

❀

*J*esus pointed out that even if we avoid actually breaking any of the Ten Commandments outwardly, there is still the little matter of what is going on in our heads. We must be careful, however, not to equate mere temptation with actual guilt. It is one thing to be tempted; it is another thing to sin. Jesus himself was tempted, but he was without sin.

There is more to what Jesus said than simply warning against being tempted by another person. The problem Jesus confronted wasn't just sexual desire. Rather, the issue was *misplaced* sexual desire combined with making plans. *Adultery* is the desire to steal someone who is not and never can be ours. Adultery, by definition, is an act counter to love. Rather than being concerned about others, the adulterer is concerned only with his or her own satisfaction, regardless of the cost to the spouse, the spouse of the other person, and the friends, family, children, and loved ones of everyone involved. Adultery is a remarkably selfish act.

It is one thing to be tempted. It is another thing altogether to plan to do it.

KEEP IT TO YOURSELF

Jesus taught his followers during the Sermon on the Mount:

"Be careful not to practice your righteousness in front of people, to be seen by them. Otherwise, you will have no reward from your Father in heaven. So whenever you give to the poor, don't sound a trumpet before you, as the hypocrites do in the synagogues and on the streets, to be applauded by people. I assure you: They've got their reward! But when you give to the poor, don't let your left hand know what your right hand is doing, so that your giving may be in secret. And your Father who sees in secret will reward you.

"Whenever you pray, you must not be like the hypocrites, because they love to pray standing in the synagogues and on the street corners to be seen by people. I assure you: They've got their reward! But when you pray, go into your private room, shut your door, and pray to your Father who is in secret. And your Father who sees in secret will reward you. When you pray, don't babble like the idolaters, since they imagine they'll be heard for their many words. Don't be like them, because your Father knows the things you need before you ask Him."

Matthew 6:1–8 HCSB

꙰

*J*esus said we should not do our righteousness in front of other people because we need to consider carefully what motivates us. We often behave as we do, not because we are concerned with others, but because we are concerned with ourselves and with what we can get from others. When Jesus healed someone, cast out a demon, or raised someone from the dead, one of the first things he'd say to the person was "Don't tell anyone about this." Jesus practiced what he preached.

It may sound cynical, but our motivations are mostly self-centered. We like the people who like us and are nice to us. We give gifts to people whom we like and are likely to give us gifts in return. How reluctant we are to be kind to those who are mean to us! We like to be praised and thanked for what we do. After all, we write not just "to" but also "from" on the gifts that we give. We want people to know who cleaned up, who contributed the money, who fixed the broken pipe. We expect gratitude and become grumpy when we don't get it. Jesus wants us to rethink how we act.

CELEBRITY APPRENTICE

Jesus taught his disciples during the Sermon on the Mount:

"The world is full of so-called prayer warriors who are prayer-ignorant. They're full of formulas and programs and advice, peddling techniques for getting what you want from God. Don't fall for that nonsense. This is your Father you are dealing with, and he knows better than you what you need. With a God like this loving you, you can pray very simply. Like this:

Our Father in heaven,
Reveal who you are.
Set the world right;
Do what's best—
as above, so below.
Keep us alive with three
square meals.
Keep us forgiven with you and
forgiving others.
Keep us safe from ourselves
and the Devil.
You're in charge!
You can do anything you
want!
You're ablaze in beauty!
Yes. Yes. Yes.

"In prayer there is a connection between what God does and what you do. You can't get forgiveness from God, for instance, without also forgiving others. If you refuse to do your part, you cut yourself off from God's part."

Matthew 6:9–15 MSG

🌼

*W*hy is God's forgiveness dependent upon our forgiving others? And why do we believe we should be forgiven when we are unwilling to forgive others? When we pray to God, we can have from him only what we believe he is willing to give. If we don't forgive others, we can't believe in forgiveness. If we have an unforgiving heart, we're not going to believe that God can forgive us.

Forgiveness is an attitude. It is a choice that we make. We free ourselves from a prison of bitterness and anger if we forgive. When God forgives us, he isn't telling us that what we did didn't matter, or that our suffering doesn't matter, or that he's okay with our actions. Forgiveness means he will not allow what we did to interfere with his relationship with us. His relationship with us is more important than the sin that would come between us. His forgiveness grows from love, from a concern for us that exceeds all else.

GET RICH QUICK

A passage from Jesus' Sermon on the Mount:

"Whenever you fast, don't be sad-faced like the hypocrites. For they make their faces unattractive so their fasting is obvious to people. I assure you: They've got their reward! But when you fast, put oil on your head, and wash your face, so that you don't show your fasting to people but to your Father who is in secret. And your Father who sees in secret will reward you.

"Don't collect for yourselves treasures on earth, where moth and rust destroy and where thieves break in and steal. But collect for yourselves treasures in heaven, where neither moth nor rust destroys, and where thieves don't break in and steal. For where your treasure is, there your heart will be also.

"The eye is the lamp of the body. If your eye is good, your whole body will be full of light. But if your eye is bad, your whole body will be full of darkness. So if the light within you is darkness—how deep is that darkness!

"No one can be a slave of two masters, since either he will hate one and love the other, or be devoted to one and despise the other. You cannot be slaves of God and of money."

Matthew 6:16–24 HCSB

*S*ome people suffer from SOS—shiny object syndrome. They are easily distracted by whatever attractive thing happens to catch their eye. It is a common human failing, of course, and an example of our general inability to distinguish between what's best for us and what will entertain us at the moment. We want to get rich quick. But the quick fix too often turns out to be nothing more than a shiny bit of glass.

Jesus asked those listening to him during his Sermon on the Mount to consider what motivated their behavior. What prompted their actions? Were they doing good for God, or were they doing good only for themselves? Were they motivated by the desire for the quick payoff? Were they good because of what the neighbors would think? Were they good because of what benefit they could derive from it? If so, Jesus argued that they weren't being good at all. Instead, they were simply working for their own selfish ends. They were working for a payment.

To serve God means to be concerned with someone besides ourselves. Our own benefit shouldn't enter into the equation at all. True righteousness means focusing on others and forgetting about what we might get out of it. We cannot be truly righteous if we're concerned only with what we're going to gain.

THE COST OF DISCIPLESHIP

Jesus went to the home of Peter, where he found that Peter's mother-in-law was sick in bed with fever. He took her by the hand, and the fever left her. Then she got up and served Jesus a meal.

That evening many people with demons in them were brought to Jesus. And with only a word he forced out the evil spirits and healed everyone who was sick. So God's promise came true, just as the prophet Isaiah had said,

"He healed our diseases and made us well."

When Jesus saw the crowd, he went across Lake Galilee. A teacher of the Law of Moses came up to him and said, "Teacher, I'll go anywhere with you!"

Jesus replied, "Foxes have dens, and birds have nests. But the Son of Man doesn't have a place to call his own."

Another disciple said to Jesus, "Lord, let me wait till I bury my father."

Jesus answered, "Come with me, and let the dead bury their dead."

Matthew 8:14–22 CEV

After Jesus healed Peter's mother-in-law, crowds of people came to be healed. Many of those who came wanted to become Jesus' followers, believing that the Messiah would solve all their physical, financial, and political problems. Jesus had to correct their misconceptions.

First, a teacher of the law approached Jesus. Such men were respected and prosperous. Jesus warned him that there were no material benefits in following him. Next, a man asked Jesus if he could follow Jesus later, after he buried his father. It's unlikely that the disciple's father was a corpse awaiting burial. The Jewish people usually buried their dead immediately, within hours of death. Rather, the father was old, and the man wanted to wait until after his father had died, so he could take care of the obligations for proper burial and the distribution of the inheritance. Jesus told him that plenty of people would be able to see to those end-of-life details. But deciding to follow Jesus couldn't wait.

Jesus did not tell those two individuals that they could not follow him. Jesus simply clarified how much it would cost. As high as that cost might have seemed to those two men, the price we pay for following Jesus is actually a bargain. We gain far more than just petty physical rewards or wealth that fades and can't possibly last. We gain eternity.

BREAKING THE RULES

Jesus left and went into one of the Jewish meeting places, where there was a man whose hand was crippled. Some Pharisees wanted to accuse Jesus of doing something wrong, and they asked him, "Is it right to heal someone on the Sabbath?"

Jesus answered, "If you had a sheep that fell into a ditch on the Sabbath, wouldn't you lift it out? People are worth much more than sheep, and so it is right to do good on the Sabbath." Then Jesus told the man, "Hold out your hand." The man did, and it became as healthy as the other one.

The Pharisees left and started making plans to kill Jesus.

When Jesus found out what was happening, he left there and large crowds followed him. He healed all of their sick, but warned them not to tell anyone about him. So God's promise came true, just as Isaiah the prophet had said,

"Here is my chosen servant! I
love him, and he pleases me.
I will give him my Spirit, and
he will bring justice to the
nations. He won't shout or
yell or call out in the streets.
He won't break off a bent reed
or put out a dying flame, but
he will make sure that justice
is done. All nations will place
their hope in him."

Matthew 12:9–21 CEV

*M*iracles will not convince people who have chosen to disbelieve. While the healed man and those who witnessed the healing praised God, the Pharisees, who saw the exact same miracle, decided that Jesus deserved to die.

The law of Moses was clear regarding the Sabbath. The one who worked on that day had to be put to death (Exodus 31:14–15). God had sent ancient Israel into Babylonian captivity for ignoring God's laws, and so the Pharisees had devoted their lives to preventing a recurrence. While rescuing an animal fallen into a ditch or saving a man's life was acceptable on the Sabbath, the man Jesus healed was not in a life-threatening situation. As far as they were concerned, Jesus could—and should—have waited until the Sabbath ended at sunset to heal him. They thought Sabbath was more important than a man's comfort or discomfort. Jesus disagreed with their priorities.

God cares about us more than anything else. God is at work in our lives every day; he never takes a day off from caring for us. God grants us the freedom to choose to live in the knowledge of his presence, or we can choose to pretend he's not there or he's not who he is. We can choose to take God for granted, or we can glory in his provision. Whether we acknowledge God's actions or not, God still acts. But God cannot make us—or anyone else—believe.

RABBIS

In a house near the Sea of Galilee, Jesus tried to describe the kingdom of heaven in many ways to his disciples:

"Once again, the kingdom of heaven is like a net that was let down into the lake and caught all kinds of fish. When it was full, the fishermen pulled it up on the shore. Then they sat down and collected the good fish in baskets, but threw the bad away. This is how it will be at the end of the age. The angels will come and separate the wicked from the righteous and throw them into the fiery furnace, where there will be weeping and gnashing of teeth.

"Have you understood all these things?" Jesus asked.

"Yes," they replied.

He said to them, "Therefore every teacher of the law who has been instructed about the kingdom of heaven is like the owner of a house who brings out of his storeroom new treasures as well as old."

When Jesus had finished these parables, he moved on from there. Coming to his hometown, he began teaching the people in their synagogue, and they were amazed. "Where did this man get this wisdom and these miraculous powers?" they asked.

Matthew 13:47–54 NIV

After Jesus gave his disciples a picture of the kingdom of heaven based on fishing, he asked if they understood him. They claimed they did. Given their record with most of the parables, we might be justified in holding on to a little bit of skepticism.

Jesus then said, "Therefore." Was he saying "therefore" in reaction to their affirmation that they understood, or was it in reaction to the parable he had just spoken? It was because they had just been instructed about the kingdom of heaven. Jesus was calling his disciples "teachers of the law." He was letting them know that because Jesus had trained them, they were now responsible as instructors.

They called Jesus "Rabbi." What a rabbi did, besides officiating over a synagogue service, was to accumulate students—disciples—who would follow him and learn his ways. The point of becoming a follower of a rabbi was to one day become a rabbi oneself. In contrast, the disciples had been thinking primarily about Jesus becoming king. But Jesus never forgot that his disciples would become rabbis like him, instructing the church that would be founded on the day of pentecost.

We have been called to become the instructors of others. We all have people with whom we spend time and share our thoughts and feelings. We are all rabbis to someone, whether it's our children, our coworkers, or our friends.

LEGALISTS

In the temple courts, during Jesus' last week in Jerusalem, Jesus condemned the religious establishment:

"You Pharisees and teachers of the Law of Moses are in for trouble! You're nothing but show-offs. You travel over land and sea to win one follower. And when you have done so, you make that person twice as fit for hell as you are.

"You are in for trouble! You are supposed to lead others, but you are blind. You teach that it doesn't matter if a person swears by the temple. But you say that it does matter if someone swears by the gold in the temple. You blind fools! Which is greater, the gold or the temple that makes the gold sacred?

"You also teach that it doesn't matter if a person swears by the altar. But you say that it does matter if someone swears by the gift on the altar. Are you blind? Which is more important, the gift or the altar that makes the gift sacred? Anyone who swears by the altar also swears by everything on it. And anyone who swears by the temple also swears by God, who lives there. To swear by heaven is the same as swearing by God's throne and by the one who sits on that throne."

Matthew 23:15–22 CEV

✳

*W*ithin a week of his crucifixion, Jesus condemned the Pharisees for their legalism, which often led them to violate the law rather than to keep it. The Pharisees rightly recognized the importance of keeping their oaths. Then they lost sight of the simple fact that God wanted people to do and mean what they said. Instead, the Pharisees began wondering what actually constituted an oath. They defined it carefully. If a promise lacked the right words, or wasn't spoken in just the right way, the Pharisees concluded that it was not an oath at all and wasn't legally binding. Rather than worrying about the intent of the heart, they became obsessed with the outward form.

Jesus berated them for their concern with finding reasons not to be bound by the promises they made. God did not create the law in order to give employment to lawyers. We do not stand before God with our attorney finding loopholes in God's commands so we can escape our commitments. There are no "technicalities" awaiting our discovery. The Pharisees, Jesus said, were blind and foolish. Many had lost sight of what really mattered—love. Despite their intent to keep the law, they had become lawbreakers.

Jesus wants us to be focused on loving God and loving people, rather than on seeking ways to get out of trouble.

HYPOCRITES

In the temple courts, just before Jesus' final Passover, he said:

"You're hopeless, you religion scholars and Pharisees! Frauds! You burnish the surface of your cups and bowls so they sparkle in the sun, while the insides are maggoty with your greed and gluttony. Stupid Pharisee! Scour the insides, and then the gleaming surface will mean something.

"You're hopeless, you religion scholars and Pharisees! Frauds! You're like manicured grave plots, grass clipped and the flowers bright, but six feet down it's all rotting bones and worm-eaten flesh. People look at you and think you're saints, but beneath the skin you're total frauds.

"You're hopeless, you religion scholars and Pharisees! Frauds! You build granite tombs for your prophets and marble monuments for your saints. And you say that if you had lived in the days of your ancestors, no blood would have been on your hands. You protest too much! You're cut from the same cloth as those murderers, and daily add to the death count.

"Snakes! Reptilian sneaks! Do you think you can worm your way out of this? Never have to pay the piper?"

Matthew 23:25–33 MSG

✳

*I*n continuing his condemnation of the Pharisees and other religious scholars, Jesus focused on the fact that they were more concerned with appearance than with substance. The word translated as *frauds* can also be translated as *hypocrites*, a word that we today use for those who say one thing and then do another.

For the Pharisee, what mattered most was how one looked. If a person dressed properly and used the right jargon, he or she was acceptable. Religious concepts needed to be expressed with standard "proper" phrases. To vary from the accepted wording meant condemnation. One also needed to avoid certain places and people, condemning them with the proper terminology.

Jesus pointed out that it was easy to keep the outside of something looking good. But what mattered was what was inside. In their motivations and attitudes, their thoughts and beliefs, the Pharisees were as wicked as those they were quick to condemn. When they protested that they would never be guilty of what their ancestors did, they were in fact condemning themselves. Those who imagine that they would be immune to human failure have failed to recognize that they are human themselves and subject to the same weaknesses all humans have. Thinking themselves to be strong, they were weak.

Jesus looks at our hearts, not at what we show the world.

CHICKENS

At the temple not long before Passover, Jesus warned the religious establishment:

"I send you prophets, wise men, and scribes: some of them you will kill and crucify, and some of them you will scourge in your synagogues and persecute from city to city, that on you may come all the righteous blood shed on the earth, from the blood of righteous Abel to the blood of Zechariah, son of Berechiah, whom you murdered between the temple and the altar. Assuredly, I say to you, all these things will come upon this generation.

"O Jerusalem, Jerusalem, the one who kills the prophets and stones those who are sent to her! How often I wanted to gather your children together, as a hen gathers her chicks under her wings, but you were not willing! See! Your house is left to you desolate; for I say to you, you shall see Me no more till you say, 'Blessed is He who comes in the name of the Lord!'"

Matthew 23:34–39 NKJV

✺

*I*n the week leading up to his crucifixion, Jesus spent time in Jerusalem teaching his disciples and the crowds. Jesus told them that he was sending them "prophets." By saying such a thing, Jesus was affirming his deity, since only God sent prophets. Then Jesus warned the Pharisees that they were going to behave just as their ancestors had and were going to miss God's presence in their midst. Rather than hearing the words of the prophets, the words of the wise, and the words of the scribes, they would reject those who came in the name of God and would kill them, just as their ancestors had killed the earlier prophets. Abel was killed by his brother in the first book of the Old Testament (Genesis 4:8), while Zechariah, son of Berechiah, was killed in the last book of the Hebrew Old Testament (2 Chronicles 24:21).

Jesus longed to protect and shelter the people of Jerusalem, but they were choosing to ignore and reject their king and their God, Yahweh, whom they claimed to worship and serve. Consequently, they would suffer for their refusal to come under his protection, for going off on their own paths, and for turning their backs on their one and only God.

God wants to take care of us and protect us. But he also gave us free will, a will that allows us to make choices both bad and good. Like baby chicks with their mother, we can huddle beneath God only if we choose to do so.

YOU NEVER KNOW

Just after Jesus left the temple, he told his disciples about the coming judgment:

"About that day and hour no one knows, neither the angels of heaven, nor the Son, but only the Father. For as the days of Noah were, so will be the coming of the Son of Man. For as in those days before the flood they were eating and drinking, marrying and giving in marriage, until the day Noah entered the ark, and they knew nothing until the flood came and swept them all away, so too will be the coming of the Son of Man.

"Then two will be in the field; one will be taken and one will be left. Two women will be grinding meal together; one will be taken and one will be left. Keep awake therefore, for you do not know on what day your Lord is coming. But understand this: if the owner of the house had known in what part of the night the thief was coming, he would have stayed awake and would not have let his house be broken into. Therefore you also must be ready, for the Son of Man is coming at an unexpected hour.

"Who then is the faithful and wise slave, whom his master has put in charge of his household, to give the other slaves their allowance of food at the proper time? Blessed is that slave whom his master will find at work when he arrives. Truly I tell you, he will put that one in charge of all his possessions. But if that wicked slave says to himself, 'My master is delayed,' and he begins to beat his fellow slaves, and eats and drinks with drunkards, the master of that slave will come on a day when he does not expect him and at an hour that he does not know."

Matthew 24:36–50 NRSV

✻

Not long before his crucifixion, Jesus told his disciples that neither he nor the angels knew when the final judgment and his second coming might be. Although Jesus is God, he had become a human being. Paul wrote that in becoming human, Jesus had "emptied Himself" (Philippians 2:7 HCSB). In his humanity, God the Son was not all-powerful or all-knowing or able to be in all places at once. As he himself said, all that he knew and all that he did, he did by the means of his Father (John 8:28 NIV).

Jesus, by becoming one of us, chose to give up his unlimited power and unlimited knowledge. He had access to the limitless only through his Father. As Christians, thanks to the indwelling Holy Spirit, we, too, have that same access to Jesus' Father. Thanks to what Jesus did on the cross, we, too, have become God's children.

※※※※※※※※※※※※※※※※※※※※※※※※※※※※※※※※※※※

BE PREPARED

Just a few days before the Last Supper, Jesus taught his disciples:

"The kingdom of heaven shall be likened to ten virgins who took their lamps and went out to meet the bridegroom. Now five of them were wise, and five were foolish. Those who were foolish took their lamps and took no oil with them, but the wise took oil in their vessels with their lamps. But while the bridegroom was delayed, they all slumbered and slept.

"And at midnight a cry was heard: 'Behold, the bridegroom is coming; go out to meet him!' Then all those virgins arose and trimmed their lamps. And the foolish said to the wise, 'Give us some of your oil, for our lamps are going out.'

But the wise answered, saying, 'No, lest there should not be enough for us and you; but go rather to those who sell, and buy for yourselves.' And while they went to buy, the bridegroom came, and those who were ready went in with him to the wedding; and the door was shut.

"Afterward the other virgins came also, saying, 'Lord, Lord, open to us!' But he answered and said, 'Assuredly, I say to you, I do not know you.'

"Watch therefore, for you know neither the day nor the hour in which the Son of Man is coming."

Matthew 25:1–13 NKJV

※

The Boy Scout motto is "Be prepared." Jesus' parable about the ten virgins was about being prepared. Jesus compared the kingdom of heaven to ten virgins with lamps who went out to meet the bridegroom so they could lead him to his bride. They had oil for their lamps, but only half of them carried extra oil.

Notice that all the virgins, both wise and foolish, fell asleep as they awaited their delayed bridegroom. Jesus' point was not that we should be on constant alert. Rather, we need always to be ready.

The foolish virgins who did not bring extra oil ended up excluded from the wedding that followed. Paul wrote that the wisdom of the world is foolishness, while what seems foolish to the world is the wisdom of God (1 Corinthians 1:20–21). In Jesus' parable, the wise virgins are those who burdened themselves with what seemed to the foolish virgins unnecessary extra baggage. There was no reason to anticipate running out of oil.

Parables are not allegories, with each bit in them standing for something else. Rather, there is a moral to the story. The moral to Jesus' parable is simple. Jesus wants us to be prepared to wait for him a long time, however long that might be. And while we wait, he expects us to live according to his law of love.

TAKING CARE OF JESUS

During his last week in Jerusalem, Jesus told his disciples:

"When the Son of Man comes in his glory, and all the angels with him, then he will sit on the throne of his glory. All the nations will be gathered before him, and he will separate people one from another as a shepherd separates the sheep from the goats, and he will put the sheep at his right hand and the goats at the left.

"Then the king will say to those at his right hand, 'Come, you that are blessed by my Father, inherit the kingdom prepared for you from the foundation of the world; for I was hungry and you gave me food, I was thirsty and you gave me something to drink, I was a stranger and you welcomed me, I was naked and you gave me clothing, I was sick and you took care of me, I was in prison and you visited me.'

"Then the righteous will answer him, 'Lord, when was it that we saw you hungry and gave you food, or thirsty and gave you something to drink? And when was it that we saw you a stranger and welcomed you, or naked and gave you clothing? And when was it that we saw you sick or in prison and visited you?' And the king will answer them, 'Truly I tell you, just as you did it to one of the least of these who are members of my family, you did it to me.'"

Matthew 25:31–40 NRSV

By speaking about separating goats and sheep, Jesus made an allusion to the words of the prophet Ezekiel. In Ezekiel 34, God compared Israel to a flock with God as the shepherd who would judge between "one sheep and another, and between rams and goats" (v. 17 NIV). God was criticizing the religious and political leadership for mistreating the weak and poor. God would judge them for it in the same way a shepherd would judge between sheep. Jesus used the same imagery to point out that God's concerns were no different in his time than they were in Ezekiel's time. He accused the religious establishment of being no better than their ancestors were. He told them they were mistreating those most in need.

God is not separated from the people of the world. Wherever we are, there he is in our midst, no matter what we are doing, no matter what we are about, no matter where we go. God feels each kindness, each blessing we bestow on those around us. As we treat human beings, created in the image of God, we treat God himself.

HE IS WILLING

In the region of Galilee, while Jesus was preaching to a crowd:

A man with leprosy came and knelt in front of Jesus, begging to be healed. "If you are willing, you can heal me and make me clean," he said.

Moved with compassion, Jesus reached out and touched him. "I am willing," he said. "Be healed!" Instantly the leprosy disappeared, and the man was healed. Then Jesus sent him on his way with a stern warning: "Don't tell anyone about this. Instead, go to the priest and let him examine you. Take along the offering required in the law of Moses for those who have been healed of leprosy. This will be a public testimony that you have been cleansed."

But the man went and spread the word, proclaiming to everyone what had happened. As a result, large crowds soon surrounded Jesus, and he couldn't publicly enter a town anywhere. He had to stay out in the secluded places, but people from everywhere kept coming to him.

Mark 1:40–45 NLT

The question for Jesus was never, "Are you able?" Rather, it was always, "Are you willing?" In the case of the leper in this reading, Jesus was willing, and so he healed the man. The question before us is the same as the question presented by this leper and the heart revealed by his question. The leper was concerned not just for his desperate need but also for the will of God. He understood that the world was filled with bigger things than only his desire for healing. He knew that God's will was more important than his own will.

The suffering that happens in the world isn't meaningless. God knows what is best for us and for the world as a whole. Whatever we face, it is all part of the grander scheme of things, part of God's overall creation, a work of tremendous beauty of which we can see but a tiny corner. What value or point there may be to endure what we must may never be clear to us. But like the leper, we should be willing to accept whatever God's will might be, whether it is the fulfillment of our deepest longing or whether it might be something else entirely. We do this because we trust that God is good and that he knows what is best. We can safely choose to submit to God's will and trust him, whatever the short-term outcome might be for us.

FASTING

Near Capernaum:

The disciples of John and of the Pharisees were fasting. Then they came and said to Him, "Why do the disciples of John and of the Pharisees fast, but Your disciples do not fast?"

And Jesus said to them, "Can the friends of the bridegroom fast while the bridegroom is with them? As long as they have the bridegroom with them they cannot fast. But the days will come when the bridegroom will be taken away from them, and then they will fast in those days. No one sews a piece of unshrunk cloth on an old garment; or else the new piece pulls away from the old, and the tear is made worse. And no one puts new wine into old wineskins; or else the new wine bursts the wineskins, the wine is spilled, and the wineskins are ruined. But new wine must be put into new wineskins."

Now it happened that He went through the grainfields on the Sabbath; and as they went His disciples began to pluck the heads of grain. And the Pharisees said to Him, "Look, why do they do what is not lawful on the Sabbath?"

But He said to them, "Have you never read what David did when he was in need and hungry, he and those with him: how he went into the house of God in the days of Abiathar the high priest, and ate the showbread, which is not lawful to eat except for the priests, and also gave some to those who were with him?"

And He said to them, "The Sabbath was made for man, and not man for the Sabbath. Therefore the Son of Man is also Lord of the Sabbath."

Mark 2:18–27 NKJV

*W*hen Jesus told the Pharisees that the Sabbath was made for man and not man for the Sabbath, he was trying to teach them an important principle that they had somehow missed in all their study of the Scriptures.

The Pharisees' concern for the Sabbath was genuine. But as well-intentioned as they might have been, they had forgotten the reason for the Sabbath. Moses himself had written, "On the seventh day do not work, so that your ox and your donkey may rest and the slave born in your household, and the alien as well, may be refreshed" (Exodus 23:12 NIV). The Sabbath existed because it was important for people to take time off. It was created in order to improve their lives. Such is the case with every law God created. He didn't come up with the rules arbitrarily. The rules exist to benefit us as expressions of his love for us so that we can live well and have the best lives possible.

❊❊❊❊❊❊❊❊❊❊❊❊❊❊❊❊❊❊❊❊❊❊❊❊❊❊❊❊❊❊❊❊❊

CONSPIRACY

Near the Sea of Galilee:

[Jesus] entered again into a synagogue; and a man was there whose hand was withered. They were watching Him to see if He would heal him on the Sabbath, so that they might accuse Him. He said to the man with the withered hand, "Get up and come forward!"

And He said to them, "Is it lawful to do good or to do harm on the Sabbath, to save a life or to kill?" But they kept silent.

After looking around at them with anger, grieved at their hardness of heart, He said to the man, "Stretch out your hand." And he stretched it out, and his hand was restored. The Pharisees went out and immediately began conspiring with the Herodians against Him, as to how they might destroy Him.

Jesus withdrew to the sea with His disciples; and a great multitude from Galilee followed; and also from Judea, and from Jerusalem, and from Idumea, and beyond the Jordan, and the vicinity of Tyre and Sidon, a great number of people heard of all that He was doing and came to Him. And He told His disciples that a boat should stand ready for Him because of the crowd, so that they would not crowd Him; for He had healed many, with the result that all those who had afflictions pressed around Him in order to touch Him. Whenever the unclean spirits saw Him, they would fall down before Him and shout, "You are the Son of God!" And He earnestly warned them not to tell who He was.

Mark 3:1–12 NASB

❊

*W*hen is the right time to do the right thing? Always. When it is within our power to right a wrong, to relieve suffering, and to encourage, that's when we can do it. There is no better time than now to be kind to another person. Whenever we see a need, we can reach out and relieve it. Is there a bit of trash that needs to be disposed of properly? Did someone drop something that needs to be picked up? Is there an elderly person needing help crossing a street? Is there a foreign tourist lost and confused who needs directions? Nothing is more important than helping those who need help. Jesus was always willing to be inconvenienced.

For the Pharisees, people and their needs often took second place to their concern for legalistic requirements. The question that Jesus wants us to ask ourselves in every situation is very simple: Is this the best thing I could do right now for this person?

THE TWELVE

Not far from the Sea of Galilee:

Jesus withdrew with his disciples to the lake, and a large crowd from Galilee followed. When they heard all he was doing, many people came to him from Judea, Jerusalem, Idumea, and the regions across the Jordan and around Tyre and Sidon. Because of the crowd he told his disciples to have a small boat ready for him, to keep the people from crowding him. For he had healed many, so that those with diseases were pushing forward to touch him. Whenever the evil spirits saw him, they fell down before him and cried out, "You are the Son of God." But he gave them strict orders not to tell who he was.

Jesus went up on a mountainside and called to him those he wanted, and they came to him. He appointed twelve—designating them apostles—that they might be with him and that he might send them out to preach and to have authority to drive out demons. These are the twelve he appointed: Simon (to whom he gave the name Peter); James son of Zebedee and his brother John (to them he gave the name Boanerges, which means Sons of Thunder); Andrew, Philip, Bartholomew, Matthew, Thomas, James son of Alphaeus, Thaddaeus, Simon the Zealot and Judas Iscariot, who betrayed him.

Mark 3:7–19 NIV

Jesus called twelve men to be his apostles—that is, to be his "ambassadors." Though some of the apostles would become famous, most of them remain obscure. They are nothing more than names on a list. No stories appear in the New Testament to tell us what James son of Alphaeus, Simon the Zealot, or Thaddaeus might have said or done. Jesus never singled them out for praise. No other author of the New Testament even mentions them. Yet those obscure men were among Jesus' closest friends while he was on earth. They were individuals whom Jesus specifically called, who served a role that Jesus needed. They were with Jesus to see his miracles, and they received the Spirit at pentecost.

Not many of us will be famous. Few of us will be remembered by anyone other than our friends, colleagues, and family. Within a generation or two, no one will even know our names. But whether our fame shines like the sun, remembered by the human race for as long as it endures, or whether we vanish in obscurity like the unknown apostles, we are important to Jesus. We serve a role that he intends, changing the world even if no one else knows what we are doing. We live for Jesus, not for fame.

LEGION

[Jesus and his disciples] came to the other side of the sea, to the region of the Gerasenes. As soon as He got out of the boat, a man with an unclean spirit came out of the tombs and met Him. He lived in the tombs. No one was able to restrain him any more—even with chains—because he often had been bound with shackles and chains, but had snapped off the chains and smashed the shackles. No one was strong enough to subdue him. And always, night and day, he was crying out among the tombs and in the mountains and cutting himself with stones.

When he saw Jesus from a distance, he ran and knelt down before Him. And he cried out with a loud voice, "What do You have to do with me, Jesus, Son of the Most High God? I beg You before God, don't torment me!" For He had told him, "Come out of the man, you unclean spirit!"

"What is your name?" He asked him.

"My name is Legion," he answered Him, "because we are many." And he kept begging Him not to send them out of the region.

Now a large herd of pigs was there, feeding on the hillside. The demons begged Him, "Send us to the pigs, so we may enter them." And He gave them permission. Then the unclean spirits came out and entered the pigs, and the herd of about 2,000 rushed down the steep bank into the sea and drowned there. The men who tended them ran off and reported it in the town and the countryside, and people went to see what had happened.

Mark 5:1–14 HCSB

✼

*B*oth Matthew and Luke have told the story about this demon-possessed man. But here in Mark, we notice something new. Jesus' first recorded words were not addressed to the possessed man, but to what was inside him. He told the "evil spirit" to depart before he ever asked it for a name.

The evil spirit's answer is worded oddly: "*My* name is Legion because *we* are many." Rather than the single spirit that began the passage, the remainder of the account describes "demons" in the plural. Did Jesus and the author of the gospel make a mistake at the beginning that they corrected as they went along?

That was not the case. The poor man was not possessed by an unruly mob of demons; he was possessed by an organized group. In the Roman army, a legion was strictly organized, with a commander and subcommanders. The demon speaking to Jesus was their commander, the leader of the evil congregation.

Jesus easily and quickly healed a man from perhaps thousands of demons. We can be confident that Jesus also can easily free us from whatever evil may have us in its grasp if we ask.

EVER MORE RULES

Near the Sea of Galilee, after the feeding of the five thousand:

The Pharisees and teachers asked Jesus, "Why don't your disciples obey what our ancestors taught us to do? Why do they eat without washing their hands?"

Jesus replied: "You are nothing but show-offs! The prophet Isaiah was right when he wrote that God had said,

'All of you praise me with
your words, but you never
really think about me. It is
useless for you to worship me,
when you teach rules made
up by humans.'

"You disobey God's commands in order to obey what humans have taught. You are good at rejecting God's commands so that you can follow your own teachings! Didn't Moses command you to respect your father and mother? Didn't he tell you to put to death all who curse their parents? But you let people get by without helping their parents when they should. You let them say that what they own has been offered to God. You won't let those people help their parents. And you ignore God's commands in order to follow your own teaching. You do a lot of other things that are just as bad."

Mark 7:5–13 CEV

The religious leaders carefully counted all the commandments of God and came up with a list of 613. To help make sure that no one would ever violate any of those 613 commandments, they devised additional rules to serve as a hedge to protect them. Exodus 23:19 commanded that a calf should not be boiled in its mother's milk, so the Pharisees decided that meat and milk products should never be consumed together. In Exodus 20:7, God said that his name should not be taken in vain. So they decided that God's name could never be spoken.

The extra laws could also be twisted to personal advantage. The Pharisees dedicated their wealth to God so that it could be used only for him. But since they considered themselves to be in God's service, the Pharisees could continue to benefit from their wealth, even as their parents were left destitute.

It is easy to drift far away from God's will even as we claim to follow him. Jesus wants us to obey God and discover his will from him, rather than obeying people who claim they know God's will for us.

WHAT'S INSIDE

Near the Sea of Galilee:

Jesus called the crowd together again and said, "Listen now, all of you—take this to heart. It's not what you swallow that pollutes your life; it's what you vomit—that's the real pollution."

When he was back home after being with the crowd, his disciples said, "We don't get it. Put it in plain language."

Jesus said, "Are you being willfully stupid? Don't you see that what you swallow can't contaminate you? It doesn't enter your heart but your stomach, works its way through the intestines, and is finally flushed." (That took care of dietary quibbling; Jesus was saying that *all* foods are fit to eat.)

He went on: "It's what comes out of a person that pollutes: obscenities, lusts, thefts, murders, adulteries, greed, depravity, deceptive dealings, carousing, mean looks, slander, arrogance, foolishness—all these are vomit from the heart. *There* is the source of your pollution."

Mark 7:14–23 MSG

*W*henever the comedian Flip Wilson's character Geraldine was caught misbehaving, she would shout, "The devil made me do it!" Jesus' response to such a claim would be, "No, he didn't."

We human beings are quick to find excuses for what we do wrong. We want to blame our parenting, the television, the Web, and the friends we hang out with. We'll blame our circumstances. But the reality is, what comes in from the outside is not what makes us do wrong. It's what comes from the inside. Not all people with bad backgrounds who play violent video games become criminals. Two people may be raised in the same circumstances, but while one becomes a criminal, the other becomes a pastor. Our appetites are what drive us, not what we choose to satisfy those appetites. If we weren't already hungry, we wouldn't try to eat. If we didn't hate, we wouldn't gossip.

Jesus used food to illustrate that what comes into us from the outside doesn't pollute us. Mark commented that Jesus' words prefigured what would become explicit later on. The dietary regulations of the Old Testament no longer mattered since food didn't actually cause uncleanness. Instead, it was what came out of people that was unclean.

Jesus warned his hearers, as he warns us, that we have no one and nothing to blame for our misdeeds but us. The devil didn't make us do it. We made ourselves do it. And we did it simply because we wanted to.

HOUSE OF PRAYER

On the following day, when they came from Bethany, he was hungry. Seeing in the distance a fig tree in leaf, he went to see whether perhaps he would find anything on it. When he came to it, he found nothing but leaves, for it was not the season for figs. He said to it, "May no one ever eat fruit from you again." And his disciples heard it.

Then they came to Jerusalem. And he entered the temple and began to drive out those who were selling and those who were buying in the temple, and he overturned the tables of the money changers and the seats of those who sold doves; and he would not allow anyone to carry anything through the temple. He was teaching and saying, "Is it not written,

'My house shall be called a house of prayer for all the nations'? But you have made it a den of robbers."

And when the chief priests and the scribes heard it, they kept looking for a way to kill him; for they were afraid of him, because the whole crowd was spellbound by his teaching. And when evening came, Jesus and his disciples went out of the city.

Mark 11:12–18 NRSV

*J*esus quoted from the prophet Isaiah when he said that the temple would be called "a house of prayer for all nations" (Isaiah 56:7 NIV). In context, Isaiah's prophecy predicted that a time would come when foreigners—Gentiles—would bind themselves to God and love his name.

When Jesus cleansed the temple of the money changers and those selling doves, his purpose was not to level an attack on making money. Jesus was not against capitalism. He was not even suggesting that selling things for religious purposes was wrong. Instead, he was attacking people who were taking advantage of the poor and the foreigners who were coming to the temple to worship God. He was attacking criminal behavior. The system that the religious establishment created around the temple was keeping those who wanted to reach God from getting to him. Rather than facilitating worship and prayer, the religious leaders were standing in its way. They were making it harder for people to find the kingdom of God.

God is not about putting up roadblocks to faith. He is about removing all the barriers that stand between him and people. He wants nothing to distract us from worshipping him, talking to him, and spending time with him. Jesus has done away with everything that could keep us away.

THE CORNERSTONE

Jesus taught his disciples in Jerusalem, just before the Last Supper:

Jesus started telling them stories. "A man planted a vineyard. He fenced it, dug a winepress, erected a watchtower, turned it over to the farmhands, and went off on a trip. At the time for harvest, he sent a servant back to the farmhands to collect his profits.

"They grabbed him, beat him up, and sent him off empty-handed. So he sent another servant. That one they tarred and feathered. He sent another and that one they killed. And on and on, many others. Some they beat up, some they killed.

"Finally there was only one left: a beloved son. In a last-ditch effort, he sent him, thinking, 'Surely they will respect my son.'

"But those farmhands saw their chance. They rubbed their hands together in greed and said, 'This is the heir! Let's kill him and have it all for ourselves.' They grabbed him, killed him, and threw him over the fence.

"What do you think the owner of the vineyard will do? Right. He'll come and clean house. Then he'll assign the care of the vineyard to others. Read it for yourselves in Scripture:

> That stone the masons threw
> out is now the cornerstone!
> This is God's work; we rub
> our eyes—we can hardly
> believe it!"

They wanted to lynch him then and there but, intimidated by public opinion, held back. They knew the story was about them. They got away from there as fast as they could.

Mark 12:1–12 MSG

❦

The people who wanted to lynch Jesus were the religious leaders in Jerusalem. They knew that Jesus' story about the vineyard was aimed at them. Like most people, they did not take kindly to criticism.

The story of the vineyard was an allusion to Isaiah's prophecy against Judah and Jerusalem that had prefigured Israel's destruction by the Babylonians (Isaiah 5). Every prophet who had ever lived had faced severe persecution from Israel's leaders. The Pharisees were quick to understand that Jesus was insinuating that they were just as blind and would therefore suffer the same fate as their ancestors.

Jesus adapted his message to the sensibilities of those to whom he was talking. How he addressed Samaritans and his disciples was different from how he addressed the religious establishment, but his goal with everyone was the same.

Jesus spoke many warm and comforting words that we enjoy reading. But his words that make us uncomfortable, that we may not enjoy reading quite so much, are just as important for us to hear. Jesus offers us both comfort and criticism, and they are equally for our benefit.

UNTRAPPABLE

Jesus taught in the temple just before Passover:

[The religious establishment] sent to [Jesus] some Pharisees and some Herodians to trap him in what he said. And they came and said to him, "Teacher, we know that you are sincere, and show deference to no one; for you do not regard people with partiality, but teach the way of God in accordance with truth. Is it lawful to pay taxes to the emperor, or not? Should we pay them, or should we not?"

But knowing their hypocrisy, he said to them, "Why are you putting me to the test? Bring me a denarius and let me see it." And they brought one. Then he said to them, "Whose head is this, and whose title?"

They answered, "The emperor's." Jesus said to them, "Give to the emperor the things that are the emperor's, and to God the things that are God's." And they were utterly amazed at him.

Mark 12:13–17 NRSV

❀

*J*esus asked a question that his critics refused to answer: "Why are you putting me to the test?" Jesus and they knew the answer to his question. They tested him in the hope that he would prove to everyone what the Pharisees already believed—that he was a false Messiah, an antichrist.

Jesus' critics were not looking for the truth. They thought they already had it, and they were simply trying to get everyone else around them to agree that they had the truth and that Jesus did not. It is one thing to test something in order to discover the truth. That sort of testing is a good thing. But how often have we heard someone ask a question that we knew was designed not to elicit information but rather to embarrass, to play "gotcha!"

Jesus wants us to seek the truth. God doesn't mind if we want proof. Gideon used fleece (Judges 6:39). In Malachi 3:10 God said, "'Bring the whole tithe into the storehouse, that there may be food in my house. Test me in this,' says the LORD Almighty, 'and see if I will not throw open the floodgates of heaven and pour out so much blessing that you will not have room enough for it'" (NIV). Testing in itself is not a bad thing. It is the *intent* of the testing that can be a problem. We may test to discover the truth, but not to attack God's character.

ENEMIES UNDERFOOT

While Jesus was teaching in the temple courts, he asked, "How is it that the teachers of the law say that the Christ is the son of David? David himself, speaking by the Holy Spirit, declared:

"'The Lord said to my Lord:
"Sit at my right hand until I
put your enemies under your
feet."'

David himself calls him 'Lord.' How then can he be his son?"

The large crowd listened to him with delight.

As he taught, Jesus said, "Watch out for the teachers of the law. They like to walk around in flowing robes and be greeted in the marketplaces, and have the most important seats in the synagogues and the places of honor at banquets. They devour widows' houses and for a show make lengthy prayers. Such men will be punished most severely."

Jesus sat down opposite the place where the offerings were put and watched the crowd putting their money into the temple treasury. Many rich people threw in large amounts. But a poor widow came and put in two very small copper coins, worth only a fraction of a penny.

Calling his disciples to him, Jesus said, "I tell you the truth, this poor widow has put more into the treasury than all the others. They all gave out of their wealth; but she, out of her poverty, put in everything—all she had to live on."

Mark 12:35–44 NIV

❈

*T*he religious leaders wanted to be honored by people, even as they dishonored those around them. They claimed to love God, even as they hated those created in his image. The problems infesting the Israelite leadership were the same problems that had infested Israelite leadership throughout its history. Though they had given up idolatry for the worship of a single God, they still didn't understand what it meant to be righteous. Prayer and tithing were good, but Jesus was concerned about their motivations.

Righteousness is not about giving money, praying long prayers, or gaining the admiration of others. Instead, righteousness is about loving God. The way we love God is revealed by how we treat those who bring us no advantage, who cannot advance our careers, who cannot offer us money or prestige. As John wrote, "If anyone says, 'I love God,' yet hates his brother, he is a liar. For anyone who does not love his brother, whom he has seen, cannot love God, whom he has not seen" (1 John 4:20 NIV). How we treat the least of God's people is how we treat God. Our behavior toward those around us is a reflection of what we believe about God.

JESUS AND THE BIBLE

When Jesus returned from the Jordan River, the power of the Holy Spirit was with him, and the Spirit led him into the desert. For forty days Jesus was tested by the devil, and during that time he went without eating. When it was all over, he was hungry.

The devil said to Jesus, "If you are God's Son, tell this stone to turn into bread."

Jesus answered, "The Scriptures say, 'No one can live only on food.' "

Then the devil led Jesus up to a high place and quickly showed him all the nations on earth. The devil said, "I will give all this power and glory to you. It has been given to me, and I can give it to anyone I want to. Just worship me, and you can have it all."

Jesus answered, "The Scriptures say:

'Worship the Lord your God
and serve only him!' "

Finally, the devil took Jesus to Jerusalem and had him stand on top of the temple. The devil said, "If you are God's Son, jump off. The Scriptures say:

'God will tell his angels to
take care of you. They will
catch you in their arms, and
you will not hurt your feet on
the stones.' "

Jesus answered, "The Scriptures also say, 'Don't try to test the Lord your God!' "

After the devil had finished testing Jesus in every way possible, he left him for a while.

Luke 4:1–13 CEV

❀

*L*uke's gospel, like Matthew's, describes Jesus' temptation in the wilderness. One detail Luke revealed that was missing from Matthew's account of the event comes at the end of the Temptation. Luke revealed that the devil left Jesus "for a while." The implication was that Satan tried again later.

The author of Hebrews explained that Jesus was tempted in every way, just as we are. Luke told us that he was tempted during the full forty days, and not just by the three temptations listed. Luke's gospel gives us a selective summary of Jesus' experiences, not an exhaustive account.

We are not tempted just once in our lives. We are not even tempted only once for the same sin. We spend our lives being tempted time and time again, usually over the same issues. When we're told that Satan left Jesus "for a while," we understand what that means. Like us, Jesus would again be faced with temptations from the devil. Our temptations may not be constant, but they are never ending and normally come without warning at the worst possible times. So be vigilant and rely on Christ, who delivers us when we ask.

DEMON OBEDIENCE

[Jesus] went down to Capernaum, a town in Galilee, and was teaching them on the Sabbath. They were astonished at His teaching because His message had authority. In the synagogue there was a man with an unclean demonic spirit who cried out with a loud voice, "Leave us alone! What do You have to do with us, Jesus—Nazarene? Have You come to destroy us? I know who You are—the Holy One of God!"

But Jesus rebuked him and said, "Be quiet and come out of him!"

And throwing him down before them, the demon came out of him without hurting him at all. They were all struck with amazement and kept saying to one another, "What is this message? For He commands the unclean spirits with authority and power, and they come out!" And news about Him began to go out to every place in the vicinity.

Luke 4:31–37 HCSB

*M*ark told the same story about the demon-possessed man in the synagogue. After the demon recognized Jesus, Jesus told the demon to "be quiet" and to "come out of him," which the demon then did without another word, without complaint, and without asking where to go.

The people were amazed by Jesus' power. And yet all Jesus did to the demon was tell it to go. The demon obeyed because of who Jesus was. Jesus derived the power to expel demons, heal the sick, preach and teach, and die for our sins from his Father, who was and is God. We often take Jesus for granted. We sometimes fail to comprehend the significance of our relationship with God. Demons will not listen to us, but they will listen to Jesus. In confronting evil, therefore, the key is to recognize that the conflict is not between us and the evil that stands before us; rather, the conflict is between evil and Jesus. When we give the problem over to him, he can overcome it. We do not have the strength to overcome our evil desires, but Jesus does.

In our lives, Jesus' power may manifest in a way that our problem goes away and never troubles us again. But it may simply mean that Jesus gives us the strength to endure it. Whichever Jesus grants us, our victory is no less complete. We can be happy with Jesus in our lives when we give him mastery over us.

GOOD NEWS

In the synagogue in Capernaum, Jesus healed a demon-possessed man:

Jesus left the meeting place and went to Simon's home. When Jesus got there, he was told that Simon's mother-in-law was sick with a high fever. So Jesus went over to her and ordered the fever to go away. Right then she was able to get up and serve them a meal.

After the sun had set, people with all kinds of diseases were brought to Jesus. He put his hands on each one of them and healed them. Demons went out of many people and shouted, "You are the Son of God!" But Jesus ordered the demons not to speak because they knew he was the Messiah.

The next morning Jesus went out to a place where he could be alone, and crowds came looking for him. When they found him, they tried to stop him from leaving. But Jesus said, "People in other towns must hear the good news about God's kingdom. That's why I was sent." So he kept on preaching in the Jewish meeting places in Judea.

Luke 4:38–44 CEV

Jesus brought good news to the people of Israel. The news was so wonderful, in fact, that huge crowds came looking for him so they could hear it. Healing the sick and casting out demons were illustrations, living parables, about God's kingdom. Jesus brought the human race relief from its blindness and from its oppression beneath the heavy boot of the evil one. Jesus rescued us from the kingdom of Satan just as God had rescued the Israelites from the kingdom of the pharaoh.

The kingdom of God is about freedom rather than slavery. It is about joy rather than sadness. It is about wealth rather than poverty. It is about health rather than sickness. But if we imagine that the kingdom of God is about a physical kingdom, physical wealth, physical health, and physical freedom, we are missing what Jesus means when he speaks of the kingdom of God. We are allowing ourselves to become distracted by things that won't endure instead of embracing what will endure forever. The kingdom is about our reconciliation, a treasure in heaven, and everlasting life. The reality of eternity begins today in our hearts because the King of the kingdom lives in us and walks with us every day. We are his ambassadors, walking the road toward the kingdom and inviting everyone we see to join us on our pilgrimage.

As we embrace God's kingdom, the kingdoms of the world will inevitably change as well. We make the world a better place and change physical reality as we help people find the way to the true King and his kingdom.

WORDS VS. DEEDS

Jesus taught his followers on a plain near the Sea of Galilee:

"You don't get wormy apples off a healthy tree, nor good apples off a diseased tree. The health of the apple tells the health of the tree. You must begin with your own life-giving lives. It's who you are, not what you say and do, that counts. Your true being brims over into true words and deeds.

"Why are you so polite with me, always saying 'Yes, sir,' and 'That's right, sir,' but never doing a thing I tell you? These words I speak to you are not mere additions to your life, homeowner improvements to your standard of living. They are foundation words, words to build a life on.

"If you work the words into your life, you are like a smart carpenter who dug deep and laid the foundation of his house on bedrock. When the river burst its banks and crashed against the house, nothing could shake it; it was built to last. But if you just use my words in Bible studies and don't work them into your life, you are like a dumb carpenter who built a house but skipped the foundation. When the swollen river came crashing in, it collapsed like a house of cards. It was a total loss."

Luke 6:43–49 MSG

❊

*W*ords do have power, but only as people act on them. We are saved by our faith. Some may wonder if that makes it "too easy." If all we have to do is believe, then why should we bother to be good? But faith doesn't stay locked up in our skulls. Real faith is more than "yes, sir." Real faith leads us to act. If we believe that Jesus has reconciled us, transformed us, and put his Spirit in us, then we can't help but start living differently.

What we really believe comes out in the way we choose to live. For instance, because we believe in gravity, we don't purposely try to set our coffee mugs down in the middle of the air. Because we believe in rainstorms and the basic principles of homebuilding, when we build our house, we will choose to build its foundations on solid rock rather than on shifting sands. What we trust changes our lives. Belief does not exist isolated from life; belief powers life. Faith is what drives us to act the way we act, to make the choices we choose to make. It may be easy to *say* "yes, sir." But our belief is real only if we also *do* "yes, sir." What we believe will manifest in our actions.

BEHIND HIS BACK

Jesus taught in the region of Galilee:

When the messengers of John had departed, [Jesus] began to speak to the multitudes concerning John: "What did you go out into the wilderness to see? A reed shaken by the wind? But what did you go out to see? A man clothed in soft garments? Indeed those who are gorgeously appareled and live in luxury are in kings' courts. But what did you go out to see? A prophet? Yes, I say to you, and more than a prophet. This is he of whom it is written:

'Behold, I send My messenger before Your face, Who will prepare Your way before You.'

"For I say to you, among those born of women there is not a greater prophet than John the Baptist; but he who is least in the kingdom of God is greater than he."

And when all the people heard Him, even the tax collectors justified God, having been baptized with the baptism of John. But the Pharisees and lawyers rejected the will of God for themselves, not having been baptized by him.

Luke 7:24–30 NKJV

❋

*J*esus praised John the Baptist, but not while any of his disciples could hear him. Jesus waited until they had departed before he began teaching the crowd about how much John the Baptist meant to the world and how there was no prophet greater than John the Baptist.

Yet having said all those wonderful things about the man, Jesus told those left listening to him that the "least" in God's kingdom was "greater" than John the Baptist. How so? What did Jesus mean by that?

Jesus did not mean that John the Baptist was not a part of the kingdom of God. John had been preaching the same message about the coming kingdom, after all. Nor was Jesus denigrating the prophet after just having praised him. Jesus was not putting John down at all. Rather, Jesus meant that being a great prophet, even one as great as John, was *nothing* compared to being a member of God's kingdom. Jesus wanted those listening to realize that the kingdom of God was greater than anything they could comprehend. John was the pinnacle of human achievement in this world, and yet the lowliest member of God's kingdom is better, greater, and more marvelous than he was.

Jesus' words suggest that we don't comprehend just how marvelous being a part of God's kingdom is, or what it will be like for us in eternity.

THE RICH GET RICHER

In the region of Galilee, Jesus taught his disciples:

"The parable is this: the seed is the word of God.

"Those beside the road are those who have heard; then the devil comes and takes away the word from their heart, so that they will not believe and be saved.

"Those on the rocky soil are those who, when they hear, receive the word with joy; and these have no firm root; they believe for a while, and in time of temptation fall away.

"The seed which fell among the thorns, these are the ones who have heard, and as they go on their way they are choked with worries and riches and pleasures of this life, and bring no fruit to maturity.

"But the seed in the good soil, these are the ones who have heard the word in an honest and good heart, and hold it fast, and bear fruit with perseverance.

"Now no one after lighting a lamp covers it over with a container, or puts it under a bed; but he puts it on a lampstand, so that those who come in may see the light. For nothing is hidden that will not become evident, nor anything secret that will not be known and come to light. So take care how you listen; for whoever has, to him more shall be given; and whoever does not have, even what he thinks he has shall be taken away from him."

Luke 8:11–18 NASB

❋

*W*hat Jesus said hardly seems fair, that the one who has would get even more, while the one who lacks will lose even the little he has. But Jesus was not talking about the redistribution of physical wealth. Instead, Jesus was talking about what happens when the message of God is taught. He was commenting on his parable of the sower and the scattered seeds: those who pay attention learn, and those who don't pay attention don't learn. Those who listened carefully to what God had to say would understand God even better, while those who didn't pay attention to God's words would lose even what limited understanding of spiritual matters they had.

Paying attention to what God has to say brings ever greater understanding to people, while ignoring God leaves them in ignorance. Jesus was merely describing the reality of teaching human beings.

It's one thing not to know; it's another thing to "know" something that isn't so. The Pharisees were in a knowledge deficit. The Pharisees were like someone who tries and fails to make a repair. When the repairman arrives, he has to undo the attempted fix before he can focus on the actual repair. We must pay attention to God's words, or we will remain ignorant or misinformed.

RECEIVING JESUS

Near the Sea of Galilee, people witnessed the healing of the demon-possessed boy:

[They] were all amazed at the greatness of God.

But while everyone was marveling at all that [Jesus] was doing, He said to His disciples, "Let these words sink into your ears; for the Son of Man is going to be delivered into the hands of men." But they did not understand this statement, and it was concealed from them so that they would not perceive it; and they were afraid to ask Him about this statement.

An argument started among them as to which of them might be the greatest. But Jesus, knowing what they were thinking in their heart, took a child and stood him by His side, and said to them, "Whoever receives this child in My name receives Me, and whoever receives Me receives Him who sent Me; for the one who is least among all of you, this is the one who is great."

John answered and said, "Master, we saw someone casting out demons in Your name; and we tried to prevent him because he does not follow along with us." But Jesus said to him, "Do not hinder him; for he who is not against you is for you."

Luke 9:43–50 NASB

❋

*J*ohn tried to keep someone who was not a disciple of Jesus from casting out demons in Jesus' name. Jesus told John that such a person shouldn't be hindered, since "he who is not against you is for you." And yet elsewhere, Jesus told his disciples, "Whoever is not with me is against me" (see Matthew 12:30; Luke 11:23). How do we reconcile the two concepts?

When Jesus commented that "whoever is not with me is against me," he was speaking about the Pharisees and their refusal to accept Jesus as the Messiah. In his rebuke to John, Jesus was pointing out that God works through whom he will, not just through those who happen to belong to the "in" group. A person cannot speak positively of Jesus and be against him at the same time. Just because a person didn't follow Jesus and the disciples around Palestine didn't mean he wasn't a believer. Besides, getting rid of demons is always a good thing. Who in his right mind would argue against that or want to stop it? John's behavior in trying to stop the man simply didn't make sense.

The practice of excluding others who minister in the name of Jesus because they are not "one of us" is wrong. Jesus was warning us against excluding those who name the name of Jesus but don't happen to belong to our particular group.

JUST BEING NEIGHBORLY

After the Transfiguration, Jesus began his journey toward Jerusalem, teaching as he went:

An expert in the law stood up to test Him, saying, "Teacher, what must I do to inherit eternal life?"

"What is written in the law?" He asked him. "How do you read it?"

He answered:

Love the Lord your God with all your heart, with all your soul, with all your strength, and with all your mind; and your neighbor as yourself.

"You've answered correctly," He told him. "Do this and you will live."

But wanting to justify himself, he asked Jesus, "And who is my neighbor?"

Jesus took up the question and said: "A man was going down from Jerusalem to Jericho and fell into the hands of robbers. They stripped him, beat him up, and fled, leaving him half dead. A priest happened to be going down that road. When he saw him, he passed by on the other side. In the same way, a Levite, when he arrived at the place and saw him, passed by on the other side. But a Samaritan on his journey came up to him, and when he saw the man, he had compassion. He went over to him and bandaged his wounds, pouring on oil and wine. Then he put him on his own animal, brought him to an inn, and took care of him. The next day he took out two denarii, gave them to the innkeeper, and said, 'Take care of him. When I come back I'll reimburse you for whatever extra you spend.'

"Which of these three do you think proved to be a neighbor to the man who fell into the hands of the robbers?"

"The one who showed mercy to him," he said.

Then Jesus told him, "Go and do the same."

Luke 10:25–37 HCSB

---

*J*esus made religious people uncomfortable. A Bible scholar asked Jesus how to gain eternal life. Jesus told him to follow these two commandments: "Love God" and "Love your neighbor." But there were many people the scholar didn't love and a lot of people the man believed didn't deserve to be loved. He wanted a definition for *neighbor* that would let him keep his hate. Jesus told him a story that let him know that wasn't possible.

Today, Jesus' story of the good Samaritan doesn't make us as uncomfortable as it did that ancient Bible scholar. After all, what's a Samaritan? Samaritans were excluded from the Jewish temple and were despised as irredeemable sinners.

If Jesus were asked the same question today, perhaps his response might be to tell the story of how a preacher and a deacon ignored the victim in the gutter, in contrast to the homosexual who helped him.

ARRIVAL OF THE KINGDOM

On the road to Jerusalem:

Jesus forced a demon out of a man who could not talk. And after the demon had gone out, the man started speaking, and the crowds were amazed. But some people said, "He forces out demons by the power of Beelzebul, the ruler of the demons!"

Others wanted to put Jesus to the test. So they asked him to show them a sign from God. Jesus knew what they were thinking, and he said: "A kingdom where people fight each other will end up in ruin. And a family that fights will break up. If Satan fights against himself, how can his kingdom last? Yet you say that I force out demons by the power of Beelzebul. If I use his power to force out demons, whose power do your own followers use to force them out? They are the ones who will judge you. But if I use God's power to force out demons, it proves that God's kingdom has already come to you."

Luke 11:14–20 CEV

✳

*J*esus told those who criticized him that God's kingdom had already come to them. The proof of the arrival of God's kingdom was the fact that he was driving out demons. Satan's authority as ruler of the world was over, and God was in charge now. Satan was a defeated foe, since only God would be capable of getting rid of demons.

The world is still full of trouble and heartache, and we eagerly await the coming of Jesus back to earth again, just as he promised. It is also true that God is ruling even now. Because of Jesus' sacrifice on the cross, he overcame the evil one. Ever since, God has connected himself permanently and intimately with all those who call on the name of Jesus.

The ambassador of a foreign nation lives in a building called an embassy. And even though the embassy is physically within the borders of another nation, that embassy is the sovereign territory of the ambassador's nation. No one may enter it without permission of the ambassador. An attack on the embassy would be the same as an attack upon the foreign nation that the embassy represents. The nation represented by the embassy reaches out across the miles and lives fully within the confines of the embassy grounds. Likewise, the future kingdom of God reaches back from the future and lives within each of us. The kingdom of God is here, now, with each one of us.

PROOF

Jesus stopped and taught people as he traveled to Jerusalem:

As the crowd swelled, he took a fresh tack: "The mood of this age is all wrong. Everybody's looking for proof, but you're looking for the wrong kind. All you're looking for is something to titillate your curiosity, satisfy your lust for miracles. But the only proof you're going to get is the Jonah-proof given to the Ninevites, which looks like no proof at all. What Jonah was to Nineveh, the Son of Man is to this age.

"On Judgment Day the Ninevites will stand up and give evidence that will condemn this generation, because when Jonah preached to them they changed their lives. A far greater preacher than Jonah is here, and you squabble about 'proofs.' On Judgment Day the Queen of Sheba will come forward and bring evidence that condemns this generation, because she traveled from a far corner of the earth to listen to wise Solomon. Wisdom far greater than Solomon's is right in front of you, and you quibble over 'evidence.'

"No one lights a lamp, then hides it in a drawer. It's put on a lamp stand so those entering the room have light to see where they're going. Your eye is a lamp, lighting up your whole body. If you live wide-eyed in wonder and belief, your body fills up with light. If you live squinty-eyed in greed and distrust, your body is a dank cellar. Keep your eyes open, your lamp burning, so you don't get musty and murky. Keep your life as well-lighted as your best-lighted room."

Luke 11:29–36 MSG

*J*esus downplayed the power of miracles to prove anything. Jesus had just cast a demon from a man who was unable to speak, but rather than believing, the Pharisees explained the miracle away as the work of the devil. Then they demanded that Jesus give them another miracle to prove they were wrong.

Instead of offering them another miracle, Jesus offered them judgment. He compared them unfavorably with people of the past—those who had repented of their wickedness and those who had traveled long distances to hear wisdom. Those people had seen no miracles at all; they had merely heard the words of a prophet and a King.

God's actions in the world can always be explained away. People can rationalize whatever they see, and they can always find an alternative explanation. God does not demand compliance; he merely requests it.

It is enough when we share the words of God and tell people how God has worked in our lives. We don't need grand eloquence or wonders to convince them. People will believe us if they choose to obey God's request.

THE EXPERTS

In a town along the way to Jerusalem, Jesus criticized the Pharisees and then turned his attention to the experts in the law of Moses:

"You experts in the law, woe to you, because you load people down with burdens they can hardly carry, and you yourselves will not lift one finger to help them.

"Woe to you, because you build tombs for the prophets, and it was your forefathers who killed them. So you testify that you approve of what your forefathers did; they killed the prophets, and you build their tombs. Because of this, God in his wisdom said, 'I will send them prophets and apostles, some of whom they will kill and others they will persecute.' Therefore this generation will be held responsible for the blood of all the prophets that has been shed since the beginning of the world, from the blood of Abel to the blood of Zechariah, who was killed between the altar and the sanctuary. Yes, I tell you, this generation will be held responsible for it all.

"Woe to you experts in the law, because you have taken away the key to knowledge. You yourselves have not entered, and you have hindered those who were entering."

When Jesus left there, the Pharisees and the teachers of the law began to oppose him fiercely and to besiege him with questions, waiting to catch him in something he might say.

Luke 11:46–54 NIV

*W*hat is the key to knowledge that the experts in the law took away? The experts in the law had a wrong interpretation of the Old Testament Scriptures. Not only did they not know the way to the kingdom of God, but they also made it hard for anyone else to find it. Their interpretation of the Scriptures created a mass of regulations. They were preoccupied with minutiae and spent no time on the key—the love of God.

Because the experts in the law failed to recognize the preeminence of God's love and the love that people should have for one another, they obscured not just God's Word, but God as well, making it hard for people to see the way of salvation. All they could see were the regulations they had no hope of keeping and the condemnation they could see no way of escaping. Instead of showing that God offered hope and a way of escape because of his great love, the experts in the law succeeded only in making people feel guilty and hopeless.

Jesus shows us the way to life and joy and peace. He lifts us up from our prisons, breaks our chains, and sets us free.

THE PROBLEM OF SUFFERING

Nearing Jerusalem, Jesus complained that the people couldn't interpret the signs of the times:

There were some present who told him about the Galileans whose blood Pilate had mingled with their sacrifices. He asked them, "Do you think that because these Galileans suffered in this way they were worse sinners than all other Galileans? No, I tell you; but unless you repent, you will all perish as they did. Or those eighteen who were killed when the tower of Siloam fell on them—do you think that they were worse offenders than all the others living in Jerusalem? No, I tell you; but unless you repent, you will all perish just as they did."

Then he told this parable: "A man had a fig tree planted in his vineyard; and he came looking for fruit on it and found none. So he said to the gardener, 'See here! For three years I have come looking for fruit on this fig tree, and still I find none. Cut it down! Why should it be wasting the soil?' He replied, 'Sir, let it alone for one more year, until I dig around it and put manure on it. If it bears fruit next year, well and good; but if not, you can cut it down.'"

Luke 13:1–9 NRSV

❋

*J*esus contradicted the popular notion, taught by the religious leaders of Israel, that suffering and disaster were necessarily the judgment of God upon sinners. Instead, Jesus taught that we can do everything right, be good people, follow all the directions, and disaster can still strike us.

On any given morning, most people will wake up and go to work. But some people will commit murder, have an affair, or embezzle money. On any given morning, some people will be doing what they are supposed to do, and some will not. One bright September morning three thousand people who went to work as usual never went back home again. Terrorists chose to fly airplanes into their workplaces that particular day. They were not greater sinners than all the other people on the planet. Jesus explained that bad things happen without warning and without reason, and it isn't because God is mad at us or loves us less than those who didn't suffer that day.

When we're driving on the freeway, traffic slows in front of us, and we put on our brakes to stop, it isn't our fault when the person behind us doesn't and plows into the back of our car. Just because we drive carefully doesn't mean our neighbor will drive carefully. As the author of Ecclesiastes wrote, "time and chance" happen to us all (Ecclesiastes 9:11 NKJV). But God sustains us through whatever comes.

THE FEW

[Jesus] was passing through from one city and village to another, teaching, and proceeding on His way to Jerusalem. And someone said to Him, "Lord, are there just a few who are being saved?" And He said to them, "Strive to enter through the narrow door; for many, I tell you, will seek to enter and will not be able. Once the head of the house gets up and shuts the door, and you begin to stand outside and knock on the door, saying, 'Lord, open up to us!' then He will answer and say to you, 'I do not know where you are from.'

"Then you will begin to say, 'We ate and drank in Your presence, and You taught in our streets'; and He will say, 'I tell you, I do not know where you are from; depart from Me, all you evildoers.'

"In that place there will be weeping and gnashing of teeth when you see Abraham and Isaac and Jacob and all the prophets in the kingdom of God, but yourselves being thrown out. And they will come from east and west and from north and south, and will recline at the table in the kingdom of God. And behold, some are last who will be first and some are first who will be last."

Luke 13:22–30 NASB

As Jesus was approaching Jerusalem to be crucified, he was asked who would enter the kingdom of God. Those who asked assumed that all the Jewish people would make it. They wondered which sinners were going to be excluded. Jesus explained that the kingdom had a narrow door that not everyone would find. Being Jewish wasn't enough. Admission was limited. Not everyone descended from Abraham would make it through the door. And once the feast of the kingdom began, that narrow door would slam shut.

To their surprise, Jesus told them that some of those entering the kingdom of God wouldn't even be Jewish. Gentiles would make it into the kingdom! Jesus wanted those listening to him to understand that entry into the kingdom was not based on their birth. Instead, entry was based upon their relationship with Jesus. Striving to get in doesn't mean that getting in is based on how hard we work. Rather, it means that admission is based on learning where the door is and then going through it. Any of us can get into God's kingdom simply by entering it. All we have to do is walk through that narrow door.

DAY 304

DUTY AND HONOR

Nearing Jerusalem, after giving the story about the rich man and Lazarus:

Jesus said to his disciples: "Things that cause people to sin are bound to come, but woe to that person through whom they come. It would be better for him to be thrown into the sea with a millstone tied around his neck than for him to cause one of these little ones to sin. So watch yourselves.

"If your brother sins, rebuke him, and if he repents, forgive him. If he sins against you seven times in a day, and seven times comes back to you and says, 'I repent,' forgive him."

The apostles said to the Lord, "Increase our faith!"

He replied, "If you have faith as small as a mustard seed, you can say to this mulberry tree, 'Be uprooted and planted in the sea,' and it will obey you.

"Suppose one of you had a servant plowing or looking after the sheep. Would he say to the servant when he comes in from the field, 'Come along now and sit down to eat'? Would he not rather say, 'Prepare my supper, get yourself ready and wait on me while I eat and drink; after that you may eat and drink'? Would he thank the servant because he did what he was told to do? So you also, when you have done everything you were told to do, should say, 'We are unworthy servants; we have only done our duty.'"

Luke 17:1–10 NIV

The apostles asked Jesus to increase their faith. He told them they already had enough. Even the smallest amount was enough to throw mountains into the sea—that is, to forgive those who had sinned against them again and again, just as God forgave us and put our sins in the deepest ocean (Micah 7:19).

Jesus then countered the notion that God somehow owes us anything. Sometimes, when people suffer, they list all the things they've done for God and demand to know how they could possibly deserve their pain. Others may try to bargain with God, promising more church attendance or Bible reading if only he'll fix their problem. With his parable of the master and his servants, Jesus pointed out that such bargaining or resentment is wrong.

Jesus died for our sins when we were still his enemies. We have done nothing and can do nothing to make ourselves worthy of his salvation. We remain unworthy of God's love that he has lavished on us. At best, we merely do our duty. We never do anything worthy of praise. As Paul said, we have nothing to boast about except the cross of Christ (Galatians 6:14).

CAMELS AND NEEDLES

Not far from Jerusalem, while Jesus was blessing babies:

An important man asked Jesus, "Good Teacher, what must I do to have eternal life?"

Jesus said, "Why do you call me good? Only God is good. You know the commandments: 'Be faithful in marriage. Do not murder. Do not steal. Do not tell lies about others. Respect your father and mother.'"

He told Jesus, "I have obeyed all these commandments since I was a young man."

When Jesus heard this, he said, "There is one thing you still need to do. Go and sell everything you own! Give the money to the poor, and you will have riches in heaven. Then come and be my follower." When the man heard this, he was sad, because he was very rich.

Jesus saw how sad the man was. So he said, "It's terribly hard for rich people to get into God's kingdom! In fact, it's easier for a camel to go through the eye of a needle than for a rich person to get into God's kingdom."

When the crowd heard this, they asked, "How can anyone ever be saved?"

Jesus replied, "There are some things that people cannot do, but God can do anything."

Peter said, "Remember, we left everything to be your followers!"

Jesus answered, "You can be sure that anyone who gives up home or wife or brothers or family or children because of God's kingdom will be given much more in this life. And in the future world they will have eternal life."

Luke 18:18–30 CEV

✳

Saturday Night Live once performed a skit about a rich man who devoted his fortune to finding a way to fit a camel through the eye of a needle so that he could get to heaven. But a camel-sized needle or pureeing a camel with a giant blender seemed to be the only solutions.

Jesus' point about the camel was to counter the prevailing notion that God's favor or disfavor was based on one's bank account and general prosperity. Most people believed that God favored wealthy people, who were certain to achieve heaven, and that God held in disfavor the poor and the sick people, who were certain to be excluded.

Instead, however, Jesus taught that salvation came from God and was dependent upon him. The disciples wondered who could be saved. Jesus affirmed that people couldn't save themselves but that God could save them. We can enter God's kingdom because of what Jesus did on the cross and for no other reason.

THE SPIRIT

During the Festival of Tabernacles in Jerusalem:

Jesus said, "I am with you for only a short time, and then I go to the one who sent me. You will look for me, but you will not find me; and where I am, you cannot come."

The Jews said to one another, "Where does this man intend to go that we cannot find him? Will he go where our people live scattered among the Greeks, and teach the Greeks? What did he mean when he said, 'You will look for me, but you will not find me,' and 'Where I am, you cannot come'?"

On the last and greatest day of the Feast, Jesus stood and said in a loud voice, "If anyone is thirsty, let him come to me and drink. Whoever believes in me, as the Scripture has said, streams of living water will flow from within him." By this he meant the Spirit, whom those who believed in him were later to receive. Up to that time the Spirit had not been given, since Jesus had not yet been glorified.

On hearing his words, some of the people said, "Surely this man is the Prophet."

Others said, "He is the Christ."

John 7:33–41 NIV

❊

To close out the Festival of Tabernacles, the priest took a gold vessel full of water from the stream of Shiloah that flowed under the temple mountain. As he poured it on the altar, he quoted Isaiah 12:3: "With joy you will draw water from the wells of salvation" (NIV).

That closing ceremony served as the springboard for Jesus' proclamation that anyone who was thirsty could come to him. During his speech, Jesus alluded to a group of scriptures. There were Isaiah's words about streams of living water flowing from within (Isaiah 44:3; 58:11). Isaiah identified that living water as the Spirit of God (Isaiah 44:3). Jeremiah also spoke about living water flowing from God (Jeremiah 2:13). And Zechariah spoke of living water pouring from Jerusalem when the Messiah came (Zechariah 14:8). That's why people who heard Jesus speaking that day were willing to identify him as the Messiah.

The people of Israel were intimately familiar with the words of Scripture. When they heard Jesus speak, they heard those same words. They recognized them and understood their implications when Jesus applied them to their circumstances. The more we read and study the Bible, the more it will start to make sense to us—and the greater our depth of comprehension will be.

CRAZY TALK

Jesus taught in Jerusalem, after the Festival of Tabernacles:

"I am the good shepherd; and I know My sheep, and am known by My own. As the Father knows Me, even so I know the Father; and I lay down My life for the sheep. And other sheep I have which are not of this fold; them also I must bring, and they will hear My voice; and there will be one flock and one shepherd.

"Therefore My Father loves Me, because I lay down My life that I may take it again. No one takes it from Me, but I lay it down of Myself. I have power to lay it down, and I have power to take it again. This command I have received from My Father."

Therefore there was a division again among the Jews because of these sayings. And many of them said, "He has a demon and is mad. Why do you listen to Him?"

Others said, "These are not the words of one who has a demon. Can a demon open the eyes of the blind?"

John 10:14–21 NKJV

❈

*J*esus had just healed a man who was blind from birth. After the religious establishment had conducted its investigation into the healing, they threw the healed man out of the synagogue and told him never to come back.

Jesus used the healing of that man from his physical blindness to teach about another kind of blindness that so afflicts human beings—the inability to see even the most obvious of spiritual truths. Sadly, those who are spiritually blind, like the religious leaders Jesus confronted, are often unaware of their disability, in contrast to the physically blind, who know it well. Jesus can open the eyes of those who are spiritually blind, even if they have been blind from birth, as easily as he can open the eyes of those who were physically blind, but Jesus was divisive. Some of the spiritually blind believed, and some didn't. Many wrongly concluded that Jesus' words were the ravings of a mad man or worse. Blindness is a terrible thing.

The pastor and poet John Newton wrote in the song "Amazing Grace," "I once was blind, but now I see." Jesus has granted us insight into the mysteries of God. What had been hidden from us, what our blind eyes had not been able to discern, Jesus has at last revealed to us, opening our eyes so that we can see.

POVERTY IS FOREVER

Six days before the Passover, Jesus came to Bethany, where Lazarus was who had been dead, whom He had raised from the dead. There they made Him a supper; and Martha served, but Lazarus was one of those who sat at the table with Him. Then Mary took a pound of very costly oil of spikenard, anointed the feet of Jesus, and wiped His feet with her hair. And the house was filled with the fragrance of the oil.

But one of His disciples, Judas Iscariot, Simon's son, who would betray Him, said, "Why was this fragrant oil not sold for three hundred denarii and given to the poor?" This he said, not that he cared for the poor, but because he was a thief, and had the money box; and he used to take what was put in it.

But Jesus said, "Let her alone; she has kept this for the day of My burial. For the poor you have with you always, but Me you do not have always."

Now a great many of the Jews knew that He was there; and they came, not for Jesus' sake only, but that they might also see Lazarus, whom He had raised from the dead. But the chief priests plotted to put Lazarus to death also, because on account of him many of the Jews went away and believed in Jesus.

John 12:1–11 NKJV

While Jesus visited the home of his friend Lazarus, Lazarus's sister poured perfume on his feet and then wiped them with her hair. The incident resembles what happened in Simon the leper's home (Matthew 26:6–12; Mark 14:3–9). Luke relates the story of a "sinful" woman in a Pharisee's house who did the same thing (Luke 7:38). Though there are similarities between all three stories, the differences are enough that most scholars assume three different woman put perfume on Jesus at three different times.

Three hundred denarii amounted to about a year's wage, and it would have aided three hundred poor people for only a day, or helped out one poor person for a year. Perhaps at that moment, focusing on Jesus, who would die in less than a week, was more important than focusing on the poor who would still be poor tomorrow.

Constantly second-guessing our choices leads to unnecessary guilt. We can do only so much. When we do a good thing, we shouldn't worry about whether there might have been some other good thing we could have done instead. We should live our lives without regrets.

REVOLUTION

After the triumphal entry into Jerusalem, when God spoke to Jesus from heaven:

Jesus answered and said, "This voice has not come for My sake, but for your sakes. Now judgment is upon this world; now the ruler of this world will be cast out. And I, if I am lifted up from the earth, will draw all men to Myself." But He was saying this to indicate the kind of death by which He was to die.

The crowd then answered Him, "We have heard out of the Law that the Christ is to remain forever; and how can You say, 'The Son of Man must be lifted up'? Who is this Son of Man?"

So Jesus said to them, "For a little while longer the Light is among you. Walk while you have the Light, so that darkness will not overtake you; he who walks in the darkness does not know where he goes. While you have the Light, believe in the Light, so that you may become sons of Light."

John 12:30–36 NASB

*J*esus explained that while his death would bring condemnation upon the ruler of the world, it would also bring life and hope—salvation—to its people. By Jesus' death, Satan was utterly and completely defeated and judged.

The crowd expressed confusion between what Jesus was saying and what they had been taught to believe about the Messiah. According to the teaching of the time, the Messiah was to endure forever, just as the kingdom he would restore for Israel would be an everlasting kingdom. Jesus solved the problem for them by explaining that the Messiah would endure forever because he would rise from the grave.

Jesus told them to believe the light while it was here so they could "become sons of Light." The darkness stood for the world without God, while "walking in the light" meant following God. Jesus alluded to the words of the prophet Isaiah, who spoke of the Messiah coming from Galilee: "The people who walked in darkness have seen a great light; those who lived in a land of deep darkness—on them light has shined" (Isaiah 9:2 NRSV). In the famous passage about the suffering and death of the Messiah, Isaiah wrote, "After the suffering of his soul, he will see the light of life and be satisfied" (Isaiah 53:11 NIV).

We now walk in the light, even as he is in the light and even as he himself is the Light—our Light forevermore.

LIGHT OF THE WORLD

In Jerusalem during the week before the Passover:

Jesus shouted to the crowds, "If you trust me, you are trusting not only me, but also God who sent me. For when you see me, you are seeing the one who sent me. I have come as a light to shine in this dark world, so that all who put their trust in me will no longer remain in the dark. I will not judge those who hear me but don't obey me, for I have come to save the world and not to judge it. But all who reject me and my message will be judged on the day of judgment by the truth I have spoken. I don't speak on my own authority. The Father who sent me has commanded me what to say and how to say it. And I know his commands lead to eternal life; so I say whatever the Father tells me to say."

John 12:44–50 NLT

✳

*J*esus made clear that his purpose as the Messiah was to save the world rather than to judge it. This contrasted sharply with the expectations of the religious establishment and most of the people of Israel, including Jesus' disciples. They believed that the Messiah had come to set the world right by destroying the wicked. Indeed, the wicked can be destroyed by killing them, but Jesus intended to set the world right by transforming the wicked through the power of God's forgiveness and redemption.

Judgment falls on people, not so much because Jesus is mad at them but simply because of their rejection of the help that Jesus offers them. Like a man who drowned because he refused to wear his life jacket, so people are judged simply as a result of their own poor choices. God does not have to reach out and strike the unbeliever; the unbeliever walks into the pit of hell all on his own, refusing to turn away from his impending doom despite all the pleading and every attempt that Jesus makes to convince him to turn around and go a different way.

Jesus' words—his words of love and hope—can lead us away from impending doom. His voice calls out to us when we are on the wrong path, instructing us to take a different way and then telling us the route we should take and how to get to it. We can walk toward God's kingdom instead of away from it.

TROUBLE IS COMING

During the Last Supper, after Judas had gone from the Upper Room, Jesus told the disciples that hard times would come after he left the world:

"I have told you these things to keep you from stumbling. They will ban you from the synagogues. In fact, a time is coming when anyone who kills you will think he is offering service to God. They will do these things because they haven't known the Father or Me. But I have told you these things so that when their time comes you may remember I told them to you. I didn't tell you these things from the beginning, because I was with you.

"But now I am going away to Him who sent Me, and not one of you asks Me, 'Where are You going?' Yet, because I have spoken these things to you, sorrow has filled your heart. Nevertheless, I am telling you the truth. It is for your benefit that I go away, because if I don't go away the Counselor will not come to you. If I go, I will send Him to you."

John 16:1–7 HCSB

🌼

*M*uch of what Jesus told his disciples ran counter to what they had always believed to be true about the Messiah. They were becoming increasingly distressed and discouraged. But then Jesus offered them some wonderful news.

Jesus never gave his disciples false hope. He gave them only realistic hope. He told them that the Holy Spirit would come to them. Though the Holy Spirit wouldn't arrive until after Jesus had left, it would actually be better than having Jesus around. Jesus, as a human being, had taken on "the form of a servant." He had "emptied" himself (Philippians 2:5–11). But the Holy Spirit would not become a finite man. The Holy Spirit, fully and completely God, would take up residence in every Christian. Christians would never be apart from or separated from the Holy Spirit. Jesus had to eat, he had to sleep, and he had to die. Jesus could be in only one place at a time. But the Holy Spirit would never leave or forsake them; they would be filled with all the power and knowledge that God had to give them.

We may wish that we could have been alive when Jesus was on earth. But in many ways, we are better off today because we now have the Holy Spirit—the Counselor—whom Jesus sent to all of us who believe. Rather than being in his limited incarnate state, God in all his fullness and power lives in us forever.

OPPORTUNITIES

Jesus was in Jerusalem just before his last Passover:

The festival of Unleavened Bread, which is called the Passover, was near. The chief priests and the scribes were looking for a way to put Jesus to death, for they were afraid of the people.

Then Satan entered into Judas called Iscariot, who was one of the twelve; he went away and conferred with the chief priests and officers of the temple police about how he might betray him to them. They were greatly pleased and agreed to give him money. So he consented and began to look for an opportunity to betray him to them when no crowd was present.

Then came the day of Unleavened Bread, on which the Passover lamb had to be sacrificed. So Jesus sent Peter and John, saying, "Go and prepare the Passover meal for us that we may eat it."

They asked him, "Where do you want us to make preparations for it?"

"Listen," he said to them, "when you have entered the city, a man carrying a jar of water will meet you; follow him into the house he enters and say to the owner of the house, 'The teacher asks you, "Where is the guest room, where I may eat the Passover with my disciples?"' He will show you a large room upstairs, already furnished. Make preparations for us there." So they went and found everything as he had told them; and they prepared the Passover meal.

Luke 22:1–13 NRSV

※

*B*oth Matthew and Luke explain how Jesus told his disciples to find the place for the Last Supper. Here in Luke, we discover that Jesus' instructions are reminiscent of the story of Abraham's servant who went to find a wife for Isaac. He prayed that she would be the one who drew water for both him and all his camels. So the location for the Last Supper was revealed by someone carrying water. That it was a man carrying a jar of water was unusual, since only women normally carried water for their households. Given the wording, "The teacher asks you, 'Where is the guest room,'" most commentators think that Jesus had already arranged for this room.

Each year, Passover celebrated Israel's deliverance from slavery in Egypt. It was no accident that Jesus was crucified during that holiday. Just as God rescued his people from physical slavery, so Jesus rescued his people from spiritual slavery.

Although Jesus was facing a horrible death, he worked on getting ready for the Passover celebration. Jesus did not worry about his tomorrow; he focused only on his today. He asked us not to worry about tomorrow as well. All we have is today, and that is more than enough to keep us occupied.

VOLUNTARY SURRENDER

In the Garden of Gethsemane with his disciples:

Jesus, knowing everything that was about to happen to Him, went out and said to them, "Who is it you're looking for?"

"Jesus the Nazarene," they answered.

"I am He," Jesus told them.

Judas, who betrayed Him, was also standing with them. When He told them, "I am He," they stepped back and fell to the ground.

Then He asked them again, "Who is it you're looking for?"

"Jesus the Nazarene," they said.

"I told you I am He," Jesus replied. "So if you're looking for Me, let these men go." This was to fulfill the words

He had said: "I have not lost one of those You have given Me."

Then Simon Peter, who had a sword, drew it, struck the high priest's slave, and cut off his right ear. (The slave's name was Malchus.)

At that, Jesus said to Peter, "Sheathe your sword! Am I not to drink the cup the Father has given Me?"

Then the company of soldiers, the commander, and the Jewish temple police arrested Jesus and tied Him up.

John 18:4–12 HCSB

*J*esus was not surprised by his arrest. When those coming to arrest Jesus announced whom they were after, Jesus identified himself with the phrase "I am He." In Greek, it is simply the two words "I am." Under ordinary circumstances, that would not signify anything. But given the reaction of those who came to arrest Jesus, it meant far more than just an acknowledgment that they had the right man. The phrase "I am" was also the one that God used when Moses asked him his name. According to the early church historian Eusebius, there was a popular legend of the time that the first time Moses spoke God's name to Pharaoh, Pharaoh fell down speechless. In the Old Testament, falling down was associated with the revelation of God in Daniel 2:46 and 8:18. It also seems to be reflected in the reactions of God's enemies in Psalms 27:2 and 56:9. Jesus demonstrated moments before his arrest that he could not have been arrested at all without his consent. Jesus' arrest happened because Jesus wanted it to happen. Jesus was willing to "drink the cup"—that is, to accept the will—of his Father and to die on the cross for our sins.

The trials and triumphs of our lives come without surprise to God. He knows everything we are facing today, and he knows what we are going to face tomorrow. That's why we have no need to worry about anything.

OPENNESS

Simon Peter and another disciple followed Jesus. That other disciple was known to the Chief Priest, and so he went in with Jesus to the Chief Priest's courtyard. Peter had to stay outside. Then the other disciple went out, spoke to the doorkeeper, and got Peter in.

The young woman who was the doorkeeper said to Peter, "Aren't you one of this man's disciples?"

He said, "No, I'm not."

The servants and police had made a fire because of the cold and were huddled there warming themselves. Peter stood with them, trying to get warm.

Annas interrogated Jesus regarding his disciples and his teaching. Jesus answered, "I've spoken openly in public. I've taught regularly in meeting places and the Temple, where the Jews all come together. Everything has been out in the open. I've said nothing in secret. So why are you treating me like a conspirator? Question those who have been listening to me. They know well what I have said. My teachings have all been aboveboard."

When he said this, one of the policemen standing there slapped Jesus across the face, saying, "How dare you speak to the Chief Priest like that!"

Jesus replied, "If I've said something wrong, prove it. But if I've spoken the plain truth, why this slapping around?"

Then Annas sent him, still tied up, to the Chief Priest Caiaphas.

John 18:15–24 MSG

༈

*A*nnas was the father-in-law of the chief priest Caiaphas. Although he had been the chief priest in the past, he did not hold that office while he was questioning Jesus. But he remained a force to be reckoned with. Jesus, however, did not recognize his authority and treated him with little respect, so much so that one of the police slapped him for it.

Jesus felt no need to defend himself before his accusers. He was a public figure, and his positions were well known. Jesus was not interested in wasting words with people who already had their minds made up. What was going to happen to Jesus was a foregone conclusion, and Jesus knew it. And it was what he wanted.

Jesus knew they had no basis for the charges against him. He had said or done nothing that wasn't true. Being right is a wonderful defense, but it does not guarantee success. People often reject what is true, preferring to believe lies. Our goal should be to speak and do what is true always. Then if we suffer, at least we suffer for doing the right thing—and we join with Jesus in the same sort of suffering he endured.

NOTHING BUT THE TRUTH

Pilate then went back inside the palace, summoned Jesus and asked him, "Are you the king of the Jews?"

"Is that your own idea," Jesus asked, "or did others talk to you about me?"

"Am I a Jew?" Pilate replied. "It was your people and your chief priests who handed you over to me. What is it you have done?"

Jesus said, "My kingdom is not of this world. If it were, my servants would fight to prevent my arrest by the Jews. But now my kingdom is from another place."

"You are a king, then!" said Pilate.

Jesus answered, "You are right in saying I am a king. In fact, for this reason I was born, and for this I came into the world, to testify to the truth. Everyone on the side of truth listens to me."

"What is truth?" Pilate asked. With this he went out again to the Jews and said, "I find no basis for a charge against him."

John 18:33–38 NIV

*S*ome people do not believe there is such a thing as universal truth. They believe instead that what is true for one person might not be true for another. It all depends upon one's point of view. People who think that way will point to the perception of beauty, taste in music, and optical illusions as evidence they are right. They will suggest that truth is in fact entirely subjective and that we can never get past it. The internal contradiction, that they are asserting a universal truth that everything is subjective, rarely occurs to them.

Pilate asked, "What is truth?" not because he thought Jesus would be able to tell him, but because he doubted that one could ever know it. From Pilate's experiences as a governor, he had found repeatedly that whenever he thought he knew the truth, often he turned out to be wrong. His experiences had made him suspicious of anyone talking about the truth. He doubted there was anything of which he could be certain. But Jesus argued in favor of universal truth. He insisted that those who recognized the truth, who considered themselves to be on the side of truth, listened to Jesus.

Unlike Pilate, we can believe that knowledge of the truth is not only desirable and possible but certain. We can have confidence in the good news that Jesus taught. We can know that Jesus' words are the truth.

GENEROSITY

On his way to Jerusalem, Paul warned the Christian leaders in Ephesus:

"I know that after my departure savage wolves will come in among you, not sparing the flock; and from among your own selves men will arise, speaking perverse things, to draw away the disciples after them. Therefore be on the alert, remembering that night and day for a period of three years I did not cease to admonish each one with tears. And now I commend you to God and to the word of His grace, which is able to build you up and to give you the inheritance among all those who are sanctified. I have coveted no one's silver or gold or clothes. You yourselves know that these hands ministered to my own needs and to the men who were with me. In everything I showed you that by working hard in this manner you must help the weak and remember the words of the Lord Jesus, that He Himself said, 'It is more blessed to give than to receive.'"

When he had said these things, he knelt down and prayed with them all. And they began to weep aloud and embraced Paul, and repeatedly kissed him, grieving especially over the word which he had spoken, that they would not see his face again. And they were accompanying him to the ship.

Acts 20:29–38 NASB

*P*aul alone gives us Jesus' words that it is "more blessed" to give than to receive. People who have enough that they can afford to give some of it away are happier than those who are in need. Needy people, after all, are dissatisfied people. But there's more to it than that. When we give, we are thinking about someone other than ourselves. By focusing on the needs of others, we shift our attention off our own problems. Loving others, doing for others, thinking about others is invigorating. How many times did Jesus and his disciples discover renewed strength as they reached out to the crowds despite being worn out?

Blessing does not come from accumulating wealth, but rather from sharing it. Jesus' words are a warning against becoming selfish. It is easy to become locked up in our own concerns and to forget about the concerns of others. True happiness comes as we spend our energy and resources on those around us, and as we learn to forget about ourselves in our concern for the needs of others. Somehow, in meeting the needs of other people, we will be surprised at how our own needs are also being met.

FALSE TEACHING

Jesus told John to write a letter to the church in Thyatira:

"To the angel of the church in Thyatira write,

'These things says the Son of God, who has eyes like a flame of fire, and His feet like fine brass:

"I know your works, love, service, faith, and your patience; and as for your works, the last are more than the first. Nevertheless I have a few things against you, because you allow that woman Jezebel, who calls herself a prophetess, to teach and seduce My servants to commit sexual immorality and eat things sacrificed to idols. And I gave her time to repent of her sexual immorality, and she did not repent. Indeed I will cast her into a sickbed, and those who commit adultery with her into great tribulation, unless they repent of their deeds. I will kill her children with death, and all the churches shall know that I am He who searches the minds and hearts. And I will give to each one of you according to your works.

"Now to you I say, and to the rest in Thyatira, as many as do not have this doctrine, who have not known the depths of Satan, as they say, I will put on you no other burden. But hold fast what you have till I come. And he who overcomes, and keeps My works until the end, to him I will give power over the nations—

'He shall rule them with a rod of iron; They shall be dashed to pieces like the potter's vessels'—as I also have received from My Father; and I will give him the morning star.

"He who has an ear, let him hear what the Spirit says to the churches."

Revelation 2:18–29 NKJV

*J*ezebel was a symbolic name for a false prophet in Thyatira. The Old Testament Jezebel had taught the ancient Israelites to worship Asherah, a fertility goddess, by engaging in intercourse with her priestesses. Many scholars believe that this new Jezebel taught a form of Gnosticism—the conviction that the body and spirit are entirely separate and that what the body does has no effect on the spirit. The Greek version of Asherah was still worshipped in the Roman Empire.

Jesus warned that those who committed "adultery" with Jezebel would die. In the Old Testament, the prophets used the word *adultery* to describe the worship of other gods in addition to Yahweh. Jezebel was mixing Christianity with Greek philosophy and Greek religion.

The beliefs and culture that we pick up from the society around us may not always be compatible with our worship of God. Sometimes following Jesus means saying no to the demands of our world.

STAYING ALIVE

Jesus' letter that he dictated to the church in Sardis:

"To the angel of the church in Sardis write: These are the words of him who has the seven spirits of God and the seven stars:

"I know your works; you have a name of being alive, but you are dead. Wake up, and strengthen what remains and is on the point of death, for I have not found your works perfect in the sight of my God. Remember then what you received and heard; obey it, and repent. If you do not wake up, I will come like a thief, and you will not know at what hour I will come to you. Yet you have still a few persons in Sardis who have not soiled their clothes; they will walk with me, dressed in white, for they are worthy. If you conquer, you will be clothed like them in white robes, and I will not blot your name out of the book of life; I will confess your name before my Father and before his angels. Let anyone who has an ear listen to what the Spirit is saying to the churches."

Revelation 3:1–6 NRSV

❋

*S*ardis was built on a mountain, and its acropolis was considered impregnable. The phrase "capturing the acropolis of Sardis" was proverbial in Greek for trying to do the impossible. Even so, it was conquered at least five times, thanks to a lack of vigilance on the part of its inhabitants. Thus, Jesus' warning about the church's failure to recognize its dangerous situation was striking. Likewise, Jesus' imagery of people not walking with "soiled" clothing and being dressed in white may grow from the fact that the city of Sardis was noted as a center for woolen goods.

Moses prayed that God would blot him "out of the book [he has] written" if God did not forgive the Israelites (Exodus 32:32 NIV). God's response was that only those who had sinned against God would be blotted from his book. Then God "struck the people with a plague" (vv. 31–35 NIV). When Jesus warned the church that if they didn't repent, they might be blotted from the Book of Life, he simply meant that they might die. The issue for the people of Sardis was not their place in heaven, but rather their continued chance for life.

The comfort in the letter is that God is selective in his punishment. He punishes only those who deserve it. The rest will receive God's blessing.

FIDELITY AND TREACHERY

Treachery, the betrayal of trust, falls short of our expectations; it comes as a surprise. The last thing we expect is a close confidant to turn on us. It comes as a shock when the one we love turns out not to love us back. By contrast, fidelity, the keeping of faith, fulfills our expectations. We expect our friends to be faithful to their commitments and to keep their promises. Loyalty is part of what love is all about, while treachery and betrayal are aspects of hate. Fidelity to the truth, to those who depend on us, isn't always easy, but fidelity is part of what love is all about.

❈

Love never fails.
1 Corinthians 13:8 NKJV

DAY 319

GOD CHOSE THE STUPID

Jesus preached in the towns of Galilee:
He began to denounce the cities in which most of His miracles were done, because they did not repent.

"Woe to you, Chorazin! Woe to you, Bethsaida! For if the miracles had occurred in Tyre and Sidon which occurred in you, they would have repented long ago in sackcloth and ashes. Nevertheless I say to you, it will be more tolerable for Tyre and Sidon in the day of judgment than for you. And you, Capernaum, will not be exalted to heaven, will you? You will descend to Hades; for if the miracles had occurred in Sodom which occurred in you, it would have remained to this day. Nevertheless I say to you that it will be more tolerable for the land of Sodom in the day of judgment, than for you."

At that time Jesus said, "I praise You, Father, Lord of heaven and earth, that You have hidden these things from the wise and intelligent and have revealed them to infants. Yes, Father, for this way was well-pleasing in Your sight. All things have been handed over to Me by My Father; and no one knows the Son except the Father; nor does anyone know the Father except the Son, and anyone to whom the Son wills to reveal Him.

"Come to Me, all who are weary and heavy-laden, and I will give you rest."

Matthew 11:20–28 NASB

Jesus' message of the good news went to the last people anyone would expect—infants. That is, people like Jesus' disciples, ordinary people from all walks of life, some wealthy, some not, some politically involved and some not. Jesus did not bring his words to the best and brightest of his generation.

Those who would listen, those who would believe, those who would accept the words of Jesus were rarely those who were in positions of power and authority. His followers most often came from the lower classes. They were the disadvantaged and the ones who were viewed with disdain by the persons in authority. Jesus found his strongest followers among the women, the children, and the "sinners" of society. That's what Jesus meant when he said that the greatest in the kingdom of God were those who were the least. He told his followers that they must become like "little children" in order to see the kingdom of God.

We can take comfort in the fact that we do not need to be special in any way for God to reach us or to use us. We are just the sort of people God wants.

GOOD GROUND

Jesus left the house and went out beside Lake Galilee, where he sat down to teach. Such large crowds gathered around him that he had to sit in a boat, while the people stood on the shore. Then he taught them many things by using stories. He said:

"A farmer went out to scatter seed in a field. While the farmer was scattering the seed, some of it fell along the road and was eaten by birds. Other seeds fell on thin, rocky ground and quickly started growing because the soil wasn't very deep. But when the sun came up, the plants were scorched and dried up, because they did not have enough roots. Some other seeds fell where thornbushes grew up and choked the plants. But a few seeds did fall on good ground where the plants produced a hundred or sixty or thirty times as much as was scattered. If you have ears, pay attention!"

Matthew 13:1–9 CEV

Good soil is fertile soil. Is there anything that good soil does to become good soil? Soil doesn't work hard to produce a hundred times the amount of seed that was planted in it. Soil doesn't plant the seed. Soil doesn't bring the rain.

Soil is simply the target where the farmer throws the seed. The farmer does all the work. God is the farmer. We are his soil. What we produce for God happens only because God gives the increase.

It is easy to forget the nature of our relationship with God. We belong to God not because we did something but because he did something. He bought us with the blood of his Son. We simply respond to God. We can do nothing more. The purpose of the story of the farmer and his field isn't to encourage us to work hard. The purpose of the story is to help us understand that God is hard at work in us. He plants and harvests. We are his field to do with as he wills and as he needs. We can have confidence, therefore, that we, being fertile fields, will produce the fruit he has sown in us.

GOD'S ENEMY

Near the Sea of Galilee Jesus taught his disciples:

He presented another parable to them: "The kingdom of heaven may be compared to a man who sowed good seed in his field. But while people were sleeping, his enemy came, sowed weeds among the wheat, and left. When the plants sprouted and produced grain, then the weeds also appeared. The landowner's slaves came to him and said, 'Master, didn't you sow good seed in your field? Then where did the weeds come from?'

"'An enemy did this!' he told them.

"'So, do you want us to go and gather them up?' the slaves asked him.

"'No,' he said. 'When you gather up the weeds, you might also uproot the wheat with them. Let both grow together until the harvest. At harvest time I'll tell the reapers: Gather the weeds first and tie them in bundles to burn them, but store the wheat in my barn.'"

He presented another parable to them: "The kingdom of heaven is like a mustard seed that a man took and sowed in his field. It's the smallest of all the seeds, but when grown, it's taller than the vegetables and becomes a tree, so that the birds of the sky come and nest in its branches."

He told them another parable: "The kingdom of heaven is like yeast that a woman took and mixed into 50 pounds of flour until it spread through all of it."

Matthew 13:24–33 HCSB

Jesus gave his disciples three pictures of the kingdom of heaven. *Heaven* was used as a metaphor for God. The members of Matthew's Jewish audience, out of fear of using God's name in vain, were accustomed to using other words to represent God rather than speaking of him directly.

First, Jesus compared the kingdom of heaven to a field of wheat that was infested with weeds. Second, Jesus compared the kingdom to a tiny mustard seed that becomes a huge bush. Finally, Jesus compared the kingdom of heaven to a bit of yeast that spread to fill fifty pounds of flour.

Jesus wanted the people to understand that the kingdom of God is made up of human beings. And as we know from our own lives, not everything we do is necessarily good. We remain less than perfect, even with the Holy Spirit living inside us. We make mistakes. We make progress slowly. Sometimes it may seem that nothing much has improved in our behavior for a long while.

The kingdom of heaven grows and spreads both in our own lives and in the world around us. There may be opposition and problems along the way, but its growth is inevitable and unstoppable.

RULES OF ENGAGEMENT

While Jesus was teaching and healing in the Galilee area:

Pharisees and religion scholars came to Jesus all the way from Jerusalem, criticizing, "Why do your disciples play fast and loose with the rules?"

But Jesus put it right back on them. "Why do you use your rules to play fast and loose with God's commands? God clearly says, 'Respect your father and mother,' and, 'Anyone denouncing father or mother should be killed.' But you weasel around that by saying, 'Whoever wants to, can say to father and mother, What I owed to you I've given to God.' That can hardly be called respecting a parent. You cancel God's command by your rules. Frauds! Isaiah's prophecy of you hit the bull's-eye:

These people make a big show of saying the right thing, but their heart isn't in it. They act like they're worshiping me, but they don't mean it. They just use me as a cover for teaching whatever suits their fancy."

Matthew 15:1–9 MSG

❀

For the Pharisees, it was critical that the Jewish people obey every one of God's 613 commandments. They spent their time discussing how to put those laws into practice. They were concerned with figuring out how they should then conduct their lives in every conceivable circumstance.

Their problem, however, came from the fact that they often looked at the laws in isolation from the other laws and in isolation from the people for whom they were created. As they decided how they must act in one circumstance, they failed to recognize how their interpretation and choices led them to disobey God's commands in other areas. In their concern for each tree, they lost sight of the forest. They focused their attention on the rules instead of on the people for whose benefit God made the laws.

Jesus wants us to understand that to honor God, there has to be an understanding of what the rules are really all about and what really matters in the larger scheme of things. Often what we think of as God's rules wind up being merely "human rules," and we allow those "human rules" to come between us and God's will. Instead of worrying about the rules, God wants us to think about him and to concentrate on one another. If we love God and if we love the people around us, we will automatically conduct our lives properly since love does no harm to others.

THE ESTABLISHMENT

Jesus was in the region of Galilee teaching; he criticized the Pharisees who had attacked him:

He then called the crowd together and said, "Listen, and take this to heart. It's not what you swallow that pollutes your life, but what you vomit up."

Later his disciples came and told him, "Did you know how upset the Pharisees were when they heard what you said?"

Jesus shrugged it off. "Every tree that wasn't planted by my Father in heaven will be pulled up by its roots. Forget them. They are blind men leading blind men. When a blind man leads a blind man, they both end up in the ditch."

Peter said, "I don't get it. Put it in plain language."

Jesus replied, "You, too? Are you being willfully stupid? Don't you know that anything that is swallowed works its way through the intestines and is finally defecated? But what comes out of the mouth gets its start in the heart. It's from the heart that we vomit up evil arguments, murders, adulteries, fornications, thefts, lies, and cussing. That's what pollutes. Eating or not eating certain foods, washing or not washing your hands—that's neither here nor there."

Matthew 15:10–20 MSG

*J*esus wasn't concerned with what most of the Pharisees thought of him, because they were not from God. Most of the Pharisees were concerned with what was outside people. Jesus' concern was with what was *inside* people.

While it is certainly the case that external circumstances—what we're taught, what we read, what we watch—can affect our lives for good or ill, Jesus makes clear that it isn't our environment or circumstances that make us who and what we are. Rather, what we are is something that comes from inside us, our human nature. The choice we make to murder or to steal, for instance, is our choice, and that choice grows from what's in our hearts and minds. We cannot blame our circumstances or argue that we couldn't help it or that we were made that way by what happened to us. We have no one to blame but ourselves.

We may have had it rough in our lives. We may have had to struggle more than our peers have had to. We may have lacked the advantages that our friends or neighbors had. But we can't blame what we did with our lives on anyone else. If we want to, we can change our lives for the better, thanks to Jesus. He can do great things through us, no matter what our circumstances.

EMPTY WORDS

After cleansing the temple, Jesus talked to the religious leaders:

"I will tell you a story about a man who had two sons. Then you can tell me what you think. The father went to the older son and said, "Go work in the vineyard today!" His son told him that he would not do it, but later he changed his mind and went. The man then told his younger son to go work in the vineyard. The boy said he would, but he didn't go. Which one of the sons obeyed his father?"

"The older one," the chief priests and leaders answered.

Then Jesus told them: "You can be sure that tax collectors and prostitutes will get into the kingdom of God before you ever will! When John the Baptist showed you how to do right, you would not believe him. But these evil people did believe. And even when you saw what they did, you still would not change your minds and believe."

Matthew 21:28–32 CEV

Words are cheap. Saying and doing are entirely different sorts of things. When we get married, we make promises to one another. It is easy for our mouths to say the words. It will be a lifetime's effort, sometimes an enormous struggle, to live up to the promises we made.

Jesus told a story—a parable—about two sons, one who told his father yes and one who told his father no. What mattered in the end was not the words spoken, but the deeds done. It is always possible to go against what we have uttered, either good or ill. The disobedient son, the one who told his father no, later thought better of his answer, and he then did what he'd been asked. Faith is more than words; faith is action. In the end, we will do what we believe. Our faith—what we really believe about God and his Word—has real-world consequences that everyone can see.

Jesus' point was that the "sinners" the Pharisees believed were lost causes had repented of their deeds and turned to God. They had heard what John the Baptist said, and they came out in droves to be baptized. But the religious establishment—those who thought of themselves as the "good" sons—had refused to believe. Belief is not about what we say; it is about what it leads us to do. Belief is the works of our hands.

FRUIT OF THE KINGDOM

During his last week on earth, Jesus taught the religious leaders in the temple courts:

"Listen to another parable. There was a landowner who planted a vineyard, put a fence around it, dug a wine press in it, and built a watchtower. Then he leased it to tenants and went to another country. When the harvest time had come, he sent his slaves to the tenants to collect his produce. But the tenants seized his slaves and beat one, killed another, and stoned another. Again he sent other slaves, more than the first; and they treated them in the same way. Finally he sent his son to them, saying, 'They will respect my son.' But when the tenants saw the son, they said to themselves, 'This is the heir; come, let us kill him and get his inheritance.' So they seized him, threw him out of the vineyard, and killed him. Now when the owner of the vineyard comes, what will he do to those tenants?" They said to him, "He will put those wretches to a miserable death, and lease the vineyard to other tenants who will give him the produce at the harvest time."

Jesus said to them, "Have you never read in the scriptures:

'The stone that the builders rejected has become the cornerstone; this was the Lord's doing, and it is amazing in our eyes'?

"Therefore I tell you, the kingdom of God will be taken away from you and given to a people that produces the fruits of the kingdom. The one who falls on this stone will be broken to pieces; and it will crush anyone on whom it falls."

When the chief priests and the Pharisees heard his parables, they realized that he was speaking about them. They wanted to arrest him, but they feared the crowds, because they regarded him as a prophet.

Matthew 21:33–46 NRSV

※

*J*esus said the cornerstone, which he identified as himself, would break those who came against it, whether they fell on it or it fell on them. The Pharisees would live to see their temple, their nation, and their power destroyed. Rather than destroying Jesus, Jesus would destroy them. He would rise from the dead, and the kingdom of God would spread throughout the world. It would consist of the Jewish people together with all humanity. As Nebuchadnezzar saw in his vision of the giant statue, God would bring a rock not cut by human hands that would "crush all those kingdoms and bring them to an end, but . . . will itself endure forever" (Daniel 2:44–45 NIV).

We belong to God's kingdom, a kingdom over which Jesus reigns, and it isn't going to be stopped. That's why Paul could write, "If God is for us, who can be against us?" (Romans 8:31 NKJV).

A TIME TO REST

Jesus was by the Sea of Galilee with his disciples when he heard the bad news:

[King Herod] sent the executioner off to the prison with orders to bring back John's head. He went, cut off John's head, brought it back on a platter, and presented it to the girl, who gave it to her mother. When John's disciples heard about this, they came and got the body and gave it a decent burial.

The apostles then rendezvoused with Jesus and reported on all that they had done and taught. Jesus said, "Come off by yourselves; let's take a break and get a little rest." For there was constant coming and going. They didn't even have time to eat.

So they got in the boat and went off to a remote place by themselves. Someone saw them going and the word got around. From the surrounding towns people went out on foot, running, and got there ahead of them. When Jesus arrived, he saw this huge crowd. At the sight of them, his heart broke—like sheep with no shepherd they were. He went right to work teaching them.

Mark 6:27–34 MSG

※

*J*esus told his disciples that they needed to get away. But when they got away to where they were going to rest, they weren't alone. Did Jesus' plans therefore get thwarted? Were Jesus and his disciples cheated out of their time of rest? Not at all.

Just as Jesus told Satan, "Man does not live on bread alone" (Matthew 4:4 NIV), the disciples would learn that *rest* did not necessarily mean getting away from it all and doing nothing. Jesus would teach all day and then feed the five thousand. But this was nevertheless a "time of rest" for both him and his disciples.

The purpose of rest is not the goofing off. Its purpose is the recharging, the being energized, the recovering from the hard work that we've been doing. In finding a crowd, in proclaiming the good news, and in feeding the multitudes, Jesus and his disciples were energized to continue their ministry.

Jesus and the disciples went on in power from the feeding of the five thousand. God will take care of our needs. He'll give us the desires of our hearts. We may be surprised and startled by how he goes about giving us what we need. We may not always realize that it is what we need. But in the end, what God gives *will* be what we need.

JUST GO AWAY

In the region of the Gerasenes, Jesus released a man from many demons:

A herd of many swine was feeding there on the mountain. So the [demons] begged [Jesus] that He would permit them to enter them. And He permitted them. Then the demons went out of the man and entered the swine, and the herd ran violently down the steep place into the lake and drowned.

When those who fed them saw what had happened, they fled and told it in the city and in the country. Then they went out to see what had happened, and came to Jesus, and found the man from whom the demons had departed, sitting at the feet of Jesus, clothed and in his right mind. And they were afraid. They also who had seen it told them by what means he who had been demon-possessed was healed. Then the whole multitude of the surrounding region of the Gadarenes asked Him to depart from them, for they were seized with great fear. And He got into the boat and returned.

Now the man from whom the demons had departed begged Him that he might be with Him. But Jesus sent him away, saying, "Return to your own house, and tell what great things God has done for you." And he went his way and proclaimed throughout the whole city what great things Jesus had done for him.

Luke 8:32–39 NKJV

*M*atthew's and Mark's perspectives on the story of this demon-possessed man were given earlier. Here, Luke made his point. Notice now who really gets what they wanted and who doesn't. The demons asked Jesus if they could go into the pigs. He gave them permission. The pigs drowned. The people of the region asked Jesus if he would please leave them, and so Jesus left them. But when the man who was freed from the demons asked to go with Jesus and leave his home, Jesus told him no.

Jesus did what the demons asked. Jesus did what the people in the region of the Gadarenes wanted.

But the demons did not actually get what they wanted. Their pigs drowned. And the people of the region of the Gadarenes didn't really get what they wanted either. The healed man stayed and told them all about what Jesus had done for him. He took Jesus' place and brought the news of God's kingdom to them.

And so, in the end, the formerly demon-possessed man was the only one who got what he wanted—a new life filled with Jesus.

God will give us what we really need. It may not always be what we thought we wanted, but in the end, we'll be thankful for what he gave us.

DISOWNED

Jesus was on his way to Jerusalem for the last time; after eating a meal in the home of a Pharisee and arguing with him and other religious leaders, Jesus finally went outside:

When a crowd of many thousands had gathered, so that they were trampling on one another, Jesus began to speak first to his disciples, saying: "Be on your guard against the yeast of the Pharisees, which is hypocrisy. There is nothing concealed that will not be disclosed, or hidden that will not be made known. What you have said in the dark will be heard in the daylight, and what you have whispered in the ear in the inner rooms will be proclaimed from the roofs.

"I tell you, my friends, do not be afraid of those who kill the body and after that can do no more. But I will show you whom you should fear: Fear him who, after the killing of the body, has power to throw you into hell. Yes, I tell you, fear him. Are not five sparrows sold for two pennies? Yet not one of them is forgotten by God. Indeed, the very hairs of your head are all numbered. Don't be afraid; you are worth more than many sparrows.

"I tell you, whoever acknowledges me before men, the Son of Man will also acknowledge him before the angels of God. But he who disowns me before men will be disowned before the angels of God. And everyone who speaks a word against the Son of Man will be forgiven, but anyone who blasphemes against the Holy Spirit will not be forgiven.

"When you are brought before synagogues, rulers and authorities, do not worry about how you will defend yourselves or what you will say, for the Holy Spirit will teach you at that time what you should say."

Luke 12:1–12 NIV

*P*aradox is a word we use to describe apparent contradictions. We face one in this passage. First, Jesus tells his followers that they should "fear" God. But then he tells them, "Don't be afraid." In Greek, the words translated *fear* and *afraid* are identical.

Jesus told us not to fear those who can merely kill us. Instead, we should fear God, who can throw us into hell. But at the same time, we don't need to fear, because God cares so much about us.

So what Jesus was really saying is that it is silly to worry when we have God with us, the God who is powerful enough to destroy us but has chosen not to. Such a God won't let mere mortals thwart us. He'll see us through whatever happens, even death, because he's on the other side of death. Those who are against God, those who want to harm us, are the ones who have something to be afraid of.

SHUTTING UP THE CRITICS

After Jesus cleansed the temple, he taught the assembled crowds:

[The religious leaders] watched Him, and sent spies who pretended to be righteous, that they might seize on His words, in order to deliver Him to the power and the authority of the governor.

Then they asked Him, saying, "Teacher, we know that You say and teach rightly, and You do not show personal favoritism, but teach the way of God in truth: Is it lawful for us to pay taxes to Caesar or not?"

But He perceived their craftiness, and said to them, "Why do you test Me? Show Me a denarius. Whose image and inscription does it have?"

They answered and said, "Caesar's."

And He said to them, "Render therefore to Caesar the things that are Caesar's, and to God the things that are God's."

But they could not catch Him in His words in the presence of the people. And they marveled at His answer and kept silent.

Luke 20:20–26 NKJV

ike Matthew and Mark, Luke tells how the Pharisees once asked Jesus whether it was right to pay taxes to Caesar. But Luke leads us to notice that the Pharisees believed they at last had a question that would be impossible for Jesus to answer right. They hoped Jesus' response would finally prove to the masses that Jesus wasn't really the Messiah.

The question the Pharisees asked was one they had already pondered. They believed they knew all the possible answers, and they were convinced that none were satisfactory. No matter how Jesus answered, they would be able to criticize him. They weren't prepared for Jesus to solve what they thought was an unsolvable dilemma. Jesus' answer was something new, something unexpected, something they didn't know what to do with. So all they could do was gape at Jesus in silence.

Toward the end of the book of Job, after Job had complained long and hard about his situation, when God finally showed up to confront him, all Job could do was respond with silence: "I am unworthy—how can I reply to you? I put my hand over my mouth. I spoke once, but I have no answer—twice, but I will say no more" (Job 40:4–5 NIV).

Like the Pharisees, our only reasonable response to God's answers is silence. There is nothing more to add once God has spoken.

DESTROYING THE TEMPLE

It was nearly time for the Jewish Passover celebration, so Jesus went to Jerusalem. In the Temple area he saw merchants selling cattle, sheep, and doves for sacrifices; he also saw dealers at tables exchanging foreign money. Jesus made a whip from some ropes and chased them all out of the Temple. He drove out the sheep and cattle, scattered the money changers' coins over the floor, and turned over their tables. Then, going over to the people who sold doves, he told them, "Get these things out of here. Stop turning my Father's house into a marketplace!"

Then his disciples remembered this prophecy from the Scriptures: "Passion for God's house will consume me."

But the Jewish leaders demanded, "What are you doing? If God gave you authority to do this, show us a miraculous sign to prove it."

"All right," Jesus replied. "Destroy this temple, and in three days I will raise it up."

"What!" they exclaimed. "It has taken forty-six years to build this Temple, and you can rebuild it in three days?" But when Jesus said "this temple," he meant his own body. After he was raised from the dead, his disciples remembered he had said this, and they believed both the Scriptures and what Jesus had said.

Because of the miraculous signs Jesus did in Jerusalem at the Passover celebration, many began to trust in him. But Jesus didn't trust them, because he knew human nature. No one needed to tell him what mankind is really like.

John 2:13–23 NLT

※

*T*he gospel writers described how Jesus threw the money changers out of the temple. Only John put the incident at the beginning rather than just before Jesus' crucifixion. John chose to arrange the story of Jesus' life in a thematic rather than a chronological order, a common choice among ancient Jewish authors.

Jesus told his critics that the only sign they would get would be his death, burial, and resurrection. Whether his critics purposely misunderstood his words about the "temple" of his body or simply chose to misinterpret them is difficult to say. But after his crucifixion, the religious leaders were concerned about getting guards for his tomb to prevent mischief. Oddly enough, his disciples didn't understand that's what Jesus meant until after his resurrection.

Jesus' words serve as a warning about how easy it can be to misunderstand Jesus. Such misunderstanding can come from being so distracted by other issues in our lives that we miss the blessing he has for us. Jesus may already have given us the answer to what is so troubling us now if only we choose to hear him.

AM I THE ONE?

[Jesus] said, "Go into the city to a certain man, and say to him, 'The Teacher says, "My time is at hand; I will keep the Passover at your house with My disciples."'"

So the disciples did as Jesus had directed them; and they prepared the Passover.

When evening had come, He sat down with the twelve. Now as they were eating, He said, "Assuredly, I say to you, one of you will betray Me."

And they were exceedingly sorrowful, and each of them began to say to Him, "Lord, is it I?"

He answered and said, "He who dipped his hand with Me in the dish will betray Me. The Son of Man indeed goes just as it is written of Him, but woe to that man by whom the Son of Man is betrayed! It would have been good for that man if he had not been born."

Then Judas, who was betraying Him, answered and said, "Rabbi, is it I?"

He said to him, "You have said it."

Matthew 26:18–25 NKJV

*D*uring the Last Supper, a Passover seder, Jesus revealed that one of the Twelve was going to betray him. Each of them asked Jesus if he was the one. Matthew's gospel alone reveals that Jesus answered only one of them: Judas.

All the disciples were going to run away from Jesus. Peter wound up denying that he even knew Jesus. But only Judas worked to destroy Jesus. What motivated Judas in his actions is unknown. The New Testament authors tell us only that Satan had entered him. His action was unexpected and startling to the other disciples. None of them suspected him.

Of the twelve disciples who asked, "Is it I?" only Judas knew the answer. If we wonder if we might go astray in some way like the other eleven, then our answer is the same as what it was for all the disciples except Judas. Those who are abandoning Jesus don't wonder whether they are doing it. They already know.

SATAN'S ENEMY

Jesus taught his disciples at the Last Supper:

"Simon, stay on your toes. Satan has tried his best to separate all of you from me, like chaff from wheat. Simon, I've prayed for you in particular that you not give in or give out. When you have come through the time of testing, turn to your companions and give them a fresh start."

Peter said, "Master, I'm ready for anything with you. I'd go to jail for you. I'd *die* for you!"

Jesus said, "I'm sorry to have to tell you this, Peter, but before the rooster crows you will have three times denied that you know me."

Then Jesus said, "When I sent you out and told you to travel light, to take only the bare necessities, did you get along all right?"

"Certainly," they said, "we got along just fine."

He said, "This is different. Get ready for trouble. Look to what you'll need; there are difficult times ahead. Pawn your coat and get a sword. What was written in Scripture, 'He was lumped in with the criminals,' gets its final meaning in me. Everything written about me is now coming to a conclusion."

Luke 22:31–37 MSG

☆

*M*ost Jewish people believed that the Messiah would raise an army against the Roman occupation. Jesus' words about buying a sword initially would have been understood by the disciples in that context. But when Peter told Jesus that they had two swords already, Jesus told him, "That's enough," which was hardly the call to arms the disciples anticipated.

Jesus never said that his disciples should literally arm themselves with swords. When an interpretation creates contradictions or absurdity, that is an indication that an interpretation is wrong.

Jesus' command to his disciples to procure a sword is best understood in a metaphorical sense. Jesus was indicating the need for his disciples to be *spiritually* armed and prepared for *spiritual* battle. Consider Paul's words that "the weapons we fight with are not the weapons of the world" (2 Corinthians 10:4 NIV). Also consider that Paul said "the sword of the Spirit" is "the word of God" (Ephesians 6:17 NIV).

We do not fight God's enemies with physical weapons. We do battle "in the Spirit." That is, we are called to challenge those who are enemies of God by bringing them the good news that Jesus died for their sins. We attack the gates of hell, not with physical swords, but with the gospel message.

YOU'LL SEE

Inside, the leading priests and the entire high council were trying to find witnesses who would lie about Jesus, so they could put him to death. But even though they found many who agreed to give false witness, they could not use anyone's testimony. Finally, two men came forward who declared, "This man said, 'I am able to destroy the Temple of God and rebuild it in three days.'"

Then the high priest stood up and said to Jesus, "Well, aren't you going to answer these charges? What do you have to say for yourself?" But Jesus remained silent. Then the high priest said to him, "I demand in the name of the living God—tell us if you are the Messiah, the Son of God."

Jesus replied, "You have said it. And in the future you will see the Son of Man seated in the place of power at God's right hand and coming on the clouds of heaven."

Then the high priest tore his clothing to show his horror and said, "Blasphemy! Why do we need other witnesses? You have all heard his blasphemy. What is your verdict?"

"Guilty!" they shouted. "He deserves to die!"

Then they began to spit in Jesus' face and beat him with their fists. And some slapped him, jeering, "Prophesy to us, you Messiah! Who hit you that time?"

Matthew 26:59–67 NLT

*J*esus' acknowledgment of being the Messiah and his announcement that he would be seated in a place of power was said to be "blasphemy" because the religious establishment didn't believe he was the Messiah. They believed he was claiming a false status and a false relationship to God. They thought Jesus was from Satan and was using Satan's power to accomplish his miracles. By claiming an alliance with God, he was, in their minds, claiming Satan had allied with God. Their belief that Jesus was a false Messiah—an antichrist—was what led them to condemn him.

The religious establishment looked at Jesus and interpreted what he had said and what he had done in ways that were at odds with reality. It is easy to misinterpret circumstances and words. It is easy to assume the opposite of how things really are. For thousands of years, human beings misunderstood the nature of the solar system, imagining the sun was in motion rather than the earth. That's why we must be careful not to misunderstand the words of Jesus, the power of Jesus, and the nature of the circumstances in which we find ourselves. We can do this by consulting the Bible, reading commentaries, and relying on a Spirit-filled community.

KEEPER OF THE WORD

Jesus' letter to the church in Philadelphia:

Write this to Philadelphia, to the Angel of the church. The Holy, the True—David's key in his hand, opening doors no one can lock, locking doors no one can open—speaks:

"I see what you've done. Now see what *I've* done. I've opened a door before you that no one can slam shut. You don't have much strength, I know that; you used what you had to keep my Word. You didn't deny me when times were rough.

"And watch as I take those who call themselves true believers but are nothing of the kind, pretenders whose true membership is in the club of Satan—watch as I strip off their pretensions and they're forced to acknowledge it's you that I've loved.

"Because you kept my Word in passionate patience, I'll keep you safe in the time of testing that will be here soon, and all over the earth, every man, woman, and child put to the test.

"I'm on my way; I'll be there soon. Keep a tight grip on what you have so no one distracts you and steals your crown.

"I'll make each conqueror a pillar in the sanctuary of my God, a permanent position of honor. Then I'll write names on you, the pillars: the Name of my God, the Name of God's City—the new Jerusalem coming down out of Heaven—and my new Name.

"Are your ears awake? Listen. Listen to the Wind Words, the Spirit blowing through the churches."

Revelation 3:7–13 MSG

*J*esus' words to the church in Philadelphia were words of encouragement for the trouble they were facing. Jesus promised that he would keep them "safe" during the "time of testing." That is, they would remain with Jesus regardless of what happened; he would never leave them or forsake them, even in the darkest of times. The open door probably refers to the opportunity for evangelism that they had.

That God would "write on them" and that they would be "pillars" may be allusions to the Maccabean revolt. The great accomplishments of Simon Maccabeus during the revolt against the Greek ruler Antiochus Epiphanes were inscribed on tablets of brass that were attached to a conspicuous place in the temple. For the people of Philadelphia, their glory and victory didn't lie in mighty deeds, but in bearing the name of God as citizens of the new Jerusalem, God's eternal kingdom.

Life can be difficult. But through everything, God never leaves us. He grants us opportunities to share the good news about the kingdom, and our names are forever written in his Book of Life.

LIFE AND DEATH

It is a paradox that we lose our lives in trying to save them, but gain them in giving them up. We are broken, usually focused only on ourselves. It is only in giving everything for another that we can be truly alive. All life feeds on death. If it weren't for the death of other living things every day, we wouldn't remain alive. Whether it is a cow to provide the hamburger for lunch or the wheat plant or the lettuce and carrots for the salad, living things give everything for us. Likewise, Jesus gave everything so we could live.

❀

If you cling to your life, you will lose it,
and if you let your life go, you will save it.
Luke 17:33 NLT

LEADERSHIP

Jesus was with his disciples near Jerusalem just before the triumphal entry:

The mother of the Zebedee brothers came with her two sons and knelt before Jesus with a request.

"What do you want?" Jesus asked.

She said, "Give your word that these two sons of mine will be awarded the highest places of honor in your kingdom, one at your right hand, one at your left hand."

Jesus responded, "You have no idea what you're asking." And he said to James and John, "Are you capable of drinking the cup that I'm about to drink?"

They said, "Sure, why not?"

Jesus said, "Come to think of it, you *are* going to drink my cup. But as to awarding places of honor, that's not my business. My Father is taking care of that."

When the ten others heard about this, they lost their tempers, thoroughly disgusted with the two brothers. So Jesus got them together to settle things down. He said, "You've observed how godless rulers throw their weight around, how quickly a little power goes to their heads. It's not going to be that way with you. Whoever wants to be great must become a servant. Whoever wants to be first among you must be your slave. That is what the Son of Man has done: He came to serve, not be served—and then to give away his life in exchange for the many who are held hostage."

Matthew 20:20–28 MSG

✳

*M*atthew and Mark record the effort of the mother of James and John to get positions of power and authority for her sons. Jesus used her request to teach his disciples about the nature of leadership and the way followers of Christ were supposed to interact with one another. Jesus was not advocating anarchy with no one in charge. He wasn't opposed to administration. He recognized the need for leadership. After all, he led his disciples.

But Jesus believed that the only motivator among his followers is our mutual love for one another. Our only concern should be what is best for our neighbors and not an attempt to maintain power. The emphasis is always to be on someone other than ourselves. Authority comes from service and from putting others first. Authority comes from not thinking about our position or our status. Certainly, there are those leaders who are gifted with administrative ability. But the methods of Christian leadership differ radically from those of a business or a government. If we want to get ahead, we need to concern ourselves with helping the people around us and focusing on their needs without worrying whether we are getting the proper respect or have an impressive title.

CLEAR PROPHECIES

Jesus and his disciples were walking on the road toward Jerusalem:

Peter began to tell [Jesus], "Look, we have left everything and followed You."

"I assure you," Jesus said, "there is no one who has left house, brothers or sisters, mother or father, children, or fields because of Me and the gospel, who will not receive 100 times more, now at this time—houses, brothers and sisters, mothers and children, and fields, with persecutions—and eternal life in the age to come. But many who are first will be last, and the last first."

They were on the road, going up to Jerusalem, and Jesus was walking ahead of them. They were astonished, but those who followed Him were afraid. Taking the Twelve aside again, He began to tell them the things that would happen to Him.

"Listen! We are going up to Jerusalem. The Son of Man will be handed over to the chief priests and the scribes, and they will condemn Him to death. Then they will hand Him over to the Gentiles, and they will mock Him, spit on Him, flog Him, and kill Him, and He will rise after three days."

Mark 10:28–34 HCSB

esus once again spoke in paradox. After the incident with the rich young man who was unwilling to sell everything and follow Jesus, Peter told Jesus that he and the other disciples had left everything. Peter's words were a hunt for reassurance.

Jesus reassured Peter that those who had left much would receive eternal life, even as they still had parents and fields in abundance—along with the persecutions that such possessions and family could bring. But Jesus was not suggesting that if we give up everything, we get more physical stuff back in return. Jesus had said elsewhere that those who do the will of God are his mothers, brothers, and sisters (Mark 3:33–35). Likewise, Jesus said the fields were white unto harvest and to pray for harvesters to go out into them (John 4:34–38). Jesus was not promising wealth and prosperity for those who sacrificed for him. Instead, he was promising what we would gain from spending ourselves for God. We gain the harvest of righteousness and the harvest of more souls for the kingdom. Inevitably, our proclamation of the good news can bring persecution.

Even though in this world we may seem to have lost everything because of our devotion to Jesus, if we go to the kingdom, we will be rich indeed. Where our hearts are, that's where our treasure is.

THE PARTY

On his way to Jerusalem, Jesus told a parable to the Pharisees:

"The older son [the brother of the prodigal son] was in the fields working. When he returned home, he heard music and dancing in the house, and he asked one of the servants what was going on. 'Your brother is back,' he was told, 'and your father has killed the fattened calf. We are celebrating because of his safe return.'

"The older brother was angry and wouldn't go in. His father came out and begged him, but he replied, 'All these years I've slaved for you and never once refused to do a single thing you told me to. And in all that time you never gave me even one young goat for a feast with my friends. Yet when this son of yours comes back after squandering your money on prostitutes, you celebrate by killing the fattened calf!'

"His father said to him, 'Look, dear son, you have always stayed by me, and everything I have is yours. We had to celebrate this happy day. For your brother was dead and has come back to life! He was lost, but now he is found!'"

Luke 15:25–32 NLT

The good son, who did what he was told and obeyed his father, became upset about the fuss being made over his wayward sibling. After living a disreputable life and wasting his part of the inheritance, the prodigal son came home to a party. The good son just couldn't make sense of what he was seeing. He couldn't see the justice of the situation.

The parable of the prodigal son was told in response to Pharisaical criticism of the time Jesus spent with "tax collectors and sinners." It followed the parables about a lost sheep and a lost coin. Jesus argued that fairness has nothing to do with how God deals with us. It isn't about settling accounts or getting what we deserve. Instead, it is all about God's great mercy. The good son—like the Pharisees he represented—appeared unmerciful, self-absorbed, and unkind. All he cared about was himself and his desires. He failed to love his brother, and he failed to love his father.

Our relationships with most people are not about settling scores and balancing accounts. Rather than focus on what's best for us or what we perceive as fair, we need instead to focus on how we can help those around us. It isn't about whether we think they deserve our help. We didn't earn God's mercy, and we can't expect anyone else to earn ours.

A RESURRECTION RIDDLE

Some of the Sadducees, who say there is no resurrection, came to Jesus with a question. "Teacher," they said, "Moses wrote for us that if a man's brother dies and leaves a wife but no children, the man must marry the widow and have children for his brother. Now there were seven brothers. The first one married a woman and died childless. The second and then the third married her, and in the same way the seven died, leaving no children. Finally, the woman died too. Now then, at the resurrection whose wife will she be, since the seven were married to her?"

Jesus replied, "The people of this age marry and are given in marriage. But those who are considered worthy of taking part in that age and in the resurrection from the dead will neither marry nor be given in marriage, and they can no longer die; for they are like the angels. They are God's children, since they are children of the resurrection. But in the account of the bush, even Moses showed that the dead rise, for he calls the Lord 'the God of Abraham, and the God of Isaac, and the God of Jacob.' He is not the God of the dead, but of the living, for to him all are alive."

Luke 20:27–38 NIV

The Sadducees believed that only the books of Genesis through Deuteronomy were scripture. Since those books seemed silent about an afterlife, the Sadducees rejected the concept.

Why is it that those five books of Moses don't talk about heaven, hell, or the resurrection? The Egyptians were obsessed with the afterlife. They believed the dead must be protected to have a good one. So they built pyramids and mummified their corpses in order to preserve them forever. They wrote a standard guidebook to the afterlife that was buried with every mummy.

Because the books of the Bible were originally written for particular individuals facing particular situations, the books of Moses didn't talk about the afterlife at all. God made a clear distinction between himself and the gods of Egypt. God didn't want his people to be obsessed with death as the Egyptians were.

God knows what we need to know, when we need to know it, and the way we need to learn it. For the Israelites in Moses' day, it was more important for them to understand how to live for God than to think about what came next. Even for us, living for God is the emphasis in the Bible. The kingdom of God isn't present only after we die or in the distant future. We experience the kingdom of God today.

THE PROMISE OF PERSECUTION

Just before his final Passover, Jesus taught his disciples near the temple:

"Nations will go to war against one another, and kingdoms will attack each other. There will be great earthquakes, and in many places people will starve to death and suffer terrible diseases. All sorts of frightening things will be seen in the sky.

"Before all this happens, you will be arrested and punished. You will be tried in your meeting places and put in jail. Because of me you will be placed on trial before kings and governors. But this will be your chance to tell about your faith.

"Don't worry about what you will say to defend yourselves. I will give you the wisdom to know what to say. None of your enemies will be able to oppose you or to say that you are wrong. You will be betrayed by your own parents, brothers, family, and friends. Some of you will even be killed. Because of me, you will be hated by everyone. But don't worry! You will be saved by being faithful to me."

Luke 21:10–19 CEV

❀

On more than one occasion, Jesus encouraged people not to worry, whether about finances, clothing, food, or even persecution. The answer to worry that Jesus gave in all instances was the same: we don't need to worry because God is with us. We know that he will give us the strength to endure whatever hard times might come. As the psalmist wrote so long ago, even though we walk through the deepest darkness, God is always with us (Psalm 23). We are never alone. God is mindful of what we're experiencing. He knows what we want, and, better yet, he knows what we need. "It is vain for you to rise up early, to sit up late, to eat the bread of sorrows; for so He gives His beloved sleep" (Psalm 127:2 NKJV). Worrying has never made anything better.

We shouldn't give in to worry. Worry is a liar and isn't our friend. Worry cannot help us and cannot fix our pain. Worry will only take and give us nothing back. Worry will not stop the sunrise, nor will it ease the nightfall. When enough tomorrows come, we'll see better and worry will seem less necessary. God will give us what we need, whether it is the perfect answer before our accusers or the food to sustain us in our hunger.

HOW TO LIVE FOREVER

Jesus taught crowds near the Sea of Galilee:

"Stop grumbling among yourselves," Jesus answered. "No one can come to me unless the Father who sent me draws him, and I will raise him up at the last day. It is written in the Prophets: 'They will all be taught by God.' Everyone who listens to the Father and learns from him comes to me. No one has seen the Father except the one who is from God; only he has seen the Father. I tell you the truth, he who believes has everlasting life. I am the bread of life. Your forefathers ate the manna in the desert, yet they died. But here is the bread that comes down from heaven, which a man may eat and not die. I am the living bread that came down from heaven. If anyone eats of this bread, he will live forever. This bread is my flesh, which I will give for the life of the world."

John 6:43–51 NIV

A day or two after feeding the five thousand, the crowds were becoming restless. They wondered if Jesus was the Messiah, and perhaps they wondered if they might get some more free food. So Jesus told them that he was the Bread of Life that came down from heaven, and he told them to stop grumbling.

Human beings become dissatisfied quickly. When the Israelites thought they were going to go hungry, God sent them manna in the wilderness. The Israelites of Jesus' day thought the Messiah would give them bread just as Moses had. But just as the Israelites became complacent and started grumbling about the manna, so the crowds became dissatisfied with Jesus' miracle of the loaves and fishes. They took what Jesus had done for them for granted and began wondering what he might do for them next.

As we grow up, we might pray to get into college, and then we might pray for a girlfriend or a boyfriend. Soon we pray to be married, have children, and get a house. At each stage along the way, we are in awe of God's answers to those prayers, but as the years pass, what had been awesome becomes ordinary. Madison Avenue knows what we are—we are always looking for the next new thing, always hoping for novelty. We would do well to remember God's wonderful work in our lives, the marvelous blessings we see each day. God has already done enough for us, and yet he continues on, whether we notice or not.

CANNIBALISM?

Near the Sea of Galilee, people from the five thousand that Jesus had miraculously fed:

They started arguing with each other and asked, "How can he give us his flesh to eat?"

Jesus answered: "I tell you for certain that you won't live unless you eat the flesh and drink the blood of the Son of Man. But if you do eat my flesh and drink my blood, you will have eternal life, and I will raise you to life on the last day. My flesh is the true food, and my blood is the true drink. If you eat my flesh and drink my blood, you are one with me, and I am one with you.

"The living Father sent me, and I have life because of him. Now everyone who eats my flesh will live because of me. The bread that comes down from heaven isn't like what your ancestors ate. They died, but whoever eats this bread will live forever."

Jesus was teaching in a Jewish place of worship in Capernaum when he said these things.

John 6:52–59 CEV

꽃

A common result of Jesus' preaching was that his audience misunderstood him. They regularly literalized his metaphors. They took what he meant spiritually and tried to understand it in purely physical terms. Thus, when Jesus told the crowd about "eating his body," they simply became confused. The literal meaning stood in opposition to biblical injunctions against murder and against consuming blood. They found what he had said so disturbing, many of those who had been following him decided to leave him.

What did Jesus mean about eating his flesh and drinking his blood? He was speaking about his coming sacrifice on the cross and what his sacrifice meant for the human race. Just as animals and plants must die before being consumed as food in order for us to continue living, so Jesus had to die in order to provide us eternal life. Spiritually speaking, we consume him. But since he was and is an eternal being, there is more than enough of his life to go around. Unlike what we ate for lunch today, he didn't stay dead.

In contrast to the life of an animal or a plant that sustains us for but a few hours before we become hungry again, Jesus' life is inexhaustible. Jesus satisfies us completely. We will never again hunger or thirst. He has provided us eternal satisfaction and an existence that can never end.

LEAVING JESUS

Jesus was teaching in Capernaum; he had just spoken of eating his flesh and drinking his blood:

When many of his disciples heard it, they said, "This teaching is difficult; who can accept it?" But Jesus, being aware that his disciples were complaining about it, said to them, "Does this offend you? Then what if you were to see the Son of Man ascending to where he was before? It is the spirit that gives life; the flesh is useless. The words that I have spoken to you are spirit and life. But among you there are some who do not believe." For Jesus knew from the first who were the ones that did not believe, and who was the one that would betray him. And he said, "For this reason I have told you that no one can come to me unless it is granted by the Father."

Because of this many of his disciples turned back and no longer went about with him. So Jesus asked the twelve, "Do you also wish to go away?"

Simon Peter answered him, "Lord, to whom can we go? You have the words of eternal life. We have come to believe and know that you are the Holy One of God."

Jesus answered them, "Did I not choose you, the twelve? Yet one of you is a devil." He was speaking of Judas son of Simon Iscariot, for he, though one of the twelve, was going to betray him.

John 6:60–71 NRSV

❦

*S*ome people followed Jesus for reasons that made it possible for them to turn away from him later. When what Jesus taught them became hard, when he didn't seem to be taking them where they wanted to go, they abandoned him.

Peter followed Jesus because he knew that Jesus was the Messiah. Peter followed Jesus because he knew that Jesus was going to bring in God's kingdom. He followed Jesus because he knew that he would have eternal life with Jesus.

But Judas—the one of the Twelve who was "a devil"—would be like the crowd who had abandoned him here. Judas would hang in for a while yet, but the day would come, just as it had come for some of the crowd, when he would decide that what Jesus was about and where he was going were not what Judas wanted.

We may not fully comprehend all the implications of what Jesus is and what he wants of us, but we know enough that, like Peter, we can't imagine being without Jesus. Jesus is the only one who can give us what we couldn't have without him—eternal life.

RAISING LAZARUS

Jesus, again groaning in Himself, came to the tomb. It was a cave, and a stone lay against it. Jesus said, "Take away the stone."

Martha, the sister of him who was dead, said to Him, "Lord, by this time there is a stench, for he has been dead four days."

Jesus said to her, "Did I not say to you that if you would believe you would see the glory of God?" Then they took away the stone from the place where the dead man was lying. And Jesus lifted up His eyes and said, "Father, I thank You that You have heard Me. And I know that You always hear Me, but because of the people who are standing by I said this, that they may believe that You sent Me." Now when He had said these things, He cried with a loud voice, "Lazarus, come forth!" And he who had died came out bound hand and foot with graveclothes, and his face was wrapped with a cloth. Jesus said to them, "Loose him, and let him go."

Then many of the Jews who had come to Mary, and had seen the things Jesus did, believed in Him. But some of them went away to the Pharisees and told them the things Jesus did.

John 11:38–46 NKJV

✳

*O*nly Jesus knew that he was going to raise Lazarus from the dead. His disciples had no expectations, and neither did any of the other people in the crowd.

Jesus' prayer to God was short. Jesus did not beg. He yelled only loud enough that Lazarus, tucked away in the dark tomb, could hear him. More than likely, it was a puzzling experience for Lazarus, who suddenly found himself in a dark, cool place, all wrapped up. He was bound "hand and foot," probably something like a mummy. So his exit from the tomb would not have been dignified. He would have had to have hopped out slowly, unable even to see where he was going since his face was covered.

Jesus had to tell the people to help him. One can imagine them standing around rather slack-jawed, so much in shock that no one thought of what to do for poor Lazarus.

The result of Lazarus's coming back from the dead was not universal belief in Jesus. Even someone coming back from the dead was not enough to convince those who rejected Jesus. Once our minds are made up, it is hard to change them, no matter how much evidence accumulates. We might want to be careful about how fast we make up our minds so we can allow God to do the unexpected in our lives.

DEATH ON PURPOSE

Jesus taught his disciples after the triumphal entry:

Jesus answered them, saying, "The hour has come for the Son of Man to be glorified. Truly, truly, I say to you, unless a grain of wheat falls into the earth and dies, it remains alone; but if it dies, it bears much fruit. He who loves his life loses it, and he who hates his life in this world will keep it to life eternal. If anyone serves Me, he must follow Me; and where I am, there My servant will be also; if anyone serves Me, the Father will honor him.

"Now My soul has become troubled; and what shall I say, 'Father, save Me from this hour'? But for this purpose I came to this hour. Father, glorify Your name." Then a voice came out of heaven: "I have both glorified it, and will glorify it again."

John 12:23–28 NASB

*J*esus wasn't suggesting that his followers seek out martyrdom. He wasn't arguing that we should love death. We would have to ignore the context of Jesus' words about "hating life" to draw that peculiar conclusion. No, Jesus' paradox that those who "love life" would lose it, while those who "hate" it would gain it, had to do with eternity. Those who focus their energy on this life, those who worry about holding on to everything they have here, are fighting a battle they can never win. If all we have is this life, we are inevitably both miserable and a failure, because all of us will inevitably die. We will lose everything we try to keep.

Jesus argued that those who serve him, follow him, and go where he goes will—even if they die—gain life, the very thing that they seem to lose. Those who belong to Christ and are part of the kingdom do not stay dead. They will live forever in paradise with Jesus. Just as a grain of wheat seems to lose its existence when it is tucked into the ground, the reality of a planted seed is something else again. That single grain of wheat comes back far greater and more impressive than it ever was before. It is multiplied a hundred times or more.

Our current lives are nothing compared to the lives we will have with Jesus forever in God's kingdom, thanks to Jesus' willingness to give his life for us.

REMEMBRANCE OF ME

Jesus and his disciples were in the Upper Room to celebrate Passover:

When the hour had come, Jesus sat down, and the twelve apostles with Him. Then He said to them, "With fervent desire I have desired to eat this Passover with you before I suffer; for I say to you, I will no longer eat of it until it is fulfilled in the kingdom of God."

Then He took the cup, and gave thanks, and said, "Take this and divide it among yourselves; for I say to you, I will not drink of the fruit of the vine until the kingdom of God comes."

And He took bread, gave thanks and broke it, and gave it to them, saying, "This is My body which is given for you; do this in remembrance of Me."

Likewise He also took the cup after supper, saying, "This cup is the new covenant in My blood, which is shed for you."

Luke 22:14–20 NKJV

Passover was a memorial service, a way for the Israelites to remember what God had done for them when he rescued them from Egyptian slavery. The sacrificial system, with its rituals and its slaughter of animals, served a similar purpose. It was a picture, a parable of what God would do through the final sacrifice of Jesus on the cross. The sacrifice of bulls and goats in the old covenant of ancient Israel never took away sins (Hebrews 10:3–4). It was simply a regular reminder of the people's sins and the fact that God was forgiving them.

The breaking of bread and the drinking of wine of the Lord's Supper serves a similar purpose. We remember what Jesus did on the cross. It is a picture for us. Likewise, the Lord's Supper does not take away sins; it reminds us that our sins have already been taken away. Jesus' death on a Roman cross takes away our sins. We remember that wonderful reality every time we share the bread and the fruit of the Vine. As often as we do it, we proclaim to all those with us the amazing love of Jesus.

JUSTICE

During the Last Supper, Jesus reminded his disciples that he said:

"The Spirit will come and show the people of this world the truth about sin and God's justice and the judgment. The Spirit will show them that they are wrong about sin, because they didn't have faith in me. They are wrong about God's justice, because I am going to the Father, and you won't see me again. And they are wrong about the judgment, because God has already judged the ruler of this world.

"I have much more to say to you, but right now it would be more than you could understand. The Spirit shows what is true and will come and guide you into the full truth. The Spirit doesn't speak on his own. He will tell you only what he has heard from me, and he will let you know what is going to happen. The Spirit will bring glory to me by taking my message and telling it to you. Everything that the Father has is mine. That is why I have said that the Spirit takes my message and tells it to you."

John 16:8–15 CEV

※

*J*esus told his disciples that humanity was mistaken about many things.

Human beings are wrong about sin because they lack faith in Jesus. That's why Adam and Eve sinned; they lacked trust. Rather than believing God, they believed the Serpent's lie that God was trying to keep them from something good. Ever since, humans have doubted that God has their best intentions in mind. Lack of trust in God is at the core of sin.

Human beings are wrong about justice—or as some translations have it, "righteousness." *Righteousness* is the opposite of sin. The religious establishment condemned Jesus, a righteous man, to death. Meanwhile, God told the human race that their righteousness is like filthy rags (Isaiah 64:6 NIV). We are barely capable of genuine righteousness.

Human beings are wrong about judgment because they think of it only in the future tense. But God has already judged Satan, the ruler of the world. Satan is already guilty, already overthrown by Jesus, as demonstrated by his power over the demons. Moreover, our sin has already been judged because Jesus was judged in our place. We stand forgiven and righteous because we died with Christ. We are not righteous in ourselves, but righteous in Christ. Everything has changed for us. Today the Holy Spirit helps us realize how things stand between God and us, and with one another.

RELIEF

At the Last Supper, Jesus predicted his death to his followers:

"In a little while you won't see me anymore. But a little while after that, you will see me again."

Some of the disciples asked each other, "What does he mean when he says, 'In a little while you won't see me, but then you will see me,' and 'I am going to the Father'? And what does he mean by 'a little while'? We don't understand."

Jesus realized they wanted to ask him about it, so he said, "Are you asking yourselves what I meant? I said in a little while you won't see me, but a little while after that you will see me again.

I tell you the truth, you will weep and mourn over what is going to happen to me, but the world will rejoice. You will grieve, but your grief will suddenly turn to wonderful joy. It will be like a woman suffering the pains of labor. When her child is born, her anguish gives way to joy because she has brought a new baby into the world. So you have sorrow now, but I will see you again; then you will rejoice, and no one can rob you of that joy."

John 16:16–22 NLT

Jesus first told his disciples that they wouldn't seem him anymore. Then he told them that after a little while, they *would* see him again.

Jesus predicted his death at the hands of the Romans—and he predicted his resurrection. He knew they would mourn not only the loss of the one they considered a friend, but also the death of their dream of national redemption. They thought he would restore the kingdom of David and would overcome the Romans. Instead, he knew the Romans would overcome their Messiah. They would never see the Jesus of their mistaken dreams again.

Jesus wanted his disciples to understand that the death of their hopes wasn't the end. They were still missing the vital reality that the kingdom of God wasn't a physical, earthly kingdom like Rome but that it was something far grander and more pervasive.

Their mourning, as sharp as it would be, would be mercifully brief. From the night he was arrested until the morning he rose from the dead, barely three days passed. Jesus compared what was about to happen to the birth of a child. The joy the disciples had after the resurrection, and the joy that we now have because of it, is a joy that will endure forever. All our sorrows from this brief lifetime of ours will be wiped away in the wonder of God's eternal kingdom. We have that eternity even now in our hearts.

A PRAYER OF JESUS

Near the end of the Last Supper, on the night before his crucifixion:

Jesus looked up to heaven and said, "Father, the hour has come. Glorify your Son so he can give glory back to you. For you have given him authority over everyone. He gives eternal life to each one you have given him. And this is the way to have eternal life—to know you, the only true God, and Jesus Christ, the one you sent to earth. I brought glory to you here on earth by completing the work you gave me to do. Now, Father, bring me into the glory we shared before the world began.

"I have revealed you to the ones you gave me from this world. They were always yours. You gave them to me, and they have kept your word. Now they know that everything I have is a gift from you, for I have passed on to them the message you gave me. They accepted it and know that I came from you, and they believe you sent me.

"My prayer is not for the world, but for those you have given me, because they belong to you. All who are mine belong to you, and you have given them to me, so they bring me glory."

John 17:1–10 NLT

⁂

*O*ne of the best ways to learn how to pray is to listen to how Jesus prayed. He used no particular formula or special words. Rather, when we overhear Jesus' prayers to his Father, what we discover is that he simply talked to him about whatever was on his mind. He told his Father the things that mattered most to him. He simply discussed his deepest concerns with his Father, expressing whatever emotions and thoughts came from deep inside him. He was not concerned with what anyone might think of his words. He was concerned only that his Father knew what was weighing on his mind.

When we pray, we needn't worry about the form of our prayers, whether our words are eloquent or our hands are folded right. We should simply tell God whatever is in our heads, without pretense, without pretending, without thinking about what we think we should be talking about to God. God already knows our needs. He already knows what is troubling us, what is important to us, and how we feel about our situation. He wants us to share these things with him. Think about how much better we feel after we unburden ourselves to a close friend. He wants to lighten our load just like that.

THE FLESH IS WEAK

Facing his crucifixion, Jesus went to the Garden of Gethsemane to pray:

He took with Him Peter and the two sons of Zebedee, and began to be grieved and distressed. Then He said to them, "My soul is deeply grieved, to the point of death; remain here and keep watch with Me."

And He went a little beyond them, and fell on His face and prayed, saying, "My Father, if it is possible, let this cup pass from Me; yet not as I will, but as You will."

And He came to the disciples and found them sleeping, and said to Peter, "So, you men could not keep watch with Me for one hour? Keep watching and praying that you may not enter into temptation; the spirit is willing, but the flesh is weak."

He went away again a second time and prayed, saying, "My Father, if this cannot pass away unless I drink it, Your will be done."

Again He came and found them sleeping, for their eyes were heavy. And He left them again, and went away and prayed a third time, saying the same thing once more.

Then He came to the disciples and said to them, "Are you still sleeping and resting? Behold, the hour is at hand and the Son of Man is being betrayed into the hands of sinners.

"Get up, let us be going; behold, the one who betrays Me is at hand!"

Matthew 26:37–46 NASB

*J*esus told his Father how unhappy he was about his circumstances. He also told his disciples how he was feeling. Even so, we sometimes wonder how we are supposed to feel about our problems. We become concerned that there's a right way to feel, and we're afraid that how we really feel isn't it.

A pastor once went to comfort parents who had just lost their only daughter in a car accident. They were grieving, but they pretended to smile. They told him that as Christians, they believed they shouldn't "mourn as the heathen do." The pastor gently suggested that the passage didn't teach against mourning; rather, that when we mourn, we should feel neither hopeless nor helpless about it, because we know God is with us and that the resurrection is coming.

Jesus knew he was the Son of God. He knew he would rise from the dead, but he still mourned his circumstances. He wished for some other way. Nevertheless, he was willing to face God's will.

What gives us strength in disaster is not pretending that we're not in pain. Our strength comes from understanding that God is with us and that he will stay with us until the end.

DAY 350

GOD'S WILL, HUMAN CHOICE

Jesus and his disciples were in the Garden of Gethsemane:

While [Jesus] was still speaking, behold, Judas, one of the twelve, came up accompanied by a large crowd with swords and clubs, who came from the chief priests and elders of the people. Now he who was betraying Him gave them a sign, saying, "Whomever I kiss, He is the one; seize Him."

Immediately Judas went to Jesus and said, "Hail, Rabbi!" and kissed Him.

And Jesus said to him, "Friend, do what you have come for." Then they came and laid hands on Jesus and seized Him. And behold, one of those who were with Jesus reached and drew out his sword, and struck the slave of the high priest and cut off his ear. Then Jesus said to him, "Put your sword back into its place; for all those who take up the sword shall perish by the sword. Or do you think that I cannot appeal to My Father, and He will at once put at My disposal more than twelve legions of angels? How then will the Scriptures be fulfilled, which say that it must happen this way?"

At that time Jesus said to the crowds, "Have you come out with swords and clubs to arrest Me as you would against a robber? Every day I used to sit in the temple teaching and you did not seize Me. But all this has taken place to fulfill the Scriptures of the prophets." Then all the disciples left Him and fled.

Matthew 26:47–56 NASB

Jesus knew that his death on the cross was inevitable. He knew that Judas would sell him out for a bag of silver.

But until the moment Judas made his decision to betray Jesus, Judas had no clue. He had been a follower, convinced that Jesus was the Messiah. One day, however, something changed for him, and so he changed too. Even though Judas was foreordained to be Jesus' betrayer, he made his choices freely. God did not force him, twist his arm, or talk him into something he didn't want to do.

Although God has absolute power and authority, he has chosen to give people their freedom. Somehow, God accomplishes his will through the choices we make, whether they're good or bad. Judas made an appalling choice, but by his choice he accomplished God's will.

Judas demonstrated that we have the freedom to make whatever choices we decide we want to make. We might want to be careful, therefore, how we exercise the freedom God has granted us.

DEATH OF A DREAM

Peter was sitting out in the courtyard. One servant girl came up to him and said, "You were with Jesus the Galilean."

In front of everybody there, he denied it. "I don't know what you're talking about."

As he moved over toward the gate, someone else said to the people there, "This man was with Jesus the Nazarene."

Again he denied it, salting his denial with an oath: "I swear, I never laid eyes on the man."

Shortly after that, some bystanders approached Peter. "You've got to be one of them. Your accent gives you away."

Then he got really nervous and swore. "I don't know the man!"

Just then a rooster crowed. Peter remembered what Jesus had said: "Before the rooster crows, you will deny me three times." He went out and cried and cried and cried.

Matthew 26:69–75 MSG

Jesus warned Peter ahead of time what was going to happen. But the warning didn't stop Peter or alter his behavior in any way.

With Jesus' arrest and with the disciples scattered, Peter suffered the loss of everything he had believed in and everything he had hoped would happen. During the whole night as he skirted about, his mind would likely have been filled with the disappointment over how things had turned out and over his own failure to act. Perhaps he wondered if he might have yet done something to change the circumstances, to fix the problem. But with each choice he made, he merely solidified the outcome and fulfilled the very words that Jesus had spoken to him, words that he couldn't believe were true—until the moment the rooster crowed and all his hopes came to nothing.

Over the course of our lives, we have doubtless received good advice that we ignored. And we have given good advice that others ignored. We have heard people tell us, "Told you so," and probably have said the same ourselves. Peter learned and came out fine on the other side of his mistakes. His misery and suffering did not have to be what it was. The night could have gone a different way for him had he understood what Jesus was trying to tell him. God won't abandon us just because we don't understand or follow his good advice, though he might tell us, "Told you so."

LIMITED POWERS

When Pilate heard that [Jesus had claimed to be the Son of God], he was the more afraid, and went again into the Praetorium, and said to Jesus, "Where are You from?" But Jesus gave him no answer.

Then Pilate said to Him, "Are You not speaking to me? Do You not know that I have power to crucify You, and power to release You?"

Jesus answered, "You could have no power at all against Me unless it had been given you from above. Therefore the one who delivered Me to you has the greater sin."

From then on Pilate sought to release Him, but the Jews cried out, saying, "If you let this Man go, you are not Caesar's friend. Whoever makes himself a king speaks against Caesar."

When Pilate therefore heard that saying, he brought Jesus out and sat down in the judgment seat in a place that is called The Pavement, but in Hebrew, Gabbatha. Now it was the Preparation Day of the Passover, and about the sixth hour. And he said to the Jews, "Behold your King!"

But they cried out, "Away with Him, away with Him! Crucify Him!"

Pilate said to them, "Shall I crucify your King?"

The chief priests answered, "We have no king but Caesar!"

Then he delivered Him to them to be crucified. Then they took Jesus and led Him away.

John 19:8–16 NKJV

✤

_P_ontius Pilate was the fifth Roman governor of Judea. As governor, he held absolute power over Jesus as both judge and jury. He could have freed Jesus just as easily as he had him executed.

Solomon wrote in the book of Proverbs, "The king's heart is in the hand of the LORD; he directs it like a watercourse wherever he pleases" (21:1 NIV). Pilate could do only as much as God would allow him to do. He wasn't the one ultimately in charge. In fact, Jesus told him that the one who had delivered him to Pilate—Judas—was far guiltier than Pilate could ever be.

Pilate demonstrated his lack of control when he faced the people of Jerusalem. Despite his belief that Jesus was innocent, he felt constrained to follow the whim of the crowd that demanded Jesus' blood. Because of Pilate's lack of character, his power was less than he liked to imagine.

In the end, God's will was done, though those who performed God's will were motivated by evil and were guilty of a great crime. In the end, we learn that God is always in charge. Nothing that happens to us is a surprise or beyond God's ability to control.

DAY 353

JESUS' WILL

[The Roman soldiers] took Jesus, therefore, and He went out, bearing His own cross, to the place called the Place of a Skull, which is called in Hebrew, Golgotha. There they crucified Him, and with Him two other men, one on either side, and Jesus in between. Pilate also wrote an inscription and put it on the cross. It was written, "JESUS THE NAZARENE, THE KING OF THE JEWS." Therefore many of the Jews read this inscription, for the place where Jesus was crucified was near the city; and it was written in Hebrew, Latin and in Greek.

So the chief priests of the Jews were saying to Pilate, "Do not write, 'The King of the Jews'; but that He said, 'I am King of the Jews.'"

Pilate answered, "What I have written I have written."

Then the soldiers, when they had crucified Jesus, took His outer garments and made four parts, a part to every soldier and also the tunic; now the tunic was seamless, woven in one piece.

So they said to one another, "Let us not tear it, but cast lots for it, to decide whose it shall be"; this was to fulfill the Scripture: "They divided My outer garments among them, and for My clothing they cast lots." Therefore the soldiers did these things.

But standing by the cross of Jesus were His mother, and His mother's sister, Mary the wife of Clopas, and Mary Magdalene. When Jesus then saw His mother, and the disciple whom He loved standing nearby, He said to His mother, "Woman, behold, your son!" Then He said to the disciple, "Behold, your mother!" From that hour the disciple took her into his own household.

John 19:17–27 NASB

Women in the first century had few rights. They were dependent upon their husbands, fathers, brothers, or sons for their survival. If a woman became a widow and there were no male relatives to care for her, she usually had but two options: begging or prostitution. Mary was a destitute widow. Jesus told John to treat his mother as if she were his own, and he told his mother to think of John as her son.

Although we may think that the social structure of first-century Palestine was barbaric, and we might think Jesus should have spoken out more explicitly against the oppression and mistreatment of women, what he did do and say was practical given the constraints of that society. And, of course, over the centuries since, in those parts of the world most heavily influenced by Christianity, the social structure *has* changed—so much so that it is now hard for us even to conceive of the problems Mary was facing. Jesus did not eliminate all Mary's problems. But he took care of her within them. Jesus can do the same for us.

THE SKULL

As [the Roman soldiers] led Jesus away, a man named Simon, who was from Cyrene, happened to be coming in from the countryside. The soldiers seized him and put the cross on him and made him carry it behind Jesus. A large crowd trailed behind, including many grief-stricken women. But Jesus turned and said to them, "Daughters of Jerusalem, don't weep for me, but weep for yourselves and for your children. For the days are coming when they will say, 'Fortunate indeed are the women who are childless, the wombs that have not borne a child and the breasts that have never nursed.' People will beg the mountains, 'Fall on us,' and plead with the hills, 'Bury us.' For if these things are done when the tree is green, what will happen when it is dry?"

Two others, both criminals, were led out to be executed with him. When they came to a place called The Skull, they nailed him to the cross. And the criminals were also crucified—one on his right and one on his left.

Jesus said, "Father, forgive them, for they don't know what they are doing." And the soldiers gambled for his clothes by throwing dice.

The crowd watched and the leaders scoffed. "He saved others," they said, "let him save himself if he is really God's Messiah, the Chosen One."

Luke 23:26–35 NLT

As he was led to the place of crucifixion, Jesus turned to the women who were mourning and warned them about Jerusalem's future. Jesus' metaphor, "If these things are done when the tree is green," pointed out that if the Romans were willing to execute an innocent man, then a guilty Jerusalem's fate when Rome crushed its rebellion would be horrific indeed. His warning resembled the warnings he had already given his disciples on the same topic. The phrase about calling upon "the mountains to fall" is a quotation of Hosea 10:8, describing the Assyrian destruction of Israel.

Jesus had told his disciples to love their enemies and to pray for those who persecuted them (Matthew 5:44). And that is precisely what Jesus himself did on the cross. He prayed for his executioners and asked his Father to forgive them. Any discussion about who was to blame or who bore the guilt for Jesus' crucifixion is misplaced, since Jesus and his Father forgave them. The purpose of Jesus' death was to bring forgiveness to everyone. Jesus' crucifixion makes no one guilty. To the contrary, his sacrifice on the cross made possible our forgiveness and opened the way for all of us to enter the kingdom of God.

PIERCED FOR OUR INIQUITIES

After [seeing to it that his mother would be cared for], when Jesus knew that everything was now accomplished that the Scripture might be fulfilled, He said, "I'm thirsty!" A jar full of sour wine was sitting there; so they fixed a sponge full of sour wine on hyssop and held it up to His mouth.

When Jesus had received the sour wine, He said, "It is finished!" Then bowing His head, He gave up His spirit.

Since it was the preparation day, the Jews did not want the bodies to remain on the cross on the Sabbath (for that Sabbath was a special day). They requested that Pilate have the men's legs broken and that their bodies be taken away. So the soldiers came and broke the legs of the first man and of the other one who had been crucified with Him. When they came to Jesus, they did not break His legs since they saw that He was already dead. But one of the soldiers pierced His side with a spear, and at once blood and water came out. He who saw this has testified so that you also may believe. His testimony is true, and he knows he is telling the truth. For these things happened so that the Scripture would be fulfilled: Not one of His bones will be broken. Also, another Scripture says: They will look at the One they pierced.

John 19:28–37 HCSB

*C*rucifixion was unknown in the Old Testament as a mode of execution. Deuteronomy 21:22–23 describes only the practice of exposing the corpse of an executed criminal by hanging it on a tree. The Persians apparently invented crucifixion. The Romans merely borrowed the practice, which they found especially useful as a deterrent against rebellion. A placard proclaiming the crime was commonly hung around the condemned person's neck. There was a degree of variation in how crucifixions were conducted, depending on the whim and sadism of the executioner.

Death by crucifixion was slow and painful. It wasn't uncommon, in fact, for the condemned to survive for several days. Death ultimately arrived from the combination of thirst, hunger, exhaustion, and exposure. And then the dead body was usually left to decay for a while.

The fact that Jesus died in a matter of hours was out of the ordinary. But a prolonged death was not necessary for Jesus to fulfill his goal. After everything was in place and ready, Jesus announced, "It is finished." Then he died for us, so that we could live forever.

THE DEATH OF GOD

From the sixth hour until the ninth hour darkness came over all the land. About the ninth hour Jesus cried out in a loud voice, *"Eloi, Eloi, lama sabachthani?"*—which means, "My God, my God, why have you forsaken me?"

When some of those standing there heard this, they said, "He's calling Elijah."

Immediately one of them ran and got a sponge. He filled it with wine vinegar, put it on a stick, and offered it to Jesus to drink. The rest said, "Now leave him alone. Let's see if Elijah comes to save him."

And when Jesus had cried out again in a loud voice, he gave up his spirit.

At that moment the curtain of the temple was torn in two from top to bottom. The earth shook and the rocks split. The tombs broke open and the bodies of many holy people who had died were raised to life. They came out of the tombs, and after Jesus' resurrection they went into the holy city and appeared to many people.

When the centurion and those with him who were guarding Jesus saw the earthquake and all that had happened, they were terrified, and exclaimed, "Surely he was the Son of God!"

Matthew 27:45–54 NIV

*T*he phrase *"Eloi, Eloi, lama sabachthani?"* was Aramaic, the language most commonly spoken in first-century Palestine. The New Testament, however, was written in Greek, the main trading language of the known world and the language most people knew. "My God" in Aramaic sounds similar to the name Elijah. But the Greek word for "my God" does not. In order that the Greek readers of the gospel would understand how the crowd misunderstood Jesus, Luke recorded Jesus' original Aramaic phrase.

That the crowd, largely made up of those who had always rejected Jesus, misunderstood his dying words isn't unexpected. They had misunderstood him during his entire public ministry. This last confusion was simply one more example of their nearly consistent inability to comprehend Jesus.

The last words of Jesus are given to remind us, if we still need reminding, that Jesus was human and that he could identify with all the challenges we face in life and in death. Dying alone on the cross, even though both he and his Father understood fully the necessity for his sacrifice, he was in pain and unhappy. We can never imagine, therefore, that Jesus doesn't understand our pain, how bad it is for us, or what it means to suffer. He does know, he does understand, and he cares.

BURIAL

It was noon, and darkness fell across the whole land until three o'clock. The light from the sun was gone. And suddenly, the curtain in the sanctuary of the Temple was torn down the middle. Then Jesus shouted, "Father, I entrust my spirit into your hands!" And with those words he breathed his last.

When the Roman officer overseeing the execution saw what had happened, he worshiped God and said, "Surely this man was innocent." And when all the crowd that came to see the crucifixion saw what had happened, they went home in deep sorrow. But Jesus' friends, including the women who had followed him from Galilee, stood at a distance watching.

Now there was a good and righteous man named Joseph. He was a member of the Jewish high council, but he had not agreed with the decision and actions of the other religious leaders. He was from the town of Arimathea in Judea, and he was waiting for the kingdom of God to come. He went to Pilate and asked for Jesus' body. Then he took the body down from the cross and wrapped it in a long sheet of linen cloth and laid it in a new tomb that had been carved out of rock. This was done late on Friday afternoon, the day of preparation, as the Sabbath was about to begin.

Luke 23:44–54 NLT

※

*L*uke, along with Matthew, reports that the curtain in the sanctuary of the temple was torn down the middle just as Jesus died. That curtain in the sanctuary was what separated the Holy Place from the Most Holy Place, where the high priest went only once a year to make atonement for the sins of the entire nation of Israel on the most holy day of the year, the Day of Atonement. *Atonement* is used to translate the Hebrew word *Kippur*, which means "to cover" or "to purify." *Atonement* meant the reconciliation of human beings with God—the replacement of punishment with forgiveness and the restoration of a relationship that had been broken. With Jesus' death, the barrier that had stood between God and the human race, symbolized by that curtain, was finally torn down. Humanity and God were reconciled, and the power of the devil was destroyed.

Jesus passed from life to death and back to life again, showing us that the way past the end of our lives is safe because the Father stands there waiting to catch us. He will not abandon us to the grave, but will instead bring us to our resurrection.

WHAT HE SAID

On the first day of the week, very early in the morning, they, and certain other women with them, came to the tomb bringing the spices which they had prepared. But they found the stone rolled away from the tomb. Then they went in and did not find the body of the Lord Jesus. And it happened, as they were greatly perplexed about this, that behold, two men stood by them in shining garments. Then, as they were afraid and bowed their faces to the earth, they said to them, "Why do you seek the living among the dead? He is not here, but is risen! Remember how He spoke to you when He was still in Galilee, saying, 'The Son of Man must be delivered into the hands of sinful men, and be crucified, and the third day rise again.'"

And they remembered His words. Then they returned from the tomb and told all these things to the eleven and to all the rest. It was Mary Magdalene, Joanna, Mary the mother of James, and the other women with them, who told these things to the apostles. And their words seemed to them like idle tales, and they did not believe them. But Peter arose and ran to the tomb; and stooping down, he saw the linen cloths lying by themselves; and he departed, marveling to himself at what had happened.

Luke 24:1–12 NKJV

When the women came to the tomb that Sunday morning, they were sad. It was the third day since Jesus had been crucified, and they wanted to prepare his body that had been buried hurriedly before the Sabbath began. With the Sabbath over, they could do the job right.

The women did not suspect, did not imagine, and did not even conceive of the possibility that Jesus' body would not be in that tomb. Given that the stone blocking the tomb entrance was large and heavy, their primary concern was wondering exactly how they'd get into the tomb to do the final tasks they thought they owed him.

The angels that met the women at the tomb wondered why they were looking in a tomb, of all places, for Jesus. They quoted Jesus' prediction of his resurrection. Even then, confronted with the reality of the empty tomb, the women had trouble understanding Jesus' words.

God often surprises us, not so much because he hasn't told us ahead of time what to expect, but mostly because we simply didn't understand what he told us. Thankfully, he isn't dependent upon our understanding in order for him to act on our behalf.

WHY CRY?

Mary stood outside the tomb weeping. As she wept, she knelt to look into the tomb and saw two angels sitting there, dressed in white, one at the head, the other at the foot of where Jesus' body had been laid. They said to her, "Woman, why do you weep?"

"They took my Master," she said, "and I don't know where they put him." After she said this, she turned away and saw Jesus standing there. But she didn't recognize him.

Jesus spoke to her, "Woman, why do you weep? Who are you looking for?"

She, thinking that he was the gardener, said, "Mister, if you took him, tell me where you put him so I can care for him."

Jesus said, "Mary."

Turning to face him, she said in Hebrew, *"Rabboni!"* meaning "Teacher!"

Jesus said, "Don't cling to me, for I have not yet ascended to the Father. Go to my brothers and tell them, 'I ascend to my Father and your Father, my God and your God.' "

Mary Magdalene went, telling the news to the disciples: "I saw the Master!" And she told them everything he said to her.

John 20:11–18 MSG

The angels asked Mary a question: "Why do you weep?" From Mary's perspective, it seemed obvious—Jesus was dead, someone had moved his body, and now she couldn't even mourn properly. An already bad situation had gotten worse.

Moments later, someone else asked her the same question: "Why do you weep?" She was distraught and had tears in her eyes. Jesus was supposed to be dead. She didn't recognize that it was Jesus himself asking the question this time.

Jesus asked her the question for the same reason the angels had. They understood she was sad, of course, and they understood why. Neither the angels nor Jesus asked for enlightenment. They asked to make Mary reexamine her situation. She didn't have a reason to weep anymore. Couldn't she see that?

When Jesus spoke her name, her tears probably didn't vanish in that instant, but they certainly took on an entirely different character. They became tears of joy.

Mary realized her circumstances were different from what she had imagined. The storms of life can buffet us so severely sometimes that we lose sight of the fullness of our own circumstances. But the storms of life will not buffet us quite as hard if we can keep our eyes on Jesus.

FOLLOW ME

After his resurrection, Jesus was spending time with his disciples by the Sea of Galilee:

Peter turned and saw that the disciple whom Jesus loved was following them. (This was the one who had leaned back against Jesus at the supper and had said, "Lord, who is going to betray you?") When Peter saw him, he asked, "Lord, what about him?"

Jesus answered, "If I want him to remain alive until I return, what is that to you? You must follow me." Because of this, the rumor spread among the brothers that this disciple would not die. But Jesus did not say that he would not die; he only said, "If I want him to remain alive until I return, what is that to you?"

This is the disciple who testifies to these things and who wrote them down. We know that his testimony is true.

Jesus did many other things as well. If every one of them were written down, I suppose that even the whole world would not have room for the books that would be written.

John 21:20–25 NIV

※

*A*fter Jesus restored his relationship with Peter—reassuring him that he loved him and getting Peter three times to acknowledge that he loved Jesus—Jesus told Peter that he would someday die as a martyr on a cross. Peter's response was to ask Jesus about the apostle John, who was following behind them.

Jesus told Peter that what John's fate in life would be was not Peter's concern. God has a purpose for each individual. God's will for one man can be quite different from his will for another. In the end, according to legend, Peter was crucified upside down in Rome during the reign of the emperor Nero. But according to tradition, John died of old age, the only one of the twelve apostles who was not martyred. After his exile on Patmos, during which he wrote the book of Revelation, John was set free and continued preaching and teaching until the day he died peacefully, surrounded by other Christians.

God works with each of us in his own separate way. We all have a part to play in God's plan. Some of us may lead lives of great turmoil, pain, and suffering. Others of us may live lives of grand excitement. And some of us will lead quiet, ordinary, and happy lives. No matter what sort of life God gives us, it will bring glory to him. And all of us, no matter the cup he gives us, are equally valuable.

THE GREAT COMMISSION

While the women were on their way, some soldiers who had been guarding the tomb went into the city. They told the chief priests everything that had happened. So the chief priests met with the leaders and decided to bribe the soldiers with a lot of money. They said to the soldiers, "Tell everyone that Jesus' disciples came during the night and stole his body while you were asleep. If the governor hears about this, we will talk to him. You won't have anything to worry about." The soldiers took the money and did what they were told. The people of Judea still tell each other this story.

Jesus' eleven disciples went to a mountain in Galilee, where Jesus had told them to meet him. They saw him and worshiped him, but some of them doubted.

Jesus came to them and said: "I have been given all authority in heaven and on earth! Go to the people of all nations and make them my disciples. Baptize them in the name of the Father, the Son, and the Holy Spirit, and teach them to do everything I have told you. I will be with you always, even until the end of the world."

Matthew 28:11–20 CEV

※

After his resurrection but before he ascended to heaven, Jesus met his disciples in Galilee and spent time teaching them. But facing the resurrected man that they had seen die on a Roman cross, some of them still entertained doubts. The Bible contains many stories about those who saw God do amazing things but who then turned around and grumbled and griped. We'd like to think that if we had been there, that if we had seen such marvelous miracles, we would be set for life. We'd never again doubt God, never again disobey, and never again complain about any suffering we ever experienced. We'd live our lives on the mountaintop.

But what we see, in fact, is the way things really are, in the real world. As Abraham told the rich man, if people don't believe the Bible, then they won't believe just because someone comes back from the grave (Luke 16:31). Doubt is where we live; it is who we are. It is human nature to doubt rather than to trust. No matter what God does, no matter how marvelously we see him act, we will always be tempted to doubt, especially as time passes and we begin to take whatever God did for granted. The novelty wears off. We must work hard and constantly strive to renew our trust.

THE DREAM IS ALIVE

After the resurrection, Jesus appeared to his disciples in Jerusalem:

[Jesus] told [his disciples], "These are My words that I spoke to you while I was still with you—that everything written about Me in the Law of Moses, the Prophets, and the Psalms must be fulfilled." Then He opened their minds to understand the Scriptures. He also said to them, "This is what is written: the Messiah would suffer and rise from the dead the third day, and repentance for forgiveness of sins would be proclaimed in His name to all the nations, beginning at Jerusalem. You are witnesses of these things. And look, I am sending you what My Father promised. As for you, stay in the city until you are empowered from on high."

Then He led them out as far as Bethany, and lifting up His hands He blessed them. And while He was blessing them, He left them and was carried up into heaven. After worshiping Him, they returned to Jerusalem with great joy. And they were continually in the temple complex blessing God.

Luke 24:44–53 HCSB

Just before Jesus returned to his Father in heaven, he carefully reviewed what the Scriptures had to say about him. He took them from the beginning in Genesis and traced himself all the way through until the end. Then he left them with final instructions about what they should be doing while he was gone.

He explained to his disciples that they wouldn't be left to do these things on their own. Instead, they'd be "empowered from on high" when the Holy Spirit arrived during pentecost, a festival also called the Feast of Weeks or Shabuoth. In Exodus 23:16 it was called the Feast of Harvest, during which the community was to show gratitude to God for the firstfruits, that is, the early harvest. The holiday followed Passover by fifty days.

Jesus did not ask his disciples to take up arms against the Romans. He did not tell them to go into politics. Instead, he told them to proclaim the good news that Jesus had died and risen and that forgiveness was available to all. It was not a complicated or difficult task.

Both young and old are concerned with discovering the will of God for their lives. But much of God's will for our lives is obvious. For all of us, one of our primary purposes, whatever else we might do, is to bear witness to others of what Jesus did for us.

REMEMBER ME

In a letter to the church in Corinth, Paul wrote:

I have already told you what the Lord Jesus did on the night he was betrayed. And it came from the Lord himself.

He took some bread in his hands. Then after he had given thanks, he broke it and said, 'This is my body, which is given for you. Eat this and remember me.'

After the meal, Jesus took a cup of wine in his hands and said, "This is my blood, and with it God makes his new agreement with you. Drink this and remember me.'"

The Lord meant that when you eat this bread and drink from this cup, you tell about his death until he comes.

But if you eat the bread and drink the wine in a way that isn't worthy of the Lord, you sin against his body and blood. That's why you must examine the way you eat and drink. If you fail to understand that you are the body of the Lord, you will condemn yourselves by the way you eat and drink. That's why many of you are sick and weak and why a lot of others have died. If we carefully judge ourselves, we won't be punished.

1 Corinthians 11:23–31 CEV

❀emember me," said Jesus as he broke the bread and shared the cup during that final Passover meal. Paul told the church in the Greek city of Corinth that Jesus wanted his people to remember him. The reason for the ceremony of Communion is to remember Jesus. Paul commented that whenever we share in a Communion meal we are telling about his death until he comes back again.

"Remember me," said Jesus. Is there a danger that we might forget him, that he had to tell us to remember? Indeed. It is human nature to become distracted with our daily concerns. We have to work, we have to sleep, we have to rest, we have to take care of our families and spend time with them, and spend time with our friends. We have much to do, and it is inescapable and entirely necessary.

Jesus told us that there was one more thing we had to do, one more responsibility in the midst of all our other responsibilities. We need to remember him. We can never forget what he did for us. Jesus died for us and lives for us. In him, we have life and have it more abundantly.

ALIVE FOREVER

Jesus appeared to John the apostle during John's exile on the island of Patmos:

In his right hand he held seven stars, and out of his mouth came a sharp double-edged sword. His face was like the sun shining in all its brilliance.

When I saw him, I fell at his feet as though dead. Then he placed his right hand on me and said: "Do not be afraid. I am the First and the Last. I am the Living One; I was dead, and behold I am alive for ever and ever! And I hold the keys of death and Hades.

"Write, therefore, what you have seen, what is now and what will take place later. The mystery of the seven stars that you saw in my right hand and of the seven golden lampstands is this: The seven stars are the angels of the seven churches, and the seven lampstands are the seven churches."

Revelation 1:16–20 NIV

❈

*J*esus said that his followers had eternal life and that they would never perish. Then he added, "No one is able to snatch them out of My Father's hand. I and My Father are one" (John 10:29–30 NKJV). At the beginning of the book of Revelation, John described his encounter with a glorified Jesus. In his hand were seven stars that represented the "angels," that is, the pastors of the seven churches in Asia Minor to whom Jesus' letters were sent.

John was in exile on a tiny island in the Mediterranean, suffering there for proclaiming the good news. Christians throughout the Roman Empire were suffering just as John was, and often they suffered far worse. Many were dying for Jesus every day. Jesus' words were comforting words for John and for the people to whom John wrote the book of Revelation. The Roman Empire might have believed itself to be in charge. But the one who was really in charge, who had the power of life and death, was not the Roman government who sent Christians to die in the arena. Instead, the real power belonged to Jesus, the one who had been killed by that Roman government but who now lives forever. Jesus proved with his resurrection that he could undo whatever the Romans might try.

God is the one who is in charge of our lives and our deaths. We can relax in his hands, comforted in the knowledge that he will rescue us from those who imagine they can control or destroy us.

THINGS TO COME

The apostle John found comfort on the island of Patmos when Jesus appeared:

After these things I looked, and behold, a door standing open in heaven. And the first voice which I heard was like a trumpet speaking with me, saying, "Come up here, and I will show you things which must take place after this."

Immediately I was in the Spirit; and behold, a throne set in heaven, and One sat on the throne. And He who sat there was like a jasper and a sardius stone in appearance; and there was a rainbow around the throne, in appearance like an emerald. Around the throne were twenty-four thrones, and on the thrones I saw twenty-four elders sitting, clothed in white robes; and they had crowns of gold on their heads. And from the throne proceeded lightnings, thunderings, and voices. Seven lamps of fire were burning before the throne, which are the seven Spirits of God.

Before the throne there was a sea of glass, like crystal. And in the midst of the throne, and around the throne, were four living creatures full of eyes in front and in back. The first living creature was like a lion, the second living creature like a calf, the third living creature had a face like a man, and the fourth living creature was like a flying eagle. The four living creatures, each having six wings, were full of eyes around and within. And they do not rest day or night, saying:

"Holy, holy, holy,
Lord God Almighty,
who was and is and is to
come!"

Revelation 4:1–8 NKJV

❈

*J*esus told John to "come up here" so that he could show John what was going to happen "after this." "After this" means after all the suffering, all the pain, and all the misery that the Christian people of the world were enduring.

The real source of power, the throne where real decisions were made, wasn't in the emperor's throne room in Rome. Instead, it was "up here." God called Moses "up here" when God called him up to the mountain to receive the Commandments. John's vision of God's throne room is a vision that would be recognizable to any Jewish person familiar with the Old Testament. The throne room as described by John makes its first appearance in Exodus 24:9–11, when Moses and Aaron, Aaron's sons, and the seventy elders of Israel see God and eat and drink with him.

Jesus asks us to "come up here," above our circumstances. There is more to life than just what we experience "down here."

Christ's words are of permanent value because of His person; they endure because He endures.

W. H. Griffith Thomas

�֎

Jesus Christ is the same yesterday, today, and forever.

Hebrews 13:8 NKJV